M. J. C.

Eugene A. Curry

1939

THE CONSUMER

AND THE

ECONOMIC ORDER

THE CONSUMER
AND THE
ECONOMIC ORDER

BY

WARREN C. WAITE
University of Minnesota

AND

RALPH CASSADY, Jr.
*University of California
at Los Angeles*

First Edition

McGRAW-HILL BOOK COMPANY, Inc.
NEW YORK AND LONDON
1939

PRINTED IN THE UNITED STATES OF AMERICA

THE MAPLE PRESS COMPANY, YORK, PA.

To

A. A. W.

and

D. J. C.

PREFACE

There has been a growing interest in the consumer and his problems in recent years, and he appears at last to have achieved a recognition long past due. We feel, however, that there has been a tendency by the discoverers of these problems to overemphasize certain of them. Frequently such emphasis is not undesirable since it brings public attention to bear upon specific things which often are subject to remedial action. The successful operation of a democracy such as ours demands, however, a well-informed body of citizens. The broad implications of particular actions by specific groups should be clearly understood as well as the ultimate results of various types of governmental action. The student should have this wide viewpoint as well as a recognition of some of the more restricted issues. In many texts, the broad character of consumer problems has not been sufficiently shown, and it is felt, in consequence, that a text providing such a view would be desirable. This is a modest attempt in that direction.

The book began as a revision of "Economics of Consumption," written by Professor Waite and published by the McGraw-Hill Book Company, Inc., in 1928. It draws heavily from the old volume for its general plan and even in certain places for subject matter. It early became apparent, however, that the contributions of Professor Cassady were so substantial and the new subject matter so voluminous that publication under an entirely new title was called for. The present work is an equal collaboration, each author having contributed the same amount of material.

Our debts to others are large. They have been acknowledged where possible, but undoubtedly some have escaped notice. The shortcomings of the book are, of course, our own responsibility.

WARREN C. WAITE,
RALPH CASSADY, JR.

ST. PAUL, MINN.,
LOS ANGELES, CALIF.,
February, 1939.

CONTENTS

THE CONSUMER AND THE ECONOMIC ORDER

CHAPTER I

THE NATURE OF THE CONSUMPTION PROBLEM

There is an economy of consumption as important from the standpoint of human welfare as the economy of production. A large portion of the waste of our economic order arises, even after goods have been produced, from poorly arranged consumption, which not only results in a loss of satisfaction and enjoyment on the part of those who consume poorly but may also result in a misuse of productive resources as well. Acceptance of the thesis that the nature of man is, in part at least, a consequence of his environment gives a vital importance to consumption. Poorly ordered consumption will produce persons less vigorous and intelligent than will well-ordered consumption. Moreover, these effects will be cumulative; for not only will better consumption result in better individuals, but also these individuals, by virtue of their greater strength and foresight, will be able to provide better environment for their children, and these in turn will be better and stronger individuals. It is just as important, in consequence, for society to consider its consuming habits and problems as to take stock of its productive equipment. And, at last, the attention of many trained observers is being directed toward this phase of man's activities.

1. Some Problems of Consumption.—Consumption is not entirely an individual matter. In fact, its most important phases transcend individual considerations. Consumption has, in other words, important social aspects. For example, much of what we consume is the result of the consumption of others. We often imitate others because we do not really know what to consume or because we wish to avoid being conspicuous through the omission of certain articles in our consumption. Moreover, if our incomes are small, our choice is limited largely to commodities that can be produced in considerable quantities because many want them. We also, in a small measure at least, contribute to the forces that determine not only the sorts of things upon which others work but also their conditions of employment. In so far as we spend our money on things that are produced under conditions degrading and harmful to the workers, we have added something to the misery of mankind; and in so far as we spend our money for things that uplift and strengthen the character of the workers, we have added something to the general welfare of mankind. The extent of our responsibility in these matters is an ethical problem, and our point of view will depend upon the particular ethical theory that we hold. We all admit that in choosing a course of action it is reasonable to make some allowance for its probable effect upon others, as well as for its effect upon ourselves, but the importance of these two sets of interests is largely a matter of personal opinion. The effects of consumption, then, are not confined within the narrow limits of our own domestic establishments, but affect many outside these boundaries as well.[1]

Consumption is a very complicated process and covers a wide range of activities. What is more, we learn about it in many ways. Perhaps the most important method in the past has been through miscellaneous facts gleaned from other fields and through individual experience. Because of the importance and complexity of the subject, however, this method is no longer adequate. Consumption is a mode of life itself. As such, it is a problem in human behavior and in human motives and might seem more properly the field of the psychologist than of the economist. The economist, however, deals with a certain portion of the field of consumption, those aspects which are related to price, either directly or indirectly. There is nothing peculiar to economics in this method of approach. Precisely the same thing is done by sociology, political science, physiology, and other studies dealing with human beings. The economist does not suppose that these economic activities can be entirely separated from the rest of man's activities. The economist deals with man as he finds him

[1] See A. C. Pigou, Essay on Expenditure of Private Income, "Essays in Applied Economics."

but concerns himself principally with this special sort of activity. The conclusions of the psychologist are accepted in all problems dealing with the relation of economic activities to other activities and with the psychological basis of these economic activities, and the economist does not attempt to change them. In other words, the economist utilizes psychological precepts in his analysis wherever necessary. There is, on the other hand, a great deal of the economics of consumption that has no relation to any theory of psychology.

2. The Economics of Consumption.—We may define economics, for our purposes, as the science that deals with the administration of resources in the satisfaction of human wants, in so far as this administration involves considerations of price or cost. Not all administration of resources is, of course, economic; much of it is technical and not a matter for economists at all. For example, the determination of the calorie content of certain foods, the setting of proper nutritional standards, and the proper preparation of food items are technical matters and are *outside* the field of economics. The calculation of the cheapest sources of certain necessary food elements and the variations in the prices of these sources are, however, *within* the field of economics.

Logically enough, the study of consumption should begin with production and distribution (in the economic sense) as a point of departure. Though it would seem to be something in the nature of a truism, much misunderstanding arises out of the failure to appreciate the fact that goods must be produced in order to be consumed. Some visionaries—Townsendites, for example—seem to labor under the impression that some sort of reallocation of purchasing power automatically brings forth goods and services sufficient for all. According to their scheme, oldsters would be taken out of industry and would be charged with the sole task of spending $200 each month. One wonders why, if such a scheme is sound, the age limit could not be dropped from sixty to (say) forty; why, if that were done, an era of prosperity such as we have never envisioned would not be forthcoming! The fact is, of course, that—just as in a family—greater average shares are possible only as greater income is produced.

The study of consumption economics also is predicated upon some understanding of distribution fundamentals. We should understand that in a modified laissez-faire society such as ours the shares going to the several productive factors are determined, fundamentally, by certain laws. We know, of course, that the owner of land receives a differential called *rent;* labor, a *wage;* the capitalist, *interest;* and the entrepreneur, a residual element known as *profits.* In general, the amount of each share is dependent upon the supply of and the demand for the particular element involved. More specifically, rent is determined by the value of a locational or fertility advantage; wages, by the marginal productivity of labor; capital, by the degree of time preference and the risk involved; and profits, by fortuitous circumstances and the enjoyment of a monopoly or quasi monopoly by the enterpriser.

Consumption may be studied in one of three different ways: in terms of prices, of the goods and services received by consumers, or of psychic states produced by goods received. We may, for example, examine and compare the expenditures or receipts of people and deal with these as matters of dollars and cents. These statements can be quite definitely made, since the monetary unit is the common means of expression used for all of them. Unfortunately, these statements will often fail to tell us what we wish to know and must be supplemented with additional data. We may, in addition, deal with consumption in terms of goods and services. Here, however, we find no common unit to which we can reduce the many things that people consume; and, since each person consumes a somewhat different set of commodities from anyone else, and even different commodities at different times, our comparisons become to some extent invalid. The best that can be done is to take certain major items of consumption, get arbitrary measures for these, and make our comparisons on this basis. Thus we might adopt cubic feet of air space per individual and square feet of window space per individual as measures of the adequacy of housing. Finally, consumption may be studied in terms of psychic states. Here we have no measures at all, and our statements and comparisons can be made only in the most general terms and with carefully stated assumptions.

Economics properly deals with only the first of these methods of approach. Unfortunately, however, a study of consumption considered from the point of price alone cannot tell us all we wish to know. Considerations of human welfare cannot be avoided in a comprehensive study of consumption, and, in consequence, the strictly economic study is expanded to include portions of the problems involved in the other ways of considering consumption. These are included always, however, with a view to explaining or clarifying certain aspects of the monetary relations of the problem. Thus, it is essential to make clear that a given quantity of money expended in different times or places usually purchases a different quantity of goods and services. It is essential to discover these differences, to measure them, and to determine the causes of the differences. Similarly, it is important to show that a given quantity of money does not correspond to a certain satisfaction and that people who consume the same quantity of goods fail to gain the same enjoyment from life. It is also important to show that there is no single exact way in which money can be spent by all consumers with each deriving the same enjoyment from those expenditures. What may be a proper expenditure of money for one person may be quite improper for another when tested by the enjoyment obtained from that expenditure.

The treatment of consumption in this study is very broad. Although the subject of consumer buying (for example) is given some space, the most important aspect is that having to do with political, rather than household, economy. The economics of consumption, from a social point of view, is concerned with three major problems. (1) The first of these is the status of the consumer in the existing economic order. The present order has important relations to consumption. The goods that are produced depend upon the desires of certain consumers. At the same time, the economic order limits and conditions consumption in many ways. The quantities of goods that a person may command are limited by his income. His income, to some extent at least, is conditioned by the success or failure of certain national policies. His choices are materially influenced by advertising and salesmen. The range of choices depends, in a large measure, upon what others consume. In short, his income, choices, and activities are modified on every side by the economic order in which he finds himself. (2) There is the problem of the manner in which goods are chosen, and the economic results of these choices. The explanation of the choice of goods must rest, in a major part, upon psychology. The economist deals primarily with the modification of these choices by prices and with the effect of changes in choices upon prices. (3) There is the problem of the relation of human welfare to wealth. This is frequently a matter of consumption in its desirable and undesirable modes. This, too, is a matter that must be viewed from the standpoint of society as a whole. In this phase, also, certain problems of social control and social betterment are recognized primarily as problems of consumption, since by such activities more and better goods and services may be extended to consumers or a proscription of harmful commodities and services may be effected. In other words, these matters come properly within the scope of economics because they impinge in an important way on economic activities. The principal economic problem in consumption, from an individual point of view, is the proper administration of the individual income. The economist does not have a great deal to say on this problem, for a great portion of the problem is technical in nature. Even here, however, guideposts can be erected. The economist can, in other words, point out general guiding principles and furnish information concerning the several technical aids that are available.

3. The Difficulties of Consumption.—When we compare production and consumption in a historical way, important differences appear. The problem of the individual as a consumer is becoming more complex. The kinds and qualities of goods offered on the market are constantly increasing. As a producer, on the contrary, his task is becoming simpler; instead of producing a range of products, he is becoming usually a specialist in the production of a small part of a single article. His tasks as a producer have become fewer and more specialized; his activities as a consumer more numerous and more complex.

The great development of technique that has taken place in production during the last century and a half has not been found in consumption. There are two principal reasons for this backwardness of consumption: (1) the very nature of the consumption problem makes it difficult to use exact measures for testing the results of individual expenditures; and (2) the home, which is the usual unit in consumption, is too small to function well economically.[1] The businessman tests the results of particular opera-

[1] See W. C. Mitchell, "The Backward Art of Spending Money," *Am. Econ. Rev.*, vol. 2, p. 269.

tions by their effect on the profits of the business. Those actions or policies are deemed effective which result in larger profits. No such exact measure is as yet available for the household. The home is, of course, operated for the well-being of the family, but well-being is such a vague thing that results can be judged only in the most general way. Moreover, the small size of the household prevents the economical operations found in industry by largely preventing the use of laborsaving devices and by causing purchasing to be less scientifically done. The usual home is much too small to utilize laborsaving devices effectively. The machine is used only a small portion of its possible working time, and it must either perform a very essential task or be very cheap to warrant its installation. In industry, a machine will often be used 12 out of each 24 hours, sometimes even more. In the household, a machine may be idle 99 out of 100 hours. Industrial purchasing has been largely specialized in the hands of expert buyers. Purchases are generally in large amounts. Therefore, close attention to prices and elaborate examinations of qualities are warranted, since the cost of such "selection techniques" can be spread over a large number of units. Household purchasing, on the other hand, falls largely upon the housewife, who not only buys in relatively small quantities but has many other complex problems and duties on which to spend her time. The two problems are essentially different. The purchasing agent in business is called upon to buy a more restricted variety of products than the ordinary housewife is called upon to purchase, and, in consequence, he can possess a much more exact knowledge of the methods of determining quality and the markets than are available to the housewife. At best, she can have only a general knowledge of prices and qualities. Business throws no exhausting labor upon those who are called upon to make its decisions; the housewife, on the contrary, is engaged in manual labor a large portion of the day.

The consumer, consequently, requires information, education, and protection. He requires many types of information. For example, since industry is organized to break down his sales resistance and direct his expenditures into certain channels, he should have sound information about goods—what they will do and which are the best buys. During the past decade, much headway has been made in these matters. In addition, however, the consumer should be given proper guidance in educational matters. He should have extended aid in his thinking concerning the several social aspects of consumption in order that he be enabled to distinguish between socially advantageous and socially harmful institutions. Thus advertising, when understood properly, has many desirable aspects. To be properly informed on such matters makes it possible for consumers more intelligently and effectively to exercise their franchise.

Consumer protection has been receiving increased attention of late, since it is recognized that certain practices which have an adverse effect upon real income, health, and even life itself are not readily discerned by consumers. Indeed, much has been accomplished in these matters within the past several years. So, besides information, the consumer requires protection in the form of certain circumscriptions and proscriptions. The most important of all of these, perhaps, is education. That is to say, the consumer requires an intelligent outlook on consumption matters. Since we are all consumers, each of us is concerned. It is the main purpose of this volume to furnish a point of view that will make for a more intelligent approach to consumer problems.

Questions

1. What activities, if any, now carried on in the home would you expect to be undertaken on any considerable scale by businesses outside the home in the near future?
2. Is technological unemployment a real problem? Write 1,000 words on the exact nature of the impact of technological change. Would it be better from the point of view of the consumer if such changes were controlled?
3. Has the introduction of laborsaving devices lightened the work of men or of women more?
4. What are the factors that make it difficult to administer the household effectively as compared with commercial production?

CHAPTER II

THE ORGANIZATION OF THE ECONOMIC ORDER

The particular task of any economic order is to secure the best possible adjustment between the wants of a society and the means of supplying those wants. Certain wants can be completely satisfied for all the members of society, as the means of satisfying those wants are supplied by nature gratuitously in sufficient quantities to provide each person with all that he desires. Thus, there is, except in certain special cases, sufficient air, water, and such things so that each may possess all he wishes. There are a great many wants, however, that cannot be completely satisfied, since the means of satisfying these wants are limited. The economic order administers this latter situation.

This administration involves two things: (1) the wants of society and its various members must be rated upon some sort of basis, and the goods which are available for the satisfaction of wants must be distributed so that only those which have been judged to be more important are satisfied; (2) the order must assign the means of production to their various uses in such a manner that the goods which are necessary for the satisfaction of the selected wants will be most effectively supplied. This means that the production of goods should be carried on by the best available technical methods. Where a want can be satisfied in several ways, the order should secure its satisfaction by the way that most effectively utilizes its resources. The means of production are limited because of physical limitations in nature and because men do not like to work or to wait. The order must, therefore, determine who will work and who will wait and how much work and waiting each must supply.

"In modern society total production has never been sufficient to supply the desires of the people for consumption. Though a few people in each age have command of all the goods and services which the twenty-four hours of the day permit them to consume, the armies of the middle and lower classes have many unfulfilled desires. It has recently been estimated [for example] that in 1933 only about 4 per cent of the families in Minnesota had incomes of as much as $2,500. If the entire production of the state were equally divided among its people, the total family income would have been only that which could be purchased with $1,500. The human and material resources of the state would need to have been used with more than 50 per cent greater efficiency in that year to produce an average family income of even $2,500."[1] A similar situation prevailed in the United States as a whole. Hence it can be seen that we can use much more than we actually produce and that the general overproduction theory is without foundation of fact. In other words, our problem is not one of distribution alone but, even more fundamentally, is one of production. An adequate supply of goods is the first essential in a program of increasing economic well-being.

1. Types of Economic Orders.—Our own economic order is but one of a number of different types of politico-economic systems or orders through which economic activities may be directed. The purpose of all, as has been stated, is that of providing a system for indicating what should be produced and how the income produced is to be distributed. Under some types of orders, the system of organization provides for relatively little central control. Under others, a maximum amount of control is required. That is to say, some orders are semiautomatic; others are operated by central authority through a system of artificial controls. It is thought by the proponents of the former that a relatively great freedom of action makes for greater economic effectiveness; by the proponents of the latter, that efficiency necessitates circumscription of individual initiative. The following paragraphs, together with those in the next section, present a brief description of the several possible types. Later, the two opposing general types of systems are evaluated.

The Autonomous Order.—"First, an economic order can at least be conceived in which goods needed by the individual are made available by his own efforts, unaided by his fellow men. Crusoe is represented as contriving to satisfy his wants, in so far as they were satisfied at all, almost wholly by the labor of *his own hands;* and it is possible that many hunters and explorers for a time

[1] R. A. Stevenson and R. S. Vaile, "Balancing the Economic Controls," p. 1.

approximate his condition. A pioneer or isolated settler also to a great extent produces the very things which he consumes and consumes nothing but what he himself produces—bakes his own bread and eats it, grinds his own flour and bakes it into bread, raises his own wheat and grinds it into flour. Such an order, where each man provides directly and entirely for the satisfaction of his own wants, may be called an *autonomous economic order*."[1]

An economic order such as that described exists nowhere in modern society. Few would advocate such a system for purposes of efficiency since it would allow for no specialization. Indeed the so-called autonomous order could be characterized as a sort of economic anarchism impossible of realization as well as economically undesirable both individually and socially.

Socialism.—Socialism, in its broadest sense, means that the principal facilities of production are socially controlled and democratically managed for the benefit of society rather than for any one group of individuals. The most important aspect of socialism is that of the socially owned and controlled production system. It is thought by the advocates of such a system that not only would production be more efficient through elimination of competitive wastes and reduction of costs (due, in turn, to production concentration) but that the benefits which did result would accrue, not to a small group of industrialists, but to the masses. It is unimportant to the present discussion whether control is obtained in an evolutionary or in a revolutionary manner. Suffice it to say that the Fabians represent one school of thought, the syndicalists the other.

Usually when one thinks in terms of socialism (in contrast to communism, for example), one presupposes a society allowing for considerable freedom of choice in the selection of consumers' goods. In practice a certain amount of limitation on consumers' choices would obtain, however, since competitive offerings would be absent and since the central authority could be expected to prohibit the production of "undesirable" commodities. In theory at least, the exercise of authority in socialism does not become fully operative until the production system begins the task of transferring manifested wants into actual goods and services. The socialistic order is not necessarily totalitarian

[1] FREDERICK M. TAYLOR, "Principles of Economics" (1925), p. 17.

although freedom of enterprise and freedom of choice are definitely circumscribed.

Under a more or less complete socialistic order, the price system would be materially altered, since state monopolies would control a large part of production; and, since production would be for the benefit of society, cost of production would become the major determinant of price rather than demand. In a socialistic order, a large percentage of incomes of the residual type would be done away with; practically all returns from the operations of the economic system would be in the form of wages or salaries earned. Social service would be expected to motivate the whole, rather than profits. Larger earnings would in theory accrue to the wage earner since it is alleged that the product would be greater and since a greater proportion would be distributed to wage earners.

Fascism.—Fascism, though not strictly a type of economic organization, has many economic implications. Fascism, in one very important sense, is a reactionary politico-economic philosophy. It is definitely mercantilistic. For example, anything that strengthens the *state*—makes it more powerful—is proper; anything that weakens the state is improper. The individuals making up society, however, are of minor importance. Indeed, the state must appear important in the society of nations, even if the individuals making up the population pay dearly for such a "front."

Both socialism and fascism advocate strong central control. Two important differences stand out, however. Socialism is a movement for the benefit of the masses; fascism has been a movement benefiting the upper and middle classes. Moreover, whereas fascism has as its primary end the strengthening of the state as such, socialism has the end of strengthening the economic well-being of the individual members.

The *modus operandi* of a fascist society illustrates its philosophy. Any type of disorder or confusion is considered wasteful and as tending to defeat the end in view. Thus there should be no "parliamentary obstructions." Hence, such democratic institutions as elections and freedom of the press and of speech are discouraged. The state even acts as "guardian" of labor and capital, outlawing strikes and providing courts to handle industrial disputes. Since democracy is considered inefficient, the control of political and economic affairs is placed in the hands of one man. One man is more efficient, it is argued, since he can be more direct and since he has a clearer conception of the ends that are being sought.

Under Italian fascism, private ownership of industrial concerns prevails, but a control through "corporations councils," made up of employers, employees, technicians, and consumers, is effected. Central control comes through the National Council of Corporations, Benito Mussolini, Chairman. Through a system of syndicates, production control is easily obtained; and, although ostensibly private enterprise continues to exist, actually the flow of capital into the several industries may at any time be guided in the interest of a rationalized industrial system. A controlled system of prices exists, and, though industrial profits may be earned, taxation may be utilized as a device for controlling their volume.

Communism.—In theory, communism differs from socialism in that the fundamental philosophy behind the movement ("from all according to their abilities, to all according to their needs") calls for arbitrary decisions concerning individual economic needs. Under such a system, in other words, society would have absolute control over consumption requirements as well as over production facilities. There would be no wages in the accepted sense of the term; "dividends" from operations would be allocated in the form of goods. The more efficient the industrial system, the more would be available for distribution to the members of society. The chief motivating factor would be the desire on the part of the members of society to raise the general scale of living.

In Russia, the communistic economic order has not been attained. Indeed, there are grave doubts whether it ever will be. After the revolution in 1917, the first phase of development was definitely communistic. Goods and services (if available) were free to workers, surpluses being commandeered for the purpose. Soon, however, it became apparent that things were not working as expected. Industry and trade had come to a standstill. The masses were in dire want. Consequently, in 1921 the New Economic Policy was launched (N.E.P., so called), being a temporary reversion to limited freedom of enterprise. Industrial activity quickened with amazing rapidity so that by 1927 leftist experiments became practicable once more. Central control was again tightened, and the first Five-year Plan was launched almost immediately.

At present, the economic system existing in the U.S.S.R. is socio-capitalistic. A dictatorship of the proletariat is the controlling force. Industry is almost entirely controlled through state monopolies and cooperatives, and, though consumers are no longer allocated goods on a rationed basis, certainly only limited quantities, qualities, and varieties are placed at their disposal. In Russia, individual preference has little effect on the types of goods produced. Although some choices can be made (as among the limited numbers of varieties offered as well as among goods of distinctly different classes), decisions regarding the use of production facilities are made on the basis of what is best for the masses rather than on the basis of manifested preferences. It is thought that such central control makes possible a much more effective planning of production.

There seems to be a distinct veering toward the right under Stalin. One manifestation of this tendency is the establishment of a differential wage system for the purpose of stimulating incentive. Another is the establishment of the controlled price system, one object of which might be that of indicating consumer preferences. Institutions in Russia, however, are still for the most part socialistic in character. It has been said that the present phase is just a step in Russia's development; that, when concentration on heavy (capital) industry is no longer necessary, consumers' goods will become more plentiful and then the next step from socio-capitalism into communism can be made.

2. The Nature of the Existing Economic Order in the United States.—Our economic order provides for the direction of production and consumption through the medium of prices. Prices determine what is to be produced, who is to consume particular products, and when these products are to be used. For the most part, the process takes place spontaneously; *i.e.*, the formation of these prices and the effects of particular prices take place within the order itself, and without direction by some outside authority such as the government. The order, in consequence, is often said to be automatically regulated. Persons are left free in most instances to make decisions on the basis of the relative importance of their own wants and to secure the satisfaction of these wants so far as their income will permit. Businessmen are free on the whole to provide the kinds of goods and services that they choose. Laborers and owners of productive resources for the most part are free to sell their services or not to sell them, as they desire. Each is dependent upon the other in this general process. Most people produce only a small portion of the goods that they consume, and a great many consume only goods that are sold in the market for money, which, in turn, gives command over goods and services produced by others. Hence, our society has been called the individual exchange-cooperative type.

The motive that drives people to this cooperation is almost entirely selfish. We do things because it is to our individual interest to do them. Those who have goods and services to sell exact the highest prices they can. Those who buy purchase from the cheapest source they know, other things remaining equal. The persons with goods or services to sell, however, are somewhat restricted in the amount that they can charge for them, since others have similar things to sell. In general, no one is obliged to buy from anyone else; and, in consequence, the prices of one seller must approximate those of other sellers, or the goods cannot be sold. This is the result of what we call competition, and it is only where competition is effective that it is safe to leave the provision of essential economic services on this purely voluntary basis. The interest of a group producing particular products might be that of exploiting the consumers of those products. Competition, if effective, however, prevents this. The pitting of each against the other in an effort to gain trade tends to ensure the supplying of these goods by those who are willing to furnish them at the lowest price.

The prospective prices of products determine which will be produced. The order leaves men relatively free to produce what they wish or to work for whomever they choose. They may be expected, at least within the limits of their knowledge, to select their most profitable alternative. Those goods will be produced which promise the producers the most profitable returns. The laborer will work where he can get the most satisfactory return for his services. There is a tendency, as a result, for our productive resources to be assigned to those uses which will yield them the most. This cannot be perfect, since society is a dynamic, changing thing; but, as rapidly as errors of estimate are discovered, an attempt is made to correct them. The force that leads to this distribution of resources is again that of private interest. We do the things promising us the largest personal gain. When there is an increase in the price of a particular product and as a result business becomes more profitable in a particular line, there is an expansion of production by the producers in that line and newcomers endeavor to crowd in. When the price of a particular product falls, some of the producers turn to the production of other things. Prices indicate to the producers the demands of consumers for particular products and changes in those demands. If consumers desire more of a product and are willing to pay a higher price for it, then the price rises in the market. If, on the contrary, consumers cease to care for an article, then it cannot be sold in such large quantities at the former price. The order provides, in this manner, for the production of goods which the consumers desire and for which they are willing to pay a sufficient price to induce someone to produce. The order also provides for changes in the quantities of the goods produced in accordance with changes in the desires of consumers for goods.

As has been suggested, price also regulates the consumption of goods by distributing these goods among the various persons who compose society. The cooperative nature of our society means that most of the goods produced must be sold to others and ordinarily, through competition, that all similar goods must be sold at approximately the same price in the market. Prices in the market must, in consequence, fall low enough to clear it of goods, and all those who are willing and able to pay the price may obtain them. If the quantity in the market is small, then prices may be high, and many either will not or cannot buy, the goods falling only into the hands of those who are willing and able to pay the higher price.

It is in this manner (rather than through arbitrary decisions as in the regimented society) that our economic system determines the relative importance of different wants. Through its system of rewards, society automatically weighs each individual and enables him to collect approximately the full economic value of his services; he is then able to command for consumption precisely the same amount of value that his services have been worth to others. If one contributes more than another in the way of economic goods, then society judges by this process that his sum of wants is of more importance than those of the less productive contributor. Within the limits of the income thus earned, he may rate and satisfy such wants as he wishes. Those who contribute a great deal are able to consume much. If society has provided all with equal opportunities, then each is said to receive all that his abilities and exertions are worth.

The fundamental tenets of the individual exchange-cooperative type of order might be summarized as follows:

a. There is no test of social worth superior to that of individual taste; hence, individuals are to be allowed freedom of choice as to consumption and production opportunities.

b. Under a system based upon freedom of contract, exchange, and enterprise, industry runs at maximum efficiency.

c. The recipients of the various productive shares will receive rewards according to their productive efficiency and competition will effectively control the amount of such rewards.

3. Criticism of the Operation and Philosophy of the Order. The existing economic order may be criticized on at least two bases. (1) It fails to function throughout in keeping with the philosophy that we have outlined as forming the fundamental basis of the order. For example, it may be argued that the rewards for efforts are not perfectly adjusted and that in many places competition breaks down. In other words, the competitive system does not operate effectively either because of monopolistic control or because of quasi-monopolistic control resulting from product differentiation, unfair methods of competition, or what not. (2) The general philosophy underlying its operation is faulty. For example, it may be argued that the rating of wants in terms of the amounts of contributions allows the irrelevant wants of the rich to be satisfied at the expense of vital wants of the poor, and again that the profit motive provides a biased and unsafe force for the general development of society, since it sacrifices the interests of the group for those of the individual.

Although these general criticisms carry considerable force, no one of intelligence proposes the complete and immediate overthrow of the existing order. It is worth while, however, to examine the system critically in order to determine its specific weaknesses and the various possibilities of remedial action. For example, we look for protection from the predatory interests of individuals through competition. In many cases, however, this protection has broken down. There are many fields of production that are clearly monopolistic. The railroads, public utilities, and a large and growing mass of industries supplying public services are already noncompetitive; their monopolistic nature is recognized; and society provides safeguards for the consumers by the legal establishment of "reasonable" rates and minimum qualities of service. In many other industries, there are trusts, less conspicuous organizations, such as trade associations, or even codes of ethics, which are designed to lessen the effect of competition and to make industry safe for the businessman. In the labor field, there are some strong organizations which occasionally have been responsible for stoppages in certain vital industries because of dispute. Although competition has not disappeared entirely, it has ceased in many cases to provide safeguards needed by society; and in these cases there is occasion for control and regulation in the interests of society as a whole.

Even granting legislative efforts designed to offset certain economic irregularities, the underlying philosophy of the order also may be criticized. It is probable, for example, that the order does not result in rating men in the best possible way for society. It is possible for each society to select and reward those whom it deems of most value to it. It may be urged, however, that our system of rewards concerns itself principally with temporary contributions and leaves only slightly rewarded those who make the most lasting contributions to our advancement. Thus, the great contributions to science or even to the arts are likely to receive only small rewards, whereas the relatively insignificant and ephemeral contribution of the popular radio comedian (say) may yield large returns. Moreover, it is quite probable that the competitive system fails in many cases to deal out the exact rewards needed to secure the supplies of the factors of production that are necessary for the goods worth making. Those who possess exceptional ability are probably paid more than is necessary to secure their services. At the same time, those of small ability are often so poorly paid that their efficiency suffers as a result.

The basis of the justice in rating men as we do lies in the assumption of an equality of opportunity. The individual alone is responsible for his life, the argument runs. Given a fair start in life, competition ensures him equal chance with others, and if he fails to make a success, the fault is his alone. Opportunities, however, are far from equal. Those of great genius rise over every obstacle, but the majority of men are mediocre and remain in the class to which they are born. There is a scarcity of capable men at the top of each profession, since to attain this level requires the unusual coincidence of great ability, the resources needed for a lengthy period of training, and the opportunity. There is an immense fund of high ability that is never realized upon by society because it is never given the proper chance of development. The system results in a much poorer utilization of our human resources than is possible, and every effort should be bent toward bringing to light and utilizing these hitherto wasted resources.

The efficiency of the present order in its administration of consumption is also certainly open to question. It has already been suggested that the rating of men on an economic basis may give an unsound criterion of the value of their wants. The institution of inheritance enables some to consume much more than their personal contributions warrant. A man may personally produce nothing yet consume much, because his ancestors produced much and acquired a property control over productive resources. Indeed, this original control may have been acquired by fraud or downright thievery from society. The methods of the valuation of wants that the order sets up breaks down here. It is when we observe the extremes in the differences of income that this becomes most clear. We find the rich indulging in whims and often actually degrading consumption while the satisfaction of wants that are necessary for their own efficiency are denied the poor. Whatever the fundamental worth of this system of evaluation, there are grievous maladjustments. All these things are matters of grave public concern and unless properly handled may in time cause the collapse of the present economic system with a loss of all the virtues that it contains.

4. The Necessity for Regulation in the Existing Order.—As has been already suggested, the purely individualistic system though eminently just in abstract form may be very unjust in its actual operation. Indeed, many injustices arise out of the competitive struggle itself. Hence, monopolies emerge, wage earners are exploited, and consumers are adversely affected. Other limitations to pure individualism arise out of a lack of incentive for furnishing certain types of services that are necessary to our modern society. Hence, our system of political economy is perforce a mixed affair; the direction of human activity and its accompanying use of resources are under *dual control.*[1] Part of the control emerges from the economic system itself, and part results from the imposition of artificial restraints by central authorities.

As has been previously suggested, there are certain forms of activity that cannot be left to individual initiative, for the reason that while they are collectively important they offer no particular incentive for an individual to perform them. Provision for the national defense, police protection, and even the education of the great mass of our citizens would not be undertaken except through governmental action. It is necessary, for similar reasons, to care for the physically and mentally defective and to furnish numerous services such as mail distribution, highway systems, and navigation facilities. In addition, we have found it desirable to formulate certain "rules of the game" to which those who choose to engage in business activity must adhere. Hence, we set up certain standards of proficiency as requisite to the entering of some fields since we believe that such requisites protect society. We also set aside certain areas in our cities for home purposes, restricting manufacturing and trading activity to segregated districts provided for the purpose. We set up certain restrictions regarding the treatment of laborers, particularly with respect to working conditions, hours of work, and wages. We have even made some headway toward establishing standards of quality for certain types of goods.

Since ours is a system depending on competition to control prices, we have antitrust laws designed for the purpose of making competition mandatory. Regulations concerning competitive practices are provided for the same purpose. In some instances, however, we recognize the advantages of monopoly by sanctioning publicly owned or publicly regulated business enterprises.

There are a great many cases, however, for which society either has not or had not until recently recognized a direct responsibility. The business machine, for example, leaves a constant stream of human wrecks by the wayside for whom until quite lately no one assumed responsibility. For one thing, new

[1] STEVENSON and VAILE, *op. cit.*, p. 7.

technological methods are introduced, with their attendant displacement of personnel.[1] There are also the inefficient and the improvident, the victims of the improvidence of others, or of misfortune (resulting from sickness or accident), and those simply ground down by the wear and tear of machine tending. Until recently there has been likewise no social responsibility for the wreckage caused by the business cycle; yet it periodically paralyzes industry and entails heavy social costs. Men remain idle who wish to work, and, as a result, the product of society is much less than it might be. Hence, we find it necessary, even in an individualistic society, to depart from the general principle of *laissez faire*. Social responsibility in such matters, though slow to be recognized in the United States, is at last being given attention.

Competition actually fails to provide adequate protection in certain cases where the consumers or laborers are ignorant. It may, in fact, act to their detriment. Where consumers cannot tell the quality of goods, there is a constant temptation to the manufacturer to adulterate or cut the quality. Indeed, competition may force him to do this very thing or be outsold by his competitors. A similar situation arises in the case of the laborer who is offering his services. Guards and safety devices are expensive, and the manufacturer who incurs extra expenses for them is at a disadvantage in the matter of costs. Though we have made some strides at setting things to rights in both cases, there still remain vast quantities of shoddy goods and injurious

[1] The problem of technological unemployment, however, is quite different from what is popularly supposed. Displacement of personnel due to technological changes arises through improvements in techniques in going industries (utilization of automatic or semiautomatic devices in certain production processes) and through the passing of outmoded industries (the carriage industry, for example). Over a period of time, personnel adjustments take place as a result of increased production volume due to a reduction of prices, the labor requirements of new industries which are continually coming into existence, and the labor requirements of industries producing the machinery giving rise to the technological change. It is interesting to note that in the United States in 1900 we employed 38.2 per cent of a population of 76 millions, whereas in 1930 we employed 40 per cent of a population of 122 millions. There is no gainsaying the individual aspects of the problem, however. That is to say, workers actually are displaced at times and have difficulty in making the necessary adjustments. Indeed, some older workers find the adjustment impossible of accomplishment.

lines of work that turn out men at middle age with their productive powers seriously reduced.

5. Comparative Efficiency of the Regimented and Unregimented Societies.—As to the comparative productive efficiency of the two general types of economic orders—capitalistic and socialistic—one can make few conclusive statements. The reason for this is quite apparent. Although the economic progress of the several countries can be compared roughly as was suggested earlier, there are few cases, if any, of purely socialistic or purely capitalistic orders. In fact, although there was a time when capitalism and socialism presented a clear-cut antithesis, such is no longer the case. Capitalism is taking on more and more "the trappings of socialism," whereas socialistic patterns have taken on a large part of "the framework of capitalistic institutions."[1]

Moreover, there never has been and perhaps never can be a controlled experiment regarding relative efficiency of economic orders. Though it is incontrovertible that Russia has with its controlled order made phenomenal progress, no intelligent person can argue that once the direction was pointed some gains could not have been made under an entirely different institutional setup. Probably much too much emphasis has been placed upon social institutions as a factor in economic progress, too little on national resources, technological developments, and the skill of labor.

Experience and logic do give us some valuable pointers with respect to comparative efficiency, however. In theory, at least, a centrally planned economy has many distinct advantages. It does make possible a reduction of waste motion. There are possibilities of reducing production and distribution wastes. A country can gird itself as if for war and carry through a Gargantuan program with tremendous enthusiasm. Moreover, security may be more effectively established in a regimented society. There are, on the other hand, limitations to such an institutional system. Rapid changes in technological processes are incompatible with economic stability, since it is through technological change that economic progress arises. Regimen-

[1] A. H. Hansen, "Economic Stabilization in an Unbalanced World," p. 324.

tation with a view to security may tend to slow down the rate of progress. Although the freezing of an existing situation would undoubtedly result in security, there is a danger that it would by that very token slow down economic advancement. There is a grave question as to whether a centralized authority would elect to scrap a well-established production program (say) in order to take advantage of newly developed techniques. If regimentation results in a failure to accept a change that promises increased product, the cost to society might be too great. In the totalitarian order, the savings at any one stage of development might be more than offset by losses resulting from a failure to progress toward a higher level of efficiency.

There are, of course, other questionable aspects of the artificially controlled economic order. There is always the question whether one man or a group of men is foresighted enough to make intelligent decisions regarding the detailed workings of a vast economic system. Mistakes made by those in central authority stand out in bold relief, for the results of such errors are not offset by the opposing actions of others. Witness the ghastly situation arising out of a combination of the exportation of wheat (for the purpose of creating foreign exchange to be used in the purchase of capital goods) and the collectivizing of the farmers (with a resulting reduction of production volume) in Russia in the early 1930's. The famine that followed the twofold program was one of the worst ever experienced. One never knows, of course, whether such errors are inherent in an artificially controlled system or whether with experience the chance of such serious errors ultimately can be eliminated.

Life under a totalitarian order would be intolerable to those who have lived under a system characterized by an absence of restraint. It has been a common experience that liberty is not appreciated until seriously circumscribed. Moreover, though savings might well result from the regimenting of consumers and the dictating of requirements, it cannot be gainsaid that "variety is the spice of life." One could conceive of vast savings resulting from the establishment of a standard calorie diet, but one shrinks at the thought of living under such a rigid discipline. To put it in another way, though the modified individualistic society may not be the most efficient possible, it probably makes for the fuller life.

That we have made excellent progress in the United States under controlled capitalism there can be no doubt. One index that is helpful in evaluating the results of our own system is that of the change in real wages in the United States. For example, real wages increased 200 per cent in this country in the 50 years 1881–1931; 400 per cent in the 100 years 1831–1931. One may infer from this that the scale of living of wage earners has been tremendously improved during the past century. In Russia, though there is little unemployment, the scale of living is "usually lower than that of workers in America and Western Europe in such bread and butter things as food and clothing, housing and transportation. Indeed the 'abolition of unemployment' might be just as plausibly, although less pleasantly described as a mass conscription of labor."[1] Though one should avoid an attitude of smugness, one cannot but recognize that the economic system under which we operate has on the whole been very effective in terms both of income produced and of the worker's share of the product.

We have, however, come to a turning of the road in our economic development. Our people seem to have indicated a strong inclination toward greater security. Part of this feeling is due to the problem having been brought into bold relief as a result of a periodic bogging down of our economic machinery, part to the increasing consciousness of the wear and tear on industrial workers of a geared-up industrial machine, and part to a recognition of the fact that the price of economic progress is technological maladjustment. We have, therefore, made many overtures toward stability. But, as Prof. Hansen warns, "We may quite conceivably find it increasingly apparent, as time goes on, that a high degree of stability can easily be purchased at too great a cost in terms of both freedom and progress. A complete autocracy which could dictate precisely what consumers must buy and which could order producers around like chessmen on a board, could without much doubt cure the evil of unemployment. But such an autocracy, whether capitalistic or communistic, would probably discover that this sort of regimentation is not the kind of life that western civilizations wish to live."[2] We probably cannot have complete security

[1] William Henry Chamberlin, "Russia's Iron Age," p. 96.

[2] Hansen, *op. cit.*, p. vii.

and the gains derived from economic progress. And we must forever remind ourselves that though we should continue to strive for improvement we must be resigned to the fact that a utopian order is impossible of realization.

Questions

1. How important is the organization of society as a factor in determining the productive efficiency of an economic order? That is, is the nature of the economic organization as important as natural resources? state of the arts? organization of the business unit? technical proficiency of workmen?
2. Who are the net producers in modern society? How many are there? What proportion of the population do they represent?
3. How much consumption is and should be provided in a communal way under state leadership?
4. Do you think that Russia's success or lack of success would be any different if the so-called individualistic type of economy obtained there? Why or why not?
5. It is said that the United States is tending toward socialism. Is this true? Is such a tendency desirable from the point of view of the consumer?
6. It is said that the regimented society is a depressionless society. Discuss this statement.

CHAPTER III

INCOMES OF CONSUMERS

The economic organization of society on a pecuniary basis gives great importance to the money income of the consumer, since the possession of this money income gives him power to command goods and services in the market. Individual consumers are, in fact, aware of a consumption problem largely because of the limitation of their consumption which is imposed by lack of funds. They ordinarily think that their problem would be solved if they could, in some way, secure a sufficiently large income. The market is uninfluenced by needs or desires unless they are expressed in offers for goods in money. Each dollar, regardless of the ethical or moral situation back of its expenditure, possesses similar power in directing the productive efforts of society. The goods of society go into the hands of those who can pay for them, irrespective of the real needs of the purchasers. The consumption problem cannot, in consequence, be understood without a knowledge of the distribution of incomes among the members of society.

1. The Concept of Income.—The most usual concept of income is that of money income. This consists of the monetary receipts for a particular period of time. The money income of a family for a year is the monetary receipts from all sources received by that family during the year. It includes the salaries or earnings of the working members, the earnings from property, gifts, etc., in short, all sums, from whatever source, that become available during the period.

Income and consumption are not necessarily the same. There is a difference between total and consumed income, which difference consists of savings and gifts from the income. Persons with large incomes generally spend a smaller proportion of their incomes than do those with small incomes. A man with an income twenty times that of another is not likely to spend twenty times as much in consumption, but much less, say ten times as much. Moreover, because one person or group has a larger money income than another, it does not follow that they are able to consume more in the way of goods and services. Certain goods and services may not be sold in the market, or, if sold, they may sell for a lower price in one place than they do in another; and, in consequence, a given money income is able to purchase more in one place than in the other. The difference appears sharply when the money incomes of cityfolk and farmers are compared. The farmer receives a great many things, such as fruits and vegetables, dairy produce, and the use of his house, which do not represent expenditures of his money income.

We may term the goods and services that a person has to consume his *real income.* The real income of people and their consumption are very similar, since savings are generally in the form of money and not of goods. Real incomes are, in consequence, of great importance in a study of consumption. When we endeavor to measure real incomes, the same difficulties arise as when we endeavor to study consumption on the basis of goods and services. There is no common denominator to which this heterogeneous mass of things can be reduced. We can describe quite precisely the income of an individual, in terms of units or pounds, in short, we can make a complete inventory of the physical things and services that he receives or consumes; but as between individuals our statements can proceed only in general terms. The best that can be done is to select certain significant items that are capable of measurement and, by weighting them arbitrarily, arrive at a general notion. Despite these limitations, comparisons of real incomes, particularly those dealing with consumption, are often desirable for many purposes, since they may yield even more pertinent information than the comparison of money incomes.

The income concept may be pushed even further, and income may be thought of as a flow of satisfaction received over a stated period of time. This may be called *psychic income.* We know little or nothing regarding the psychic income of individuals. The psychologists have provided us with no unit for the comparisons of reactions, and, in consequence, statements regarding psychic incomes are merely guesses. We may suspect that the satisfaction which one person receives from a good is different from that of every other individual, or that psychic incomes are somewhat proportional to real incomes—our conclusions in either case depend upon our assumptions at the outset. We have, as an additional difficulty in income comparisons, the fact that the various concepts are neither proportional nor equal. Thus, the same money income does not provide the same real income, and, moreover, it is not likely to do so. Similarly, the same real incomes may yield quite different psychic incomes. In consequence, we can hardly solve one portion of the problem in terms of one sort of income and another part of the problem in terms of a different sort of income and make close comparisons. Comparisons can be made only in a most general way, and then only when all the assumptions and implications are clearly stated.

2. Estimates of the National Income.—Various estimates have been made of the money income for the United States as a whole and for various other countries. Among recent attempts for the United States, those of the U.S. Department of Commerce and of the National Bureau of Economic Research are perhaps the best. These estimates are described as follows:[1]

"National income may be defined as the net value of commodities and services produced by the nation's economic system. It is net in that the value of output of all commodities and services is reduced by the value of commodities (fuel, raw materials and fixed equipment) consumed in the process of production. And it refers, by design, to the net product of the economic system, which, for the advanced nations during recent decades, may be identified with the market economy; provided market is understood broadly as the meeting place of all buyers and sellers, no matter how much freedom of transactions may be curbed by custom or regulation.

"We include not only monetary payments but also some payments that appear in the form of commodities or services: (1) farm produce retained by farm families for their own consumption; (2) payments in kind to employees; (3) services of houses inhabited by their owners. On the other hand, we exclude some incomes that appear in the form of money but that represent payments for activities that are unproductive when judged by the most lenient standard of productivity: (1) illegal activities

[1] SIMON KUZNETS, "National Income, 1919–1935," *Nat. Bur. Econ. Res. Bull.* 66, p. 1, Sept. 27, 1937.

(theft, robbery, prostitution, murder, etc.); (2) such activities as, while legal, represent largely shifts of income among individuals rather than additions to the command over goods (gambling, speculative gains from the sale of assets by non-professional groups); (3) speculative gain of any type resulting from a general change in the price level. Finally, we add to these incomes disbursed to individuals the net savings of enterprises."

Examples of these estimates for selected years are shown in Table 1.

TABLE 1.—NATIONAL INCOME, TOTAL AND PER CAPITA[1]

Year	Total national income (millions of dollars)		Per capita in 1929 prices
	Current prices	1929 prices	
1919	60,161	56,424	$538
1924	70,557	69,978	616
1929	83,631	83,614	689
1934	47,960	59,684	472
1937[2]	69,800	77,550	601

[1] SIMON KUZNETS, "National Income, 1919–1935," *Nat. Bur. Econ. Res. Bull.* 66, p. 2, Sept. 27, 1937.

[2] *The Annalist*, vol. 52, No. 1338, p. 336, Sept. 7, 1938.

The reduction to terms of 1929 dollars provides a rough measure of comparative physical volumes. It is at once apparent that, however viewed, income provided by the general social economy even in good years in as prosperous a country as the United States is pitifully small and emphasizes the necessity of a much greater production before the level of consumption can be materially raised for the entire group.

The major source of this income is attributable to human effort. It has been estimated, for example, that roughly 80 per cent of the national income in 1929 went to reward current effort and approximately 20 per cent went to owners of property.[1] These rewards to current effort include wages and salaries and an estimate for the share of the individual enterprisers' income attributable to their efforts and aside from their returns on invested capital.

[1] M. LEVEN, H. G. MOULTON, and C. WARBURTON, "America's Capacity to Consume," p. 35.

Comparisons are frequently made, as has just been done, of money incomes between different periods of time in the same country. Important errors may be involved if these comparisons are used to imply similar differences in real incomes or relative welfares, disregarding even the impossibilities of an accurate summation of the money income. There is a certain income that escapes both notice and assessment in any calculation of money incomes.[1] (1) There are certain unpaid services furnished in the order, particularly those of women. The services of the housewife are as much a source of real income as though they had been purchased in the market, and they amount to (say) one-fifth of the value of goods bought and sold in the market. (2) There are differences in the qualities of goods. The comparison of money incomes over a period of time fails to reflect properly these improvements. The workingman now spends his income for commodities quite different from those for which the workingman in 1850 spent his. Comparisons between countries are rendered inexact for similar reasons. (3) The money income fails to account for such things as leisure, more congenial occupation, improved personal relations, the growth of freedom, good government, and education. Leisure, for example, although not directly purchased, is nevertheless a quasi commodity and one to which people divert their consumption as their incomes become larger. It is a well-established fact that the high-wage countries and industries are the countries and industries of the shortest hours and at the same time those in which the least labor of women and children is used to supplement the family income. (4) There are certain items to be balanced against these uncounted items. A greater proportion of goods and services is now sold in the market than formerly. Similarly, although the number of hours of working has been lessened, there has been a speeding up of tasks. (5) The general level of prices, as will be subsequently pointed out, may have changed, and this can be only roughly measured over any considerable period. History cannot record nor statistics measure the precise difference between two periods or places; at best only a rough estimate based on plausible assumptions is possible.

3. The Inequalities of Money Income.—It is evident from common observation that large differences exist among persons

[1] See William Smart, "The Distribution of Income," Chap. XI.

and families in the amount of their income. The table below shows the estimates made by the Brookings Institution for 1929.

TABLE 2.—PERCENTAGE DISTRIBUTION OF INDIVIDUALS AND FAMILIES BY INCOME CLASSES, 1929[1]

Income class	Percentage of individuals	Percentage of families of two or more persons
Under $1,000	39.8	21.5
1,000 to 2,000	41.0	38.0
2,000 to 3,000	10.9	18.9
3,000 to 4,000	3.2	8.9
4,000 to 5,000	1.5	4.5
5,000 to 10,000	2.3	5.9
10,000 and over	1.3	2.3
Total	100.0	100.0

[1] M. LEVEN, "The Income Structure in the United States," p. 145.

The inequalities of these money incomes, which are at once apparent, arise from two principal sources—differences in innate abilities of individuals and differences in the inheritances of property and environment. Psychological data indicate that people differ greatly in their innate capacities and that, if these capacities could be completely tested and compared, we would find people grouped around the typical curve of normal distribution regarding them. In this curve, the largest number would be near the center, and as the capacities became higher or lower there would be fewer persons in each group as we passed to the extremes. One would expect from the distribution of capacities that the income curve would be of a similar shape. The table shows that this is not true and that the income curve is very one-sided.

The principal cause of the difference in these curves is inheritance. Those who have no particular ability may be high on the income curve through inheritance. The numerous moron sons of wealthy parents are examples. The inheritances that affect incomes are of two types—the inheritance of wealth and the inheritance of environment and opportunities. The effects of the inheritance of property are obvious; they increase the income of the inheritor with little regard to his ability. The effects of the inheritance of environment and opportunity are less obvious but much deeper and more important. A mediocre person raised in a superior environment with good opportunities and assisted by the advantage of sound training is assured of a place in a moderately high-income group. It is true that low incomes do not necessarily mean poor environments for children and large incomes good environments. It is also true that especially gifted individuals push themselves to the top from even the lowest groups. But, in general, the income of the parents has a great deal to do with the environment and opportunities of the children. The importance of this point cannot be overemphasized, since if it is true it constitutes a serious indictment of our present economic system. If rewards and opportunities for development are largely matters of inheritance, then the system fails to make the best use of our human resources. It is, of course, the belief that larger incomes or better utilization of those incomes will make available latent abilities among the mass of those who constitute the low-income groups, which gives the social importance to a study of consumption.

Wages are the principal source of income for the lower income groups, and there are considerable variations among them. In all countries, the lowest wages generally prevail in agriculture, and these are usually from one-half to three-fourths of the wages of unskilled industrial workers. Living costs in the country are usually less than in the city, so that real wages do not differ so much. There is a higher rate of natural increase in the country, with a labor movement toward the city. There is also a large difference among industries, although less pronounced than that between agriculture and industry. Wages in mining and the textile industries are generally lower than the national average and in the construction industries considerably higher. Another important and fairly stable difference is that between skilled and unskilled labor. A normal differential in the United States appears to be about 30 per cent in terms of the average for skilled workers, but this may fail to account for the greater stability of employment in the skilled trades and hence be too low. There has been a tendency toward a lessening of this differential since the war. Salaries, on the whole, are higher than wages, but here again the differences have tended to lessen. There are, of course, variations among individuals in their rates of pay even in the same general lines of work. The variations are greater among the skilled than among the semiskilled, and among the semiskilled than among the unskilled. The differences also tend to be greater among adult males than among women and children and among those receiving piece rates as compared with time rates.

Economic opportunities differ by regions, and, in consequence, we find differences in the average money incomes in various geographic areas in the United States. These incomes are relatively high in the Middle Atlantic, New England, and Pacific states, and relatively low in the South. The predominance of agriculture in the South is one of the reasons for these differences, and there may be real differences in productive capacity. The regional averages for 1929 are shown in Table 3.

TABLE 3.—INCOME OF INDIVIDUALS, BY GEOGRAPHIC DIVISIONS, 1929[1]

Geographic Division	Per Capita Income
United States	$750
New England	907
Middle Atlantic	1,107
East North Central	831
West North Central	562
South Atlantic	466
East South Central	344
West South Central	476
Mountain	664
Pacific	999

[1] M. LEVEN, H. G. MOULTON, and C. WARBURTON, "America's Capacity to Consume," p. 38.

There also appears to be a rather high correlation between the size of the community and the income of employed workers in that community. An example is afforded by a Michigan study made in 1934. The median annual income reported for 1.4 million persons was $840, but the median income for those in cities above 40,000 was $980, and this was more than twice the income of those living in rural townships. This type of difference was found for all the occupations for which separate tabulations were made.

The income of the individual in so far as it depends upon his own productivity shows a well-marked change with age. The normal course is a gradual increase from a low beginning to a peak in middle or post-middle age, and then a decline until retirement or death. Table 4 gives the median incomes reported

TABLE 4.—MEDIAN INCOME OF EMPLOYED WORKERS IN MICHIGAN BY AGE AND CERTAIN OCCUPATIONS, 1934[1]

Age group	Professional	Clerical	Skilled	Semi-skilled	Unskilled
15 to 24	$585	$631	$705	$505	$321
25 to 34	1,273	1,077	1,087	819	521
35 to 44	1,666	1,285	1,178	861	588
45 to 54	1,731	1,271	1,137	829	560
55 to 64	1,606	1,178	1,065	732	519
65 and above	1,519	980	955	590	448

[1] M. LEVEN, "The Income Structure of the United States," p. 156.

by the Brookings Institution for the Michigan study of 1934. The peak of incomes for most groups appears to have been at about forty years of age. For the clerical personnel it was between forty and forty-five, and with the professional group it was just below fifty years.

The social cost or loss resulting from unequal incomes becomes most apparent when the extremes of incomes are compared. On the one hand, senseless and often degrading luxuries are indulged in; and at the other extreme, individuals lack the minimum necessary to maintain physical efficiency. For example, in Great Britain, Sir John Orr estimates the number of those living "near or below the threshold of adequate nutrition" as a result of deficiency of income as about 10 millions.[1] In the United States, Miss Stiebeling found that 61 per cent of the families in the lower income group of employed wage earners and low-salaried clerical workers in the 1934–1936 study had C grade diets, or diets that were deficient in some important elements.[2] Infant mortality is high in the lower income groups; housing is usually poor, with overcrowding and, in a large number of instances, failure to meet most of the accepted, even if arbitrary, minimum standards. There is little doubt that, so long as society's income as a whole is not diminished, within wide limits an increase of income enjoyed by the poor at the expense of a

[1] "Final Report of the Mixed Committee of the League of Nations on Nutrition," p. 266.

[2] HAZEL STIEBELING, "Diets of Families of Employed Wage-earners and Low-salaried Clerical Workers Living in Industrial Communities in Three Regions of the United States, 1934–1936," *Bur. Home Econ.*, 1937.

similar decrease in the income of the rich would increase the welfare of society.

The unequal distribution of income not only modifies consumption by giving some the power to consume more than others but also modifies the character of the goods chosen on each income level. This is due to the tendency of men to ape their superiors; thus, since consumption offers, in many cases, a very visible way of imitation, it leads to excessive indulgence. The rich, therefore, possess not only the power to consume more than the poor but also the power to modify materially the goods that are bought by the poor with their income.

An increase in the income of the poor, relative to the income of the rich, would affect industry by leading to a change in the proportion of goods of different kinds produced. There would be a smaller production of expensive luxuries and a greater production of necessary articles. "Rare wines would give way to bread and meat, new machines and factories to clothes and improved dwellings."[1] Goods that depend largely for their importance on the fact that few consume them would decrease in importance and price. Such things as diamonds would decrease materially in value.

It is not to be assumed that an absolute equality of incomes would be desirable. The income of every civilized nation when balanced against its population is, after all, pitiably small. Per capita income in money terms in the United States even in a year of high prices such as 1929 was estimated at around only $700, and such a money income is considerably larger than the per capita incomes of European countries. The chief disadvantage of a more equal distribution of incomes lies in its probable effect upon the accumulation of capital. The great bulk of savings comes from the larger incomes, since a larger portion of the smaller income is consumed. The increase of the lower incomes would be quite small since there are a great many in the low-income groups, and the amount of savings would be decreased. The Brookings Institution report their estimates for 1929 as follows: "The upper 10 per cent of the families, including those with incomes above $4,600, made about 86 per cent of the total savings. The second group, with incomes from $3,100 to $4,600, accounted for 12 per cent of the savings. The remainder, saved

[1] A. C. Pigou, "Economics of Welfare," 2d ed., p. 76.

by 80 per cent of the population, amounted to only two per cent of the total."[1] Although these estimates probably overstate the importance of the high-income groups, they, nevertheless, are instructive as to their very predominant importance.

Capital accumulation is proceeding at a more rapid rate under an unequal distribution of incomes than it would be likely to under a more equal distribution. It is, in consequence, often argued that when we adopt a long-time view of society this inequality of incomes secures a more rapid progress than we would have under a more equal distribution of incomes. It must not be overlooked, however, that much of the increase of the income of the poor, if it were at the expense of the larger incomes, though it would not be saved and appear in the form of capital, would, nevertheless, be invested in a very real sense. Better homes and living conditions would be provided, and more would be expended on education. It is quite possible that these investments might yield even more to social well-being and progress than similar investments in material equipment.

4. Comparisons of Money Incomes.—Reasons have already been indicated for the probable failure of estimated money incomes to reflect properly the real income of persons or of the community. Several of the more important differences may again be noted. (1) The real income of society must exceed the goods and services represented by the money income because of the omitted or uncounted items. The money-income estimates are based on only the 48 million gainfully employed, and certainly the remainder of the 122 million of our population produce a considerable amount. The services of the housewives are an outstanding example of an omitted item. (2) The usual estimates of money incomes overstate the fluctuations of the real income of society during the cyclical changes. Real income does not fall so low in a depression period as money income, even after adjustment for changes in the level of prices is made. People continue to use their durable goods even though they do not replace them as before. Automobiles, for example, are run longer before being dismantled; houses, clothes, and equipment are repaired and made to last longer. Although the quality of service rendered probably declines, nevertheless these things are made to yield services when under better conditions they would

[1] LEVEN, MOULTON, and WARBURTON, *op. cit.*, p. 96.

have been discarded for newer articles. Moreover, people in these periods do for themselves things they previously chose to buy in the market; housewives preserve fruits and vegetables and mend more, and the men make repairs and do more small construction work. Thus the real volume of goods and services does not decline so much as the decline in money income indicates. (3) Though real incomes are very unequally distributed, the differences are not so great as those indicated by the distribution of money incomes. The lower income groups do for themselves many things for which the rich pay in the market: more household production goes on in the poor households; those on lower incomes save a smaller portion of their money income and are more likely to receive uncounted assistance.

Questions

1. What factors other than income also limit consumption?
2. In a period of falling prices, would the real income of society or its money income decline more?
3. Turn to some standard text in economics, and determine the distinction between wealth and income. Now discuss the proposition that all consumption is equally destructive of wealth.
4. Are savings part of the national income?
5. Is the dissatisfaction with our personal income all a matter of relatives, *i.e.*, the greater amount that someone else has?
6. Per capita incomes in 1929 were estimated as nearly three times as large in the Middle Atlantic states as in the East South Central states. What could account for such great differences?

CHAPTER IV

PRICE BEHAVIOR AND THE CONSUMER

It is a familiar fact that the prices of commodities change. When the prices of large numbers of commodities are observed over a period of time, a great many changes will be found to have taken place. When one year is compared with the preceding year, some prices will be found to have risen, some to have fallen, and some to have remained the same. The range covered by these fluctuations may be very large; for example, in 1896 the average wholesale price of potatoes fell 54.6 per cent and the price of coke rose 41.5 per cent as compared with their average wholesale price in 1895. Among these many sorts of price changes, we are able to distinguish two general groups: those which affect only one or two commodities, and those which are widespread and general and influence all commodities. We speak of the latter as a change in the general price level or the purchasing power of money, by which we mean that in general the dollar will purchase more or less goods than formerly.

1. The Measurement of General Price Changes.—It is difficult, because of the diverse changes in prices, to say whether the dollar will purchase more at one time than at another. It will purchase more of some commodities and less of others. A summary or average of these many changes must be made in order to determine what the change, in general, has been. An index number is the device by which these changes are summarized and expressed. Index numbers may be used to express other changes as well as changes in prices; for example, changes in the physical volume of production or the volume of business, but their more common use is in connection with prices. The prices to be included in the index depend upon the particular purpose for which the index is prepared. For example, an index of the general price level will require that all prices be represented, or at least the prices of all the more important commodities. Some indices, on the contrary, will deal only with the prices of a particular group of products; for example, an index of the cost of living will include only the prices of the commodities that the consumer purchases. The problems involved in the construction of index numbers are complex and can only be briefly mentioned here.

Index numbers are of two general types:[1] (1) those in which the prices of individual items have each been reduced to a percentage of the price or size of those items in a year or period, called the *base*, and an average taken to represent the change in the group; and (2) those in which the group of items is represented by an appropriate average or total, and these averages or totals expressed as relatives of the averages or totals in the base periods. Index numbers of the first type are averages of relatives, and of the second type ratios of averages, or aggregates.

Let us suppose the problem to be that of measuring the changes of the retail cost of dairy products relative to their cost in 1935, and we have the following data:

Kind of dairy product	Average retail price of dairy products, cents		
	1935	1936	1937
Milk per quart	10	11	12
Butter per pound	25	35	30
Cheese per pound	20	30	25

1935 is taken as the base period. In the first type of index, the average of relatives, we would consider the price of each kind of dairy product in 1935 as representing 100 per cent, express the price in each following year as a percentage of the 1935 price, and take an average of these relatives, thus:

Kind of dairy product	1935	1936	1937
Milk	100	110	120
Butter	100	140	120
Cheese	100	150	125
Total	300	400	365
Average	100	133	122

[1] See A. A. YOUNG, in H. L. Rietz, "Handbook of Mathematical Statistics," Chap. XII, Index Numbers.

In the second type of index, we would simply sum or average the actual prices and express as relatives as follows:

Kind of dairy product	Price		
	1935	1936	1937
Milk	$0.10	$0.11	$0.12
Butter	0.25	0.35	0.30
Cheese	0.20	0.30	0.25
Total	0.55	0.76	0.67
Relative	100	138	122

A simple summation of prices is seldom sufficient to constitute a desirable index. If people generally consume five times as much butter as cheese, the decrease of 5 cents in the price of butter in our illustration would have had five times the significance of the 5-cent decrease in the price of cheese. Commodities, in consequence, are usually "weighted," or multiplied by some number that indicates their relative significance for the particular purpose for which the index is being prepared. The result is a *weighted* index number. Hence the effect of weighting is an index number which indicates proportional changes. When the prices are not weighted, the index is called a *simple*, or *unweighted*, index. Indices using actual prices will be weighted by quantities, and indices constructed from relatives will use relative expenditures as weights. The significance of an actual price change depends upon the quantity of the product affected by that change, whereas the importance of a relative change in price depends upon the relative expenditure upon that commodity. Indices constructed on this basis are shown below:

Kind of dairy product	Weighted average of relatives				Ratio of weighted aggregates			
	Weights	1935	1936	1937	Weights	1935	1936	1937
Milk	10	1,000	1,100	1,200	25	2.50	2.75	3.00
Butter	5	500	700	600	5	1.25	1.75	1.50
Cheese	1	100	150	125	1	.20	.30	.25
Total	16	1,600	1,950	1,925	31	3.95	4.80	4.75
Index	..	100	122	120	..	100	121	120

Where index numbers are prepared for special purposes, such as to show changes in the cost of living, they are nearly always weighted. It has sometimes been argued that where index numbers of prices in general are constructed by an average of relative prices weighting may be dispensed with. The unweighted index number, however, is sensitive to abnormal variations of unimportant prices and is too little influenced by large variations of important prices. Usually, therefore, index numbers are more accurate when weighted.

An additional opportunity for variation in index numbers arises because of the different averages that may be used to summarize the data. The most common is the arithmetic mean, or ordinary average, derived by dividing the sum of the individual items by the number of items or by the sum of the weights in the weighted index. The other average that is frequently used is the geometric mean, where all the prices or ratios for a given date are multiplied together and the nth root extracted, n standing for the number of commodities included. The geometric mean for 1936 for our unweighted average of relatives would be $\sqrt[3]{110 \times 140 \times 150} = 132$. The geometric mean is widely used for averaging price ratios, since equal weight is given to equal ratios of change. This is equivalent to saying that equal weight is given to a price that doubles and a price that falls one-half.[1] Medians, modes, and harmonic means are occasionally used in preparing index numbers. The figures may also be left as an aggregative instead of striking an average.

The most widely used index of the general price level in the United States is the Wholesale Price Index of the U.S. Bureau of Labor Statistics. The recently revised number is a weighted aggregate index of 784 quotations of wholesale prices. Each quotation is weighted by an estimate of the annual amount marketed during the years from 1923 to 1925. The sum of these items for each period is expressed as a relative of the sum in 1926. Subtotals are found for nine commodity groups, and these also are expressed as indices. The Federal Reserve Board publishes index numbers compiled from prices collected by the U.S. Bureau of Labor Statistics, using the U.S. Bureau of Labor Statistics methods but grouping the data into separate indices of

[1] See C. M. Walsh, "The Problem of Estimation," for a classic presentation of the arguments in favor of the geometric mean.

raw materials, producers' goods, and consumers' goods. A large number of indices are prepared by various private agencies. There are, for example, indices published by Dun & Bradstreet, Fisher, the Harvard Bureau of Economic Research, *The Annalist*, Snyder, and numerous others.

Index numbers have many uses. The conditions of economic life are complex, and we need summary expressions to indicate clearly exactly what has happened. Index numbers are utilized for this purpose in various sections of this book. For example, when it is desired to show the growth of advertising in the United States, to picture *changes* in real wages over a period of time, or to indicate the degree of change in national income during the depression, the device is utilized.

2. Types of Price Movements.—When the general level of prices is observed for a considerable period of time, three distinct types of price movements appear. Some of these can be distinguished in Figs. 1 and 2.

(*a*) There are periods when prices rise violently and very far. Such rises appeared, as may be seen on the accompanying chart, during the World War period, from 1914 to 1921, and the Civil War period, from 1860 to 1870. These violent movements of prices might be called *periods of inflation and deflation.* (*b*) There are certain sustained general movements of the price level, continuing over a period of time. For example, from 1873 to 1896 the general trend of prices was downward, and from 1896 to 1914 the trend was upward. These general movements of prices are spoken of as *secular trends.* (*c*) There are wave-like movements of prices above and below the secular trend which last from 3 or 4 to 10 or 12 years. These are called *cyclical movements* and are related to and correspond closely with the so-called *business cycle.*[1]

The secular changes in the price level are explained by the economist principally by the quantity theory of money. The price level is thought to depend upon the relation between

[1] Another important type of price movement is the *seasonal.* This type is not a *general* movement but occurs in certain kinds of commodities only and at different times for different goods. Seasonal movements are very important to consumers, however, since purchasing savings accrue to those who properly time their buying. Hence some space is devoted to this subject in Chap. XVII, The Problem of Purchasing.

the amount of money and credit, its velocity of circulation, and the quantity of commodities that are bought and sold. The greater the quantity of money (in the broad sense) relative to a given quantity of goods, the higher the price level is likely to be. If the quantity of goods increases more rapidly during a given period than the quantity of money, other things remaining equal, prices may be expected to fall. If the opposite condition obtains, a rise in prices can be expected. It has been contended that, previous to the World War, an annual increase of 3 per cent

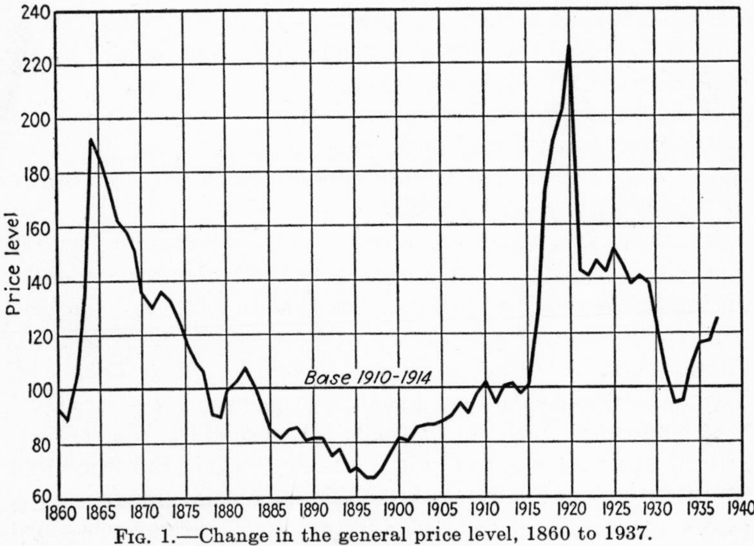

FIG. 1.—Change in the general price level, 1860 to 1937.

in the actual stock of gold in existence would have been necessary in order to keep prices steady.[1] When the stock of gold (according to the argument) increased at a lower rate than 3 per cent annually the general level of prices fell, and when the stock of gold increased more rapidly than 3 per cent annually the general level of prices rose. The period from 1873 to 1896, for example, was one of declining gold production; goods were increasing rapidly, and in consequence prices fell. Gold was produced at an increasing rate beginning with 1896, following the discovery of deposits in South Africa and Australia, and prices rose gradually until the inflation period of the World War. The supply of

[1] See G. A. CASSEL, "Theory of Social Economy," pp. 441–454.

gold has now an effect on general price levels quite different from that which it had before the World War—exactly how much different has not been determined definitely. Currency conditions have altered. Not only is there no gold in circulation in most countries, but also it is recognized that the central banks of the world keep much larger gold reserves than they are likely to need. Added to this is the fact that some countries have revalued gold at a lower level. Thus we may expect a higher level of prices now than previous to the World War. Indeed, since the quantity of money can be more easily controlled by central authorities, artificial inflationary movements actually can be induced. Thus . . . "since it is the tendency of the dominant elements in a competitive economy to favor monetary expansion, the abundance of gold reserves is likely to provide relatively easy money conditions. In other words, the monetary conditions are likely to prove distinctly favorable to expansion—to a secular rise in prices."[1]

Periods of inflation usually result from very large issues of paper money. When this money cannot be exchanged for gold as formerly, the general price level ceases to depend directly upon the stock of gold; the principal factor is now the quantity of paper money. Inflation frequently accompanies wars; for wars call for expenditures much larger than the ordinary revenues of the state, and the issuing of money provides the state with a quick means of purchase.

3. Effect of Changes in the General Price Level on Various Classes.—Changes in the general price level are of great significance in the economic life of the people. Any change of considerable magnitude shifts purchasing power among groups, resulting in benefits to some and hardships to others. This is because all prices do not change with equal rapidity or to the same extent. A considerable group of prices, such as those of annuities, interest payments, and public-utility rates, change very slowly, and the groups concerned with such transactions are influenced particularly.

The most marked changes take place in the relationship of debtor and creditor. The debtor gains on rising prices. His obligations may now be paid with the equivalent of a smaller

[1] F. B. Garver and A. H. Hansen, "Principles of Economics," rev. ed., p. 346.

quantity of goods than before. Thus if wheat is 50 cents a bushel, it would require 2,000 bushels of wheat for a farmer to pay a debt of $1,000, whereas if wheat were $1 a bushel the debt could be retired for the equivalent of 1,000 bushels. During a period of falling prices, creditors gain. The amounts borrowers must repay will now purchase more than at the time the loan was made.[1] Those who are on fixed incomes are in the same situation as the creditor class; in fact, most of those who have fixed incomes secure them by loaning money to others or by the purchase of bonds or annuities, which is an analogous operation. There are, moreover, many salaried people who for considerable periods of time are essentially in a similar situation. Debtors naturally prefer prices to rise, whereas creditors and those with permanent posts at fixed salaries favor falling prices.

Business generally gains when prices rise. The businessman is usually in a debtor position, and many of the payments he must make for things such as rents, salaries, and interest do not rise so rapidly as the prices of goods that he has for sale. Profit margins tend to widen, and business activity is stimulated. If we include the farmer in this group, we find him affected most of all because of his generally important debtor situation and because of a tendency of agricultural prices to rise faster and fall faster than industrial prices. The opposite situation prevails when prices fall, and generally losses are incurred.

The situation of the wage earners is somewhat more complex. The employed worker gains on falling prices and loses on rising prices because his wages usually lag. But because of the changes in business activity, which usually are associated with price movements, employment generally increases with rising prices and declines with falling prices. Thus, while wage rates lag, the number employed increases on the upswing and the laboring group gains in total purchasing power, whereas the reverse occurs when prices are falling. The gain from reemployment

[1] It is possible, in extreme circumstances, for a price rise to wipe out the holding of creditors. The price rise in Germany in the 10 years following 1913 was so great, for example, that, by 1923, 4 million paper marks had a purchasing power of 6 prewar marks. A creditor with an equivalent of 1 million dollars of securities actually could have been repaid by his debtors with currency having purchasing power sufficient to buy only a moderate-priced dinner for two.

would be largest in the early stages of the price increase and the losses from the wage lag greater for the group in the later stages.

A movement of prices thus affects each group in the community and changes their position relative to other groups either favorably or unfavorably.[1] It is not surprising, then, that movements of the general price level are associated with unrest in particular groups and sometimes with class disturbances. There is usually labor unrest when prices are rising. City people are dissatisfied, and there is much talk about the high cost of living. There is agricultural unrest when prices are falling and much talk about the unjust debt situation. The period from 1870 to 1896 was one of downward trend in prices. Farmers organized the Greenback party and put candidates into the field for President and Congress from 1876 to 1884. Silver had been demonetized in 1873, and this was assumed to be one of the causes of the lower prices. Farmers referred to the "Crime of 1873" and pressed first for silver-purchase laws and later for free coinage of silver at 16 to 1. The drive culminated in 1896 in the presidential campaign of W. J. Bryan and his famous cross-of-gold speech. From 1896 to 1920, prices rose and labor strengthened its unions. The American Federation of Labor had less than ½ million members in 1897, but by 1920 over 5 million. Toward the close of the period and during the war there was great complaint about the high cost of living. From 1920 to 1933 there was again great agricultural unrest which gradually subsided in the rise from 1933 to 1937. The later period was again a period of labor unrest.

4. The Business Cycle and the Consumer.—The cyclical changes in the general level of prices above and below the secular trend are, in a large measure, due to the variations in business called the *business cycle*. In these fluctuations, there are periods

[1] From the point of view of the individual the problem often is even more complex than it first appears, since some consumers find themselves in the position of being at once creditors (investors in securities, for example), debtors (mortgaged property owners, say), and wage earners. Individuals of this type might be adversely affected by price declines (say) in their capacities as debtors and—under some conditions—wage earners, and favorably affected in their capacities as creditors. Conversely, for some consumers price increases may improve their positions in one of their several roles, yet adversely affect their positions in one or more of their several others.

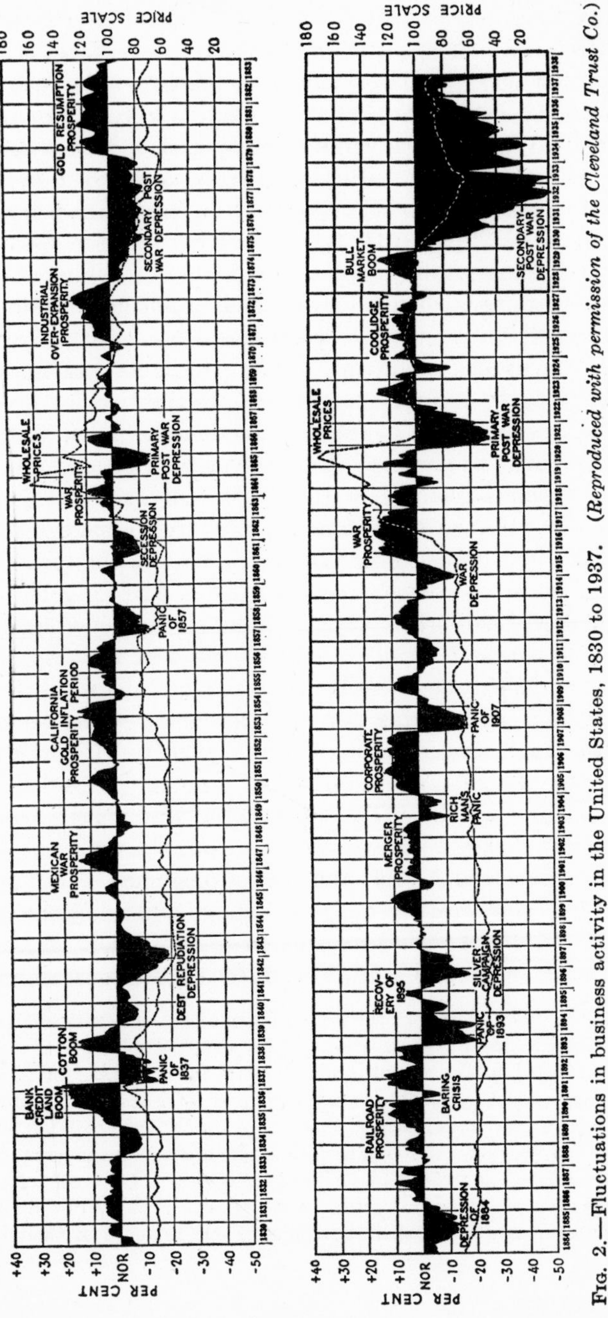

FIG. 2.—Fluctuations in business activity in the United States, 1830 to 1937. (*Reproduced with permission of the Cleveland Trust Co.*)

of considerable expansion and contraction of credit by banks. During a portion of the cycle, bank credit expands the means of payment for goods more rapidly than goods are increasing, and here we find rising prices, and in another phase we find the greater contraction of credit and falling prices. There are many other factors, such as the general business psychology, which influence these short-time movements, but bank credit probably plays a dominant part.

Cyclical fluctuations in business activity are indicated by changes in the general price level about as well as by any other single index. The business cycle, however, consists of a great deal more than simply a change in the general price level. There are changes in employment, rates of wages, volume of production, profits, interest rates, volume of credit, and other important relationships. Consumers will be variously affected by the cycle and in different portions of it. This is because the term *consumers* includes everyone, and different groups are affected differently by the cycle and its stages. As has been suggested, incomes and the prices of the products that are purchased with those incomes do not change simultaneously, and in consequence real incomes vary.

These fluctuations in business activity follow one another in a fairly definite succession. The cycle is generally divided into four stages: periods of depression, of recovery, of prosperity, and of liquidation. There is no constant length for the entire cycle nor for any of the stages of the cycle. Each cycle is distinct in itself and differs from other cycles in important details. There is no sharp break between the different stages of the cycle—they pass gradually from one to the other. The stages, however, differ somewhat in their lengths; the period of recovery, for example, is generally the longest, that of liquidation the shortest.

The relations between the production of goods, their consumption, the accumulation of stocks of goods, and the prices of goods vary during the cycle. If we begin with the period of depression, we find that it is characterized by small production, low prices, and low profits. There is a great deal of unemployment. The volume of physical production in some industries frequently falls to as low as 50 or 60 per cent of the average production. There are large stocks of goods accumulated from earlier phases of the cycle. These consist of consumers' goods, partially processed goods, and raw materials. Consumption is low, relative to other periods, but is greater than current production. The real income of society is low for nearly all classes. Since current production is less than current consumption, the existing stocks of goods must be cut down; and, after they have been exhausted, goods must be produced at an increased rate if the current rate of consumption is to be maintained. The increase in production is not immediately accompanied by a rise in prices, since many of the plants have been operating at only a part of their capacity and may actually lower their unit costs as they expand operations. Sooner or later, however, additions to plants and repairs become necessary, and the industries making producers' goods increase their activity. Prices now begin to rise, and the cycle has passed into the so-called *recovery stage*.

The increase of employment that begins during the period of depression and extends through the period of recovery and well into that of prosperity brings an increasing real income to labor as a class. The increase in the rates of wages comes somewhat after the increase in prices has begun, and the rate of increase continues to lag behind that of prices. The laborer who has been previously employed thus suffers a decrease in real income, since the prices of the goods that he is purchasing are rising more rapidly than his wages. The amount paid laborers as a total, however, is increasing, and increasing even more rapidly than prices, because of the greater employment of labor, and in consequence the real income of labor as a whole is increasing. Profits are also increasing, since wages, rents, and capital costs are lagging behind prices. This means that the real income of the employing class will be increasing.

The rising prices stimulate the production of consumers' goods and greatly intensify the activity in the production of producers' goods as well. Dealers, manufacturers, and even consumers begin to expect the increase of prices to continue and begin to accumulate stocks. This continues through the period of prosperity. For this to take place, the production of goods must exceed the current consumption. Prices now rise rapidly. The period of recovery passes into that of prosperity. During the early phase of this period the real wages of labor are high, both because more are employed and because the rates of wages begin to creep up to the level of prices. Men may also move into higher grades of employment. It is quite common during periods of prosperity, when labor is scarce, for laborers to advance beyond their accustomed class. For example, an unskilled laborer may secure a job as a skilled laborer. The income of the employing class probably begins to decrease during the period. Certain producers begin to recognize that their lines are overcrowded and lessen their activities toward expansion. This affects materially the demand for production equipment and the buying power of the laborers in these industries.

There is now a rapid passage into the period of liquidation. Dealers try to work their stocks off and cease buying. Industries shut down as far as possible. Employment decreases very rapidly. The rates of the wages fall, but not so rapidly as prices, so that the real wages of those who remain employed are higher. The great increase of unemployment and part-time work, however, lowers the real income of the laboring class a great deal. Workers also change from higher to lower grades of work, which lowers real incomes even though the rates of pay for each type of work remain the same. Heavy losses are sustained by many businessmen, and the incomes of this class are seriously curtailed. The period of depression has arrived, which is turned into a period of increasing activity in the manner that has been indicated. A chart showing fluctuations in business activity from 1830 to 1938 is given in Fig. 2.

5. Consumption and Depression.—As is evident from the foregoing discussion, consumption is profoundly influenced by a depression. Production of certain commodities declines greatly, the usual demand and supply relationships are disrupted, and incomes change materially, with the result that there is a considerable shift in consumption patterns.

The great decline in real income for the community as a whole is well illustrated in Table 5, which shows an index of the national income in terms of 1929 dollars. This index, however, is one of income produced. The real income in consumption terms could not have fallen so low, for the consumer received services from durable goods already in his possession, such as houses, automobiles, and household equipment. The services provided by these goods in the latter part of the depression were not so efficient as in the early part because of obsolescence and depreciation but nevertheless were of considerable magnitude. Likewise, as

TABLE 5.—INDEX OF THE NATIONAL INCOME IN THE UNITED STATES, 1929–1935[1]
(1929 = 100)

Year	Index	Year	Index
1929	100	1933	79.2
1930	86.5	1934	75.3
1931	76.7	1935	79.0
1932	63.0		

[1] Data on national income produced are from U.S. Department of Commerce Bureau of Foreign and Domestic Commerce, deflated by cost-of-living figures of National Industrial Conference Board.

has previously been noted, the household at such times provides services of its own where formerly it purchased in the market.

Another very important phase of the effect of depression on consumption is manifested in a decline in individual money incomes. Table 6 gives figures showing the shifts in family incomes from 1929 to 1933.

The italic figures show the percentage of those who were originally (in 1929) falling in a particular income group and who remain in that classification in the depression year 1933. From these data, it can be seen readily that those who are in the lower income groups in good times tend to retain the *status quo* when depression sets in and those in the higher brackets find it very difficult to retain their positions. For example, of those families whose incomes were under $500 in 1929, 74.2 per cent still fell within that classification in 1933, and 14.9 per cent had moved to the next higher classification, 3.7 per cent climbed into the $1,000 to $1,199 grouping, etc. Of those in the $500 to $999 class in 1929, 64.1 per cent were still there in 1933, and 25.2 per cent had dropped into the lowest grouping and only a little over 10 per cent moved into higher brackets. Of those earning $1,000 to $1,199 in 1929, however, only 32.6 per cent remained in that classification in 1933, 11 per cent shifting into higher brackets and the remainder—over 55 per cent—slipping back into the lower income groups. This latter tendency is even more marked in the data for families in the still higher income groups.

This picture of the effect of depression on individual incomes is probably typical. If so, it helps to explain many things that are mentioned later in this section. The causes of the tremendous

TABLE 6.—PERCENTAGE DISTRIBUTION OF FAMILY INCOMES OF 17,769 IDENTICAL CALIFORNIA FAMILIES 1933 COMPARED WITH 1929[1]
(Total in each income group in 1929 = 100)

Family income, 1929	Per cent in each group, 1929	Percentage of families who, because of changes in net family income from 1929, were redistributed in 1933 into the following income groups												Total 1933
		Under $500	$500 to $999	$1,000 to $1,199	$1,200 to $1,499	$1,500 to $1,999	$2,000 to $2,499	$2,500 to $2,999	$3,000 to $3,499	$3,500 to $4,999	$5,000 to $6,999	$7,000 to $9,999	$10,000 and over	
Under $500	100.0	*74.2*	14.9	3.7	2.8	2.1	0.8	1.0	0.1	0.2	0.1	0.1	0	100.0
500 to 999	100.0	25.2	*64.1*	6.0	2.9	1.1	0.4	0.2	0.1	0	0	0	0	100.0
1,000 to 1,199	100.0	16.3	39.6	*32.6*	7.2	3.3	0.7	0.1	0.1	0	0.1	0	0	100.0
1,200 to 1,499	100.0	11.1	27.1	22.3	*32.2*	5.5	1.2	0.2	0.1	0.2	0	0	0.1	100.0
1,500 to 1,999	100.0	7.6	17.4	13.5	21.4	*34.6*	3.9	1.0	0.3	0.1	0.1	0	0.1	100.0
2,000 to 2,499	100.0	6.3	11.9	9.4	15.5	27.5	*26.1*	2.2	0.5	0.5	0.1	0	0	100.0
2,500 to 2,999	100.0	4.6	8.4	5.6	13.2	19.9	22.0	*22.3*	2.1	1.3	0.4	0.1	0.1	100.0
3,000 to 3,499	100.0	3.9	6.9	6.5	7.3	12.1	18.7	18.1	*21.6*	4.3	0.5	0	0.1	100.0
3,500 to 4,999	100.0	4.2	6.9	3.9	6.6	9.9	11.9	12.2	13.2	*29.0*	1.8	0.4	0	100.0
5,000 to 6,999	100.0	4.2	3.6	3.0	3.3	6.4	8.6	10.0	10.6	20.9	*28.7*	0.7	0	100.0
7,000 to 9,999	100.0	2.6	3.2	2.3	2.3	4.6	4.6	8.1	9.4	21.1	16.9	*23.0*	1.9	100.0
10,000 and over	100.0	1.6	1.6	1.6	2.5	2.7	2.0	3.3	4.7	6.9	13.9	14.7	*44.5*	100.0

[1] Adapted from P. A. Dodd and E. F. Penrose, "Economic Aspects of Medical Practice in California," p. 132.

decline in sales of many types of products, for example, become quite clear in the light of individual income data. Such a disruption of the individual-income pattern engenders lack of confidence, and the latter, in true vicious-circle fashion, makes for further declines in business activity, which in turn causes fresh declines in income. Consequently scales of living are adversely affected, and there is a resulting pressure on living standards. That depression has an extremely serious effect on consumption there can be no doubt. That some classes of individuals are affected much more seriously than others (in terms of a departure from an established level) is equally certain.

The effect of the depression upon individual items may be examined by noting the changes in consumer expenditures on the items and also on the physical volumes of sales. The former gives an indication of the rearrangement by consumers of their expenditures, and the latter, physical changes in consumption. Tables 7 and 8 bring together data on the latter phase.

TABLE 7.—PHYSICAL CHANGES IN CONSUMPTION OF VARIOUS ITEMS, 1930–1936[1]
(1929 = 100)

Commodity	1930	1932	1934	1936
Electricity (nonindustrial)	112	122	131	158
Electric refrigeration	183	390	625	
Electric toasters	80	64	115	
Gasoline	102	100	109	114
Cigarettes	100	87	106	122
Meat	97	96	101	91
Wheat flour	101	93	93	92
Butter	99	104	103	
Vacuum sweepers	75	35	58	90
Passenger automobiles	65	30	39	69
Radios	86	59	91	
Visitors to national parks	102	93	111	
Departures from the U.S.	105	82	60	
Motion-picture attendance	116	63	74	

[1] Compiled by Prof. R. S. Vaile of the University of Minnesota from various sources, mainly from the U.S. Department of Commerce.

As will be noted, the commodities included in the accompanying tables represent two different types of consumers' goods. These are known respectively as *transitory* and *durable* consumption goods. The behavior of the two types in depression is usually in contrast. Specifically one may draw the following interesting conclusions from the consumption data that have been presented:

TABLE 8.—INDICES OF DEPRESSION CONSUMPTION OF SELECTED COMMODITIES[1]
(1929 = 100)

Commodity	1932	1934
Rayon	111	173
Fruits and vegetables	107	109
Milk	104	100
Silk	89	74
Boots and shoes	86	97
Cotton	70	76
Cigars	67	69
Wool	66	65
Automobile tires	52	69

[1] Compiled by Prof. R. S. Vaile from National Bureau of Economic Research figures.

1. Total consumption of certain types of goods changed very little during the depression, as evidenced by the figures for meat, wheat flour, fruits and vegetables, and milk. These agricultural products are perishable or costly to store and, in consequence, must be used as produced. Agricultural production continues in nearly full force during a depression.

2. The consumption of cigarettes (another example of transitory goods) declined less drastically than most products. This is a type of goods for which the individual unit of purchase is small, and habits firmly established.

3. Sales of durable consumption goods (with the exception of electrical refrigerators), on the other hand, suffered serious declines, as evidenced by the figures for electrical appliances and automobiles.

4. The *use* of automobiles seems not to have declined, however, as is indicated by the physical volume of gasoline sold. Thus, although new cars could not be purchased, the relatively small immediate outlay permitted the utilization of the old ones.

5. The figures for automobile tires sold reveal a marked decline despite evidence of a maintained position in automobile mileage. This is no doubt due to a combination of (*a*) improved tire quality and (*b*) more complete utilization of the product.

6. An interesting change is revealed in the use of different types of textiles, the use of rayon having increased tremendously whereas cottons, woolens, and silks suffered marked declines.

7. The domestic use of electricity increased materially in the face of declines in the sales of appliances, indicating that the *use* of appliances remained at predepression levels following 1929.

8. In recreation the consumer tended to (*a*) confine his traveling to America and (*b*) reduce the frequency of his visits to the motion-picture theater. Although figures are lacking, unquestionably there have been increases in the patronage of libraries and in the size of radio audiences.

That there has been unmistakable evidence of consumers attempting to maintain a certain scale of living during depression times there can be little doubt. One bit of evidence is the tendency of consumers to give institutions having a reputation for lower prices a greater proportion of their patronage.

TABLE 9.—PERCENTAGE OF SALES THROUGH CHAIN STORES BY KINDS OF STORES

(Total sales of all stores in each line = 100)

Type of store	1929	1933
All stores	20.0	25.2
Combination grocery and meats	32.2	43.7
Cigar store	25.1	33.9
Shoe store	38.0	46.2
Drugstore	18.5	25.1

Table 9 gives data on the proportion of chain to total sales in certain lines, 1929 and 1933. Though some of the change indicated is in part a manifestation of a long-term trend, part is very probably due to the fact that the consumer has been attempting to make his dollar go further.

"With the decreasing incomes, there seems [also] to have been a general movement to maintain a scale of living by relinquishing some of the niceties of quality. There was the accompanying tendency on the part of the manufacturers to produce and among retailers to handle products at lower prices, made possible in part by poorer quality. This lowering of quality was especially noticeable in the loading of silks and reducing of rayons by using cheaper yarns as well as by reducing the count in the weave by stretching.

"In the study at the University of Minnesota comparing expenditures in 1931 with those of 1929, it was found that the sales of exclusive and high-priced goods had sharply declined whereas sales of medium- and low-priced goods in almost all lines were approximately equal to the 1929 figures. . . . This cheapening of quality was not limited to any particular line. There has been jerry-building in housing with its counterpart in furniture and home furnishing. Men's clothing and women's apparel, particularly the latter, has suffered a general decline in quality standards [also]."[1] The student is challenged at this point regarding the social desirability of such a situation: Aside from the possibility of a higher real cost of cheap merchandise, might not the offering of cheap, unattractive merchandise have created a

TABLE 10.—INDICES OF CONSUMER EXPENDITURES ON SELECTED COMMODITIES, 1929–1937
(1923–1925 = 100)

Commodity	1929	1931	1933	1935	1937
Gasoline	115	95	88	108	137
Cigarettes	113	117	97	128	159
Telephones	119	120	99	103	120
Wheat flour	92	57	86	114	
All meats	110	85	60	78	93
Butter	106	74	54	73	82
Oleomargarine	118	56	39	83	92
Furniture	93	47	25	30	54
Furs	85	40	19	19	28
Hotels	99	75	52	62	75
Life insurance	110	94	64	70	70
Autos	115	68	43	79	116
Residential construction	75	32	9	19	35

[1] R. S. VAILE and H. G. CANOYER, "Effects of Cyclical Movements on the Consumer" (mimeographed ed.), pp. 17–18.

disinclination to purchase and, hence, have acted as a deterrent to recovery?

Indices in terms of expenditures are shown in Table 10. They indicate considerable rearrangement of consumer expenditure. Food expenditures fell about the same amount as total income, indicating that the constant consumption was maintained by lower prices. The expenditures for such things as gasoline, cigarettes, and telephones were maintained and considerably increased by 1937. The larger purchases such as furniture and furs fell very greatly.

In conclusion, some of the effects of the depression in consumption might be briefly summarized as follows:

1. National income declined, but not so greatly as might be expected when the figures are corrected for price change. Moreover, national income paid out holds up better than actual income produced since, during depression times, we are dipping into surplus, indeed, in some instances, into capital.

2. There are tremendous shifts in individuals' incomes during depression times, a small percentage increasing but most declining. From a study of the figures, one is particularly struck with the difficulty of maintaining a predepression level of income; it is especially difficult for those who were formerly in the medium and high brackets to maintain a level previously established.

3. The figures for consumption of goods exhibit marked differences in behavior. Although food consumption, in most instances, remained practically constant and such items as gasoline, domestic electric power, and rayon increased, durable consumption goods such as automobiles and radios suffered drastic declines.

4. Recreational-activities figures indicate large shifts, even the movies suffering drastic declines and this despite such artificial stimulants as price reductions, bank nights, and double features.

5. Shifts in patronage from independent to chain establishments were manifest; although a part of this is undoubtedly a trend phenomen, most, one would assume, is due to an attempt on the part of the consumer to protect a certain established living standard.

6. A decline in merchandise quality is clearly evident. This condition also indicates an attempt by the consumer to maintain a certain living scale. Once a certain scale of living has been

attained, the average consumer evidently prefers, when income decreases, to spread his expenditures over a wide variety of low-quality goods rather than to concentrate his buying power on fewer items of higher quality.

Questions

1. If the general price level should rise by 50 per cent during the next two years, as some expect, how would you be affected? Are all consumers affected uniformly?
2. Which fluctuates more, the production of goods or their consumption?
3. Study the Cleveland Trust Company chart carefully, and draw conclusions concerning (*a*) the length of depressions, (*b*) how often they occur, (*c*) the causes of some of the major ones, and (*d*) the behavior of prices in relation to cyclical fluctuations.
4. Specifically how is consumption affected in time of depression?

CHAPTER V

THE COST OF LIVING AND ITS EFFECT UPON REAL INCOME

The changes that take place in the prices of commodities cause changes in the cost of living of the consumer. The term *cost of living* is, however, somewhat ambiguous. The cost may refer to the money expenses of living, which is the sense in which the term will here be employed, except where specific exceptions are made, or it may refer to the effort or the real cost involved in procuring the means for a living. Thus, if the prices of products purchased by the consumer remained the same and his wages for the same effort increased, we would say that the real cost of living had fallen, for he could now procure the same things with less effort. There can be no such thing as *the* cost of living, meaning a single general cost of living. There are many different manners of living, and each of these ways will have a different cost. We do not gain much idea of these costs by simply comparing the expenditures and incomes of people, since all we find then is that those with large incomes have large expenditures and, hence, high cost of living. It is necessary, in consequence, to set up some outside measure of living, not related to income or prices, for determining what the costs of living are. There will be many of these costs of living, since there will be many different ways of living.

1. Measurement of the Cost of Living.—A usual way of measuring costs of living is to set up a certain quantity of goods, which constitute a particular way of living or the measurable items of a certain way of living, and price these goods. For example, the U.S. Bureau of Labor Statistics in 1922 determined a minimum standard quantity budget which they judged to represent the quantities of goods needed to maintain a family of five at the minimum level of health and decency. This budget was priced in many places and used to determine the cost of living at a minimum standard. Most of these sorts of studies have been made of costs at a minimum standard. A few, however, include other standards; for example, in general the National Industrial Conference Board studies have included a more liberal standard as well as a minimum standard.

Changes in the cost of living, like changes in the general price level, are customarily measured by index numbers. There are two important index numbers of the cost of living of low-income city dwellers in the United States. One is prepared by the U.S. Bureau of Labor Statistics, and the other by the National Industrial Conference Board. Also, an index of the cost of things bought by farmers for family living is prepared by the U.S. Department of Agriculture. None of these indices proceed exactly upon the basis of pricing a specific bill of goods at different times or places. Instead, certain items of each of the general budget groups are priced, and an index of the changes of each budget group is determined. These are then combined to give the general index by weighting according to the relative importance of each group as disclosed in certain budget studies.

The U.S. Bureau of Labor Statistics Index of the Cost of Living is made up of the cost of food, clothing, housing, fuel and lighting, furniture and furnishings, and miscellaneous items. An index is prepared for the United States as a whole and for each of 32 cities. An index of each of the included groups relative to their cost in the period from 1923 to 1925 is first prepared. A weighted average of these relatives is used for the total-cost figure. The weights at present used are the average percentages of the total expenditures of the family for each group as determined from the 1918–1919 study of family expenditures. The group weights for the United States are as follows: food, 31.6; clothing, 14.1; housing, 19.8; fuel and light, 6.0; furniture and furnishings, 4.8; and miscellaneous, 23.7. The individual cities have slightly different weights, depending upon their geographical location. These weights will be changed as the results of the latest family-expenditure study become available. The index is now published four times a year—in March, June, September, and December. The index of housing costs is calculated from rental figures obtained on 400 to 2,500 houses and apartments in each city, by special representatives of the bureau who visit agents and secure the data directly from their records. For clothing, house furnishings, and miscellaneous groups, 4 or more quotations are secured on a large group of articles in each city. Wherever possible, more quotations are secured, but for such items as streetcar fares, telephone rates, and newspapers several quotations are not always possible. The food index is made up of 20 to 25 quotations in each city on 84 articles. Prices of the items included in the food, fuel, and light indices are obtained by mail, all others by personal representatives of the bureau. In pricing, the type of goods has been varied from city to city in conformity with the purchasing habits of the families. The kind and quality of goods priced are held constant from year to year as far as possible. The indices thus furnish no information as to the differences in absolute cost among the 32 cities but do indicate the comparative rates of change in the cost of goods purchased by low-salaried workers in these places.

The U.S. Bureau of Labor Statistics index of the price of food is prepared for 51 cities and for the United States as a whole. The actual retail selling prices of 84 articles of food are obtained from dealers in these cities on the fifteenth of each month. The number of articles included in the index was 43 in the years 1921–1934 and 22 prior to 1921. The dealers selected represent the different classes of stores found in a given city, the sample showing approximately the same proportions of types of stores as are found in the whole city. For the larger cities, at least 25 stores are used; for the smaller cities, the number is occasionally reduced to 15. Difference in consuming habits in various portions of the country is taken into account by the difference in weights used in the different cities. The index for each city is an aggregative reduced to a relative of the 1926 base.

The cost-of-living index of the National Industrial Conference Board is very similar in its method of construction to that of the U.S. Bureau of Labor Statistics. The groups included in the index are food, shelter, clothing, fuel and light, and sundries. The food index used is that of the U.S. Bureau of Labor Statistics, but the indices for the other groups are independently determined. Quotations are gathered by the questionnaire method from a larger number of cities than those included in the U.S. Bureau of Labor Statistics indices, but, in general, fewer quotations are procured from each city, and from fewer regular sources. The base of the index is 1923. The weights were arrived at by taking the percentage of the total expenditures spent for each group after examination of a number of expenditure studies. The index is published monthly for the United States as a whole.

The index of the cost of things bought by farmers for family living is computed in a manner similar to the previously described cost-of-living indices. Individual relatives are determined for each of the included budget groups on the basis of fixed-weight aggregatives of actual prices. The indices for the various groups are combined by weighting each group by its relative importance in the farm family budget. These weights are determined from farm cost-of-living studies in various parts of the United States made from 1920 to 1929.

It is clear that an index must compare the same sort of quantities. Thus we can price the same bill of goods at two periods, or we can average rates of change in prices between two periods. A more elaborate attempt has been to measure changes in the cost of a given quantity of satisfaction at different prices. If it can be assumed that we deal with an individual whose tastes remain unchanged throughout the period of observation and for whom all other circumstances capable of affecting choice, except prices, also remain unchanged, the relative income required at the two times can be established within fairly narrow limits. It has been shown by several investigators that this ratio of incomes must lie between the values shown by an index of the weighted aggregate of a constant bill of goods of the type purchased by the individual in the base period and an index of the weighted aggregate of a constant bill of goods of the type purchased in the compared period.[1]

The cost-of-living index may usually be taken to represent the number of dollars that are necessary to purchase the same quantity of the same kind of goods as were purchased in the base period, the expenditures being made in the manner assumed by the index. When prices are high, each dollar will purchase less goods than when prices are low. We may estimate the purchasing power of the consumer's dollar by the reciprocal of the cost-of-living index. When the cost-of-living index is high, the purchasing power of the consumer's dollar is low; and when the cost-of-living index is low, the purchasing power of the consumer's

[1] See A. C. Pigou, "Economics of Welfare," Part I, Chap. V, Measurement of the National Dividend; also "International Comparisons of the Cost-of-Living," *International Labour Office Series N, No.* 20.

dollar is high. The purchasing power of the consumer's dollar shows the quantity of goods that a dollar will purchase relative to a dollar expended in the base period, when expenditures are made in a manner assumed by the index. A more proper computation would be to construct a new index in the form of a weighted harmonic mean of prices with the base-year expenditures as weights.[1] This would give us an index showing the changed quantity of commodities that would be purchased if the same amounts of money were paid for them. The results would differ from the reciprocal of the cost of a constant bill of goods because the latter in assuming constant quantities to be bought gives more weight to price changes in expensive articles, whereas the weighted harmonic mean in assuming constant expenditures gives greater weight to price changes in the cheaper articles. We have, however, no indices computed on this basis. The idea of the purchasing power of the consumer's dollar must not be confused with the idea of the purchasing power of the consumer. The latter depends upon the number of dollars that the consumer has, as well as upon the prices of goods; the former depends solely upon the prices of goods. Even though the purchasing power of the consumer's dollar might decrease, the purchasing power of the consumer would still increase if the number of dollars that he had was increasing more rapidly than prices were rising.

2. Changes in the Cost of Living in the United States.—The indices of the cost of living for the United States as estimated by the U.S. Bureau of Labor Statistics are shown in Table 11.

Living costs nearly doubled during the World War period, declined rapidly in 1921–1922 by about 15 per cent, and then changed little until the depression, with marked declines in 1931–1933 and a subsequent slow partial recovery.

The various budget groups which comprise the expenditures of the consumers differ in their fluctuations and at times these differences become very large. Thus, in the period 1930–1933, food fell the most rapidly of all the groups, and miscellaneous hardly at all. The fall in rents began in 1926 and continued for some time after.

[1] See W. F. FERGER, "Distinctive Concepts of Price and Purchasing-Power Index Numbers," *J. Am. Statistical Assoc.*, vol. 31, p. 258, June, 1936.

TABLE 11.—ESTIMATED ANNUAL AVERAGE INDICES OF COST OF GOODS PURCHASED BY WAGE EARNERS AND LOWER SALARIED WORKERS IN 32 LARGE CITIES COMBINED, 1913–1937[1]
(Average 1923–1925 = 100)

Year	All items	Food[2]	Clothing	Rent	Fuel and light	House-furnishing goods	Miscellaneous
1913	57.4	63.1	55.7	61.4	53.9	47.7	50.1
1914	58.2	64.6	56.1	61.4	54.3	49.0	51.2
1915	58.8	63.9	57.4	61.9	54.5	51.3	52.8
1916	63.2	71.7	62.9	62.6	56.6	57.2	55.5
1917	74.4	92.4	75.6	62.1	63.0	66.9	64.2
1918	87.2	106.2	102.5	63.2	73.3	85.9	76.7
1919	101.1	120.2	135.7	68.4	79.4	108.2	86.3
1920	116.2	133.1	161.6	80.4	93.1	132.8	99.1
1921	103.6	101.6	124.4	92.4	99.3	111.8	102.8
1922	97.2	95.0	101.0	95.1	98.6	94.8	99.7
1923	99.0	97.9	101.2	97.5	100.3	101.8	99.3
1924	99.2	96.9	100.4	101.0	99.1	100.1	99.9
1925	101.8	105.0	98.4	101.5	100.6	98.1	100.8
1926	102.6	108.5	97.0	100.5	102.2	95.9	101.1
1927	100.6	104.5	95.1	98.9	100.6	93.6	101.7
1928	99.5	103.3	93.7	96.5	98.9	91.3	102.3
1929	99.5	104.7	92.7	94.3	98.2	90.2	103.1
1930	97.0	99.6	90.7	91.7	97.2	87.9	103.5
1931	88.6	82.0	82.7	86.9	95.1	79.2	102.7
1932	79.8	68.3	73.2	78.0	90.4	68.9	100.2
1933	75.8	66.4	70.9	67.2	87.4	68.0	97.0
1934	78.6	74.1	77.5	62.9	88.6	74.9	96.7
1935	80.7	80.5	77.9	62.9	87.5	76.4	96.7
1936	81.6	82.1	78.7	64.2	87.5	77.8	96.5
1937[3]	84.3	85.1	82.4	67.4	86.6	84.9	97.8

[1] "Changes in the Cost of Living in the United States," U.S. *Bur. Labor Statistics Serial R* 749, p. 7.

[2] Covers 51 cities since June, 1920.

[3] Preliminary.

The rates of change in the various budget groups also vary greatly from city to city. As previously pointed out, the values of the indices cannot be taken to represent differences in the cost of a given level of consumption in the different cities. There are considerable technical difficulties in measuring differences in the cost of living from one section of the country to the other, and the U.S. Bureau of Labor Statistics has not undertaken them.

The indices are adequate, however, to show the great difference among cities in these rates of change. For example, as is shown in Table 12, food prices in Minneapolis in June, 1937, were less than 6 per cent below their level in 1923–1925, whereas in Los Angeles they were more than 20 per cent lower than in 1923–1925. This, it should be noted, does not say which city was higher at either period.

TABLE 12.—HIGHEST AND LOWEST REPORTED INDICES OF COST OF BUDGET GROUPS REPORTED JUNE 15, 1937, BY THE U.S. BUREAU OF LABOR STATISTICS[1]
(1923–1935 = 100)

Item	Highest index		Lowest index		Difference
	City	Index	City	Index	
Food	Minneapolis	94.2	Los Angeles	79.4	14.8
Clothing	San Francisco	90.7	Houston	76.8	13.9
Rent	Washington, D.C.	88.0	Birmingham, Ala. Los Angeles	53.1	34.9
Fuel and light	Pittsburgh	100.6	Atlanta	70.3	30.3
House furnishings	New Orleans	95.2	Chicago	76.8	18.4
Miscellaneous	Baltimore	104.3	New Orleans	91.6	12.7
All items	Cincinnati	89.0	Los Angeles	79.4	9.6

[1] "Cost of Living in the United States," *U.S. Dept. Labor Serial R* 605, p. 9.

The Works Progress Administration attempted to determine living costs on an *emergency* and on a somewhat higher *maintenance* level, for a four-person normal worker's family in 59 cities of the United States at March, 1935, prices.[1] For this purpose an elaborate synthetic budget was priced in each city. The cost of living at the maintenance level ranged from a high of $1,415 in Washington, D.C., to a low of $1,130 in Mobile, Ala., and averaged $1,261 for the entire group of cities. The cost of the emergency level was also highest in Washington, D.C., at $1,014, but was lowest in Wichita, Kans., at $810. At both levels, necessary outlay in the most expensive city averaged about 25 per cent above the least expensive. In more than half the

[1] M. L. STECKER, "Intercity Differences in Cost of Living in March, 1935, 59 Cities," *WPA Preliminary Rept.*, 1937.

cities, living costs were within a range of $100 a year. The budgets priced were the same in all cities except for a few items. Transportation allowances had to be adjusted for city size and area, and allowances made for fuel and ice to take account of climatic differences.

3. Measurement of Real Income.—We have defined real income as consisting of goods and services and have pointed out that it is impossible to compare real incomes directly since these goods and services vary among persons and times. The amount of real income is, however, a matter of sufficient importance to warrant even a crude attempt at estimation. Two general methods are available. One is to determine the amount of money necessary to purchase a given quantity of goods and services and to compare this with the money income of the group. The other is to use the consumption of selected goods and services as indices. The former is the more generally used and as a rule takes the form of a division of the money income by a cost-of-living index, with the resulting quotient expressed as an index. This represents what we have termed the *purchasing power of the consumer*.

The most elaborate attempt to examine real income in the United States by this method is the study of Prof. Paul H. Douglas.[1] Professor Douglas estimates the average annual money earnings of employed workers for each year of the period 1890–1926 and divides these dollar incomes by an index of the cost of living. The results for selected years are given in Table 13. Average annual real earnings appear to have increased between 1900 and 1914 by only about 4 per cent, but these earnings were obtained in an appreciably shorter work day. Between 1920 and 1926, there appears to have been an increase of 35 per cent, which came from a gain of 23 per cent for those remaining in the same industry and a 12 per cent gain by workers shifting to better paid industries. The gains varied greatly by industries. To these gains, Douglas would add for the period a 5 per cent gain arising from a decrease in the size of the worker's family, 14 per cent for increased free income from the government, 2 per cent for increased private philanthropy, and 7 or 8 per cent for a lower rate of unemployment. All told, there appears to have been about a 55 per cent larger real income for the ordinary wage

[1] P. H. Douglas, "Real Wages in the United States, 1890–1926."

Table 13.—Relative Real Annual Average Earnings of Those Attached to the Manufacturing, Transportation, and Coal-mining Industries after Allowing for Unemployment[1]

(1914 = 100)

Year	Real Earnings
1890	107
1895	100
1900	103
1905	110
1910	112
1915	102
1920	123
1925	134

[1] P. H. Douglas, "Real Wages in the United States, 1890–1926," p. 468.

earner in 1926 than in the 1890's. The principal criticisms of this study have been in respect to the adequacy of its data. It was necessary to compute a cost-of-living index for the period before 1913, and Douglas's index has been questioned on the grounds of inadequate sampling, *i.e.*, the inclusion of data only from the large cities, and also because of an insufficient number of commodities. The estimates of annual money earnings of employed workers have been attacked on the grounds that our data of unemployment are so meager and unreliable as to vitiate any conclusions.

A variation of this method has been employed by the International Labour Office in an attempt to compare standards of living of workers in various countries of the world.[1] The comparison was made for 21 principal world cities, on the basis of skilled trades similar in technique the world over. These were: in the building trades, masons and unskilled workers; in the engineering trades, fitters and unskilled laborers; in the furniture trades, cabinetmakers and unskilled laborers; and in the printing and bookbinding trades, hand compositors, machine compositors, and unskilled laborers. For all the occupations covered for each town, the average time wage for a 48-hour week was determined. This wage is then compared with the cost of a "basket of provisions" customarily consumed by workers to determine how many baskets such a wage would purchase. Some variation in the contents of the basket of provisions is permitted for

[1] "Report on the Standard of Living of Workers in Various Countries," C.E.I. 26, International Labour Office, Geneva, 1926.

differences in consuming habits, and an allowance is made for differences in the costs of housing. An indication of the resulting indices is given in Table 14.

TABLE 14.—PURCHASING POWER OF WORKERS IN SELECTED OCCUPATIONS IN VARIOUS WORLD CITIES, OCT. 1, 1926[1]
(London = 100)

City	Index
Philadelphia	177
Sydney	137
Copenhagen	111
Berlin	61
Warsaw	45
Rome	43

[1] "Report on the Standard of Living of Workers in Various Countries," p. 29, C.E.I. 26, International Labour Office, Geneva, 1926.

The critics of this study have maintained that the indices overstate the real differences between cities. It has been pointed out, for example, that the items not included in the comparison, such as rents and other living costs, are lower on the Continent than in the United States. The representativeness of the included classes as an indication of the situation regarding other workers has also been questioned on the grounds that the wages in these trades in the United States are higher relative to the general average of wages than in the compared countries. This is because these trades were well organized in the United States, whereas the great mass of the remaining workers were generally unorganized. In Europe, trade unions were relatively more important in these other lines and the wages closer to those in the included groups. It was also suggested that the European laborer had more security in the way of unemployment insurance and old-age pensions. All these elements act to give greater equality to the real wage than that indicated by the indices.

An example of the comparison of real incomes by selected items or groups is found in M. K. Bennett's study.[1] In this, the following 14 statistical series were reduced to relatives and included: deaths per 1,000 inhabitants (inverted); births per 1,000 inhabitants (inverted); percentage of population engaged in professional service; percentage of population aged five to twenty attending elementary and secondary schools; pieces of

[1] M. K. BENNETT, "Measurement of Relative National Standards of Living," *Quart. J. Econ.*, vol. 51, p. 317, February, 1937.

mail per capita handled by postal services; telephone instruments per 1,000 inhabitants; mileage of telephone and telegraph wire per 100,000 inhabitants; telegraph messages sent per 1,000 inhabitants; railway locomotives per 100,000 inhabitants; motor vehicles per 1,000 inhabitants; raw sugar per capita domestically retained; tobacco per capita domestically retained; tea, coffee, and cocoa per capita domestically retained; and citrus fruits and bananas domestically retained. The first 5 series were used

TABLE 15.—INDICES OF REAL INCOME IN VARIOUS COUNTRIES

Country	Professional services	Transportation and communication	Luxury-food consumption	General index
United States	147	187	163	166
British Isles	128	135	143	135
Denmark	133	133	120	130
Switzerland	139	123	112	125
Holland	132	76	153	118
Belgium	117	117	120	118
Sweden	108	124	97	110
Germany	147	104	73	110
Norway	109	120	88	107
France	99	123	93	106
Finland	53	55	40	50
Italy	45	44	60	49
Spain	27	41	82	48
Portugal	16	19	55	28

as an index of professional services, the following 5 as an index of transportation and communication, and the last 4 as an index of luxury-food consumption, and all were combined in a general index. These indices are given in Table 15. They show an appreciably higher real income from these sources in the United States than in other countries, the British Isles, Denmark, and Switzerland being grouped at a high level, Holland, Belgium, Sweden, Germany, Norway, and France in a modal group, and Finland, Italy, Spain and Portugal at very low levels. The limitations of the comparison are obvious: the narrow range of included items and the arbitrary weighting.

Several of the budget groups offer another indirect measure of real income. The item of *sundries* or *advancement*, for example, shows great elasticity. When the percentage of income spent on such items increases, we have an indication of an increase of real income. If we observe the same class over a period of years and find that the percentage spent for sundries or advancement is increasing, we may quite safely conclude that the real income of the group is increasing.

Rowntree suggests a minimum health standard as a means of measuring real income. Such a measure may be accurately defined and remains the same over a period of time. Substitutions may be affected in the things consumed that go to maintain the standard of health, but the measure in itself does not vary. The costs of maintaining it do vary with changes in the price level. As the surplus above this minimum increases, the standard ceases to be a satisfactory standard of real wages. The percentage of the total budget that is required to maintain the minimum health standard is a possible measure for comparing real incomes.

The death rate may also be used as an indication of the amount of real wages. For a considerable range in the low incomes, an insufficient income is quickly manifested in a high death rate, whereas higher incomes show lower death rates. This measure is useful only among people of low-income groups. Among higher income groups, a curtailment of real income is manifest not in the curtailment of subsistence items but rather in the items of advancement or sundries. These latter, of course, have no effect on the death rate.

Studies of real income or purchasing power have come into increasing use as measures of the position of various groups and classes and as guides to governmental action. The recent Soil Conservation and Domestic Allotment Act has as one of its stated purposes, for example, "to reestablish and maintain the prewar ratio between the per capita purchasing power of farm and non-farm income."

Questions

1. Secure more recent data from a U.S. Bureau of Labor Statistics cost-of-living report, arrange in the form of Table 12, and explain the differences in rates of change in as many of these cost items as you can for the cities showing the largest and smallest changes from the base period.

2. Is the cost of living now above or below that of 1923–1925? Above or below the prewar period?

3. One of the stated purposes of the Soil Conservation and Domestic Allotment Act is . . . " (3) to reestablish and maintain the prewar ratio between the per capita purchasing power of farm and non-farm income." What data or material would be needed for determining when this point had been reached?

4. What differences would you expect to find in fluctuations in the cost of living of high-income and low-income groups?

5. The following data are important indications of the money incomes of factory workers and farmers and the indices of their cost of living.

	1929	1930	1931	1932	1933	1934	1935	1936
Average per capita weekly earnings, manufacturing B.L.S. (employed workers). .	$27.36	$29.39	$22.51	$18.18	$17.60	$19.12	$21.03	$22.36
Index of factory pay rolls (Federal Reserve Bull.).........	109	89	67	46	49	63	71	82
Cost of living B.L.S...........	99.5	97.0	88.6	79.8	75.8	78.6	80.7	81.6
Net farm income, U.S. (billion dollars), (U.S.D.A.)........	5.67	3.86	2.39	1.49	2.68	3.47	4.54	
Index of prices paid by farmers for things used in living.....	158	148	126	108	109	122	124	122

Prepare a short discussion of the changes in purchasing power of these two groups during the depression.

CHAPTER VI

MONOPOLY AND THE CONSUMER

The economic organization of society around a system of prices places the interest of the consumer and the producer in conflict, especially with respect to the most desirable volume of production. The consumer desires the largest possible volume of production and the lowest possible prices. The seller on the other hand desires a restricted output with higher prices, resulting in larger profits to himself. Whenever possible the seller will develop devices to restrict the competition from others in his market. He will seldom be able to do this completely but often will achieve some partial limitation, particularly for short periods of time. Examination will ordinarily disclose competitive forces running through all these situations and preventing a monopoly from being retained for long periods.

The interests of the consumer will usually be best served by competition, since this will produce a larger output and generally lower prices than would result when monopolistic conditions are present. This is not always true. It is possible that the monopoly may not use its power to oppress the public; it may simply prevent cutthroat competition in the industry and be content with a normal rate of return on its investments. Such instances are, however exceptional. It is also possible that the monopoly through its larger scale of operations may be able to reduce costs sufficiently so that, even though it charges a monopoly price, this price may be lower than the price which would have prevailed with a larger number of smaller competing concerns.[1] Simple competition will be found when there are a relatively large number of sellers in a market, dealing in a perfectly standardized product or one in which it is impossible to associate qualities with a particular seller, to which market new sellers may enter freely. Merely to enumerate these conditions discloses the rarity of simple competition in modern society and likewise indi-

[1] See A. Marshall, "Principles of Economics," 8th ed., p. 484.

cates the principal methods by which competition is broken down.

1. Market with a Single Seller.—The production of each seller under simple competition is such a small part of the total that any variation he makes in his output will have an infinitesimal influence upon price. The demand curve as far as his operations are concerned is thus nearly perfectly elastic, and each proportionate increase in his output will increase his total revenue in the same proportion.[1] He finds it profitable to expand production as long as each unit of his increase adds more to total revenue than to total cost. He is thus led to expand production to a point where his costs have increased sufficiently per added unit to equal selling price.[2] If there is a single seller in the market, however, the situation is changed with respect to the demand curve. It now has a lower elasticity, and, as restriction of supplies on the part of the seller takes place, prices rise. If the curve is inelastic, the total revenue rises and probably total costs fall as output is restricted; hence the net revenue of the seller is increased by some output less than under competition. Even though the elasticity of the demand exceeds one, restriction will be desirable when total costs fall more rapidly than total revenue. The output under monopoly will thus be smaller than under competition, with higher prices resulting. The monopoly will also make less demand for labor and capital than it would under competitive conditions, and these must find employment in other fields that are open to them. The effects of the monopoly are not, in consequence, confined to the higher prices charged in the monopolized industry but extend to other fields as well.

A single seller will seldom be able to secure complete control of a market, and then if secured the control will usually be difficult to hold. There appear to be four circumstances under which complete monopolies may be established:[3] (1) The first is the rare case where one group has control of one or more essential raw materials entering a final product. (2) The second occurs when the state grants an exclusive patent for some mechanical

[1] The influence of elasticity of demand is explained in Chap. X.

[2] It is to be recognized that uncertainties enter to upset calculations in the short run.

[3] See Garver and Hansen, "Principles of Economics," rev. ed., p. 189.

device or a copyright to the work of an author. Such rights in the United States have limitations as to the time over which they extend. (3) There may be economies arising from large-scale production which permit the larger plant because of lower costs to drive competitors from the field, and this is an important source of monopoly in restricted markets. (4) The most important group are those secured by a grant by governmental authority of an exclusive right to sell a commodity or service in a particular market. The public utilities, such as telephones, street transportation, and the supply of gas, water, or electricity to the public, are common examples. Most of the so-called monopolies in the United States, except those arising from patent rights or the public utilities, are in reality partial monopolies.

The public-utility monopolies are important because of the considerable proportion of the consumer's income that is expended for their services. The National Bureau of Economic Research estimates around 10 per cent of the national income is produced by privately owned public utilities.[1] The characteristics that generally distinguish the businesses designated by the legislatures and the courts as public utilities are (1) that the business must be one which supplies some service essential to a civilized existence, although not necessarily an absolute necessity; (2) that the service also must be one sold generally to the public; and (3) that there must be a tendency for the business to become a monopoly. The utility usually operates under an exclusive grant to supply services in the community. The measures used in setting the rates for utilities have been explained in Chap. VII.

A seller sometimes secures not only a monopoly but also an ability to discriminate or to charge different consumers different prices for the same product. Such a monopoly is known as a *discriminating monopoly*, in contrast to a simple monopoly where a single price must be charged all customers.[2] The advantages of such a division of the market are more definitely pointed out in the discussion of demand.[3] If this power were benevolently exercised, a great deal of good might be done, but it will seldom be in the interest of the monopolist to exercise his

[1] SIMON KUZNETS, "National Income 1919–1935," *Nat. Bur. Econ. Res. Bull.* 66, p. 5, Sept. 27, 1937.

[2] See A. C. PIGOU, "Economics of Welfare," 1st ed., pp. 240–256.

[3] See Chap. X.

power in this way. A discriminating monopoly will yield the monopolist a larger profit than a simple monopoly, and, in consequence, the monopoly will classify its customers and charge each class a different price whenever possible.

It does not follow that price discrimination is always bad for the consumer. Sometimes it permits production where none would be possible under a simple monopoly.[1] If a comparison is made with simple monopoly, discrimination is advantageous to the group who secure a lower price because of it and detrimental to the group whose price is raised by it. If for some reason we judge the gains to one group more important than the losses to the other, as we might if the group to which the price was lowered was composed largely of poor people and the one to whom the price was raised largely of rich people, then we might decide that discrimination was desirable. Furthermore, in special cases, prices in the higher priced market may be lowered when costs fall because of enlarged output, and this may be the case where the more elastic market is an export market in which exported goods compete with local production.[2] Any advantage the consumer may gain from discrimination is incidental to the gains of the monopolist, although output will, in general, be greater under a discriminating than under a simple monopoly.

2. Monopoly with Several Sellers.—When there are two or more sellers in a market, the probability of developing monopoly gains declines greatly and becomes less as the number of sellers increases. When the product sold by all firms is identical, one of two general conditions may develop: either the firms reach an agreement with respect to prices, which will usually contain a considerable element of monopoly; or they compete freely in the market, with competitive or cutthroat prices resulting, and sometimes elimination of competitors by a subsequent monopoly.

One of the devices developed in these situations has been the trade association. These are organizations of firms producing similar lines of goods and are found in a wide variety of fields. Some are relatively unimportant while others, such as those in the iron and steel and electric-power fields, are of great importance.

[1] "It may happen, for instance, that a railway would not be built, or a country doctor would not set up in practice if discrimination were forbidden." See Joan Robinson, "Economics of Imperfect Competition," p. 203.

[2] See Robinson, *op. cit.*, p. 205.

Through the association, or *institute* as it is frequently called, the members exchange information and oppose legislation and taxes believed detrimental to the group. The associations also seek to discourage ruinous competition among the members, and at times have no doubt succeeded in establishing monopoly prices and practices in the industry and have kept inefficient producers in existence. In other cases, the provision of information has no doubt led to improved techniques and more orderly production. Unless carefully restrained, however, the associations are certain to result in the development of monopolistic practices detrimental to the consumer.

The National Industrial Recovery Act of 1933 was hurried through Congress with the advent of the new administration and approved by the President on June 16 of that year. It was regarded at the time of enactment as one of the cornerstones of the New Deal program. The act provided for many of the things sought by trade associations for their groups but which were previously illegal. The National Recovery Administration was the organization set up under the act. Its objective was to place industry under codes that provided industrial self-governing agencies and to ensure compliance with these codes by the use of the powers provided the NRA. The NRA was the government's answer to the declaration of business leaders that if they were permitted to form effective trade associations they would be able to stimulate industry and bring about needed reforms.

The codes for the industries were written by the industries themselves, with, of course, collaboration of the NRA. The governing body of the industry was the code authority selected in some manner by the industry. The codes varied greatly in their details although there were certain essential similarities. Nearly all authorized the code authorities: to adopt and enforce fair-trade rules, including price-control devices; to collect and report business statistics to governmental agencies; and to recommend to the administrator measures for planning, including stabilization of employment. The NRA changed greatly during its short life and possessed both good and bad features. Prices at times appear to have risen too rapidly, and the devices designed for consumer protection proved woefully inadequate. The code authorities had great difficulty in enforcing the fair-price provisions, and eventually price fixing was abolished altogether.

Reflection on the operation of the act shows it to have fostered many monopolistic practices and to have resulted in provisions in the codes that would have enabled many of the larger business groups to eliminate competition of a type especially irksome to them.

In some lines, a single large concern dominates the market with a number of relatively small competitors. The United States Steel Corporation would be an example, likewise the large oil concerns in certain sections of the country, and a single distributor in some milk markets. It is usual in such circumstances for the large concern to set the price for the market and the others to adjust theirs accordingly. Often the smaller concerns sell for lower prices but are unmolested because they are not expected to survive, because of their relative inefficiency or because they are too small to merit consideration. Should the small concerns become important, measures would probably be taken to drive them from the market by means of a price war.

Where the products of one seller can be differentiated from those of other sellers, increased scope of monopolistic action is possible beyond that possible when all products are identical. A product is differentiated when any significant basis exists for distinguishing the goods of one seller from another. The basis may be real or imagined but is of importance so long as it results in any preference on the part of the buyer. As is indicated in the chapter on advertising, differentiation of product is a primary objective of that activity. Typical examples would be the cases of Bromo-Seltzer, Alka-Seltzer, and Sal Hepatica; Ford, Chevrolet, and Plymouth; and Chesterfield, Old Gold, Lucky Strike, and Camel. There has been some degree of restriction of competition between the products because of consumer preferences. The development of a special market provides scope for limited monopolistic action on the part of the seller, and such differentiation and the resulting special market will be sought whenever possible. The results have been well stated by Garver and Hansen as follows:

"As long as many customers prefer one seller's wares to those of another, so long will the seller be able to reduce output and confine his sales to those who are willing to pay higher prices. When this condition has prevailed for a time, the sellers may become so numerous that none can sell a sufficient output to enable him to reach lowest total unit cost, even though he should offer to sell at a price equal to that cost. There is not enough volume of demand to go around. By contrast, pure competition would force price down to the lowest total unit cost of the typical sellers. It would do this by eliminating some of the sellers—by assumption, the least efficient. It therefore appears that the building of clienteles is one of the causes of chronic overcapacity in certain lines of business, chiefly those in which manipulation of demand is most easily accomplished."[1]

The result of such monopolistic competition will be a higher normal price than under pure competition, and where expenditures are made for advertising and differentiation a price still higher will result. The volume of output will usually be less than under competition, but not necessarily so if selling costs are incurred, although even here the greater probability is that output will be less. The prices, however, are lower and output greater than they would be under the monopoly of a single seller or an agreement among the sellers. The extent to which prices are higher than under competition depends upon the special circumstances in particular cases. The prices of drugs, tooth paste, and cosmetics are evidently greatly higher, but one suspects that automobiles may not be appreciably so.

Location may also provide a partially sheltered market. A retailer may supply services to the neighboring community, but there may not be enough business for two or more concerns to operate efficiently in the locality. The new competitor will not enter unless he believes that he can operate more efficiently and drive the present retailer out, and in consequence no local competition is likely to appear. This situation provides the present business with some slight monopoly advantages. The retail market, particularly with convenience goods, is largely of such a character.

3. Market Exclusion.—It will be to the advantage of a group operating or selling in a market to build barriers to the entry of others into that market in order to provide a monopoly or a partial monopoly for themselves. Except in a few special cases, such as some health and sanitation requirements which safeguard consumers, market exclusion will be detrimental to the consumer by forcing him to pay higher prices for commodities and services

[1] Garver and Hansen, *op. cit.*, p. 200.

than would be necessary without this exclusion. The extent of these practices in the modern economy is seldom realized.

One of the more important and most widespread types of market exclusion is that provided by tariffs. Our import duties place burdens upon the sale of certain foreign-made goods in the United States. Tariffs wherever effective must be bad for consumers since they raise the price of the commodities in question. The results of a tariff depend a great deal upon the type of goods on which it is levied. Some goods are produced at lower costs in the United States than in other countries and are in consequence exported. A tariff placed on such goods by this country will have no influence on prices or domestic consumption since none of these goods are imported anyway. Another type of goods, such as bananas, tea, and silk, are not and cannot well be produced in this country because of costs, and some quantities are likely to continue to be imported even in the face of higher consumer prices. If the foreign producers have no other markets in which they can sell and cannot shift to the production of other products, then as long as they continue to supply the same quantities to us as formerly and other things except for the tariff are unchanged, they must take a lower price while the domestic price remains the same. If, however, the producers curtail sales in this country, then our prices will be higher. If these producers have many alternative markets or other productive opportunities, then our own price will be raised by nearly the full amount of the tariff. The government will receive as revenue at least as much in the form of import duties as the increase in the cost to the consumers. Any justification of such a tariff must be on the grounds that these imported goods form the basis of or a part of a desirable system of raising revenues.

The majority of the commodities on which tariffs are levied are those which can be produced both in this country and in other countries as well. The tariff then permits production in this country when none would otherwise be possible or permits a larger proportion of the supply to be produced domestically than would otherwise be possible. If the tariff is high enough to keep out all imports, then the government derives no revenues from it and the increased price paid by consumers is a bonus to the domestic producers. In case the goods are partly produced in this country and partly imported, the higher price paid by the consumer increases the tax revenues of the government on the imported goods and acts as a bonus to the domestic producer on the goods produced in this country.

The calculation of the cost of a particular tariff to domestic consumers is a matter of considerable technical difficulty. As long as goods are imported, domestic prices will exceed prices in world markets by the amount of the tariff. This may be occasioned by a rise in domestic prices or a fall in world prices because of our smaller takings, or more usually by a combination of the two. Their relative importance appears to depend to a large extent on our relative importance as an importer of that commodity in the world market and the alternative opportunities of the producers of the product. The greater our relative importance as an importer and the less the opportunities of the producers to switch to other lines of production, the less likely are our domestic consumers to bear the full burden of the tariff.

Sugar may be taken as an example; with respect to this commodity Secretary Wallace has written:[1]

"It is estimated that at current prices American consumers are obliged to pay more than $350,000,000 per annum in excess of of the value, at world prices, of their annual sugar supply (without allowance for the estimated net revenue of approximately $47,000,000 represented by the difference between disbursements under the Sugar Act of 1937 and receipts from the tariff and the 50¢ tax on sugar, or for the possible increase in world price that might result from changed conditions). This is equivalent to a tax of approximately $2.70 per capita on a population of 129 million persons. It means on the average a levy of more than $10 per family. . . . "

Another frequently used device for market exclusion is that of taxation. If taxes are laid on the competing product or marketing agency, then the costs or prices of that commodity or agency are raised and competition from this source lessened or eliminated. The taxes on oleomargarine are an example. The Federal government imposes a tax of 1/4 cent a pound on uncolored oleomargarine and 10 cents a pound on yellow or colored oleomargarine. In addition there are special taxes on manufacturers

[1] Letter of Secretary Wallace to Hon. Robert J. Bulkley, U.S. Senate, Mar. 1, 1938.

and handlers.[1] Twenty-eight states in 1935 had taxes on oleomargarine in some form. Nine states have taxes that apply generally to all oleomargarine sold within the state, ranging from 5 cents per pound in Iowa to 15 cents per pound in Washington and Wisconsin. In other states, taxes are levied on special kinds, such as those containing foreign fats or oils or more than a certain percentage of vegetable oils. The effect of such a tax must be to exclude oleomargarine from many markets and enhance the competitive position of competing fats and oils.

Often taxation is employed to limit the expansion or eliminate certain types of marketing organizations. The chain-store taxes, discussed elsewhere, are examples. In 1937, anti-chain-store legislation existed in 22 states, and bills were pending in 7 others.[2] In addition a number of cities and towns levy additional taxes on organizations operating chain stores in them. Such taxes were first used in 1925 and were moderate, but beginning about 1930 the legislation has become increasingly drastic. The taxes in Louisiana, Florida, Iowa, and Pennsylvania have been especially heavy. In Pennsylvania the tax per unit was $500, and this led to the immediate closing of a large number of stores. The Twentieth Century Fund has said:

"The present chain store taxes illustrate special interest legislation that is basically unsound. . . . If chains have a competitive advantage owing to the economies of the chain type of organization, the public benefits from it in low prices. We oppose the use of the taxing system, or any other device, to maintain the status quo for the benefit of those who would be injured by new methods of competition that benefit the public. The chain store taxes seem to have been used for this purpose."[3]

The license fees charged hucksters and peddlers, roadside-stand operators, and others are frequently designed to eliminate them from the market rather than for any regulatory or revenue purpose.

[1] Manufacturers are subject to special taxes or licenses at the rate of $600 a year. Wholesale dealers handling colored oleomargarine pay $480 a year and those handling uncolored $200. Retail dealers pay $48 a year to handle colored oleomargarine and $6 a year for selling the uncolored product.

[2] Federal Trade Commission, "Final Report of Chain-store Investigation," pp. 80–81.

[3] Twentieth Century Fund, "Facing the Tax Problem, 1937," p. 503.

A somewhat analogous situation is found in the case of resale price maintenance. Resale price maintenance permits the manufacturer to specify the price at which goods sold by him are to be sold by both the wholesaler and the retailer. It is aimed primarily at curtailing the activities of agencies depending largely upon attracting consumers by low prices, such as the chain stores, mail-order houses, and department stores. More than 40 states now have laws permitting resale price maintenance, mostly passed within the last few years; and the Tydings-Miller Act of 1937 is a Federal act permitting manufacturers to make resale contracts with retailers in states that have "fair-trade laws" without fear of Federal antitrust laws. These laws tend to exclude certain types of agencies from the market, although they are not nearly so drastic as the tax legislation in the case of chain stores.

Sellers of products may agree among themselves to a restriction of supplies or proration of the market. Sometimes these are gentlemen's agreements and sometimes marketing devices utilized by cooperatives having a considerable portion of the supplies. In the case of agricultural products, there has also been some legal sanction. Thus the marketing and licensing provisions of the Agricultural Adjustment Act and the California Agricultural Prorate Act legalize such procedures. Under these, a central body decides upon the total quantities to be sold and their allocation to particular markets, presumably selecting an arrangement that will raise the returns to producers.[1] Such a plan prevents some from selling the quantities or qualities or at a time when they otherwise would. It is a form of discriminating monopoly. Under the AAA there have been 25 distinct products for which active operations have been undertaken in the *general crops* group.[2]

[1] Among the devices commonly used are the following:

1. Exclusion of inferior grades or sizes from shipment.
2. Temporary embargoes on shipments.
3. Restriction of supplies in specified markets.
4. Curtailment of shipments during specified periods.
5. Limitation of total supply whose shipment or sale will be permitted during the whole marketing season.
6. Diversion of part of the crops to secondary uses.

[2] E. G. Nourse, "Marketing Agreements under the AAA," p. 358.

Examples of voluntary agreements among a large group and through cooperative action are found in the milk markets of nearly all the large cities. In these markets there is usually a large cooperative organization of producers negotiating the prices to be paid members by the dealers and distributors in that market. Where the cooperative controls a large portion of the supply, it may be difficult for outsiders to find a purchaser for their milk even though they might be willing to sell at lower prices. Various devices may be used to make it difficult to become a member of the cooperative. It is also alleged that in a number of markets the health departments have refused to inspect the farms and herds of new producers who desire to sell in the market. Where the ordinances require inspection, this proves an effective method of exclusion. More formal controls have been instituted in a number of markets in states having milk-control boards and in a smaller number of markets in which there is considerable interstate commerce by orders from the Secretary of Agriculture of the United States. In most of these there are provisions allowing restriction of free entry to the market.

The Agricultural Adjustment Act of 1938 makes provision for marketing quotas on five important agricultural commodities. The conditions under which the quotas may be established are specified for the individual commodities by the act. In the case of corn, for example, when the Secretary finds that the corn supply on October 1 will exceed normal supply by more than 10 per cent, quotas are to be in effect in the commercial corn-producing area. A referendum of the farmers subject to this quota must be held, and the quota will be in force unless more than one-third of those voting are against it. A penalty of 15 cents a bushel is levied against sales by any farmer above his marketing quota, in order to hold supplies on the domestic market in check. In years in which quotas are voted, commodity loans by the government are to be available on these products within certain ranges of a calculated parity price. Prices will thus tend to be higher in years in which these provisions are utilized.

4. The Control of Monopolies.—Monopolies have become an increasingly important problem in the modern economy, and with their growth have come problems of control. At the present time, a major fallacy seems to permeate our thought. Each group regards its problem from its own individual viewpoint and appears to believe that it may improve its relative position by a smaller output sold at higher prices. Thus the labor group through their unions demand a higher wage per unit of time and shorter hours, the farm group favors proposals designed to curtail production, and businessmen endeavor to establish sheltered markets through advertising or exclusion of competitors. In cases where elasticity of demand and cost reductions are favorable, an individual group restriction will improve the relative position of that group, but undertaken over a range the effect must be detrimental because it reduces the total volume of production. The increasing growth of monopoly in our society must be a matter of grave concern to the consumer. The extension of monopolies cannot fail seriously to influence the level of consumption of the people as a whole.

There is growing evidence that we will be increasingly driven to methods of more direct control of our monopolies. The present methods of control are outlined in Chap. VII. The huge corporation has come to dominate most major industries, if not all industries, in the United States. It has been estimated that the 200 large corporations in this country control 49 per cent of all corporate wealth, 38 per cent of all business wealth, and 22 per cent of the total wealth of the country.[1] The policy of indirect control has evidently failed to maintain competition in many fields, and newer and more drastic controls must be sought.

Questions

1. The barbers in Minnesota secured a law authorizing them to agree on a price for haircuts; if two-thirds of a community agreed on this price, all shops would be forced to charge at least as much. Is such a law desirable?
2. Would the public be better off with a large number of small partial monopolies or a few larger ones, *e.g.*, more Standard Oil companies or a few larger ones?
3. It is sometimes argued that in the case of exhaustible resources monopolies are desirable. Why might this be so?
4. A number of years ago when Old Golds were introduced on the market, $5,000,000 was set aside for advertising. Do you think the public gained from the introduction of this new brand into the field? Would they have done well to support it, or should they have continued to buy the old brands?

[1] See A. A. Berle and G. C. Means, "The Modern Corporation and Private Property."

5. In a monopolized industry, say a milk market, would it make any difference to consumers if the laborers organized as a monopoly—*i.e.*, would labor monopoly operate simply to divide the monopoly profits, or would it increase prices to consumers as well?

6. Are there any reasons for supposing that agreements among farmers to restrict sales are not so dangerous to consumers as agreements in other fields?

7. A real estate company in Los Angeles has control of one of the more desirable residential districts. Though there is an overplus of residential building lots in most sections of the city, the tendency seems to be to move into the section controlled by this one company. Is there likely to be any element of monopoly in the price of the lots sold by the controlling company? If so, how much?

CHAPTER VII

CONSUMER PROTECTION

The economic organization of society around a system of prices permits exploitation of the consumer in two general ways: (1) when, as has already been pointed out, the supply of a particular good is principally in the hands of a powerful group, and a monopolistic or quasi-monopolistic price is exacted; and (2) when the consumers themselves are unable to judge the character of the goods that they are buying. The situation regarding the consumer is quite different now from what it was 100 years ago. For one thing there are now many more goods from which to choose, and hence intelligent choices are more difficult to make than heretofore. Moreover, goods are now made in so many grades to accommodate the varying standards of living that one is hard put to it to distinguish properly between the several grades offered. In addition, the purchaser no longer is acquainted with the seller and thus cannot rely so much upon his integrity. Consequently, the purchaser to a great extent depends upon the unsupported claims of the vendors for his information about the commodities and services purchased. As a result of these and other factors, we have in the United States what has been referred to earlier as a dual system of control. Competition is still the basis of our economic society, but governmental supervision of many activities in the market place has been substituted for complete freedom of enterprise.

In order to decide whether the consumer is *adequately* protected, one must first find out to what *extent* he is protected. But first let us summarize the more specific ways in which the consumer *may* be adversely affected in our present economy:

1. The consumer may become the victim of a sales idea and make an important purchase on the basis of it. Example: The Octane selector advertised by certain automobile companies a few years ago was nothing more than a spark lever, but since a spark lever possessed no sales appeal the device was given this important-sounding name.

2. The consumer may purchase an article for which (because of a monopolistic situation or because of his own ignorance) he is charged an inordinately high price. Example: Bayer's aspirin, though little if any different from any other acetylsalicylic acid, is often priced five times as high as the lowest-priced aspirin.

3. The consumer may be the victim not only of an excessive price (when judged in terms of a sound product), but at times the good or service that he buys is *worthless.* Example: A few years ago Sanatogen was being sold as . . . "a scientific compound every particle of which represents the finest concentrated tissue constructing nutriment . . . [which] . . . contains over 700% more tissue building, life-sustaining nourishment than wheat flour." That this statement was somewhat oversanguine was demonstrated when a laboratory analysis revealed that $1 worth of wheat flour contained as much energy as $197 worth of Sanatogen.

4. The consumer actually ailing might purchase a so-called *cure* possessing only palliative powers and, hence, not discover the limitations of the product until it is too late. This is a particularly fruitful field for the quack because: (*a*) the consumer of this type of product is not in a normal psychological state and is therefore more amenable, and (*b*) many people to whom (say) cancer advertisements might appeal cannot afford expert medical advice.

5. The consumer might be the victim of the purchase of a definitely dangerous product (not only exorbitantly priced, not only worthless, but definitely harmful!). Example: a commodity of this type was LashLure, which when applied caused, in at least one case, total blindness.

1. Protection of the Consumer-buyer by Law.—Before mentioning the several specific agencies designed for the purpose of protecting consumers, it seems advisable to review very briefly the law that applies in the sale of merchandise. As will be seen, the consumer-buyer is not without legal protection. He should, however, avoid shady situations and exercise reasonable care in making his bargains so that an invocation of legal remedies will be unnecessary. In other words, although the consumer as a buyer is granted some legal protection, the necessity of resorting to such remedies should be avoided if possible.

1. *Breach of Warranty.*—"As matters stand, the buyer is armed with all the varieties of remedy known to the law today,

and well armed. Let us take the simple case in which a misstatement is made by a seller: the article that was said to be pure silk turns out to be partly artificial silk. However innocently or casually the statement may have been made, and regardless of whether it was oral or in writing, on a label in a printed advertisement or in a radio broadcast, or only by implication as when the dealer hands the goods to the buyer in response to the buyer's description of what he wants, without himself saying a word—regardless further of whether the misrepresentation was made by the seller in person or by an employee, and, if made by the latter, regardless of the instructions and cautions given and other precautions taken by the employer to prevent the employee from making misstatements—the buyer can rely in the first instance on the breach of warranty which the Uniform Sales Act in force in the majority of our states reads into the transaction.

"Whatever the law may have been in 1606 as to the distinction between a bare affirmation and a warranty, this is the law today: 'Any affirmation of fact or any promise by the seller relating to the goods is an express warranty if the natural tendency of such affirmation or promise is to induce the buyer to purchase the goods, and if the buyer purchases the goods relying thereon.'"

There are also liberal implied contracts of correspondence with description, conformity to sample, fitness for particular purposes, merchantability, and compliance with trade usages and customs.

To understand the tremendous meaning of breach of warranty under the Sales Act, let us consider the courses open to the disappointed buyer.

First, he may keep the goods and sue or set off for the breach.

Second, he may regard the warranty as a condition (this is an idea brought into the English act from Scotland and then copied into the American act) and refuse to accept the goods, or if he has accepted them he may return them and refuse to pay or be otherwise bound by the contract, or, if he has paid, he may demand his money back.

Third, if he has suffered damages from the breach of warranty (remember, a 10-cent purchase might conceivably cause thousands of dollars' worth of damages), he can sue for the actual damages reasonably foreseeable, though far in excess of the purchase price.

Fourth, in a proper case he might demand specific performance with the aid of equity, though in the highly simplified illustration used here it is improbable that a court of equity would see any reason for intervening, as the remedy at law seems adequate.

In the face of such a drastic law of warranty, it is difficult to understand why critics persist in accusing the law of washing its hands and piously saying *caveat emptor*.

2. *Fraud*.—"If we add one detail to the misrepresentation of the seller of the artificial silk, namely, what the lawyers call *scienter*—the knowledge that the statement was false or a reckless disregard of its truth or falsity—we have a case of fraud. Fraud opens many possibilities for redress. There is the tort action for deceit. There is a possibility of criminal proceedings for obtaining money under false pretenses, or whatever the crime happens to be called in any particular state. In fact, many crimes are built on fraud, false advertising, misuse of the mails, misbranding, or exposing for sale without some notice that may be required by statute—more likely to be found in the case of such foodstuffs as oleomargarine than in the case of cloth. Details are statutory, but the general principle is practically universal. . . .

"[It must be admitted however that] fraud is hard to detect and harder still to prove. The law wisely refrains from giving it an exact definition, for that would be the signal for tricksters to exercise their misguided ingenuity. When fraud is relied upon for the setting in motion of criminal law, the whole procedure, particularly the mode of proof, becomes darkened by the long tradition of the presumption of innocence. Even in civil proceedings, from the very nature of the case we must anticipate difficulty in uncovering fraud, for it is the essence of fraud to conceal fraud. . . .

"Finally, the cost and the trouble of fighting such a case for the small transactions of the consumer are prohibitive. The reputable dealer is likely to take the stand that the customer is always right, and the disreputable dealer is likely to escape altogether."[1]

As we shall see later, however, specific governmental agencies—the U.S. Post Office Department, the U.S. Food and Drug Administration, and others—organize their efforts in the direction

[1] Quoted without footnotes from Nathan Isaacs' excellent article, "The Consumer at Law," *Ann. Am. Acad. Political and Social Science*, vol. 173, pp. 180–182, May, 1934.

of controlling fraudulent activities. Through such agencies fraud can be more effectively dealt with than is possible by private suit.

2. Protection of the Consumer from "Unfair" Prices.—One way that the consumer may be harmed is through excessive prices. The prices charged by the monopoly are generally higher than those which would have obtained had competitive conditions existed in the industry, and in consequence some control is desirable.

There are in general four courses open to government in facing the monopoly problem: (1) Monopolies may be "let alone"—as is done in some European countries—on the assumption that competition will, in time, take care of the situation. (2) They may be destroyed and unfair practices tending toward monopoly proscribed. (3) They may be tolerated but regulated (on the grounds that it is to the consumer's advantage since in some types of industries costs decline as volume increases). (4) They may be taken over entirely by the government as publicly owned and managed enterprises.

We have in the United States utilized each of the last three policies in our attempt to handle the monopoly problem. In other words, under some circumstances we in the United States have tried to make competition mandatory by forcing monopolies from the field; under others, we have recognized the social advantage of allowing a regulated monopolization of the field; under still others (in only a few, to be sure), we have retained control of a field, declaring the activity to be a government monopoly. Our method has been *chiefly* that of attempting to maintain competition, however.

1. *Antitrust Legislation.*—The method of indirect control consists of the prevention of combinations, the dissolution of "combines" already in existence, and the maintenance of the conditions of fair competition by the prevention of unfair business practices. As long ago as 1890, the Sherman Antitrust Act was passed, forbidding, in the field of interstate commerce, all contracts, combinations, or conspiracies in restraint of trade and all monopolies or attempts to monopolize. This type of legislation was strengthened somewhat in 1914 by the passage of the Clayton Act and the Federal Trade Commission Act.

The Sherman Antitrust Act as now interpreted by the courts takes into account the famous Rule of Reason, and hence the language of the act is modified to that extent. In other words, the Supreme Court came to the conclusion in 1911 that monopolies were not necessarily bad; that, in fact, some monopolies had gained control of the market not by unfair means but by producing a superior commodity or service. The court, therefore, distinguished between "good" and "bad" trusts, *i.e.*, those which achieved dominance through superior management or the good reputation of a superior product as opposed to those which gained their position through exploitation of the consumer or of labor or through unfair competitive tactics. If the monopoly is good, argued the court, there is no reason for dissolution unless it subsequently exerts the monopolistic power that it gains. On the other hand, if the monopoly is bad, it should be dissolved or at least its monopolistic influence should be circumscribed. Though mere size in itself is not considered inimical to public interest, the court has warned the large companies that they must be doubly careful lest they utilize their strength unfairly.

The chief instances of outright dissolution by the courts have been in the cases of the Standard Oil Company and the American Tobacco Company. The Standard Oil Company was simply broken up into a number of similar concerns in which those having stock of the holding company received shares, but in later cases greater efforts have been made to see that the stock was put in the hands of really separate groups. *Consent decrees* have been more numerous than judicial dissolutions. Examples of these are the case of the International Harvester Company, in which the company agreed to amend its policy by selling certain of its lines to independent groups, and the packers case, in which the five largest packers consented to divest themselves of the ownership of any public stockyards, market companies, stockyard-terminal railroads, stockyard-market newspapers, or public cold-storage warehouses that they owned (except where essential for their meat business) and agreed not to engage in the distribution of certain foodstuffs not directly connected with the business of meat packing.

There seems to be some tendency on the part of the government of late to condone the activities of business entities regardless of size while condemning cooperative action by several separate units. "In recent years, [for example] not a single case is on record where an actually functioning business merger has been dissolved."[1] On the other hand, agreements by several on price matters have been condemned regardless of whether the form of organization was the gentleman's agreement, the trustee trust, the pool, or what not.

In general, then, the antitrust laws forbid a group of individuals to act in concert with respect to price matters. This applies to trade-association groups as well as to informal groups of large industrialists. Thus, in the so-called Hardwood (1921), Linseed (1923), and Trenton Pottery (1927) cases the courts condemned schemes which had as their purpose a restriction of production and a fixing or maintenance of prices and have taken this stand regardless of the reasonableness of prices so fixed. This principle was reaffirmed in the Sugar Institute Case (1936) when it was decided that an open price plan was illegal if accompanied by agreements not to deviate from reported prices. On the other hand, in the Maple Flooring (1925) and Cement (1925) cases the courts condoned the exchanging of past cost data in an absence of agreement regarding prices. And, in addition, in the Appalachian Coal case (1933) they tentatively whitewashed a cooperatively operated sales agency in an absence of monopolistic control.

The courts, then, seem not to condemn associational activities which tend to raise the level of competition. Thus, they allow the gathering and dissemination of credit information although, presumably, they would condemn concerted action in granting or refusing credit to individual applicants. They also allow group action in advertising the product of an industry, but in general would refuse to condone the establishment of a uniform price for the product. Moreover, trade-associational effort may be expended legally in regard to standardization and simplification, commercial and industrial research, the exchanging of information in traffic matters, the handling of disputes by means of commercial arbitration, and the improvement of trade-practice standards. Cooperative buying may also be practiced but might become illegal if monopsony power were exerted.

[1] Willard L. Thorp, "Government Regulation of Enterprise," pp. 701–702, in Spahr and others, "Economic Principles and Problems," 3d. ed., vol. II.

The status of agricultural cooperatives in regard to antitrust matters is somewhat different. The Clayton Act of 1914 provides that antitrust laws were not to be construed as prohibiting the formation and operation of nonstock, nonprofit agricultural associations. The Capper-Volstead Act of 1922, though perhaps not completely clear constitutionally, goes further. In effect, it excuses such associations from some of the rigors of the antitrust statutes by legalizing market operations by agricultural associations provided that either (1) no member is given more than one vote or (2) the association pays dividends of not more than 8 per cent per annum. However, the law prohibits monopolistic control, the result of which is to enhance prices unduly. In fact in such cases the Secretary of Agriculture is instructed to issue orders to cease and desist; if necessary, petition the district court to enforce his order and finally, where such action is required, place the matter in the hands of the Department of Justice. Thus, there seems to be some contrast in the application of antitrust laws to agricultural and to industrial groups. This contrasting treatment, no doubt, rests on an assumption of a fundamental difference between the "small impotent farmer" and the "large powerful industrialist." In one, presumably, cooperative action is socially beneficial; in the other it tends to be monopolistic—thus harmful.

With few exceptions, antitrust laws have lain dormant for half a decade. As this is written (June, 1938), the government is about to launch a sweeping investigation into monopolistic trends and practices. For this purpose, a temporary economic committee has been created by joint congressional resolution for investigatory purposes. The committee will consist of 12 members—3 each from the House and Senate, 1 each from the Justice, Commerce, Labor, and Treasury Departments, and 1 each from the Securities and Exchange and the Federal Trade Commissions. What can be expected of this is impossible to state at this early date.

The Federal government has been active recently in the control of rackets. Racketeering activities have most often been carried on through trade associations controlled by unprincipled gangsters whose purpose has been to gouge legitimate businessmen and, hence, the public. Much of this racketeering has been centered in New York City. Through the invocation of Federal laws requiring registration of certain types of firearms and through the antitrust statutes, the Federal income-tax law, and the Antiracketeering Statute,[1] the situation has been cleaned up considerably. Much of the credit for the success of the government in this drive has been due to the ingenious gathering of evidence and the administration of the several existing laws by the present District Attorney Thomas E. Dewey of New York.

Ever since the enactment of the Clayton and Federal Trade Commission legislation, there is the growing endeavor to control unfair trade practices that *tend* toward monopoly. As will be seen later, unfair trade practices include: (1) cutting prices below cost in a locality in which competition appears; (2) discriminating in favor of merchants who agree to discriminate against competitors' products or to refuse to handle them; and (3) producing special ("fighting") brands, sold at very low prices for the purpose of driving competitors' products out of the market. The use of threats or other forms of intimidation and the employment of spies to ascertain the details of competitors' business transactions are also considered inimical to public welfare since they may lead ultimately to price control.

2. *Public-utility Regulation.*—The difficulty in the control of public utilities lies principally in the determination of the precise rate to be set for the service offered. The rate should not be set too high, since the consumers would in that case pay more than would be necessary for the services rendered. If, on the other hand, the rate were set too low, the earnings of the company would be small and the capital of the company inadequate, enterprise would be discouraged, and the service and equipment would become dissipated. Such an error might result in an actual confiscation of capital and in the long run would be disadvantageous to the consumer. The goal that is aimed at under this type of control, then, is the setting of a *normal* price, a price based upon cost of production.

[1] The popular name of the statute enacted by Congress, June 18, 1934, which, though exempting labor unions, proscribes the obtaining of money through the use of force, violence, threats, or coercion, the obtaining of the property of another with his consent if induced by wrongful use of force or fear, or the committing of acts of physical violence to person or property in furtherance of either of the foregoing schemes, if such activities affect interstate commerce (18 U.S.C.A., 420*a*–420*e*).

The price should be such as would yield competitive earnings for the type of enterprise in question. Quite obviously, this is a difficult price to determine. It involves the determination not only of the rate of earnings but also of the amount of capital upon which the rate is to be based, both of which are controversial matters. It involves in addition the determination of total operating costs, a figure somewhat more ponderable. In determining the rate base, the market value of the concern cannot be taken, since the market value of any business is the present worth of its anticipated earnings at the competitive rate of interest and the earnings quite obviously depend upon the rates that the business is allowed to charge. Capital value for purposes of rate control is thus quite different from capital value for other purposes, say taxation. It must, in some way, then, have reference to the amount of money invested in the past. This is almost impossible to obtain in established businesses, since the capital may have been watered and the books manipulated in such a way as to disguise the real facts. It is customary, in consequence, to take either the estimated *cost of reproduction* of the plant or a value ascertained by a direct physical valuation and add to this a more or less arbitrary allowance for investments, for good will, promotion expenses, patent rights, etc.

Rates are usually established by public authority, but the final decision as to the reasonableness of a rate rests with the courts. There are several government commissions that deal with things coming within their power. The Interstate Commerce Commission, for example, regulates the rates to be charged by the railroads in interstate business. The Federal Power Commission has to do with interstate nonaffiliated operating power companies. The Federal Communications Commission has control over interstate telephone and telegraph companies. In addition, each state has commissions that perform similar functions for matters lying entirely within the state.

By a system of holding companies, a relatively few management groups have in the past been able to organize and control their public-utility properties to their own advantage. Through purchases (at arbitrary prices) from nonoperating affiliates and through other charges levied upon subsidiaries—for management, engineering, accounting, and legal services—operating costs have been inflated. In addition, holding companies have frequently acquired new property from corporate insiders at inordinately high prices.[1]

It was for the purpose of controlling such questionable practices that the Public Utility Act came into being in 1935. This was considered to be a Federal matter since holding companies sell securities in interstate trade, since their subsidiaries sell gas and electricity in interstate channels, and since their contracts are made through the mails. In any case, their activities extend over the several states and cannot be controlled by the laws of any one state.

Originally those drafting the bill contemplated the actual elimination of holding companies by Jan. 1, 1940, but the final draft—the one enacted into law—was not nearly so drastic. According to the law, the SEC is given wide powers of supervision and control, some of which are preventive and some remedial. Periodical reports must be rendered to the commission, making possible such control. On the preventive side—unless it is purely an intrastate transaction—it is necessary, in order that a holding company acquire an interest in an operating company, to receive permission from the commission. The commission may refuse such permission if it feels that a concentration of control will be detrimental to public interest. On the remedial side, the commission is authorized (among other things) to (1) establish regulations regarding the payment of dividends by operating companies to holding companies and (2) establish regulations concerning construction and other contracts existing between the affiliated companies. Each of the several powers granted the commission is to ensure that purchasers of service are not charged exorbitant prices and that holders of operating-company securities are given a fair return on their investment. Neither

[1] The following is a more specific listing of holding-company practices that have been criticized ("Owens on Business Organization and Combination," p. 463): "(1) Loading the fixed capital account of operating utilities with arbitrary amounts in order to establish a base for excessive rates. (2) Engaging in transactions for the purchase or sale of property or securities with controlled or subsidiary companies for the purpose of recording arbitrary profits or fixing valuations unjustified by market values. (3) Disregard of prudent financing in excessive issues of bonds, imperiling the solvency of the subsidiary and involving excessive charges for interest and commissions. (4) Deceptive methods of dividing earnings as between operating companies and the parent company. (5) Intercompany financing on a basis disadvantageous to the operating company."

of these ends is accomplished when a small group of men operate the affairs of their companies to their own selfish ends. This legislation, therefore, is admirable in its purpose.

The establishment of prices by governmental authority takes place only in industries of a monopolistic nature. The interests of the consumers of other products or services are assumed to be sufficiently protected under the operation of full competition. A regime in which all prices were established by governmental authority would be undesirable. The reason for this should be quite clear. Unless the price established by the government were the same as the competitive price, there would be an excess of product over the amount demanded at that price, or less product would be supplied than buyers wished to buy at that price. In other words, if the established price were lower than the competitive price, consumers would try to buy more of the product than was produced and some would have to go without; if the established price were higher than the competitive price, producers would produce more than could be sold at that price and some of the product would remain unsold. Only under an elaborate, and probably unworkable, system of taxes and bounties would it be possible to set up a regime in which there could conceivably be a better arrangement of prices than under the purely competitive system.

3. Protection against Product Misrepresentation and Inferior Quality.—Consumers are often exploited because they lack knowledge of the market, or are unable to judge the qualities of goods in relation to their prices. The wide range of the purchases that the consumer is called upon to make and the limited time at his disposal for studying each of these purchases preclude any close knowledge of the prices or qualities of any one of them. Furthermore, many of the differences in the qualities of goods are not directly visible and are revealed only after elaborate tests. Relatively little has been done directly to ensure consumers adequate knowledge of the proper price for an article. During the World War, lists were prepared of "fair" prices for a considerable number of articles, but this particular activity has been dropped. The consumer must now secure his own information, which he receives principally from the merchants whom he patronizes, from advertisements, or from special agencies of the consumer-research type.

There are a number of times when both consumers and producers would gain by a more adequate knowledge on the part of consumers. In the case of seasonal crops, for example, consumers need to be instructed as to when is the proper time to buy for canning or preserving, or when the crop is particularly low in price or exceptionally high in quality. The dissemination of such information would be mutually advantageous. Some of the large cooperatives and trade associations are taking steps in this direction.

1. *Federal Trade Commission.*—The most important legal agency in the control of trade practices in the United States is the Federal Trade Commission.[1] Coming into existence in 1914 this quasi-judicial body was set up not as a consumer-protection agency but as one designed to protect competitors. Recently, however, the act was amended to deal with practices affecting the public.[2] Although the act originally was designed to furnish protection to manufacturers and tradesmen, its administration was even then advantageous to consumers. In other words, the activities of the commission protected consumers by indirection since the test as to whether a competitor had been harmed was whether the consumer had been deceived to the disadvantage of the competitor.[3] Before the existence of the Federal Trade Com-

[1] Other functions of the commission are: (1) to make investigations at the direction of Congress, the President, the Attorney General, or upon its own initiative; (2) to report facts in regard to alleged violations of the antitrust laws; (3) to prevent discrimination in price and other forms of discrimination in violation of the Robinson-Patman Act amending the Clayton Act; (4) to prevent exclusive dealing contracts, capital-stock acquisitions, and interlocking directorates in violation of the Clayton Act; and (5) to administer the Webb-Pomerene or Export Trade Act, aimed at promotion of foreign trade by permitting the organization of associations to engage exclusively in export trade.

[2] Approved on Mar. 2, 1938, the Wheeler-Lea Amendment (S. 1077, Seventy-fifth Congress) improved procedure and granted new powers to the commission. The more important provisions of the amending legislation are: (1) broadening the act to deal with unfair practices adversely affecting the public; (2) insertion of a section dealing specifically with "false advertising of foods, drugs, devices, and cosmetics"; (3) improving the method of procedure in the handling of cases; and (4) strengthening the power of the commission to enforce final "cease and desist" orders by introducing a civil penalty of $5,000 for their violation.

[3] If no competition existed—if monopoly conditions obtained—the commission could not prove injury. Hence, theoretically at least, in such cases the respondent could continue the practice with impunity.

mission, it was possible, for example—therefore, of course, it was a usual practice—to sell imitation linoleum as genuine linoleum because the practice was not directed against any particular competitor and there existed in consequence no sufficient interest to prevent the fraud. Such practices are now, in part at least, suppressed by the action of the commission.

The commission has instituted over 25,000 inquiries since its inception. An appreciation of the method by which the consumer is protected by the commission's activities is gained from the following list of some of the types of cases handled:

1. Misbranding of commodities with respect to quality, quantity, origin, nature of manufacture, etc.

2. Passing off goods or articles for well- or favorably known products of competitors through appropriation or simulation of such competitors' trade names, labels, etc.

3. Selling rebuilt, secondhand, renovated, or old products or articles made from used or secondhand materials as new.

4. Schemes to create the impression in the mind of the prospective customer that he or she is being offered an opportunity to purchase under unusually favorable circumstances when such is not the case. For example:

a. Sales plans in which the seller's usual price is represented to be made available on some pretext for a limited time or to a limited class only.

b. Misleading trade names calculated to create the impression that a dealer is a manufacturer or grower, is selling directly to the consumer, and is passing on the resulting savings.

5. Imitating or using standard containers customarily associated in the mind of the consumer with standard weights or quantities, but selling the public less than such weights or quantities.

6. Giving products misleading names so as to create value in the minds of consumers, *e.g.*, implying falsely that a product

a. Is so named because it was made for the government.

b. Is made in or came from some locality famous for the quality of such products.

c. Was made by some favorably known process when, in fact, it was made only in imitation of such process.

7. Selling below cost with the intent and effect of hindering, stifling, or suppressing competition.

8. Giving products a purported unique status of special merit through misleading and ill-founded scientific tests.[1]

The commission usually does not enter a complaint of its own initiative but generally awaits a protest by an interested party. Protests are nearly always from competitors, since they are the only ones who are likely to find it worth while to incur the trouble and expense of making a complaint. If the practice is one that injures the consumer alone, and that the bulk of the trade indulges in, the practice may continue indefinitely before coming to the attention of the commission. After a complaint has been filed, the commission proceeds much like a court. Evidence bearing on the claims made for the article—its performance and composition—is presented and passed upon. The commission then hands down its decision based upon the majority vote of its members. The particular dealer is either ordered to cease and desist from the particular practice or, if the commission does not find against him, is permitted to continue that practice. Until recently, decisions, together with the report of any scien-

[1] Federal Trade Commission, "Annual Report," pp. 67–71, 1936. It might be well to mention a few cases specifically in order that the student may have more firmly in mind the type of protection that has been afforded the consumer by the Federal Trade Commission: (1) A hosiery company was selling cotton goods under such labels as *men's merino*, *gray wool*, and other similar terms. An order by the commission to cease and desist the practice was upheld by the courts, since such deceptions tend to injure competitors. Obviously, however, the consumer was protected by indirection. (2) A company selling aspirin in advertising its product not only exaggerated the benefits of its product, according to the commission, but attempted to induce the belief that aspirin sold by other manufacturers was not genuine and even implied that the competitors' product might be dangerous. Considering the fact that aspirin is only acetylsalicylic acid and that there are few differences except in price between the various vendors' brands, both implications were unwarranted. The complaint, of course, was made on the basis of injury to competitor, but the consumer was protected as well. (3) Automobile finance companies were advertising their services in such a way as to give the public the distinct impression that the cost of financing through these concerns amounted to only 6 per cent simple interest. The fact is, however, that as in all instances of automobile financing the 6 per cent was discounted, which meant that the effective interest paid by the customers of these concerns amounted to almost twice that amount. Again the commission frowned on the practice and asked for stipulations, on the same grounds that customers were deceived to the disadvantage of the companies' competitors. Again the consumer was given protection.

tific investigations made, were published. Recently, there seems to be an increasing tendency on the part of the commission to deal quietly with the offending firms and to entertain stipulations or agreements on the part of respondents that they will cease unfair practices.

Through its trade-practice-conference procedure, the commission may entertain rules of fair competition for an entire industry. The rules adopted are of two types: (1) those which have to do with unfair practices and hence, when approved by the commission, are enforceable through court action, and (2) those which are concerned only with unethical practices and are thus enforceable only through cooperation of the group.

One of the most interesting of the recent groups of rules is that emerging from a conference on the rayon industry. In this the commission went further than usual in its conference procedure by promulgating rules concerning the wording used in the advertising of the product. Thus, Rule I declares it to be unfair trade practice to represent or sell rayon as "(1) not being rayon; or (2) as being something other than rayon." Indeed, a positive statement that a rayon product or material actually is rayon must be made clearly on the label and in the advertising and sales promotional material.

Rules were promulgated recently (June, 1938) by the commission for the fur industry also.[1] These rules cover in great detail labeling, advertising, and merchandising practices and make it mandatory to use correct names in describing furs, to avoid the term *genuine* except where actually appropriate, and to eschew misleading and fictitious pricing practices. Similar rules may be expected for other industrial groups as time goes on.

Even before the Wheeler-Lea Amendment, the commission instituted a system to control more effectively the publishing and dissemination of untruthful advertising matter by individual firms. In 1929, a special board of three members was set up for this purpose by the Federal Trade Commission. With the purpose of reducing false and misleading statements to a minimum, this board reviews all advertising matter published in newspapers and magazines and broadcasted over the radio. To this end the board examined 96,939 advertisements and

[1] Copies of trade-practice-conference rules may usually be had on request from the Federal Trade Commission.

noted 9,074 as containing statements appearing to be false or misleading during the year 1935–1936. These 9,074 advertisements formed the basis of 1,865 prospective complaints. During the same year the board received copies of 337,443 commercial broadcasts by radio stations of which 19,572 were marked as representations appearing to be false or misleading. Of these, 1,304 became cases for further review and procedure in instances that appeared to require it.

The procedure in such cases is as follows: If a periodical or radio advertisement appears to be misleading, the commission sends a questionnaire to the advertisers requesting a sample of his product, a quantitative formula, and copies of all advertisements published during the year. Upon receipt of these data, the claims, sample, and formula are sent to one of the technical agencies of the government for scientific opinion. If the advertiser is proved to be justified in his claims, the case is tentatively closed; if not, he may enter a stipulation or be asked to cease and desist. In the latter instance, the case may finally have to be settled in the courts. The commission is of the definite opinion, probably justified, that its work in this field has contributed to the general improvement in the character of advertising that has been manifest in the last few years.

All the foregoing activity with respect to untruthful advertising has been carried on through general commission powers. The recent amendment gives the commission specific powers for controlling false claims. It is now declared unlawful to disseminate false advertising through the mails, in commerce, or by any other means, for the purpose of inducing the purchase of food, drugs, devices, and cosmetics. False advertising is defined as that which is misleading in a material respect. The definition includes not only acts of commission but acts of omission also. That is to say, not only affirmative false statements are punishable but the failure to reveal material facts as well.

It would be fruitless to speculate upon the effect of the new sections upon industry and the consumer. A great deal will depend upon the character of enforcement given them by the commission. This much might be said, however: According to the law, whenever an advertiser publicizes an offering of food, drugs, devices, or cosmetics, the advertisement must contain no false statements, must not fail to disclose facts material to the consequences that may result from the commodity's use. Moreover, no retailer may, in the future, rely upon the statement or assurance of the manufacturer of an article; exact and scientific knowledge is required. Since, in addition to the specific proscriptions, better enforcement procedure has been provided, this legislation is an important step toward more effective consumer protection.

2. *Pure Food and Drug Laws.*—The Federal government makes an attempt to protect the consumer in his purchases of food and drugs by means of the Pure Food and Drug Law, the Meat Inspection Law, and various Federal and state acts standardizing containers, weights, and measures. As in the cases of the legislation dealing with monopolies and unfair trade practices, the Federal laws deal only with articles handled in interstate commerce. There are in all the states, as we shall see, pure food laws more or less like the Federal law, and in addition many municipalities regulate certain articles through their own ordinances.

The Federal Pure Food and Drug Law of 1906 (with its various earlier amendments),[1] though recently expanded and improved by Congress, remains in effect in most respects until June, 1939. The old law endeavors to protect the consumer by forbidding the adulteration and misbranding of food and drugs that enter interstate commerce. According to this law, a product has been adulterated if it has been damaged or rendered inferior by mixing a substance with it, by substituting another substance for it, by abstracting any valuable constituent from it, by so treating it as to conceal inferiority, by adding poisonous or deleterious

[1] Up to June, 1938, the most important amendments to the 1906 act were as follows: (1) the Sherley Amendment (1912), which proscribed statements on labels regarding the therapeutic or curative effect of such articles when such statements are false and fraudulent (this is the so-called *fraud joker*); (2) the Net Weight Amendment (1913), which made it mandatory in most instances to state plainly and conspicuously the terms of weight, measure, or numerical count on packages of food; (3) the McNary-Mapes Amendment (1930), which provides for the promulgation of standards of quality, condition, and fill of container of canned foods (except meat and canned milk) and conspicuously labeling such canned food indicating where appropriate that the tinned food falls below the standard established; (4) the Sea Food Amendment (1934), which provides for permissive government inspection of sea food and for authorization of a statement on the label that the goods have been inspected (in effect in the shrimp and oyster industries at present).

substances to it, and in any case if it contains any substance unfit for food. Legally, a product is misbranded: if the package bears a false or misleading statement or is falsely branded as to its place of manufacture; if it is in imitation of, or offered for sale under the distinctive name of, another article; if it is labeled or branded so as to deceive the purchaser. If in package form, it is misbranded also if the quantity of the contents is not marked in terms of weight, measure, or numerical count or if the package or its label bears any false or misleading statement.

While it is no longer possible to prepare a soothing syrup containing morphine to keep the baby quiet, the labels describing the contents of many foods and drugs, though truthful, have told us little regarding their relative merits. There have been in addition several other definite limitations to the food and drug legislation under which we have been operating. For one thing, the law has been extremely weak in the area of consumer protection against false therapeutic claims. The reason for this weakness has been that fraud has had to be proved in such cases. That is to say, the government has had to establish the fact, not only that a medicament was useless in the treatment of the disease for which it had been sold, but that the vendor knew that it was without merit. An unprincipled vendor often could bring in witnesses who were quite willing to swear that they had been cured through the use of his product. Indeed, some of the customers probably actually believed that they were cured through the use of the compound. There are always available hypochondriacs who are continually contracting, treating, and "curing" diseases. Such a burden of proof has been often too great to overcome. Considering the handicap, it is a wonder that the government has been able to win any cases at all.

One other outstanding weakness of the old Federal act has been its lack of power in controlling the sale of dangerous (or even deadly!) compounds in the absence of mislabeling. This weakness was brought forcibly to the attention of the nation recently as a result of the sale of the deadly "Elixir Sulfanilamide" and is probably one of the reasons for the enactment of new legislation at this time. The case is particularly interesting in this connection since it illustrates clearly one of the weaknesses of the old law.

Ironically, the drug sulfanilamide is one of the really valuable discoveries of the decade. The "elixir"—containing diethylene glycol—proved to have a definite lethal effect, however, during September and October of 1937 at least 73 persons having died as a direct result of its use. Twenty other persons who took the elixir died, but it has not been clearly established that this drug was exclusively responsible for these deaths. "Elixir Sulfanilamide" was first distributed commercially on Sept. 4, 1937; the first word of deaths from an unidentified sulfanilamide preparation reached the Food and Drug Administration on Oct. 14, six weeks later. On Oct. 16, an investigator for the administration telegraphed from Tulsa, Okla., that 9 persons had died in that locality after taking "Elixir Sulfanilamide." Seizure of all outstanding shipments was immediately ordered. Since, until recently, the Federal Food and Drug Act contained no provision against dangerous drugs, seizures had to be based on a charge that the word *elixir* implied an alcoholic solution, whereas this product was a diethylene glycol solution. Had the product been designated a *solution*, rather than an *elixir*, no charge of violating the law could have been brought. *Before the elixir was put on the market, it was tested for flavor but not for its effect on human life.* The old Food and Drug Act then neither required that new drugs be tested before they were placed on sale nor authorized the seizure of dangerous drugs unless their label misrepresented them.

The new legislation—S5, Seventy-fifth Congress—was signed by the President on June 25, 1938. Although there are some exceptions, as was mentioned previously, the law goes into effect June 25, 1939.[1] There is no question but that the new legislation improves the consumer's position tremendously. Let us briefly outline the more important provisions of the new food and drug legislation.

The new amendment to the 1906 law broadens the authority of the Pure Food and Drug Administration in several ways and probably improves enforcement procedure as well. For one thing, it now brings cosmetics under the supervision of the

[1] The 1938 act completely replaces the old legislation on June 25, 1939. However, the "hair-dye" provision goes into effect 90 days after the signing of the bill; the provision regulating the issuance of new drugs, that having to do with adulterated cosmetics, and that broadening misbranding to include drugs dangerous to health when used as prescribed are effective immediately.

administration and proscribes the shipment of those cosmetics which are injurious, adulterated, or misbranded. With respect to drugs, the definition is now expanded to include articles (other than food) that are intended to affect the structure or any function of the body of man. This provision is designed to get at the sale of devices—such, for example, as bowleg straighteners—but without question will bring obesity "cures" within the scope of the administration's authority as well. If so, the activities of Mr. Hayes (in selling his Marmola; see footnote, Chap. VIII, pages 130–132) will at long last be circumscribed.

The new law broadens the authority of the administration in several other ways. The section on new drugs, for example, prohibits their introduction until an application has been filed with the Secretary of Agriculture and has become effective.[1] Drugs that the Secretary finds unsafe for use under conditions as prescribed are prohibited from being shipped in interstate commerce.

Perhaps the most important provisions of the new law from the standpoint of the consumer, however, is the one that eliminates the "fraud joker." Under the new legislation (instead of providing, as the old law did, that an article is misbranded if the statement of its curative or therapeutic effect is *false* and *fraudulent*), a drug is misbranded if the label is false or misleading in any particular. This certainly is an important victory for the consumer. According to the new law, a drug also is misbranded if it is dangerous to health when used as prescribed on the label; it is misbranded likewise when it fails to bear certain statements where appropriate. For example: (1) Package drugs must bear the name and address of their manufacturer or distributor, and the statement of quantity must be readable. (2) The statement "Warning—may be habit-forming" must appear on packages containing narcotic or hypnotic substances. (3) Unofficial drugs must bear their common or usual name, and such compounds must contain the names of active ingredients. (4) All drug labels must bear adequate directions for use and adequate warnings against misuse.

[1] Each application will become effective on the sixtieth day after filing unless the secretary postpones the effective date. This provision in effect requires proof of safety in use as a prerequisite to the introduction of new drugs.

There is also a provision in the act relative to cautionary labeling of coal-tar hair dyes. According to the law, such a product must bear on its label, "Caution—this product contains ingredients which may cause skin irritation on certain individuals and a preliminary test according to accompanying directions should first be made. This product must not be used for dyeing the eyelashes or eyebrows; to do so may cause blindness." Moreover, the new legislation provides that germicides must actually possess germicidal powers. This would seem to be a very reasonable provision, but that certain so-called germicides have not had such powers in the past there can be no doubt. Indeed, in some cases the administration has found preparations in which germs were actually propagating!

Regarding foods, the new legislation proscribes the shipment of *all* foods injurious to health. (The old law applied only where a poisonous substance had been added.) Moreover, in cases where it is necessary to add poisons (*e.g.*, with some sorts of spray), definite provision may be made for the extent of tolerance. In addition, labels on food (except butter, cheese, and ice cream) must declare artificial coloring and chemical preservatives; dietary foods must be informatively labeled. Incidentally, confectionery containing trinkets is outlawed under the act.

One of the very important new provisions of the amending act permits the setting up of definitions and standards of foods. Although the degree of success depends largely upon the administration of this provision, much may come of it. Foods for which there are no standards will have to bear labels disclosing their ingredients. This applies to proprietary foods or those which are sold under distinctive names.

As was mentioned previously, some of the administrative features of the Food and Drug Law have been strengthened also. For example, criminal penalties have been increased and may now be imposed even on the first offense; heavy fines and prison sentences are prescribed for cases of second or wilful offenses. In addition, multiple seizures have been provided for under certain circumstances.[1] One important administrative

[1] The multiple-seizure device is one that has been employed in the past in flagrant cases of grossly misbranded drugs and ones which are definitely dangerous to health. The 1906 act is silent on this subject, and, since

provision (though of seeming unimportance) is that having to do with minor violations. According to the new act, such violations may be settled by written notices or warnings. The importance of this lies in the natural hesitancy in "utilizing a 16-inch gun to shoot a sparrow." That is to say, unless special provision is made, officials generally dislike invoking laws carrying drastic penalties in attempting to circumscribe the activities of minor violators. Publicity may also be used as a punitive device by the administration in cases involving danger to health or gross deception of consumers.

Probably the most important weakness of the new law is its provision for court review. The original (Tugwell) bill did not mention court review. Written by the administration, this bill envisioned a finality of secretarial orders.[1] The present provision is the result of a compromise. Before it was changed at the last minute, any person affected by an order of the Secretary could seek an injunction in any one of the 85 Federal district courts. Obviously this would have been very unsatisfactory since, theoretically at least, antagonists could enter one injunction after another against an order, timing them in such a way as to tie the hands of the administration entirely. Coupled with this would have been the expense and burden of carrying evidence and exhibits all over the United States and the very good chance of a lack of homogeneity of decision, both of which would have been intolerable. As the bill was finally enacted, it provides that an appeal from an order may be entered in any one of the 10 Federal circuit courts within 90 days after the issuance of the order. The court may order additional evidence taken before the Secretary and will have the power to modify or set aside any order temporarily or permanently.

---

it says nothing about it, there has been nothing to prevent it. What the term actually means is that, since each shipment constitutes an offense, many seizures can be made on the same product and a separate case can be predicated on each seizure. Incidentally, if the government so desired, it could actually put a company under by means of this device. Indeed, in some instances this probably would be socially desirable.

[1] Injunctions could, of course, be brought against a secretary's order under the general law. Since the legal residence of a secretary is usually Washington, D.C., however, such a suit would have to be entered in the District of Columbia.

If a review section is essential in order to protect business from an arbitrary exercise of power by a government official (and perhaps it is), the provision in the bill as enacted is definitely preferable to that contained in the earlier draft. There are, of course, fewer courts—10 instead of 85—and therefore less expense and burden on the government in handling various cases. Also, since the circuit courts have a multiple-judge system, presumably a higher quality of decision will be forthcoming.

There is no question at all but that the Food and Drug Administration has been working under a terrific handicap ever since its inauguration. The law that the group has been required to administer has been completely inadequate, and as in most other regulatory agencies, it has almost continually been working shorthanded. There is little question that the new amendment strengthens the powers of the administration. Given adequate financial support, we may expect more effective control of antisocial acts of unprincipled food and drug vendors as a result of the enactment of this measure.

Another piece of legislation leveled at impurity of foods is the Meat Inspection Law (1907). This act provides that meat entering interstate trade be inspected by well-trained veterinary inspectors and that the product be so marked. Hence, the consumer is usually safe in the purchase of meat that is labeled "U.S. Government Inspected." Often state governments have inspection machinery for intrastate supplies, and in many instances all meat going through a packing plant whether for intra- or interstate trade is inspected. Thus, there is another area in which consumer-protection legislation is in effect. Although the consumer is in no sense protected from excessive price by legislation of this type, he is definitely given some measure of protection from dangers arising out of the consumption of harmful food products.

Several other laws having to do with food and drugs might well be mentioned at this point. One—the so-called Haugen Amendment (1923)—provides a statutory definition for butter. Thus, this product is defined by law as "the food product usually known as butter, and which is made exclusively from milk or cream or both, with or without common salt, and with or without additional coloring matter. [and containing] . . . not less than 80 per cent by weight of milk fat, all tolerances having been allowed for." In addition we have laws which declare unlawful the importation of adulterated or spurious drugs (1848), impure tea (1883 and 1897), and unhealthy or unwholesome meats (1922). Moreover, horse meat (since 1919) may not be transported unless it is labeled as such. Also an import milk act (1927) exists which provides protection by means of a regulation of milk importation through mandatory inspection and licensing.

Some of the existing food laws exert control through the taxing power of the Federal government. Filled cheese (since 1895) is heavily taxed as is (since 1898) mixed flour. Many of these, while ostensibly consumer protective, actually are designed to protect industry. For example, the Oleomargarine Act (1886) places a discriminatory tax on colored margarine over white. The consumer-protective aspects of legislation of this type are quite secondary to their producer-protective aspects. There are, however, certain consumer-protective features contained therein. Without legislation, for example, unprincipled producers in the margarine field might actually succeed in selling their product as butter; might at least (if product were attractive enough in appearance) succeed in charging prices somewhat higher than would be possible otherwise.

Questions

1. Is the present antitrust legislation consumer protective? If not, what should be done in order to make it protective of consumer interests? Can any law be devised in an economy such as ours fully to protect the consumer against prices containing an element of monopoly?
2. Why is the existence of rackets inimical to consumer interest?

CHAPTER VIII

CONSUMER PROTECTION (*Concluded*)

4. Other Federal Agencies.—There are many other types of consumer-protective legislation designed to protect quality, which should be mentioned. Some of this legislation is of the general type protecting consumers from fraudulent enterprises of all kinds. Most, however, is for the purpose of protecting consumers in the purchase of specific types of goods and services. Some of these pieces of legislation are new and therefore cannot be judged finally as to their adequacy. Each, however, should be given some attention by the student of consumption economics in order to see just what exists in the way of legal protection.

1. *Postal Department.*—One of the most important of the existing consumer-protective legislative devices is the power of the postal service to control the use of the mails. Thus, the department is legally charged with the responsibility of proscribing the use of the mails in connection with fraudulent enterprises. This legislation is administered through the Inspection Division and Solicitor of the U.S. Post Office Department. The legislation covering this phase of consumer-protective activity is very broad indeed. The use of mails in direct connection with a fraudulent scheme (*i.e.*, the mailing of the article purchased, by the vendor) is not necessary in order that a vendor be involved. The section is more broadly interpreted to mean that the use of the mails *in the furtherance of* or *in connection with* any fraudulent enterprise is in violation of the law.

"It is entirely safe to say that every day witnesses the abstraction from the pockets of our citizens of far more money by the use of cunningly devised printed statements than is removed at the point of a gun or by threats of bodily harm. Complete statistics are not available, but it is a matter of record that in only 97 of the 3,643 mail-fraud cases investigated in the fiscal year 1936, more than $36,000,000 was filched from the victims of the schemes.[1] An examination of the palpably fraudulent schemes currently being advertised in the columns of magazines and periodicals enjoying a nationwide circulation will convince the most skeptical that enough is not yet being done under the mail-fraud statutes to protect the uninformed and the unwary. . . . The Post Office Department can not be said to be performing its full duty to the citizen until it takes cognizance of such advertisements and suppresses such fraudulent schemes before the pockets of the swindlers have become filled with the savings of their victims."[2] The department brings the full force of the mail-fraud statutes to bear upon racketeers and other swindlers who conduct their operations through the mails. A total of 6,252 mail-fraud investigations were authorized during the fiscal year 1937, an increase of more than 35 per cent over the number for 1936. Arrests for fraud during 1937 increased from 824 to 927 and convictions from 563 to 638.[3]

The postal authorities have two ways of handling fraud cases: (1) prosecution through the U.S. Department of Justice on a basis of evidence gathered by postal inspectors, and (2) issuance of a fraud order. Each of these methods is used extensively. The former is somewhat slow, and since speed is essential in many of these cases the method loses much of its effectiveness. The latter is a particularly effective device when speed is neces-

[1] Such activities include failure to furnish merchandise as promised, sale of worthless or deceptively worded insurance policies, sale of worthless securities, mythical estates, "work-at-home" schemes, fake cures, etc.

[2] "Annual Report of the Postmaster General," pp. 75–76, fiscal year ended June 30, 1936.

[3] As an example of the type of cases handled by the department: just previous to the opening of the fiscal year 1937 there became very active in many sections of the country a particularly vicious swindle practiced on elderly persons. Securing names of victims both through personal inquiry and from spectacle peddlers who received commissions, two of the swindlers would visit the victim and convince him that he had a cataract that might cause blindness or paralysis. They would fill the eye with argyrol or other solutions and place a piece of thin rubber or skin from the inside of an eggshell on the eye. The rubber or skin would then be taken off and exhibited as proof that the cataract had been removed. For a pretended operation of this kind the swindlers obtained from $50 to $500. The department now feels that this racket has been effectively suppressed. Thirty-five of the bogus eye specialists have been convicted and sentenced to terms of imprisonment totaling 177 years. Others are awaiting trial.

sary. For example, a fraudulent enterprise is started and is receiving a continuous stream of checks from its victims. Prosecution may be resorted to and will be in time, but meanwhile the money continues to pour in. Citing the individual to appear in Washington within (say) 10 days to show reason why a fraud order should not be issued and the subsequent issuance (in the case of failure legally to justify his activity or in case of failure to appear) of a fraud order quickly deprive him of the use of the mails. All mail addressed to him is marked *fraudulent* and returned to the sender.

One limitation to any scheme designed to protect the consumer against himself is the consumer's own gullibility. One case illustrates the point: A fraud order was issued against a company that was selling fake oil shares. Despite the fact that mail was returned to the senders marked *fraudulent*, many of the victims were annoyed by the interference of the postal authorities and actually circumvented the regulating activities of the department by sending their money to the vendor by wire.

The postal regulation as a consumer-protective device has several additional limitations. For one thing, most of the cases handled by the department originate through complaints. In other words, someone must complain, in most instances, before investigation is made. This limitation, it would seem, should be remedied. There ought to be some agency that actually examines advertising copy. Perhaps there ought to be closer cooperation between the special board (now advertising investigation bureau) of the Federal Trade Commission and the Postal Inspection Unit. This type of cooperation, though practiced in some instances, should be extended. It could be carried on effectively not only between the U.S. Post Office Department and the Federal Trade Commission, but also among several protective agencies, including the SEC and the Pure Food and Drug Administration.

Though it is generally agreed that the mail-fraud statutes law affords the consumer a great deal of protection, one must admit further limitations. For one thing, the Postal Inspection staff is too small for completely effective work. For another, the U.S. Post Office Department procedure is somewhat inflexible. By the simple process of changing the name of the company disreputable dealers have at times kept one jump ahead of the law. One would imagine that if the postal authorities were impotent in such circumstances, one of the other governmental agencies (the Federal Trade Commission or the Pure Food and Drug Administration, say) would be in a position effectively to act. And often this is the case. Occasionally, however, commercial knaves have been able to circumvent the regulations of all three agencies.

2. *Federal Housing Administration.*—One of the newer agencies whose activities are of a consumer-protective nature is the Federal Housing Administration. Inaugurated in June, 1934, for the purpose of inducing recovery, this organization offers very effective protection to the homeowner, from the time the lot is selected and the house is planned until it is fully paid for and title is delivered to the purchaser. When a house is to be built and an application for mortgage insurance filed with the FHA, through any FHA approved private-lending institution of the borrower's choice, trained technical experts launch a carefully planned program to safeguard the buyer's interests.

First consideration is given location, to ensure that the house is not in a neighborhood likely to become undesirable in a short time. The entire appraisal system of this governmental agency is based not only upon the present worth of the property, but upon its probable value in future years when it is paid for in full. Attention is given to every feature of the building lot—the neighborhood; surrounding developments; sewage disposal; water supply; electricity, gas, and telephone service; nearness to schools and shopping centers; transportation facilities; and all other features that have a bearing upon the value of the property.

Meanwhile the FHA architectural staff, composed of competent specialists who know what should go into a well-planned, well-constructed house, carefully review the plans and read the specifications to assure practicability of design, livability, and compliance with the government's minimum standards of building. Approval by the architectural staff means that plans, in its opinion, are sound and that specifications call for good building materials.

Few who invest in homes really know whether their houses actually are being built in accordance with the plans and specifications. For instance, few laymen would recognize the difference between green and seasoned lumber, few would know if foundations were properly laid, whether framing is sufficiently strong, whether good quality building materials were being used, and the thousand other details that make the difference between a good house and a shoddy one. But the purchaser may be reasonably assured that the FHA architectural inspectors will look into such matters. They make periodic inspections of the house during construction to ensure strict compliance with the approved plans and specifications.

Further protection to the purchaser is provided by the FHA mortgage-risk department, which concerns itself with the financial structure behind the house to be built or bought. For this purpose, the regular income of the applicant is compared with the proposed investment and the monthly payments that must be met to pay off the insured mortgage. It is considered safe budgeting in most instances when investment in a home does not exceed two and one-half times the annual income and when the monthly payments required to amortize an insured mortgage do not exceed 25 per cent of the monthly income. In other words, in an average case, an applicant of acceptable credit standing regularly earning $200 a month safely could invest up to $6,000 in a home, establishing sufficient equity so that the payments would not exceed $50 a month, including taxes and insurance. But, if he were seeking to build a house out of proportion to income, on which the monthly payments would become an unbearable burden, the applicant would be so advised and mortgage insurance denied on the excessive amount applied for. To protect the purchaser and to safeguard his investment, payments called for on an insured mortgage should not exceed what the applicant safely could budget as rent.

For the individual, probably the greatest safeguard of the FHA insured-mortgage system lies not so much in the strict regulation of interest rates and other charges as in the fair and unbiased valuation system. This is the heart of the FHA insurance plan and offers the consumer protection against exploitation by unreliable builders and unscrupulous lenders. Although the right of real estate brokers and builders to a fair and legitimate profit is thoroughly recognized, the FHA appraisers make a definite attempt to prevent an inflation of values. The purchaser might not be able to detect price inflation, but the careful analysis given the transaction by the FHA's trained experts is a reasonably adequate safeguard against hidden charges and exorbitant profits.

The FHA insured-mortgage system offers many economic advantages. It makes possible not only the lending of a greater percentage of the appraised value of house and lot than under previous conditions but also the writing of the mortgage for a longer term of years. Thus, the purchaser is protected against periodic renewals, with its accumulating fees, bonuses, and commissions. The debt is reduced with the very first payment, and the mortgage is gradually whittled away. The interest and carrying charges, taxes, and fire insurance are included in the fixed installments, which are paid monthly, just as rent is, until the property is free and clear.

Protection to the purchaser by the FHA insured-mortgage system extends even further. Should misfortune overtake the purchaser in the form of loss of income to the extent that he could not conveniently meet the monthly payments, the FHA continues to protect his interest in the property. That is to say, the buyer's equity under such a condition is not necessarily terminated. Should sale of the property become necessary, any amount remaining after the payment of first claims must be returned to the original borrower.

The FHA insured-mortgage system offers the borrower as much protection as it does the lender. Those who build or buy a home under the FHA appraisal system are given reasonable assurance that they are not overcharged or made to pay for value not received. The building plans and specifications must be complete in every detail. A contractor building a home must abide strictly by these specifications. Materials must be precisely of the specified type or quality. The buyer, in other words, is assured of getting the kind of house he has agreed to pay for.

3. *Securities and Exchange Commission.*—Another area of consumer protection now exists in the field of security selling. Previous to 1933, the purchaser of securities had little specific protection. The consumer, of course, has been protected against fraudulent issues to the extent that vendors have utilized the mails in the furtherance of such schemes. In addition, there are in practically all states blue-sky laws whose purpose is to prevent the issuance of worthless bonds and shares. But these, to a large

extent, were ineffective. Part of the weakness of state laws lies in their poor administration, but part, certainly, results from the fact that security selling transcends state lines.

The sale of securities in interstate commerce is now regulated through the provisions of the Securities Act of 1933 and the Securities and Exchange Act of 1934. The SEC was organized on July 6, 1934, to administer the Securities Act of 1933 (formerly a function of the Federal Trade Commission) and the Securities and Exchange Act of 1934. Since its organization, it has been charged with the additional responsibility of administering the Public Utility Act of 1935. Thus the supervision of registration of security issues and the suppression of fraudulent practices in the sale of securities, the supervision and regulation of transactions and trading in securities, both on the stock exchanges and in the over-the-counter markets, and the regulation of public-utility holding companies are properly commission functions.

One of the main purposes of security legislation is that of making it mandatory for investors to be provided with more and sounder information about the character of securities offered. Hence, according to the law, securities cannot be sold in interstate commerce until such information is provided. One of the difficulties the consumer has always experienced in the purchase of securities was the overenthusiastic representation of the issue by the vendor. Under the existing Federal legislation, all pertinent facts must be truthfully given the SEC by the issuer, these data being used as the basis of a factual prospectus. The prospectus must be made available to prospective security purchasers. Originally, not only the corporation but even accountants and engineers employed by it were held responsible for misrepresentations. Indeed, the liability provisions were so drastic that they were amended somewhat in the 1934 act.

Two points regarding Federal regulation of security issues should be kept well in mind by the consumer. (1) The commission does not guarantee a security issue. The commission does not even imply by its approval that it is a sound issue. The commission merely insists that full and true facts concerning the issue be made available to investors. Even if an issuer of securities were to admit an actual absence of quality in the issue, the commission, if furnished with full and truthful information, could publicize the facts only; it could not circumscribe the activities of the concern. (2) All securities are not subject to SEC regulation. For example, Federal, state, and municipal bonds; securities of railroads, commercial and savings banks, and building and loan associations are excepted as well as securities not publicly offered. Moreover, issues of $100,000 or less may be exempted by the commission.

On those securities coming within the commission's scope, the investor now has a sound basis upon which to judge, however. He now may intelligently choose between a speculative security offering a chance for unusual gains and one that is relatively safe and that offers a chance for only small returns. But the purchaser must still use sound judgment. The only difference is that *caveat vendor* now has been substituted for the old *caveat emptor*.

4. *Deposit-insurance Corporations.*—Closely allied to investment in securities is investment of funds in banks and in building and loan associations. The consumer now is offered a greatly increased measure of protection in this field also. Though banking institutions have been the subject of increased regulatory effort for a century or more, not until recently have deposits been insured by a branch of the Federal government. The Banking Act of 1933 made provision for a temporary and a permanent plan of deposit insurance. Over 14,000 banks in the temporary plan became members of the permanent plan in 1935. The Federal Deposit Insurance Corporation chartered by the Federal government is the guaranteeing institution. Maximum coverage for one depositor in one institution is $5,000. All national banks must be members; most state banks have elected to participate.

Probably the most important phase of the deposit-insurance system is the provision for regulating the operations of participating banks. A successful guarantee system requires strict regulatory control of the insured banks. The Federal plan is no exception. Thus, the legislation is preventive in the sense that it establishes high operating standards in order to reduce the chances of failure. Regulation covers loan and investment policies, the payment of interest on deposited funds, the carrying of certain types of insurance, etc. In general, participating nonmember state banks are subject to the same supervisory and regulatory requirements as those which are members of the

Federal Reserve System, which means that operating policies of participating state banks will, in general, receive a higher quality of supervisory control than that provided for by the banking codes in their own states.

In 1934, legislation was enacted the chief purpose of which was to strengthen the savings-and-loan-association system. Through this act, Congress authorized the creation of an insurance plan to guarantee the savings accounts in Federal and participating state building and loan associations. Thus, accounts in building and loan associations are insured by a public concern known as the Federal Savings and Loan Insurance Corporation. Through the insurance of bank as well as building-and-loan deposits, the consumer is given some measure of protection in still another of his economic activities.

As can be seen readily, Federal legislation of the consumer-protective type extends into many fields. Each type has been presented in such a way as to give the student a survey of its nature and scope. Since an attempt is being made to present a more or less complete account of the important legislation whose purpose or effect is that of protecting consumers in their purchasing transactions, it seems advisable to mention briefly several additional functions of Federal agencies that either directly or indirectly protect the consumer:

1. The control of the advertising and labeling of spirituous liquors, wines, and malt beverages by the U.S. Treasury Department Federal Alcohol Administration.

2. The regulation of the importation, manufacture, production, compounding, sale, or giving away of narcotics by the U.S. Treasury Department Bureau of Prohibition.

3. The control of the labeling of the caustic poisons by the U.S. Department of Agriculture Pure Food and Drug Administration.

4. The supervision and control of the sale of biological products as well as of the quality of drinking water on interstate common carriers by the U.S. Treasury Department Public Health Service.

5. The requiring of the installation of proper safety equipment on American vessels (in order that the consumer be assured of safe passage) by the U.S. Department of Commerce Bureau of Marine Inspection and Navigation.

6. The development of standards of weights and measures and the sponsoring of labeling plans by the U.S. Department of Commerce Bureau of Standards.

5. State and Municipal Legislation.—State and municipality regulations are accomplished by the governmental exercise of the police power. Within a state, the police power may be exercised by the state itself or by the units of local government, such as cities and counties. The extent to which any particular governmental unit may exercise the police power must be determined by constitutional and statutory provisions provided for its exercise. Under the California constitution (Art. 11, Sec. 11), for example, all counties and cities may make all local police and sanitary regulations not in conflict with general laws, *i.e.*, not in conflict with statutes passed by the state legislature on the subject. In addition, under constitutional grants of home rule (California Constitution, Art. 11, Secs. 6 and 8), chartered cities have *complete* police power in municipal affairs to the exclusion of the state legislature.

Within their respective spheres, cities, counties, and the state exercise the police power. That is to say, they see to the protection of the health, safety, and morals of the public. Police regulations must be reasonable and, in addition, nondiscriminatory. What is reasonable depends a great deal upon popular belief in and conception of the necessity for such regulation and upon acquiescence, at least, in the type of remedial action provided by a statute. Whether there is such a need primarily is a question for legislative determination. This the courts will not overthrow simply because they doubt the wisdom of the measure. It is only where the court finds that the regulation in question has no reasonable relation to public health, welfare, and safety that it will strike down a statute on constitutional grounds unless, as was said previously, there is discrimination.

With respect to the nondiscriminatory phase, governmental bodies have a wide discretion in classifying businesses and practices for the purpose of regulation, as long as they bear equally upon all members of a class. The most usual contention set up against the exercise of police powers is that the regulation takes property without due process of law or that interferes with contractual obligations.

These problems, however, are technical and need not be discussed further in a work of this sort. It will be sufficient for our purposes to indicate the various types of police-power regulations that government—either state or local—has created for safeguarding the purchasing public. These (based upon a law in California) for our purposes are classified as follows:

I. State laws that protect consumers' health:
- *A.* Pure food and drug regulations.
- *B.* Regulations covering food-dispensing establishments (meat markets, restaurants, etc.).
- *C.* Meat inspection requirements.
- *D.* Regulations concerning the canning of foods.
- *E.* Milk inspection and pasteurization.
- *F.* Regulations designed to protect watersheds and water supplies from contamination.
- *G.* Quarantining shellfish during certain seasons.
- *H.* Definition of purity of wines.
- *I.* Prohibition of sale of diseased and infected fish.
- *J.* Restriction of the cultivation, sale, possession, distribution, and use of narcotics.
- *K.* Regulation of the manufacture and restriction of the sale of certain types of secondhand goods. (Regulation of the remaking of mattresses; selling secondhand furniture without fumigating.)
- *L.* Control of the bacteriological count in swimming pools.
- *M.* Prevention of the use of sulphur containing arsenic in the spraying of fruits and vegetables.
- *N.* Regulation of clinics, dispensaries, barbershops, etc.
- *O.* Prohibition of the advertisement of venereal-disease "cures."
- *P.* Establishment of professional standards (for chiropodists, chiropractors, cosmetologists, dental hygienists, dentists, midwives, nurses, obstetricians, optometrists, osteopaths, pharmacists, and physicians and surgeons).

II. State laws that provide for the safety of consumers:
- *A.* Safety to persons.
  1. Prohibition of the sale of certain drugs without prescription.
  2. Requirement of underwriters' standards in the sale of electrical equipment.
  3. Bonding of common carriers for the safe transportation of passengers.
  4. Regulating the sale of poisons.
  5. Restriction and regulation of building.
  6. Provision in theaters for proper fire and safety equipment.
- *B.* Safety to property.
  1. Prohibition of frauds.

2. Regulation of weights and measures.
3. Regulation of insurance companies, state banks, building and loan associations, etc.
4. Prohibition of the issuance of false financial statements.
5. Blue-sky legislation; bucket-shop prohibition.
6. Requirement for the providing of bonds by warehouses.
7. Establishment of standards.
   a. Butter.
   b. Apple containers.
   c. Establishment of specific-gravity standards in gasoline (Los Angeles).
   d. Defining the weight of loaves of bread.
   e. Prohibition of the adulteration of paints and varnishes.
8. Requirement for labeling.
   a. Imported eggs.
   b. Commercial feeds; fertilizers.
   c. Marking secondhand furniture as such.
   d. Statement of *variety* of raisins.
   e. Nomenclature of wines.

This is by no means a complete listing of state and municipal consumer-protective legislation but should be suggestive in indicating the type of legislation that exists. Both state and local regulations are made and enforced in regard to all of these concerns, as was indicated before. The location of the dividing line between Federal, state, and local authorities depends upon constitutions and statutes. It might be well, however, briefly to indicate some of the fields in which municipal and county regulation has been employed. The city of Los Angeles, for example, having municipal home rule, has extensive regulations designed to protect the consumer against unsafe building structures and equipment. It prohibits certain types of advertising devices that tend to defraud the public. It regulates auctioneering, the sale of foods, secondhand automobiles (makes vendors register automobiles and put up bonds for the protection of the public in the delivery of the pink slip or title). It licenses baggage carriers and regulates bail-bond brokers, bakeries, restaurants, barbershops, and beauty parlors. To protect the public, it requires bonds to be given by heating contractors, house movers, motorbus and taxicab operators, ticket sellers, and personal-property brokers. It attempts to control even fire and "come-on" sales.

Smaller cities without home rule, in addition to enforcing existing state law with regard to consumer-protective matters, regulate the sale of food products, prescribe the standards for building, regulate the operations of itinerant vendors, etc.

6. Nonlegislative Consumer-protective Agencies.—Besides the governmental agencies, there is a growing control being exercised by business itself through the development of codes of ethics.[1] The economic groups that have the most explicit and effective codes are the professions, chiefly the legal and medical groups. Some of the codes established by businessmen are quite effective also, for the organizations behind them are well able to enforce them. Radio broadcasters, for example, operate under a code of ethics that among other things prohibits the broadcasting of "matter which is barred from the mails as fraudulent, deceptive or obscene" and makes it mandatory that "each member station shall refuse any advertising matter regarding products or services injurious to health." So, too, there are codes in scientific research and in the teaching professions, codes for engineers, architects, accountants, and less exact codes for dentists, brokers, advertising agencies, and real estate dealers.

Certain trade associations have taken it upon themselves to indicate certain articles in their field capable of passing specific tests. For example, the fire underwriters have established a thoroughgoing service, testing and certifying appliances involving fire and casualty hazards. A set of specifications, technical reports, and a regular listing of approved products are maintained. The label "Approved by the Underwriters' Laboratories" implies protection with reasonable certainty, particularly with respect to fire hazard.

There are a considerable number of similar agencies in other lines, but they operate chiefly for industries and little for consumers. There are few examples of such agencies that serve the consumers direct. The Educational Buyers' Association, for example, serves large consumers such as universities, analyzing particular makes of articles and assembling the data and presenting them to their clients so that they may more readily secure the greatest value for their money. Consumers' Research and Consumers' Union, discussed in another chapter, serve the ultimate consumer in somewhat the same capacity.

Certain institutes also are operated, at least nominally, in the interests of the consumer. Organizations like the Good House-

[1] See J. M. Clark, "Social Control of Business," pp. 223–238.

keeping Institute and the New York Herald Tribune Institute usually function by "guaranteeing" the articles advertised in the journals supporting them. *Parents' Magazine* performs a somewhat similar service. These agencies catch the obvious frauds, but that is about all. Very often articles bearing their seal of approval will possess some merit, but one cannot be sure that he is not grossly overcharged for them. Such institutes cannot represent the consumers in an unbiased manner since they derive their subsistence from the advertisers.

Another type of organization carrying on consumer-protective activities is that represented by the American Institute of Laundering. In order to earn the right to utilize this institute's seal of approval, a manufacturer's product must presumably measure up to certain standards of quality, construction, color-fastness, shrinkage, and launderability. If the efforts of the institute are sincere, the results will be advantageous in every direction. For one thing, manufacturers of sound products will be distinguished from those selling shoddy items, and, as a consequence, retail store buyers can more intelligently purchase their requirements. But, what is more to the point, the consumer when requiring first-grade merchandise will be enabled to obtain it. Undoubtedly this is another step in the direction of more effective consumer protection.

The American Medical Association is an example of still another type of consumer-protective organization. "The American Medical Association through its Council on Pharmacy and Chemistry sets up standards for proprietary and unofficial preparations to determine whether or not they are correctly stated. Standards are also established whereby the identity and purity of such products may be determined and controlled. Its publication *New and Non-Official Remedies* describes preparations which the council approves and in addition contains a list of those which it does not sanction. Many articles which are harmful or worthless are exposed in the official journal of the association and its publication *Quacks and Nostrums*."[1]

The American Medical Association also has established standards for satisfactory advertising of foods. When advertising is found to be consistent with the nature of the food, the

[1] Jessie V. Coles, "Standardization of Consumers' Goods," pp. 247–248.

producer is permitted the use of a label stating that the food is "approved by the American Medical Association." Such approval indicates that consumers can rely on the statements appearing in the advertising. This service has been of particular interest because until very recently Federal legislation did not cover advertising. Up to May, 1932, 792 foods had been tested by the association, 295 of which had been accepted. The association publishes the names of accepted products as well as the names of those which have been refused approval on the grounds that the producer was unwilling to change the advertising to meet the standards of the association. This service undoubtedly protects the consumer from merchandise of inferior quality; but, in common with the others previously mentioned, provides little in the way of protection against overpricing.

Considering the fact that much of the criticism leveled at industry has to do with advertising, it is interesting to note the many efforts of businessmen to raise advertising standards. Advertisers are realizing more and more that truthful advertising is helpful to the entire profession. Self-regulative efforts of such organizations as the Advertising Federation of America and the Proprietary Association should be extremely encouraging to the consumer, for they indicate that the businessman himself at least recognizes the need for higher ethical standards in the vending of his wares. And despite the natural bias of such groups, more has been accomplished by them than is generally realized.

The work of the Better Business Bureaus is perhaps one of the best examples of this type of activity. Financed solely through membership support of business firms, including banks, industrial plants, and retail establishments, the bureaus of which there are 62 today, are expected to:

1. Promote accuracy in advertising through cooperation with advertisers, advertising mediums, and properly constituted authorities.

2. Expose fake promotions and aid in prosecuting fake promoters.

3. Warn the public against endless easy-money schemes.

4. Aid in the elimination of unfair competition.

5. Provide a medium for the settlement of disputes between business concerns and their customers.

The bureaus' most important weapon is publicity, although prosecution can always be resorted to. Complaints may be made by customers or competitors. The bureaus probably succeed in cleaning up some of the worst of the sales-racket cases (such as permanent "going-out-of-business" sales, "farm-it-by-proxy" propositions, or the sale of cheap machine-made cotton rugs as "genuine Orientals"). The bureaus' slogan regarding investments is advice of the wisest sort—"Before You Invest—Investigate." Hence the bureaus' work is another link in our consumer-protective system.

7. Standardization and Simplification.—It is desirable that the beginnings that have been made in consumer protection be extended much further. Where consumers are unable to judge the qualities of goods, they are open to exploitation in two ways: (1) through the adulteration of products and (2) through the misrepresentation of the powers or services of a particular good by those selling it. The consumer can be protected under such circumstances only by the development of standards, together with their enforcement and a dissemination of knowledge of the precise meaning of the standard in relation to the performance or character of the good concerned. Standards should be worked out from the viewpoint of the consumer, and the labeling of goods in terms of these standards required for as many things as possible. This not only would offer the consumer much-needed protection in the goods that he purchases but would also greatly facilitate the solution of his problem of what to buy and thus ensure a better satisfaction of his wants. It would make it unnecessary for him to be an expert judge of the qualities of many of the products that he purchases. He could, for example, find that a certain grade would fulfill his particular requirements, and he would be able to call for that particular grade or quality without the expert knowledge required to determine whether the article fell in this particular grade or class. This would result in a great saving of time and effort and leave the consumer more time and energy for recreation or for work in his special field. Moreover, it would eliminate the competitive advantage of the quality cutter and give a greater advantage to the producer who could supply goods of standard quality at the lowest price.

Standardization is not the visionary concept that some people suppose. Indeed, there are many instances of workable standards existing in consumers' goods today. For example, the U.S. Pharmacopoeia and the National Formulary compilations of standards in medicines are official and are used as a basis for enforcement of the Federal and state food and drug laws. In fact, Sec. 7 of the 1906 Federal law provides that a drug is adulterated if it differs from the standard of strength, quality or purity set down in the official U.S.P. or N.F.

Another example of standardization in consumers' goods is found in canned goods. Unfortunately, however, this phase of the work has not been carried far enough. Under authority of the McNary-Mapes Amendment, the Pure Food and Drug Administration has begun to set up a series of standards below which no commodity may fall unless it be so marked. The Secretary of Agriculture under this amendment is authorized to promulgate a minimum standard of quality, condition, and fill of container for every class of canned foods except milk and meat products. Brands that fail to meet the standards are required to carry a special label which for vegetables reads, "Below U.S. Standard, Low Quality but Not Illegal" and for fruits "Below U.S. Standard, Good Food—Not High Grade." Ninety per cent is the standard set for fill of containers. Goods falling below this standard must be marked *slack-filled.* As no money has been specifically appropriated for enforcement of the McNary-Mapes Amendment, grades have been established thus far for only a few items—peas, tomatoes, dried peas, peaches, pears, apricots, cherries, and mushrooms. The Canned Fruit and Vegetable Grading Service of the U.S. Department of Agriculture Bureau of Agricultural Economics also carries on some standardization work. Although it has no authority to enforce standards, the service does have authority to promulgate standards and to issue certificates indicating that the goods coincide with the established standards.

Other standards have been established nationally or in various sections of the country for milk, tea, meat products, butter, cheese, ice cream, breads, spices, edible oils, coffee, chocolate, carbonated beverages, etc.[1] One of the most interesting developments along these lines is the mandatory grading of meat by municipal ordinance. In the city of Seattle, for example, meat grading is compulsory. The city of New York is considering a

[1] For a full and excellent discussion of standardization of consumers' goods, see JESSIE V. COLES, *op. cit.*, especially Chaps. 14–17.

similar ordinance.[1] Such a law is definitely consumer protective since, where it is in effect, the housewife when buying meat not only knows what she is getting but, quality being known, is enabled to purchase what she needs at the store offering the lowest prices.

The Federal government and a number of states have defined the character and size of a number of containers used as measuring devices in the sale of fruits and vegetables. Other standards either exist or are in the process of development in many other lines, including textiles and clothing. Further development of standards, in foods particularly, has been provided for by the recent Federal pure food and drug legislation.

Standards without a doubt are very important to the consumer. Minimum standards are protective. Various grades resulting from standardization are helpful to the purchaser. It should be recalled that everyone is not interested in buying the highest quality of a product. Standards allow the purchaser to buy precisely the quality required, actually to compare values. But standards need not always be complex. For example, a shirt manufacturer might establish a standard based upon the number of launderings that the material will stand. Thus, shirts may be graded as 30, 40, or 50, indicating the number of launderings it will withstand. In some instances, of course, ultrasimple standards are impossible. In cases of the latter type, consumer education is required. Even where grades of food are actually designated, consumers must learn the meaning of the various designations. This point becomes somewhat clearer when one learns that grades are sometimes identified by such terms as *special*, *prime*, or *choice* and quite obvious when one considers the confusing grade names selected by some packers. What could be more ridiculous, for example, than the terms selected by olive packers—*medium*, *large*, *extra large*, *mammoth*, *giant*, *jumbo*, and *colossal!*—for describing the several grades of their product?

There is also much to be gained from a reduction in the number of varieties of goods that the consumer purchases—*i.e.*, from simplification. An excessive number of the varieties of the same product needlessly increases manufacturing costs, retailing expenses, and the difficulties of choice by the consumer. The

[1] *Consumers' Union Repts.*, June, 1938, pp. 6–9.

U.S. Chamber of Commerce estimated at one time that one-quarter of all industrial effort in America is wasted because of irrelevant overdiversification of styles, types, and sizes. Obviously, a world of entire uniformity would be a monotonous place. With hats, furniture, clothes, and houses all the same, we could count the increased production we would gain as dearly paid for. Standardization and simplification do not necessarily mean this, however. Standardization means simply the determination and enforcement of standards that will enable the consumer to judge more intelligently and to fit the things offered in the market more easily and exactly to his needs; simplification, merely the reduction in the number of needless varieties and sizes in order that production and marketing efficiency may be attained. There is need for an organization or government department that will seriously devote itself to this task. Standards should be worked out following research on consumer requirements rather than on the convenience of productive methods. Specific goods should be tested against these standards and the findings published. Manufacturers and sellers should be required to label their goods conspicuously in terms of these standards.

Some idea of the savings that might accrue to the consumer following such a program may be grasped from the savings attributed to the work of the U.S. Department of Commerce Bureau of Standards, which performs tests on industrial commodities and articles purchased by the Federal government. In one year, its staff of 800 scientists and technicians performed 180,000 tests, covering, among other things, electric batteries, lamps, clocks, watches, insulating materials, fuels, lubricants, optical instruments, paper, leather, rubber, textiles, brick, cement, sugar, and gasoline pumps. The bureau is estimated to have saved the government $100,000,000 in a period of a year on the purchase of supplies and equipment for various governmental agencies and to save particular industries large amounts through its work in simplification and standardization. It is estimated, for example, that its work on builders' hardware, which resulted in the reduction of 100 nonstandard finishes to 25 standard finishes, has saved the industry around $10,000,000 a year. All this, of course, benefits the consumer indirectly; but there is, in addition, need for an organization that will approach the problem from his viewpoint and place the results before him in such a way that he can use them.

8. Final Criticism of Consumer Protection.—Unbridled competition is not completely dependable in protecting the consumer against high-priced and poor-quality goods and services. The reason for this is that the consumer because of his specialization has not the time to learn about the thousands of items which he requires in his daily living. Vendors, therefore, can in many instances make claims about goods wholely unsupported by fact. Moreover, even granting a nation of discriminating purchasers, the "guinea-pig" method of testing products leaves in its path the unfortunate victims of experimentation. Even though the company dispensing a deleterious nostrum is forced out of competition as a result of lack of custom in time, the harm already has been done. Hence, consumer-protective laws are required.

The old cry of some of the critics of our system, "There ought to be a law," is utterly ridiculous. There is a law. Indeed, there are hundreds of laws whose primary or secondary purpose is that of protecting the consumer. Many of these are quite adequate. Some, however, require amendment. Some, undoubtedly, require better enforcement procedure. In a few instances, perhaps, entirely new legislation is required.

Much can be expected of the new Federal Trade Commission and Pure Food and Drug amendments. Undoubtedly, many of the legislative gaps existing in the past have now been plugged up.[1] Presumably, many of the states will follow the lead of the Federal government and modernize their intrastate regulations

[1] As an example of the loopholes that existed previously, the following (from Ruth de Forest Lamb's excellent "American Chamber of Horrors," pp. 5–9) is presented:

"Widely advertised for years as an obesity cure, *Marmola* is composed essentially of thyroid extract and bladderwrack, a seaweed rich in iodine. Unquestionably, *Marmola* does reduce weight, but not without serious prejudice to health. By supplementing the natural thyroid secretion and stimulating the gland itself to greater activity, it causes the body tissues, including the fat, to be burned up at an abnormally rapid rate. Naturally, the weight goes down. But that is not all that happens! With a person whose thyroid gland is normal, the use of *Marmola* constitutes overdosage of two dangerous drugs. With one whose thyroid is already overactive, its use may bring about nervous and digestive disturbances, heart symptoms, headache, delirium, fever, and even collapse, coma and death.

also. Moreover, if the various Federal agencies develop cooperation techniques in handling cases arising in their various jurisdictions, even more can be expected.

Unquestionably, we have made progress in nonlegislative consumer protection also. Partly because of governmental activity, partly because of an awakened social consciousness, and partly because people in the trades have discovered it to be good business, many business groups have taken definite steps away from the philosophy *caveat emptor*. This, too, is extremely encouraging.

It should be borne in mind, however, that the consumer cannot be protected fully in anything short of a completely regimented society. The reason for this is simply that the consumer cannot be protected against his own poor judgment. He insists on buying large new cars when he should be purchasing better food for his family. He buys goods in the lowest priced lines, when

---

Obviously, it is not a product to be taken indiscriminately and without the advice of a competent physician.

"The nostrum is exploited by Edward D. Hayes, whose earliest ventures were with 'lost-manhood' cures when he was operating as the Dr. Knapp Medical Company and the Dr. Raynor Medical Company. . . . Hayes' case history serves admirably to show under what circumstances the Post Office can exercise control. For in 1904, when Hayes was using the mails to operate 'a scheme or device for obtaining money or other property by means of false or fraudulent pretenses, representations or promises,' the Post Office was able to interrupt his activities—for a time. This was accomplished by issuing a fraud order against his companies. . . . The fraud order, however, did not bother him much. He simply changed the name of his firm and went on as before until the Post Office caught up with him again. By one technicality or another, he seems to have kept a jump or two ahead of his pursuers until 1914. Then, the Post Office cracked down on his Interstate Remedy Company with a criminal prosecution. This time, he pleaded guilty and was fined $5,000. Worse still, from his point of view anyway, his precious sucker list numbering half a million names was ordered destroyed. . . .

"The Federal Trade Commission came into the picture in 1918 when it issued a complaint against the Raladam Company, as Hayes now called himself. In consequence, the company was ordered to stop advertising *Marmola* as 'safe, effective and dependable in use, when the present knowledge of thyroid as a remedial agent does not justify such representations.' Hayes promptly appealed—continuing, meanwhile, to rake in his profits. (He was doing a business of $600,000 a year.) Luckily for him, the appellate court decided that there was no basis in law for the action of the Commission,

the quality of goods must of necessity be low. Consumer education in purchasing is needed. The consumer must actually be taught to pay higher prices for goods in some instances.

Poor judgment is manifest at every turn. We often criticize the old-time advertiser who mulcted the public out of its dimes by offering a complete sewing machine for 10 cents and who upon receipt of the money delivered a needle. Should we not condemn the consumer who used such poor judgment in responding to such an obviously impossible offer?

It is the opinion of the authors that definitely harmful products are much less common now than they were a quarter of a century ago and that so-called *cures*, particularly for malignant diseases, are offered much less frequently than heretofore. The great bulk of consumer deception at present is in the relatively less serious area of overenthusiastic brand promotion and its common attendant, inflated price. As a corollary, there undoubtedly exists a great deal of short-weighting in retail transactions. Some of this is due to laxity in governmental departments charged with the responsibility of controlling dishonest practices. Some, however, results from the consumer's carelessness or ignorance. In a society such as ours, consumer education is probably just

---

and vacated the order. While it would be to the interest of the public for *Marmola* to be put out of business, so the court reasoned, the Federal Trade Commission, under the powers given it by Congress, was not the agency to do it. This time, the Commission appealed. In a decision hailed with glee by the patent-medicine men and their trade papers, the Supreme Court decreed that the business of the Federal Trade Commission is to protect competition—though not necessarily that between knaves! Since it had failed to show any competition, the Commission had no power to act.*

"The Federal Trade Commission can do nothing about *Marmola*, the Post Office can not touch it—how about the Food and Drug Administration? It has no jurisdiction, either. Incredible as it may seem *Marmola* is not a 'drug' within the meaning of the Food and Drugs Act. The condition it is 'intended to cure, mitigate or prevent'—that is, obesity—is not one generally recognized as disease; its labeling (which means not only the label itself, but the printing on the carton and any folder inside) bears no other curative claims; nor does the stuff purport to be a food and therefore subject to the food provisions."

* [Though this was not the end of governmental action in this case, because] "In May, 1935, the Federal Trade Commission issued a new complaint against the Raladam Company." *If this won't stick, maybe action under the amended law will!*

as essential as protective legislation. That is to say, training in an intelligent approach to marketing problems is necessary if consumer protection is to be completely effected.

Questions

1. To what extent is the consumer adequately protected in his purchasing activities in the United States at the present time?

2. In what areas is protection most inadequate—dangerous products, poor-quality commodities, excessively priced items? Give the reasons for your answer.

3. Is complete standardization of consumer goods practicable? Would the consumer position be improved greatly if such a program were carried through?

4. "With only its existing authority the postal inspection unit of the Post Office Department could, if given adequate man power, protect the consumer completely." Do you agree? Why or why not?

CHAPTER IX

THE CHOICE OF GOODS

We know relatively little of the causes leading to the choice of goods. It is quite generally accepted that we start life with a certain inheritance of primitive fundamentals that are called *instincts.* There is no general agreement as to precisely the things that constitute these instincts. Each book on psychology contains a list of instincts, and most of the lists differ. Instincts comprise hunger, fear, rage, sex, gregariousness, etc. Upon these instincts, more complex reactions are built up from the experience of our environment. The learning process begins so early that it has been nearly impossible to differentiate between the part of our reaction that is inherited and the part that is environmental. These instincts are, without doubt, of considerable importance in influencing certain broad lines of our expenditure, but they have little to do with our selections of specific commodities. The latter are primarily the results of our environment and seem to be made principally because of habit, impulse, or imitation, and only slightly upon the basis of any rational calculation.

1. Psychological Basis of the Analysis.—Whether desires are instinctive or acquired is not particularly important to this analysis. It is important, however, that we recognize the various motives which affect choices of goods. The following list is the result of an inventory of human desires.[1]

[1] Adapted from Dunlap's and Poffenberger's lists, Albert T. Poffenberger, "Psychology in Advertising," Chap. IV. William H. Lough, "High-Level Consumption," p. 90, furnishes the following simplified classification: (1) subsistence (covering all the prime requirements); (2) enjoyment (including all expenditures for personal and family pleasures and comforts); (3) approval (including entertaining the "right" people, dressing and living in correct style, and driving a car in the "right" price class); (4) prominence (covering expenditures designed to make a person preeminent and, if possible, to allow him to keep up with and even pass the pace-setting Joneses); (5) security (including any expenditures or reserve designed to make the future more secure).

Alimentary desire.

Excretory desire.

Desire for rest and comfort.

Desire for security from danger (including the desire for good health).

Desire for activity (including play).

Desire for clothing and shelter.

Desire to be with people (gregariousness).

Amatory desire.

Parental desire.

Desire for preeminence.

Desire for conformity.

Desire for cleanliness and for beauty.

Desire for economy.

Wants may be classified in several ways. One way—that of distinguishing between instinctive and acquired wants—has already been mentioned. Another is that of separating fundamental requirements from those which are more specific. In doing this, the former method of classification can be utilized admirably for explanatory purposes. Thus wants may be classified as follows:

1. *Basic Requirements.*—That is to say, man has certain fundamental needs to satisfy if he is to exist. He experiences hunger and must have food; he is sensitive to cold and to heat and must protect himself from the elements; he experiences sexual desires and finds it necessary to satisfy them. These are wants with which man is born; he has no alternative but to satisfy them in some manner.

2. *Desires for Particular Types of Goods.*—Man may exist indefinitely—just as other animals do—with few refinements. Actually, since refinements emerge from environment, he chooses certain goods that *particularly* satisfy his desires. Thus he is not satisfied to exist on bread alone. Not only does he elect to satisfy physical hunger in various ways (choosing from a variety of vegetables and meats) but also to satisfy other types of requirements as well. Hence, depending upon the circumstances—produced by social or physical environmental conditions—he spends more or less on clothing, food, transportation, education, etc. Some of these requirements are also practically involuntary. Thus, fuel and overcoats become necessary in cold climates, and

even transportation (because the development of metropolitan areas has been predicated upon it) has become a necessity. The combination of desires is known as man's standard of living; the degree of attainment, his scale of living.

3. *Desire for Specific Items.*—Man's choices become even more specific in modern society since usually he is not satisfied to choose indiscriminately (say) *any* food. He has developed certain tastes within each of the general classifications. That is to say, he prefers certain types of foods to others. Such preferences are probably largely the result of environment also. But man's choices are even more specific than this. As a result of product differentiation his choices between items—often identical except for the container—are greatly affected by the persuasive efforts of vendors. The consumer then chooses not only between products in different generic groups (*e.g.*, automobiles vs. furniture) or between different products in the same group (meat vs. vegetables) but between similar items in the same group (Royal Gelatine vs. Jello). Though man possesses certain innate wants, the problem of choice indeed is very complex.

As has already been suggested, " . . . it is always difficult to say whether a given desire is natural or acquired. The criterion which is generally relied upon to determine whether certain forms of behavior and certain motives or desires are natural is their universality. If, in spite of differences in race, in geographical location, in traditions and customs of peoples, certain motives for action always crop out, one is pretty safe in assuming that they are natural . . . [But, whether natural or acquired, desires are quite stable]; what undergoes change in the course of life is not so much the desire but the means of satisfying it. Our training cannot change the desire for food and drink, but it can determine whether the means of satisfying it shall be by eating raw meat or Campbell's soup, by drinking water from a spring or by sucking Coca-Cola through a straw."[1]

The scale of commodities that a person consumes is built up in a more or less haphazard manner. Some of the commodities are acquired by a trial-and-error method. The consumer comes to expect a certain amount of satisfaction from a commodity from his previous experience with it. As has been suggested, certain commodities are included because other people are

[1] Poffenberger, *op. cit.*, pp. 50–51.

observed to be consuming them, and we think we shall derive something of the enjoyment that others seem to derive from their consumption; certain things widely consumed and whose omission in our consumption we believe would make us conspicuous are also included. These are often consumed with but little thought of the satisfaction that the goods themselves yield. For example, many of the articles of our apparel are uncomfortable, and, left to ourselves, we would not choose to wear them; but in order not to appear conspicuous, we comply with the whims of society.

There is no common quality of goods that makes them desirable. Desirability is solely in the reaction of the individual to the good and depends upon the individual and his environment rather that upon the good itself. For example, certain people like olives, and others do not. The differences are in the individuals and not in the olives. The power that certain goods have to satisfy a want is called *utility* by the economist. Since this utility is purely psychic, we have no direct measure of it. We can only observe the effects as they become expressed in price, and, from these, draw certain inferences. Thus, if we observe that a man is in doubt as to which of two things to spend a dollar on, we may infer, without great error, that they have about equal utility to him or, if he buys one in preference to the other, that the purchased goods possess the greater utility to him.

It is quite probable that each person derives a quite different satisfaction from the consumption of a particular kind of goods. This precludes any comparison of the satisfactions derived from the consumption of certain goods or a group of goods among different persons or of any total or social summation of satisfaction. Moreover, since environment is constantly changing the individual, a person's desires at any one time may be quite different from those he has at some other time. There is not even any satisfactory unit of measurement by which an individual can compute the absolute amount of satisfaction that he derives from certain goods. This means that we cannot even sum up or total the satisfactions that a person derives from his income. A person calculates this satisfaction in terms of other goods. Thus it is impossible for one to tell another the satisfaction he derives from the consumption of a piece of candy or even to calculate it himself except in terms of other goods. One may, however, prefer the candy to a package of cigarettes or three packages of gum.

Many psychologists and economists object vigorously to the notion that individuals are at all rational in their attitudes toward goods; that they make conscious choices among goods on the basis of the utility which they have for them.[1] Men's motives, they say, are little understood, are very complex, and cannot be accounted for in hedonistic terms. Human behavior, according to these men, is not rational but is determined largely by the environment or circumstances in which man happens to be placed. It is a product of an unstable and irrational complex of reflex actions, impulses, instincts, habits, customs, climate, and fashions. People do not, in other words, make fine and precise calculations respecting the probable satisfactions to be obtained by the purchase of various goods. They are influenced, rather, by suggestion, advertising, accident, and many other factors. Their choices and price offers are determined more by custom than by the relative marginal utilities of goods.

The truth of these statements cannot be denied. They hold true within considerable ranges of our expenditures, and, in consequence, the notion of the comparison of utilities cannot be pushed very far. But, at the same time, men are not completely irrational in the sense in which the man in the street uses the term. He does learn and build up a system of expenditures. He does select certain goods and thus does choose in the ordinary sense of the word. Although these are serious limitations to the development of a satisfactory theory of consumption, they do not completely destroy the usefulness of the concept of utility. There still remain certain relations that may quite safely be stated and that lead us to concrete and useful conclusions. The first of these is the principle of diminishing significance, or, as it is more often called, of diminishing utility, or, even better, of *diminishing marginal utility*. This principle, based upon the law of satiety, is simply that where a good is consumed or where its consumption is contemplated in varying amounts

[1] See J. B. Watson, "Psychology from the Standpoint of a Behaviorist"; F. H. Allport, "Social Psychology"; T. Veblen, "The Limitations of Marginal Utility," *J. Political Econ.*, vol. 17, pp. 620–636; J. M. Clark, "Economics and Modern Psychology," *J. Political Econ.*, vol. 26, pp. 1–30, 136–166; W. C. Mitchell, "Human Behavior and Economics," *Quart. J. Econ.*, vol. 29, pp. 1–47.

each unit of that good will generally possess less significance relative to other goods, the larger the amount. That is to say, each added unit to a stock of goods (suits, dresses, radios, etc.) possesses less utility or want-satisfying power than the previously added unit. And since all units in the stock are identical, the utility of each is determined by that of the marginal unit. This is a general principle, verifiable by observation of the happenings in the market place. The principle of diminishing utility applies to the consumption of a good in successive increments at a particular period of time. Thus as oranges are eaten successively there is less and less utility for each successive orange. Since this is true, additional amounts of goods will be accepted by consumers only at lower prices. Hence, the existence of this principle explains the shape of the demand curve discussed in a later chapter.

The principle of diminishing marginal utility is very helpful in pondering the problem of choice. The rational individual will attempt to maximize his satisfactions by selecting goods in such a way as to produce the highest possible total utility. In other words, he will avoid adding too much of a certain type of goods; he will, instead, acquire other items whose marginal utility (due, in part, to the small amount possessed) is higher. Since utility is largely a subjective matter, different individuals will react differently to problems of choice. One person, for example, imputes tremendous importance to health and, hence, is most interested in maintaining an excellent table; another, affected perhaps by the Joneses' conspicuous consumption scale, forgoes more or better foods in order to acquire greater amounts of clothing or a finer motorcar.

These are, however, limited applications, and the more important application of the theory is to our consumption when considered over a period of time.[1] When consumption is considered for a considerable period of time rather than for a particular short period of time, things are consumed at certain rates. As these rates of consumption of particular goods are varied, there is a change in the significance or utility of each unit of the goods, and, in general, the utility per unit at the higher rate is less than the utility per unit at the lower rate. The statement, of course,

[1] See H. E. Miller, "Utility of Curves, Total Utility, and Consumers Surplus," *Quart. J. Econ.*, vol. 41, pp. 292–316.

includes the assumption that there has been no significant change in the character of the consumer or acquirer during the period.

2. The Effect of Price on Choice.—Nearly all the goods used by the consumer are purchased in the market; and, since the consumer has a limited income, he must choose between these goods and apportion his expenditure among the various lines. He cannot consume all. In consequence, he buys some goods at the ruling prices and eliminates other goods at the ruling prices. It is quite evident that the consumer is influenced in his purchase by the price of these particular goods. We observe that if the price of certain goods drops, more is likely to be sold; and if it rises, less. These reactions may not be immediate, but for the market as a whole are certain.

Within a considerable range of price and period of time and depending upon the particular good, individual consumers, however, do not pay so much attention to changes of price as is often thought. They find from experience about what a certain range may be expected to be, and it is only when prices lie outside this range that any considerable thought is given to the matter. For example, a man may have come to consider from $8 to $10 as his range for shoes in the market. He may give no thought to paying either $8 or $10 for a pair. He has come to expect to buy shoes for approximately that price. If he should find shoes selling for $15, however, he will consider other courses of action. He may decide to make the old shoes last a little longer, buy the new shoes with the expectation of using them more carefully than the old ones, or buy shoes of lower quality.

The operation of the principle of decreasing significance is responsible for the wide variety of things that we find an individual consuming.[1] As has been suggested, the consumer is interested in deriving the largest possible satisfaction from the expenditure of his income. If he spends an excessive amount on one thing, he derives less satisfaction from that expenditure than he would if he had spent a portion of it for other things; for, as he expands his consumption of this particular thing, its relative significance per unit decreases, and his dollars, in consequence, buy less satisfaction. He discovers that if he spends too much on this one particular line he will not have enough to spend on other

[1] See H. R. Seager, "Principles of Economics," 1st ed., p. 74.

lines, and he will feel quite definitely the lack of these goods. He learns with some definiteness the approximate amounts that can be spent on each thing. If a person has a fairly regular income, he is taught by this experience the possibility of buying a certain amount of satisfaction in the market from each dollar that he spends. This provides him with a crude measure for judging the desirability of purchasing goods.

In order to derive the maximum satisfaction from his income, the consumer endeavors in his haphazard way to derive the greatest possible satisfaction from each dollar. This as we have indicated he does through his apportionment of expenditures. If certain of the goods that he has been purchasing drop in price, his dollars will purchase more satisfaction in this line of expenditure than formerly; and, if the decrease has been large enough to draw his attention, he will expand his consumption. The principle of diminishing significance, depending upon the rate of decrease, sets a limit to this expansion, since as he consumes more of this single item its unit importance decreases. Through the operation of this principle, then, a point is reached where his dollars purchase about as much satisfaction for him as they would have if he had expended them for other goods. Conversely, his purchases would be restricted if the price of the article rose. An exception to the general rule—that, if a large quantity of certain goods is to be disposed of in the market at a given time, the price must be lowered—is found in certain cases where the customer is unable to judge the quality of the goods directly and takes the price of the article as an indication of its quality. Too frequently with this type of commodity more can be sold at the higher than at the lower price.

There are a great many difficulties in balancing expenditures with any degree of fineness. This fact appears particularly in comparing large and small units of expenditure. The comparison of the purchase of a package of cigarettes with that of a raincoat strikes one as foolish. No consumer makes such comparisons directly. Selections between articles of nearly the same cost are quite readily made, but not so easily between large and small units. Another difficulty arises in fitting goods that yield many different services, such as automobiles or pianos or radios, into our scheme of expenditure. It may happen that we would quite willingly purchase a few of the services of these articles if we could buy them separately, but if we have to purchase the entire bundle of services contained in the goods, we may have to sacrifice so much in other goods that we do not care to do so. This difficulty is in part overcome through the hiring of the services of goods. One may, for example, be quite willing to hire a taxi to transport one when coming home late at night from the theater in the rain. Yet the ownership of a car might be beyond one's reach in expenditure. This one service is desirable enough to appear in one's scale of purchases, but that of a ride to an afternoon picnic or the ball game is not. For many things, however, this solution of hiring individual services is impossible, and the whole group of services must be purchased or none may be had.

The extent to which expenditures are balanced and compared is difficult to determine and undoubtedly differs with individuals. For most of us, it is probable that a great many of the necessary purchases are made with no conscious evaluation of other alternatives. They are largely a matter of habit. The usual consumer takes little account of the constant minor fluctuations of prices in the market. In fact it would be impossible for him to keep informed of all of them. Within a considerable range of changes of price, in consequence, he continues to buy approximately the same amounts. Thus, an individual merchant might raise the price of sugar considerably before it became reflected in decreased sales. Sometimes, however, the price increase is so widely advertised that there is a considerable slump in sales followed by a gradual increase as it ceases to hold the attention of many people. Dealers of milk in Minneapolis, for example, observed that, when the price per quart was increased, there was a considerable decrease in the quantity taken. This decrease seemed to continue for about two weeks, and then the quantity taken rose gradually to about the former amount. If the price changes involve items of considerable unit value, the consumer must, of course, rearrange his expenditures with a view to maintaining the proper balance among the various lines.

The importance of a dollar to an individual depends not only upon the nature of the person, but a great deal upon the number of dollars which he possesses.[1] The loss of a few dollars from the income of a poor family may cause intense suffering, whereas

[1] See A. Marshall, "Principles of Economics," 8th ed., p. 95.

the same loss would be scarcely felt in the income of a rich man. We say, in consequence, although always recognizing that there undoubtedly are exceptions, that the dollar has a much greater significance to the poor man than to the rich man. It is interesting to note that divisible articles, such as meats, are varied in smaller units of size and price in shops appealing to the low-income groups than in shops catering to those with higher incomes. The dollar itself may not be a sufficiently large unit to impress maladjustments in expenditure upon a person. This depends upon his income. The larger his income, the larger must be the maladjustment before it attracts his attention. A student may weigh the possibility of consuming a piece of pastry at the noon meal against a larger dinner in the evening, while the businessman may give no thought to paying either $75 or $100 for a coat.

3. Limitations to Consumption.—It is said, at times, that wants are insatiable. This, however, is not true. "No sound need is insatiable. The quantity of goods required to satisfy it completely is even smaller than might be expected. Consider, for example, the desire for knowledge. The mental receptivity of the masses is ordinarily very limited. Only a small minority aspires to better things. The great intellects whose aspirations are unbounded are few indeed. Even a Faustian intellect is satisfied by the known truth and is insatiable only in the sense that it searches in ever new directions and kindles new needs.

"There are degenerate needs that demand new sensual pleasures and constant change of refinement. Such needs are creative in augmenting methods of enjoyment. But wherever man is influenced only by his own being, human nature prescribes narrow limits which cannot be permanently exceeded. Desires are only inflated to immeasurable proportions when the social degenerations of variety and love of fame are brought to bear."[1] This concept becomes much more practicable when, assuming a certain structure of society, one looks for the specific factors limiting consumption. In addition to the limitations of income and of physical satiety, one discovers many factors which affect the wants of individuals.[2]

[1] Friedrich von Wieser, "Social Economics," p. 25.

[2] For a stimulating discussion of the several factors mentioned in the text see Walter B. Pitkin, "The Consumer—His Nature and his Changing Habits," pp. 85–244.

For example, time limits the amounts that each consumes. There is, in other words, a tremendous competition for the consumer's time in modern society. Goods are not usually acquired just to have them. They are most often purchased for the purpose of consumption. And, it must be admitted, "You cannot eat ripe, red cherries and drink sweet milk at the same time. You cannot climb an Alp and go swimming in one and the same instant. You cannot watch a motion picture while you are sleeping, nor can you grow chrysanthemums while you are flying in an airplane."[1]

Time, of course, is not the only limiting factor. Intelligence and skill are probably just as important. An absence of intelligence often affects incomes, for one thing, and also directly affects requirements. The unintelligent, often, do not experience wants of a higher order. Certain types of goods—books, for example—are not required by such individuals at all. Lack of requisite skill is a corollary. One need not ponder long the popularity of the radio. By the same token, one wonders whether there will be any considerable demand for pianos 50 years from now.

Moreover, energy and health must be considered as conditioning the capacity to consume. "The energy required to manufacture one unit of a commodity shrinks daily; but the amount needed to use up the commodity remains constant. Dancing, automobiling, touring, attending the opera, driving motorcycles, airplanes, racehorses, or steam yachts, and many other pleasures are exceedingly strenuous."[2] Much the same can be said of other types of consumption. Obviously, health also affects consumption. For most things—foods, even—the point of satiety is reached much sooner if one's health is adversely affected. For other things—drugs, say—the rule works the other way. The healthy individual—the individual who is mentally and physically well—has no need for drugs at all.

Then there are the constitutional preferences and habits. There is no gainsaying the preference of Americans for wheat rather than corn. There are other preferences just as strong which limit the consumption of certain types of commodities. Habits are closely allied phenomena. Individuals who habitually

[1] *Ibid.*, p. 91.
[2] *Ibid.*, p. 96.

consume particular commodities can only with difficulty be induced even to try another that serves the same purpose. Considering the fact that absolute limits exist in the total consumption of food by individuals, preferences and habits positively affect the amounts of particular foods required.

Age, finally, limits consumption. One has only to consider the physical limitations of the old to grant the truth of this assertion. That is to say, old people are usually inactive and therefore *cannot* consume certain types of goods. Indeed, even the consumption of food often is circumscribed. And one needs few powers of perception to recognize the consumption limitations of children.

There are, then, many specific factors that tend to limit the wants of individuals. The law of satiety is of great importance in this connection. But so also are the limitations of time, energy, habit, and age. Perhaps the most important single influence, however, is that of a limitation of income. Despite other limitations, in other words, people could consume much more than they do at present if only they possessed purchasing power.

4. Some Special Problems.—Articles that last for a considerable period of time and cost large amounts may cause great inconvenience in purchase. If the payment must be made in a lump sum, it might, for example, demand more than the current income of the family. The shorter the period in which payments are concentrated, or the larger the payments relative to the income, the more burdensome they are likely to be. For example, the sacrifice involved in the purchase of a pair of shoes by a really poor family is more than is readily realized by those better situated. If the price must be taken from the sum allowed for food for a single week, the sacrifice will be more than it would be if spread over several weeks. It follows from the principle of diminishing utility that the sacrifice of other utilities necessary for the purchase of a commodity costing a considerable sum is much less if the same amount is taken in small sums over a period of time rather than in one lump sum. The system of installment buying is in accord with this principle. Although we generally spend more in total in installment payments, the inconvenience that we suffer may be less through the spreading of our payments over a considerable period of time. It is not true that installment purchases are always desirable. As has been suggested in another connection, they open the possibilities of wise expenditures to the wise, but they also provide a dangerous means of foolish expenditure to the foolish.

The sacrifice of other goods that is entailed by large purchases often prevents the purchase of an article even though single small purchases of the article may have to be made subsequently. Thus, a poor family might, with great economy, purchase coal by the ton if at the beginning of the period it had the money that it will subsequently spend on coal. Since it does not have this money at the beginning of the period, it must adopt the more expensive procedure of purchasing coal in smaller lots or, perhaps, on credit. It has often been said, and with some degree of truth, that economy is a luxury of the rich.

Closely allied to the foregoing is the pressure on consumers of low income who, if they are to satisfy a broad scale of desires, are forced to purchase merchandise of low quality.

Considering the fact that incomes are limited, the consumer is faced with the problem of choice arising out of the alternative of acquiring a relatively few items of high quality or a larger number of items of low quality. The course chosen by the individual depends to a great extent upon his own particular standard of living, the latter depending upon a myriad of environmental influences. A great deal of intelligence is required to maintain a rational attitude in this matter. Unquestionably, some consumers maximize their satisfactions in choosing a large number of mediocre goods. But, often, despite a rational attitude an individual is not strong enough to withstand the tremendous pressure exerted by vendors of various goods. Consequently, he chooses irrationally and as a result receives much less than maximum satisfaction.

Another general phenomenon that appears in the choice of goods by the consumer is his preference for present goods over future goods of like kind and quality.[1] When the consumer is presented with the alternative of having certain goods now or waiting until a later period, and the later situation is expected to be essentially the same as the present one, he almost invariably elects to have the goods now. Future events appear less impor-

[1] See F. A. FETTER, "Economic Principles," pp. 235–261; A. C. PIGOU, "Economics of Welfare," 1st ed., Part I, Chap. II.

tant than present ones. The longer the period, the greater the sum of goods in the future necessary to balance in the consumers' mind a certain sum of goods now. These conditions are demonstrated by observation and operate in typical cases. They do not hold for every individual or for the same individual in all cases, but, in general, they are true. They do not even depend upon any particular psychological hypothesis. The extent to which men undervalue the future with reference to the present is spoken of as their *time preference.* Those who prefer most strongly goods now rather than in the future have a high rate of time preference. Those who would be almost as willing to accept goods in the future as now are said to have a low rate of time preference. Typically, the poor and the improvident have high rates of preference; the middle-aged and those whose needs are expected to rise while income remains constant have low rates.

The practical effect of this inverse telescopic faculty of looking at things is that persons sacrifice large quantities of goods in the future for the sake of smaller quantities of goods now. This may reduce very materially the total quantity of goods that an individual is able to consume during his lifetime. The general social result is that the creation of new capital is checked and people are encouraged to use up existing capital to such an extent that great future advantages are sacrificed for smaller present ones.

It follows from the principle of diminishing utility and the endeavor of the consumer to derive the largest possible satisfaction from his income that whether he buys a commodity and how much he buys depend upon: (1) the size of his income, (2) the relative expected satisfactions and his habits in buying commodities, and (3) the prices of this and other articles. The quantity of a particular commodity that a particular consumer will buy, other factors being unchanged, will vary with the price of the commodity. The quantity of a commodity that a consumer will take off the market at a given price is his individual demand for the commodity. The quantity of goods that buyers stand ready to take off the market at a particular price—and that is the sum of the individual quantities at that price—is called the *demand* at that price. At any one time there is a whole series of demands for the commodity at the various prices. As will be seen later, these demands may be arranged in the form of a table showing the different quantities that will be taken off the market at various prices. Such a table is commonly known as a *demand schedule.* The demands may be expressed graphically by means of what is known as a *demand curve.* Both of these express the demand situation at a particular period of time. *Demand* in the sense in which the economist uses the term is to be differentiated from *want* or *need,* neither of which is demand.

Questions

1. What are the fundamental factors influencing the choice of goods? To what extent does marginal utility condition choices?

2. Support or argue against the contention that wants are insatiable? If prices were low enough, would unlimited quantities of goods be taken?

3. Cheap, shoddy goods are inimical to the welfare of consumers and hence should be proscribed. Argue for or against this contention.

4. In the Army and Navy there has existed a great deal of usurious lending by private individuals who offer (say) $5 to be repaid with $6 on payday. What is the psychological basis for the existence of such a practice? Is the willingness on the part of the borrower a proper justification of the practice?

CHAPTER X

THE ELASTICITY OF DEMAND FOR COMMODITIES

The amount of a commodity taken off the market by consumers at a particular time depends upon a large number of factors. A useful classification of these factors would include (1) the psychology of the consumers, (2) the number of the consumers, (3) the price of the commodity in question, (4) the price of other commodities, and (5) the incomes of the consumers. In the analysis of most problems, the influence of the price of the commodity upon the quantity taken is of special significance. This relationship, in consequence, calls for a special concept, the demand curve for the commodity. This is a statement of the various quantities of the commodity that would be taken from the market at a given time under various circumstances.

The changes in the quantities of goods taken off the market, accompanying a given change in price, vary with different commodities. The nature of this relationship is described by the elasticity of demand for the commodity. Some commodities are so firmly embedded in the consumption pattern that their purchase continues with little change in quantity in the face of large price changes. For other commodities, especially for those for which there are numerous substitutes, a small change in price will cause a large change in the consumption. If there is a large change in the quantity taken off the market accompanying a small change in price, the demand is said to be *elastic*. If a small change in quantity taken off the market accompanies a large change in price, the demand is said to be *inelastic*.

The factors that are ordinarily associated with the elasticity of demand of a particular commodity are three in number. (1) The number of uses of a commodity is of great importance. Commodities with many uses will tend to have more elastic demands. (2) Much will depend upon the number of substitutes, those commodities for which there are many substitutes generally having more elastic demands. Substitution is possible between a great many food products and a number of such things as fruits, vegetables, and meats having considerable elasticity. (3)

The importance of the expenditure on the commodity relative to the consumer's income influences elasticity; the greater the amount taken by the commodity, the more elastic the demand is likely to be. Habit and the feeling that a particular good is a necessity, of course, tend to produce an inelastic demand. Marshall has pointed out that demand is, generally speaking, very inelastic for absolute necessaries and for some of the luxuries of the rich that do not absorb much of their income.[1]

The most probable assumption of the demand curve of an individual buyer for ordinary commodities would be that the curve is inelastic at low prices, with the elasticity greater at the higher prices. The individual consumer is likely to reach a saturation point at some point where the price becomes low relative to his income, and below these prices his demand curve is vertical.[2] The demand curve for the whole market will depend a good deal upon the number of classes in the market and how high the price is, relative to their incomes. If the market has a number of classes differing in income so that a fall in price not only results in a larger purchase by present consumers but also induces new groups to purchase the commodity who formerly refrained from purchase because of the high price, then demand will probably be elastic. The larger the new group relative to the old, the more elastic will the demand curve be. If the market is composed of buyers all alike in income and taste, then the elasticity is likely to decline as price falls.

1. Differences in Elasticity and Their Importance.—The elasticity of demand of a commodity is expressed numerically by taking the ratio of the rate of change in quantity to the rate of change in price.[3] Roughly, if a 1 per cent change in price is

[1] A. MARSHALL, "Principles of Economics," p. 109.

[2] *Ibid.*, p. 109: "The elasticity of demand is great for high prices, and great or at least considerable for medium prices; but it declines as the price falls; and gradually fades away if the fall goes so far that satiety is reached."

[3] The following equations may be taken as defining the elasticity of demand:

$$1.\ e = \frac{dq}{q} \div \frac{dp}{p} = \frac{dq}{dp} \times \frac{p}{q}$$

$$2.\ p^e q = c$$

where q = quantity.
p = price.
e = the elasticity of demand.
c = a constant.

accompanied by a 1 per cent change in the quantity taken off the market, the elasticity of demand is 1. If a change of 1 per cent in price is accompanied by a ½ of 1 per cent change in the quantity taken off the market, the elasticity of demand is ½. If a 1 per cent change in price is accompanied by a 2 per cent change in the quantity taken off the market the elasticity of demand is 2. The elasticity applies only to small changes in price. In precise terms elasticity is a concept from differential

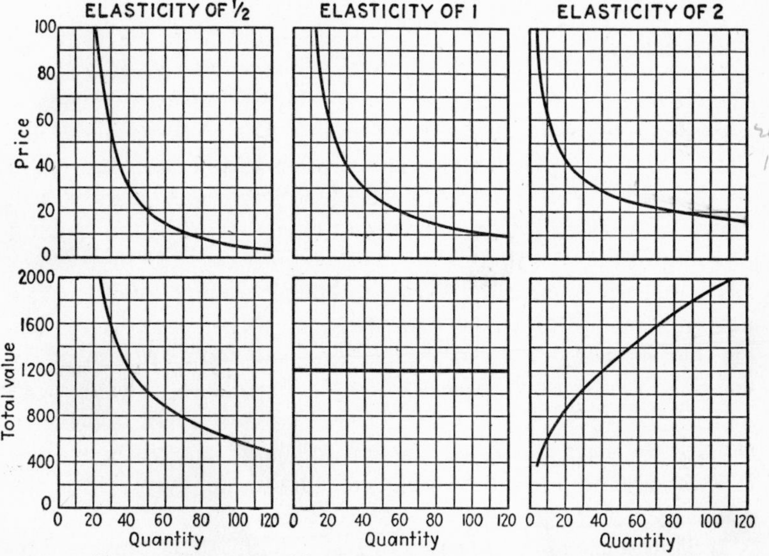

FIG. 3.—Examples of demand curves of different elasticities.

calculus and refers only to a point on the demand curve. Most demand curves have different elasticities in different portions of the curves.

The elasticity of demand of a commodity is particularly significant as an indication of the changes in the total value of sales accompanying changes in price. When the demand curve has an elasticity of demand of 1, the total expenditures of consumers for that commodity will be the same, regardless of the prices of the commodity. When the elasticity of demand for a commodity is less than 1, the total expenditures of the purchasers of that commodity will increase as the price rises. When the elasticity of demand for a commodity is greater than 1, the total expenditures of consumers for that commodity fall as the price rises.[1] We may examine these circumstances for a particular commodity either in terms of the total expenditures, the total revenue curve, or the changes in total revenue, *i.e.*, the marginal or additional revenue curve, selecting the particular expression that best serves our purpose in the analysis.[2]

2. Elasticity of Demand and Monopoly Action.—Whenever control can be exercised over the quantity offered for sale in the market, the elasticity of demand evidently enters as a factor determining the most desirable quantity to be offered. As long as the elasticity of demand is less than 1, gross revenue will be increased by raising price and curtailing the quantity sold. If the elasticity of demand is 1, raising the price and curtailing the quantity sold will yield the same gross revenue as a larger quantity of sales at a lower price; whereas if the elasticity of demand is more than 1, raising the price or curtailing the quantity sold will decrease gross revenues.

The possible success of a production-restriction program such as that instituted under the AAA depends very much upon the elasticity of demand for the particular product. Where the commodities have elasticities of demand of less than 1, the smaller

[1] This may be readily shown as follows:

$$pq = V$$

where V = the total gross sales.
p = the price.
q = the quantity.

This identity may now be used to transform our earlier definition of elasticity, $p^eq = c$, to the form $p^{e-1}V = c$. Examination of this equation shows that V must remain constant under all prices when e equals 1, decline in value as p increases when the elasticity is greater than 1, and increase in value as p increases when the elasticity is less than 1.

[2] The marginal receipts curve is the first derivative of the total receipts curve. The principal relationships between the demand or average receipts curve, the marginal receipts curve, and the total receipts curve may be summarized algebraically for curves of constant elasticity as follows:

Average receipts or demand curve.	$p = c^{\frac{1}{e}}q^{-\frac{1}{e}}$
Total receipts.	$V = q^{1-\frac{1}{e}}c^{\frac{1}{e}}$
Marginal receipts.	$M = \left(1 - \frac{1}{e}\right)q^{-\frac{1}{e}}c^{\frac{1}{e}}$

quantities will result in larger total consumer expenditures and there is considerable probability that this would result in larger net returns for producers. If the restriction were in the case of a commodity having an elastic demand, there would be much less probability of an increase in the net revenue of producers, for total expenditures for the commodity by consumers would fall, and total costs would have to fall even more rapidly in order to increase these net returns. In the case of commodities with elasticities of demand of 1, the gain would be such savings in costs as resulted from the production of a smaller volume.

Whenever a total market is divisible into sections or smaller separated markets with different elasticities of demand or of varying size, an arrangement of prices or quantities can usually be found that will produce a larger gross revenue from the sale of a given quantity of goods than when a uniform price prevails in all the markets. The principle to be followed in order to secure the greatest possible net income for a given supply is to equalize the marginal net returns in each market. If goods sold in one market would produce larger net returns if sold in another market, there would obviously be gain by their diversion.

In some cases, the division may be secured through alternative uses for the product or raw material. An example may be taken from city milk markets. Bottled fluid milk is thought to have generally an inelastic demand, cream an elastic demand, and manufactured dairy products elasticities of demand close to 1. Let us assume a market in which milk may be used interchangeably in these various ways. In a competitive market, the amount of milk used for the various purposes would be adjusted so that the same price for milk would be secured in each of the uses. A single price for milk as a raw material would prevail. Otherwise advantage would accrue from shifting milk in the relatively low-return class to the class or classes where it possessed higher value. If a single distributor had a monopoly, however, he could increase his returns above the competitive level even though he disposed of the same total quantity of milk as before. This would be accomplished by raising the price of the bottled milk, curtailing the quantities sold, and thus increasing total consumer expenditures for fluid milk, while if the diverted milk were placed in a use having an elastic demand total revenues from this source would also be increased.

Another important group of cases is where there is a protected or home market for the producer and a larger open or world market to which he can export or dump such quantities as he desires without influencing the home market price. Even though the elasticities of demand are the same in both markets, because the domestic seller is only one of many suppliers on the larger market, the demand curve for his product will be more elastic than the total demand curve for the whole market. A doubling of the quantity of his sales may increase the supplies in the market as a whole by only a few per cent with a consequent minor influence upon price. Wheat may be used as an example since it is a commodity that probably has an inelastic demand in the United States and in the world as a whole. An overhead marketing organization with control of all the wheat to be sold by producers in the United States could, disregarding antidumping laws and other retaliatory measures, under the protection of our tariff curtail wheat sales in this country, thus raising domestic prices, and dispose of the resulting surplus together with our usual exports on the foreign market, depressing the world price only a little. The result would be to increase the total sales value of a given crop of United States wheat.

The advantage of this sort of arrangement leads every businessman to endeavor to create a special or protected market for his product and to seek a larger market elsewhere in which he can dispose of his excess production. The various devices and procedures followed are described in other chapters.

3. Determination of Elasticities of Demand for Particular Commodities.—The nature of the demand curve as we have defined it and its elasticity are not known precisely for any commodity. This must necessarily be so since the demands in any situation do not remain the same, but in fact change. The only recorded fact that we are able to grasp as a statistical datum is that at a certain period a given supply was disposed of in a market. This sets one point upon a demand curve; the others are, however, tentative or hypothetical, the quantities that would have been disposed of at other prices, which prices in fact did not occur. Nevertheless, because of the great usefulness of such knowledge, attempts are made to arrive at a notion of the approximate character of the curves for the more important commodities.

The most usual method is by a statistical comparison of past production, or sales, and price. The method consists in the comparison of prices and quantities of goods for comparable past periods, months, years, or seasons. After proper statistical correction for changes between these periods, the data are presumably upon a basis that represents what the relationship between prices and quantities would have been in any one of these periods. Since because of unusual or unmeasurable factors the corrections are not complete, the particular observations of prices and corresponding quantities do not all lie on a perfect curve, and it is necessary to draw or fit a curve to the observations. The accompanying chart shows the relationship between the price and production of potatoes as determined by one investigator.

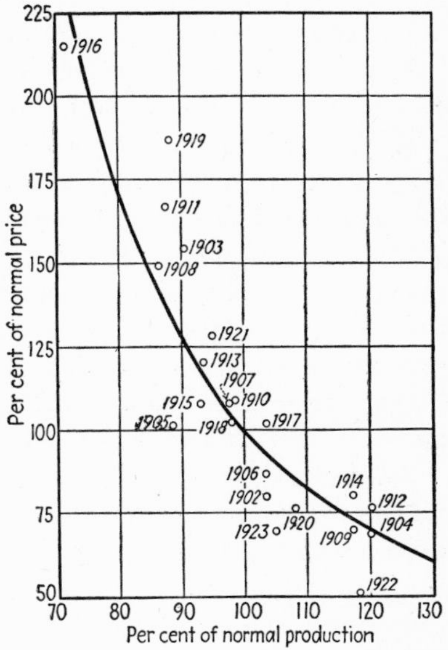

FIG. 4.—A "statistical" demand curve for potatoes in Minneapolis and St. Paul.

The curve that is determined by this method cannot represent the demand curve that is described by the economist. The statistician's demand curve represents a series of equilibrium points between demand and supply, usually the relation between the particular annual quantities and the seasonal average prices, and this curve may be quite different from the actual demand curve at a particular period of time. This is illustrated in the next diagram, in which the actual demand and supply situations are represented by the dotted lines. The curves are assumed to shift between periods, and the resulting statistical demand curve is obtained by connecting these equilibrium points.

The difference in the particular demand curve that the statistical method yields depends largely upon the variability of the demand and the supply curves during the period. If the demand curve had remained constant throughout the period and the supply curve alone had varied, a "true" curve would be given. But when the demand curve changes, or varies in its position, even though retaining the same shape, then the curve yielded by the statistical method cannot be the actual curve at any one period. The degree to which the actual curve is approached by the statistical curve depends largely upon whether, during the periods from which the data are drawn, the uncorrected variation has been greater in the supply or in the demand curves. If the variation has been principally in the supply curves, the statistical curve will closely approach the curve existing at any one period.

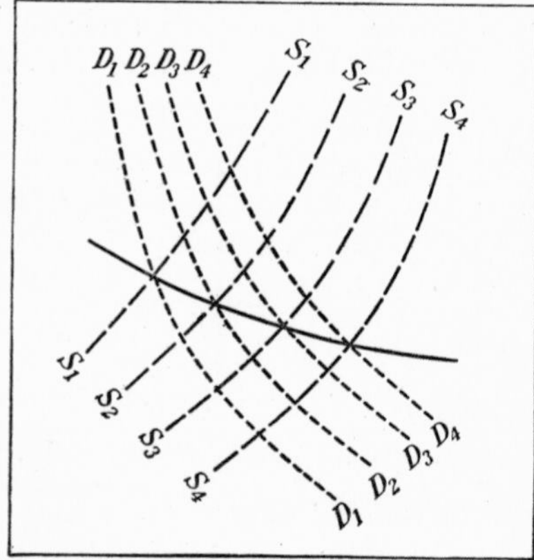

Fig. 5.—Relation of demand and supply curves considered by the economist to the statistical curve resulting from past quantity and price relationships.

The statistical demand curve differs from the economist's demand curve in another important aspect. The economist's demand curve represents the quantities of the particular article varying in price that would be taken at different prices for that article, while all other commodities remained the same in price. The statistician's curve, however, is a curve that represents the quantities of this commodity taken at various prices with the price of other commodities varying in the manner in which they have varied in the past.

At various times, a number of commodities, chiefly agricultural products, have had their elasticities of demand computed by various investigators. The following table presents a summary of some of these results.

TABLE 16.—ELASTICITIES OF DEMAND DERIVED IN CERTAIN STATISTICAL STUDIES IN THE UNITED STATES

Commodity	Market	Years	Elasticity
Milk	Boston, class I	1922–1931[1]	0.07
Milk	Several markets, fluid	1934–1935[2]	0.27
Wheat	United States	1922–1929[3]	0.27
Lemons	California	1910–1927[4]	0.33
Potatoes	Minneapolis	1902–1924[5]	0.46
Potatoes	United States	1915–1929[6] (ex. 1917–1921)	0.31
Sugar	United States	1890–1914[7]	0.50
Corn	Chicago	1897–1929[8]	0.59
Rice	New Orleans	1914–1929[9]	0.65
Coffee	Import price	1881–1913[10]	0.75
Pork	United States, retail	1922–1930[11]	0.93
Peaches	United States, farm	1910–1915 to 1921–1925[12]	1.20
Apples	New York, wholesale	1898–1899 to 1914–1915[13]	1.42
Lambs	United States	1907–1926[14]	1.58
Beef	United States	[15]	1.97
Bananas	New York, wholesale	1897–1914[16]	2.56

[1] J. M. CASSELS, "Fluid Milk Program of the A.A.A.," *J. Political Econ.*, vol. 43, p. 416 (1935).

[2] GAUMNITZ and REED, *U.S. Dept. Agr.*, D. M-2. "Some Problems Involved in Establishing Milk Prices," p. 44.

[3] H. SCHULTZ, "Shifting Demand for Agricultural Products," *J. Farm Econ.*, vol. 14, pp. 201–227, April, 32.

[4] H. R. WELLMAN and E. BRAUN, "Lemons," *Univ. of Calif. Bull.* 460, p. 20.

[5] H. WORKING, *Minn. Tech. Bull.* 29, p. 13.

[6] H. SCHULTZ, *op. cit.*, pp. 201–227.

[7] H. SCHULTZ, "Statistical Laws of Supply and Demand," p. 200.

[8] R. W. COX, "Factors Influencing the Price of Corn," *Minn. Tech. Bull.* 81, p. 23.

[9] E. J. WORKING, "Changes in Demand," *J. Farm Econ.*, vol. 14, p. 244, April, 1932.

[10] E. W. GILBOY, The Leontiff & Schultz Methods, *Quart. J. Econ.*, vol. 44, p. 233, November, 1930.

[11] WORKING, *op. cit.*, p. 246.

[12] E. M. DAGGIT, *Yearbook of Agriculture*, p. 566, 1926.

[13] G. F. WARREN and F. A. PEARSON, *Farm Econ.* No. 48, p. 777.

[14] M. EZEKIEL, "Factors Relating to Lamb Prices," *J. Political Econ.*, p. 241, April, 1927.

[15] M. EZEKIEL, Reported by G. F. Warren and F. A. Pearson in *Cornell Bull.* 466.

[16] G. F. WARREN and F. A. PEARSON, *op. cit.*, No. 48 p. 778.

It has also been suggested that the relative elasticity of demand may be roughly determined from the rates of increase in expenditure on a commodity and the increase in income. This is based upon the assumption that a rise from a lower to a higher level of income with prices unchanged is equivalent from the point of view of the individual to a proportionate lowering of all prices with income remaining the same. A coefficient similar to that for the elasticity of demand may be used to express the relationship[1] and for convenience may be called the *elasticity of consumption.* The results of the computations of such a coefficient for a number of commodities are assembled in Table 17. The data are from recent studies of family expenditures in the United States.

TABLE 17.—EXAMPLES OF ELASTICITY OF CONSUMPTION

New England states[1]		Southwest[1]	
Article		Article	
Sugar	0.15	Milk, cream, ice cream	0.29
Potatoes	0.20	Bread	0.34
Flour	0.24	Sugar	0.35
Bread	0.25	Potatoes	0.35
Milk, cream, ice cream	0.29	Butter	0.46
Butter	0.36	Eggs	0.55
Eggs	0.66	Flour	0.59
Meat, poultry, fish	0.66	Fresh vegetables	0.76
Fresh vegetables	1.16	Meats	0.79
Fruits	1.20	Fruits	1.13

[1] Computed from data in *Monthly Labor Rev.*, vol. 42, p. 892, April, 1936. Expenditures per consumption unit are used, rather than income.

There are certain important differences in the measures derived by these two methods, as well as between them and the demand curve of economic theory. The theoretical demand curve presumes to state the relation between price and quantity removed

[1] We may write this

$$\phi = \frac{dc/c}{dI/I}$$

where c = the amount of consumption.
I = the income.

The amount of consumption may be represented either in units of physical quantity or in amounts spent. ϕ will be positive when increases in income lead to increases in expenditure on the commodity and negative when increases in income lead to decreased expenditures on the commodity. When ϕ is more than 1, increases in income lead to increased proportions of the total income spent on this commodity, and when less than 1 to decreased proportions of the total income.

from the market, with all other things except the price of the commodity in question remaining the same. The studies of past prices and quantities show the changes that have accompanied changes in quantity in the past in the market as a whole with other prices and elements, changing as they have in the past. The expenditure method indicates for a class the probable changes in quantities, with all prices, including the price of the commodity in question, changing in the same proportion. The statistical results in all methods appear to be open to a wide margin of error and are in all cases to be interpreted with great caution. Fortunately, for many problems it is necessary to know only the elasticity within wide limits to indicate the nature of the solution, and for this the statistical results are generally of sufficient reliability.

4. Some Further Applications of Elasticity.—The elasticity of demand is a factor of importance in a number of economic problems. We have already indicated its significance in the case of the action of the monopolist. The effect of a laborsaving device upon the laborers employed in the industry in which the device is introduced turns largely upon the elasticity of demand for the commodity they are producing. If the demand is inelastic, labor is certain to be forced out of this industry, while if the demand is elastic even more labor may be employed than before the device was introduced. Thus, early introductions of machinery in the manufacture of cotton appear to have increased the amount of labor used in that industry. Prices of cotton at that time were relatively high and the demand was elastic. Later introductions of machinery after the price had become relatively low and the demand inelastic appear to have forced labor out of the industry.[1]

The elasticity of demand also has an important bearing on the results of a tax. If the commodity has an elastic demand, then, if there is an increased price for the commodity as a result of the tax, the quantity taken by consumers will decrease greatly, and the tax base will shrink. If, however, the commodity has an inelastic demand, nearly the same amount of the commodity will be taken despite the higher price. As is pointed out later, the ease with which a tax may be passed to the consumer in the form of a higher price depends on the elasticity of demand for the

[1] A. C. Pigou, "Economics of Welfare," p. 717.

article. If the demand is inelastic the consumer is likely to bear nearly the full burden of the tax in the form of a higher price, while if the demand is elastic a very large share of the burden will probably be borne by the producer of the commodity.

Another situation in which the elasticity of demand is of great importance is found in Secretary Wallace's recent suggestion for a "two-price" plan for certain agricultural products. In this plan the high-income group would pay one price, while the low-income group would be aided in their consumption by a subsidized lower price. Since the plan has for its objective an increase in the income of agriculture and an enlarged consumption by the low-income groups, the successful operation of the scheme would necessitate an inelastic demand for the product by the high-income group and an elastic demand in the low-income group, in the relevant price ranges. Rearrangement of a given volume of a product in such a situation would permit prices resulting in a larger total consumer expenditure and expanded consumption by the low-income group. If the high-income group had an elastic demand and the low-income group an inelastic demand, the plan could not obtain its objectives. These few examples will serve to suggest the importance of a knowledge of the elasticity of demand in the solution of specific economic problems.

Questions

1. If a commodity with an inelastic demand, say wheat, were heavily taxed and the price in consequence increased, how would you expect the demand for other commodities to be affected? Explain.

2. How would the elasticity of demand for various commodities be a factor in the setting of rates by a group having a monopoly of the transportation to an otherwise isolated community?

3. Warren and Pearson have said that large crops generally bring the producer less and cost the consumer more than small crops. What demand situation would make this possible?

4. Which would you expect to have the greater effect upon its price, a restriction in the supply of nails or a similar restriction in the supply of lumber?

5. Would a flat sales tax of (say) 2½ per cent affect all businesses similarly?

CHAPTER XI

DEMAND MANIPULATION AND THE CONSUMER

The irrationality of consumers and their susceptibility to suggestion in their consumption habits provide an opportunity for the individual businessman to attempt an increase in his sales through aggressive advertising and salesmanship. A large part of consumption is, in consequence, directed to a considerable degree by such sales-promotional efforts. One writer has estimated that consumers have conscious wants for about half the things they consume and that they depend upon suggestion and direction for the selection of the other half.[1] This direction of consumption by the businessman for his own profit is probably not entirely desirable since consumers may be made to want and consume goods that are not for the best interests of society. The seller of a particular product cares little whether the consumer might better expend his income along other lines if only an increase in the sale of his particular product can be obtained. The motives that are exploited for the purpose of selling goods are not always the characteristics that it is most desirable to have exploited. The seller, through study and subsequent trial and error, selects those appeals that are likely to prove most effective in the sale of his product and is probably more apt to exploit human weakness than to develop desirable characteristics. A greater number of appeals, for example, are made on the basis of sex emotions than on the basis of intellectual or moral values.

It should be quite clearly understood at the outset that, in general, advertising and salesmanship have only one fundamental purpose—that of increasing the desire of the consumer for particular products. From a technical economic point of view the advertiser's aim is twofold. He attempts (1) to move his whole demand schedule to the right (create an actual increase in demand) and (2) to "perpendicularize" the demand schedule (create a more inelastic demand) for his product. Regardless

[1] See G. B. Dibblee, "The Law of Supply and Demand," Chap. XV.

of the techniques employed, these are the basic purposes of sales-promotional endeavor. Though originally the term *advertising* signified *communication,* it now connotes some sort of persuasion, and almost every known method of attack—deception, cajolery, vulgarity, and even truth—has been used in the persuasion process.

1. Expenditures for Demand Manipulation.—In the broad sense, demand manipulation includes *all* sales-promotional activities. That is to say, the cost of advertising is only one part of the total cost of selling. It is, however, impossible to isolate certain types of sales costs. The cost of personal selling, for example (particularly the persuasive phase), is practically imponderable. Because of this, and since advertising is both insidious and ubiquitous,[1] attention in the following discussion will be directed toward the nonpersonal type of demand-manipulative activity. Many of the points, however, apply with equal force to personal demand-manipulative efforts.

TABLE 18.—ESTIMATED TOTAL EXPENDITURES FOR ADVERTISING IN THE UNITED STATES, 1929, BY MEDIUMS[1]

Type of Advertising	Expenditure
Newspapers	$792,000,000
Direct	400,000,000
Periodicals	320,000,000
Business papers	75,000,000
Outdoor	75,000,000
Radio	75,000,000
Premium, program, directory	25,000,000
Street-car	20,000,000
Total	$1,782,000,000

[1] "Recent Social Trends in the United States," p. 872.

The expenditure for advertising has increased tremendously over a period of years. Advertising expenditures in the United States in 1929 were more than eight times those of 1900 and probably were in excess of 1¾ billions in 1929. The figures in Table 18 are estimates indicating the dollar expenditures in each type of medium in that year. The total advertising figure

[1] Advertising differs from most other types of demand manipulative effort in that (1) it invades the home when one's defenses are down and (2) it is impossible to avoid because of its universality. One needs only to listen to a broadcast to appreciate the former contention; to pick up a magazine, turn on the radio, or go out riding (past thousands of billboards) to appreciate the latter.

for 1929, amounting as it does to less than 2 per cent of the national income, seems somewhat insignificant at first glance.

Several points should be kept in mind in this connection, however. (1) If there is any waste in advertising, it should not be condoned on the ground that it is only a minor percentage of national income. (2) The social effect of advertising may be much greater than is indicated by the amount of the expenditure. (3) As is shown by the figures in Table 19, advertising expenditures in certain fields in terms of a percentage of the consumer's dollar are quite significant.

TABLE 19.—TYPICAL PERCENTAGE SHOWING RELATIONSHIP OF ADVERTISING APPROPRIATION TO TOTAL SALES VOLUME IN DIFFERENT LINES[1]

Classification	1929	1930
Drug and toilet articles	21.2	19.6
Electrical and radio	5.9	5.9
Jewelry and silverware	5.7	5.7
Food	5.8	5.6
Hardware	4.4	4.7
Travel and transportation	4.6	4.6
Clothing	3.8	3.8
Automotive	3.5	3.5
Leather and shoes	3.1	3.2
Financial and insurance	1.0	1.1

[1] A. E. HAASE, "The Advertising Appropriation," p. 176.

2. Advertising—Beneficial or Harmful?—Because of its nature —the fact that it is continually in the public eye—advertising is a subject of constant debate. Some argue that it is one of the greatest causes of waste in our economic system. Others contend that it is an extremely efficient economic tool, that, instead of being a wasteful device, it actually increases economic well-being. One reason for divergent views regarding advertising is that often each school of thought argues from particular cases; that each argues without benefit of a satisfactory theoretical analysis. Another reason, very closely allied to the first, is that each approaches the problem from an entirely different point of view. One is biased by *individual* considerations; the other looks only at *social* consequences. One sees a definite advantage accruing to the businessman, who, by means of advertising, sells a million boxes of "cold-prevention" tablets; the other recognizes the social loss resulting from the sale of such a worthless compound.

The Individual Point of View.—There is little question that, for some types of commodities and under certain circumstances, advertising can be used effectively in the sale of goods of individual sellers. Advertising is being constantly and successfully utilized in the process of:

1. Increasing the number of users of products.
2. Increasing the number of uses to which products may be put.
3. Increasing the frequency of use of commodities.
4. Lengthening the period of season during which the product is used.
5. Enhancing sales through

   a. Increasing the units of sale of those products already in demand.

   b. Introducing new products to accompany the one already effectively advertised.

The accomplishment of a specific purpose is not attained under all circumstances. Different vendors utilize advertising with varying results. The interest that the seller may secure from the consumer in regard to his product varies from mere recognition of the product brand to an insistence upon the purchase of the particular product. The ideal of every manufacturer, of course, is that of creating such a regard for his product that his customers will *insist* upon his particular brand. If such were the result, he would enjoy a monopolistic control of the market. Actually, his success in achieving this result is only fair. Consumer interest shades by imperceptible steps from (1) consumer recognition, through (2) consumer preference, to (3) consumer insistence. In goods that are essentially similar in character and that are made by a number of different manufacturers, the best any one manufacturer can hope, often, is consumer recognition or preference.

Even consumer recognition increases the possibilities of sales, however, since the consumer upon being presented with a choice of several articles is often swayed in his purchase toward the one that he actually recognizes. The manufacturer who can develop a consumer preference to the extent of getting consumers to inquire for his good or brand still further strengthens his sales possibilities.[1] Consumer insistence, if and when it exists, yields the vendor even greater returns, since he not only is assured of a large sale volume but is able to exact tribute in the form of a monopolistic or quasi-monopolistic price.

In the sale of small items, which are constantly bought with little thought being paid to the purchase, consumer recognition, preference, or insistence can be maintained only by constant advertising. St. Jacobs Oil and Pearline are the classic examples of this among advertising men. Both obtained a wide sale a number of years ago through extensive advertising by their founders. In each case, however, when the properties were passed on to the heirs of the deceased founders, the latter decided the products were well enough known to continue to sell without the benefit of advertising. Each product was unsalable within a short time, and, in each case, the plants were closed.

As has been suggested previously, the buying motives of consumers are a subject of constant study by advertising technicians. These motives, though many and varied, may be classified into two types, rational and emotional. Emotional motives—emulation, pride in one's appearance, love of the romantic, social ambition—have their origins in human instincts where responses are unreasoned and impulsive. Rational motives, on the other hand, are based on reason and include such objective factors as economy in the purchase of goods and their durability.[2]

[1] In order to create a preference for an item of merchandise, one need not necessarily have an unique or even a superior product. In "My Life in Advertising," pp. 101–103, Claude Hopkins tells the story of the successful Van Camp's beans advertising campaign: "Van Camp's offered no unique arguments. They were like other pork and beans. When we met in the factory and served a half dozen brands, not a man present could decide which was Van Camp's. But we told facts which no one else ever told. . . .

" . . . We told just the same story that any rival could have told, but all others thought the story was too commonplace. . . . We could . . . bake better beans than any woman could ever bake at home [even though] we could not bake better beans than our rivals. So we centered our attack on the weak spots, made Van Camp's seem the one way out. And we created an enormous demand. Not only that, but *the Van Camp's brand commanded a much higher price than our rivals'*." (Italics supplied.)

[2] Other important motives according to studies made by Dr. Melvin T. Copeland are as follows: *Emotional*—social achievement, personal proficiency,

There is, of course, no basis for judging the relative importance of these appeals in personal selling. In the case of advertising, however, some idea of their relative importance may be gained by comparing the per cent of advertisements utilizing the two types of appeals. This Prof. Copeland did some time ago for 668 advertisements in national magazines with the following results:

Emotional	72.0%
Rational	28.0%
	100.0%

Table 20 gives the results of a similar but somewhat broader study directed by one of the present authors. It can readily be seen from these data that in the sale of consumers' goods emotional appeals are utilized much more extensively than are rational appeals. One might even infer from the figures that many advertisers believe that their products would not fare so well if judged by the consumer on a purely objective basis. And such probably is the fact. One can say, with little fear of contradiction, that advertisers do seek out the emotional foibles of the consumer and then play upon such weaknesses.[1] One must conclude, also, that the individual and social viewpoints are often in definite conflict; that advertising may "measure

TABLE 20.—ANALYSIS OF 800 ADVERTISEMENTS BASED ON APPEAL AND TYPE OF COPY IN DIFFERENT MAGAZINES, 1937[1]

Dominant appeal	Per cent	Type of advertising copy	Per cent
Emotional	86.0	Persuasive	85.0
Rational	14.0	Informative	15.0
Total	100.0	Total	100.0

[1] General, women's, movie, humor, class, news, business, parent, pulp, and social.

maintaining and preserving health, proper care of children, satisfaction of appetite, security from danger, pleasure or recreation, and obtaining opportunity for greater leisure. *Rational*—economy in use, efficiency in operation or use, dependability in use or quality, enhancement of earnings.

[1] See KENNETH GOODE, "Manual of Modern Advertising" (p. 433): "Speaking broadly, no advertiser who hopes to make a large success dealing with people in commercial quantities need waste a second thought on any

up" from the one point of view while dismally failing when measured in terms of the other.

The Social Viewpoint.—Since the trend of expenditures for demand manipulation is steadily upward, the question whether such activities yield an advantage to society becomes particularly pertinent. One may even enquire whether demand manipulation may not actually operate to the detriment of society. The problem is an extremely difficult one, and the only hope of solution lies in analyzing this important force from a number of different socio-economic aspects.

One must continually bear in mind that nearly all sales effort is competitive in nature;[1] that a very large part is *purely* competitive. Much of this effort, in other words, is designed to draw trade away from a rival and to lead to the substitution of a particular concern's goods for those of a competitor. If goods and services are approximately equal in their capacities to satisfy the consumers' wants, successful effort in this direction probably leads to no immediate gain to consumers. There may be, however, certain subsequent developments arising out of this change of patronage that may very definitely affect subsequent consumers. It is contended, for example, that expansion (even at the expense of other firms) is good, since this results in a concentration of business in a smaller number of larger units and that these larger business units will be able to operate at lower cost.

3. Advertising and Commodity Prices.—Let us attempt an evaluation of sales-promotional activity and its effect upon prices.

---

motives except . . .

1. Self-preservation—This includes hunger and thirst.
2. Sex
3. Emulation."

He argues further that the clever advertiser will stir the emotions of the prospective customer but will, at the same time, furnish him a basis for rationalization. Thus clever advertising psychologists discover that (p. 435) " . . . reasoning to justify an emotional decision, is very important . . . Even in penny chocolate bars, eaten for sheer pleasure, the thought of food value and energy can be utilized with profit. A blatant sex appeal page selling a cheap 'Doctor's book' in a popular magazine, drugs the reader's conscience with a final paragraph, 'What shall we tell our Growing Children?' "

[1] A. C. Pigou, "Economics of Welfare," 1st ed., pp. 172–175.

Advertising practitioners argue that advertising (and, indeed, any type of sales effort) increases sales volume, that this has the effect of decreasing production costs, and that, since costs decline, selling prices must necessarily follow. According to this contention, then, the effect of demand manipulation is that of reducing costs and, hence, prices.

In order to test this theory it is necessary to refresh our memories with respect to certain aspects of our production system. It should be recalled that industries (or processes) may be classified into three types. These are known as industries of *increasing*, of *constant*, and of *decreasing* cost. Increasing-cost industries are those in which increasing unit costs may be expected to accompany an increase in volume. This phenomenon is due to the fact that in such industries (*e.g.*, in agriculture) the most important factor of production is one that is definitely limited. As this factor (land or other natural resources) is utilized more intensively (or as an increasing amount of an inferior quality is placed in production), the law of diminishing returns is brought into play and higher costs follow. Hence, an increase in demand can be satisfied only at an increase in unit costs.[1]

Industries are by no means always of the increasing-cost type. Some are said to operate in such a way that costs remain constant regardless of volume. So-called constant-cost industries are those in which increased demand can be satisfied with no change in unit costs. Theoretically such a condition can obtain when relatively little fixed capital needs to be utilized in the production process, when there is a plentiful supply of labor available at constant rates, when required raw materials are plentiful and freely reproducible, and when production methods are stable and unchanging. Actually, one is hard put to conceive of an industry genuinely of the constant-cost type.

[1] There are, however, certain forces that counteract the tendency toward increasing costs. It must always be assumed in considering the principle of increasing costs that the state of the arts remains the same from one point of time to another. Remove this assumption, and labor and capital costs will perhaps be affected in such a way as to offset increasing tendencies. Again, prices of agricultural products, for example, are made up not only of production costs (in the narrow sense of the term) but of expenses arising out of processing and marketing. Each of the latter phases of activity might be of a decreasing-cost nature and, thus, might offset actual increases arising out of the increasing-cost phase of the production process.

Decreasing-cost industries, on the other hand, are those in which increased volume will be accompanied by a decrease in unit costs. There are several factors that may cause decreasing costs. One is the possibility of a more effective use of the production facilities accompanying large volume. The producer enjoying a large volume can utilize his plant and equipment more continuously and his management more fully. He can utilize specialized labor more effectively and can often buy fuel and supplies at lower prices as a result of volume purchases. Another factor, closely allied to the first, is the possibility of *adapting* existing technical equipment for use in the industry under question as production volume increases. The conveyor system (in existence years before the automobile industry came into being) could not have been effectively utilized, *e.g.*, by motor manufacturers, unless volume had been sufficient to utilize the device intensively. Diminishing returns in this type of industry, though not absent, usually remains latent until tremendous volume is attained. That is to say, in industries of the decreasing-cost type no one factor of production is definitely limited. Hence, the effect of diminishing returns is postponed.

Since most manufacturing industries are of the decreasing-cost type, one is tempted without further analysis to give advertising a clean bill of health. In other words, it seems highly plausible that an increase in demand resulting from advertising in such industries would inevitably result in lower prices. But such a conclusion at this stage of the analysis is by no means tenable. When attempting to evaluate the social aspects of demand-manipulative effort and decreasing costs, one must consider, not one, but three questions.

1. Assuming some advertising effectiveness, how is the increased sales volume distributed among the several firms within the industry? For if advertising is effective only in increasing the sales of one firm as against another, a cost advantage to one may be offset by a disadvantage to another. Socially there may be no change arising out of such a shift in volume. The advertising of tire manufacturers seems to be largely of the type that succeeds only in increasing sales of one company at the expense of another, since the demand for tires is a derived demand. Ordinarily one is not influenced by

advertising to purchase a new set of tires although one may indeed be influenced to buy the product of a certain manufacturer when one's old tires are worn. Gasoline probably is in the same category. Other examples should suggest themselves.

Advertising might indeed be effective in increasing the sales in a whole industry, however. If so (and if optimum size were not already attained), one might expect a reduction of costs in the several plants in the industry. Even in the absence of a general increase, advertising effectively utilized may actually concentrate production in the hands of a relatively small group with a resultant cost advantage to the individual firms constituting the group. Without advertising, in other words, there might exist hundreds of small plants, each serving its own local market. Publicity on a national scale extends markets and makes for larger sales volume and hence operations on a larger scale. In this way, the level of costs may be forced downward also.

2. Is the industry actually one of decreasing costs? If not (at least, if a part of the total production process is not of the decreasing-cost type), then increased volume coming about as a result of demand-manipulative activity obviously cannot be expected to bring about decreasing costs. Indeed, increased volume might actually raise instead of lower costs. In such a case, clearly, lower prices do not accompany increased volume.

As has been suggested previously, however, the principle of decreasing cost may actually operate in certain phases of an increasing-cost industry. It would be possible, in other words, to have decreased cost result from increased volume even in certain phases of extractive industries. Decreasing costs might even more than offset increasing-cost tendencies. Lumbering may be considered as an example of an industry of this type.

3. Are the savings coming about as a result of lowered costs passed on to the consumer in the form of lower prices? This introduces the whole question of advertising or brand monopolies. Prices, instead of being decreased as a result of an effective advertising program, may indeed be increased. There is no doubt whatever that in practice a differential gain accrues to companies whose sales-promotional programs are successful enough to establish the name of their products in the minds of

consumers.[1] Although the total amount of such gains does not arise out of lower costs resulting from increased volume, some part, no doubt, does. Part, of course, comes from the quasi-monopolistic prices that can be exacted by such companies.[2] Regardless of the specific source of the differential, however, the result is inimical to the interest of the consumer. Advertising in such cases (even though the industry be one of decreasing costs) is antisocial, since the consumer instead of receiving a portion of the gains resulting from advertising in the form of lower prices is actually paying a penalty in the form of higher

[1] For example, a study by E. T. Grether of the University of California some time ago revealed that the annual net profit of the Lambert Company, manufacturer of Listerine, was almost nine times the value of the physical property of the company; that the Coca-Cola interests, whose tangible assets were worth some $5,000,000, were acquired by a banking group for a sum approximating $25,000,000; that the William Wrigley Company had at the time a balance of $9,000,000 available for dividends, with assets of $43,000,000 and physical property of only $10,750,000; and that Lehn and Fink paid $6,250,000 for intangibles. Although there is no way of separating the effects of advertising from the effects of product quality, good management, and merchandising methods, the effects of advertising cannot be gainsaid. Besides the higher price that can be exacted from consumers (even for products whose qualities are absolutely indistinguishable from those of competitors), the following other differential gains may result: (1) Companies may be able to command the services of dealers at a lower margin. (2) Other products of an allied nature may be more effectively sold by trading on established good will. (3) Such producers are partly protected from competition by newcomers since potential competitors are faced with the prospects of expending huge amounts of effort and money in order to earn a place in the sun.

[2] The following price and cost data based upon analyses made by the Bureau of Health of the State of Maine and reported in Ruth de Forrest Lamb's "American Chamber of Horrors," pp. 339–349, are, perhaps, somewhat typical of the price situation obtaining in the field of highly advertised cosmetics:

Item	Approximate cost at retail	Selling price
Coty dusting powder	$0.1570	$0.75
Elizabeth Arden Venetian lip paste	0.0240	1.00
Harriet Hubbard Ayer special astringent	0.0884	1.75
Evening in Paris perfume	0.2680	2.75
Luziers' Lu Mar (massage cream)	0.1404	3.00

prices.[1] Brand dominance occurs most often in convenience and specialty-goods lines; less often in the sale of shopping goods; very seldom in the industrial field.

To summarize then: In analyzing the effect of the advertising on prices, one needs to inquire into: (1) the effect of advertising—whether increased sales accrue to the entire industry or to one producer at the expense of others; (2) the type of industry—whether it is one of increasing, constant, or decreasing cost; (3) the disposition of the product of increased efficiency—whether the consumer is actually given the benefits or whether, on the other hand, efficiency savings are retained in the form of profits by the firms effectively utilizing the sales-promotional device.

That prices of many advertised products have been reduced over a period of years there can be no doubt. One can mention scores of instances, automobiles offering an outstanding example. A great deal of the cost (and price) reduction in such cases, however, has resulted from inventions and improvements in technical skill—many of which could have been utilized with no great increase in sales volume. In other words, some of the reductions in costs appearing in so-called decreasing-cost industries have probably had little connection with increased sales volume. One must distinguish cost reductions that are functions of increased volume from those resulting from extraneous causes.

Advantages accruing to industry as a result of increased volume are not limitless in any case. Not only does the decreasing-cost line tend to level off as volume increases (due to an eventual attainment of optimum size), but additional offsetting factors come into being as well. "(1) The purely supervisory staff increases more rapidly, after a time, than does output. (2) The relations between different departments and plants become more complex and more likely to involve misunderstandings. (3) The number of regimenting rules and regulations, the red tape, becomes greater and leads to increased cost and to inefficiency. (4) Lack of a feeling of responsibility and a growth of evasion of

[1] It must be admitted that the *level* of prices, even in such cases, may decline as a result of large volume since brand monopolies are incomplete. The point is, however, that, because of their enjoyment of a quasi-monopolistic control the producers of those products which are in particular favor need not pass on *all* of the volume savings. They may, in other words, charge prices which are somewhat higher than those which would exist at the competitive level.

responsibility also make their appearance in organizations beyond a certain point."[1]

4. Advertising and the Business Cycle.—It has been argued by advertising protagonists that demand manipulation is a valuable economic tool since it has the power to smooth out cyclical movements in business. If the contention has merit, advertising is, indeed, of tremendous social value. Certain studies of this phase of advertising have been made,[2] but due to an absence of sufficient factual data the results are still somewhat inconclusive. Though it can be demonstrated that there is a correlation between advertising and sales volume in individual instances, the various causes of such phenomena cannot be isolated. If one compares advertising appropriations and sales, one may find in certain instances that those firms which increase their appropriations enjoy an increase in sales and those which decrease their appropriations suffer a decrease in sales. There are, however, certain limitations to the inferences that may be drawn from such findings:

1. There is no way of determining which is cause and which is effect. In other words, the question remaining unanswered is, Do increased sales follow increased appropriations, or vice versa?

This question must be seriously considered, since many firms base their advertising appropriations upon past or prospective sales volume. Though some sales undoubtedly result from such expenditures, the increased expenditures, made as they are on a basis of enhanced volume (resulting from a combination of causes), are artificially controlled, thus making for a possible spurious correlation between sales and advertising.

2. The results of advertising in time of depression might well (and probably, in many instances, do) increase sales of one company as against those of another, having no effect on the industry as a whole. It has been demonstrated often that one firm can improve its position in an industry even in the face of declining sales for the industry as a whole. The result in such a case is an advantage to one firm at the expense of another and is probably of little value in ironing out cyclical fluctuations except from a purely individual point of view.

[1] F. B. Garver and A. H. Hansen, "Principles of Economics," rev. ed., p. 235.

[2] See particularly R. S. Vaile, "Economics of Advertising," Chap. VI.

3. The type of commodity probably has a great deal to do with the potentialities of advertising as a stimulus to sales in time of depression. In a study made by the University of Minnesota[1] in 1933 it was found that though food production in the United States had decreased only 11 per cent and textiles 13 per cent, and though tobacco production had actually increased some 13 per cent from the beginning of the depression, the production of iron and steel, lumber products, and machinery and metals had decreased 52, 71, and 74 per cent respectively. This is typical of the contrasting effect of the depression on consumption and capital-goods industries. It can be seen readily that the type of industries needing stimulation in time of depression are the so-called heavy industries. And these are the industries in which advertising can least effectively be used. Imagine, for example, the U.S. Steel Corporation launching a campaign to "use more steel," or, equally ridiculous, some large machinery-manufacturing concern placing its trust in advertising when owing to general industrial inactivity prospective customers are utilizing their plants at (say) only 50 per cent of capacity. The fact is that under these conditions no inducement (let alone advertising!) would be effective in the sale of such equipment.

The authors can see little in the argument that advertising can help very much in ironing out cyclical fluctuations in business. Indeed, the figures in Table 21 indicate that the businessmen themselves have no overabundance of faith in advertising in time of depression.

TABLE 21.—INDEX OF VOLUME OF ADVERTISING IN THE UNITED STATES, 1929–1935[1]
(1929 = 100)

Year	Index of Advertising
1929	100
1930	86.1
1931	73.3
1932	58.6
1933	53.1
1934	61.8
1935	65.7

[1] Adapted from Printers' Ink Combined Index, 1936 Supplement, *Survey of Current Business*, p. 21.

5. Truth in Advertising.—That much advertising is not strictly truthful there can be little doubt. As has already been indicated,

[1] R. S. VAILE, ed., "Impact of the Depression."

advertisers use every known appeal in seeking custom for the products offered consumers. Some advertisers create a false sense of danger ("impure" toilet tissue); others, a false sense of security (weak antiseptics); in fact, many of our present-day plagues are products of the imagination of some copywriter. Acid indigestion (Phillips' milk of magnesia), body odor (Lifebuoy soap), coffee nerves (Kaffee Hag), cosmetic skin (Lux soap), smokers' teeth (Bost toothpaste), intestinal fatigue (Fleischmann's yeast), paralyzed pores (Lady Esther face cream), and intestinal toxicity (Eno Salts) are a few of the many "diseases" discovered, if not invented, by the advertising fraternity. Nor is that all. Advertising at times makes possible the sale of deleterious nostrums which are dangerous either directly or indirectly. That is to say, dire results may actually follow their use, or by reason of their worthlessness therapeutically users attempting self-diagnosis thus forego sound medical advice until it is too late.

Untruthful advertising is by no means a new phenomenon.[1] In fact, advertising is not nearly so mendacious now as heretofore. As a result not only of group effort on the part of the advertisers but also of governmental regulation,[2] serious misrepresentation is on the wane. Much advertising even now is "puffed," however. Hence each advertiser's product is *the best, the most durable, the greatest value*, and what not. Table 22, based upon a study of 10 different types of magazines, indicates (according to the opinion of the investigator) that while only 11 per cent of the advertisements analyzed were out-and-out untruthful almost 50 per cent were puffed.

Consumers are not the only ones who look upon untruthful advertising with disfavor. Thoughtful advertising men abhor

[1] One could cite scores of examples of untruthful advertising down through the years. A particularly interesting one published in 1657, a facsimile of which appears in Frank Presbrey, "The History and Development of Advertising," p. 49, holds forth in the following fanciful way on the virtue of coffee as a drink. "It suppresseth Fumes exceedingly, and therefore good against the *Head-ache* and will very much stop and *Deflection of Rheums*, that distil from the *Head* upon the *Stomach* and to prevent and help *Consumption*, and the *Cough of the Lungs*. It is excellent to prevent and cure Dropsy, Gout and Scurvy . . . [and] *to prevent miscarryings in child-bearing women.*"

[2] See Chap. VII.

this type of advertising, at least theoretically, on the grounds that the effectiveness of all demand-manipulative effort is undermined by the untruthful statements of a few. The reason is apparent. The effectiveness of advertising depends upon the faith of the consumers. If their faith in advertising declines, the guiltless suffer with the guilty. In general, if advertising is ineffective the sums thus ineffectually expended are a social waste.

TABLE 22.—PERCENTAGE OF TRUTHFUL, UNTRUTHFUL, AND PUFFED ADVERTISEMENTS IN 10 DIFFERENT TYPES OF MAGAZINES, 1937[1]

Degree of Truth	Percentage
Apparently truthful	34.0
Puffed	48.0
Untruthful	11.0
Indeterminable	7.0
	100.0

[1] General, women's, movie, humor, class, news, business, parents, pulp, and social.

6. Advertising as an Informational and Educative Device.—There is a tremendous contrast between advertising as it could be and advertising as it actually exists. That is to say, advertising has tremendous potentialities which are not fully realized. Advertising informs the consumer at times but misinforms him at others. Education connotes the teaching of the truth. Advertisers not only are biased but also lack the social responsibility of true educators. It seems very unfortunate that advertising cannot do a completely satisfactory job of informing, because the consumer in our present society has great need of informative news concerning the offerings of vendors. In other words, the consumer is a specialist, often making nothing that he uses directly; hence, he requires truthful information as to goods and services that are available to him. As a matter of fact, the consumer's reliance on information supplied by advertisers is quite essential because that very fact—the knowledge that information concerning goods will be available—makes it possible for him to specialize.

One should not conclude that advertising is not at all educative. "There are . . . certain ways in which advertising might be educative—and doubtless sometimes is. The principal possibilities may be listed as follows:

"1. Methods of use of product, including its own care and upkeep.

"2. Announcement of new products, new inventions, new processes.

"3. Announcement of new uses for old products and of [product] improvements.

"4. Announcement of a product to a market where it has not previously been available.

"5. Announcement to a constantly changing public, *i.e.*, the people who are just becoming old enough to make use of a product.

"6. Listing of the place and explanation of the method of purchase and sale.

"7. Information concerning [prices], stocks on hand and tendencies in supply and demand.

"8. [Announcement of] Style changes and trends.

"9. The popularization of a new custom as a part of the standard of living.

"10. [The furnishing of] Objective measurements of performance."[1]

As has been suggested, most of these possibilities actually are utilized by advertisers at one time or another. Informative (in contradistinction to persuasive) advertising undoubtedly increases the degree of perfection of the market by improving the position of the ordinarily uninformed or poorly informed consumer-buyer. Indeed, in a society based upon specialization, the dissemination of information through advertisements is absolutely essential.

Advertising of the purely informational type then is not completely absent in our economy. Want advertisements for example are usually essentially informative, as are the descriptions of merchandise appearing in mail-order catalogues. Indeed, retail advertising in general is, to a considerable extent, informative. There is, of course, still much room for improvement. It is encouraging to note, however, that more sound information is being given consumers in retail advertisements than heretofore.[2] Still more can be expected in the future.

[1] Vaile, *op. cit.*, pp. 45–46.

[2] As an example of a genuinely objective advertisement, the following specimen is submitted:

"Lady Pepperell Sheets & Cases

Tubtested by the makers of Rinso, Lady Pepperell sheets, after 200 washings

7. Advertising and Living Standards.—It is sometimes argued that advertising raises standards of living. There can be little quarrel with the statement if the word *affects* may be substituted for the word *raises*. It is assumed, of course, that one actually means that *standards* rather than *scales* of living are affected by advertising. One can hardly dispute the contention that advertising along with many other environmental factors has marked influence upon the creation and strengthening of *desires* for more and better worldly goods.

It is probably even true that advertising affects *scales* of living. There are several possible ways in which it does so. (1) If reduced prices do actually result from larger sales volume (coming about as a result of advertising), consumers are enabled to buy additional goods with the resulting savings. (2) In cases where advertising actually increases volume, it is (at least theoretically) possible that part of the efficiency savings resulting from such increases would be passed on to workers in the industry so affected. In other words, volume operations made possible by effective advertising expenditures may bring efficiency differentials, part of which may be distributed to workers.

(3) By virtue of their increased desire for worldly goods (brought about, in part at least, by advertising), workers may strive harder and thus produce more.[1] There is little question

---

(equivalent to eight years' normal wear) emerged snowy white and almost sturdy as new. See how they compare with U.S. requirements for high count sheets":

Type	Weight per square yard, ounces	Thread count warp filling	Breaking strength, pounds	
			Warp	Filling
U.S. government.......	4.3	69 62	65	60
Lady Pepperell........	5.6	76 68	75	95

[1] Quite pertinent in this connection is this story: An American—a cigarette manufacturer operating a factory in Mexico—was faced with a serious employee-absentee problem. He discovered that his workers—mostly girls—would work for a few days, then "feeling wealthy" would take a few days off. He discovered, in other words, that their wants were

that such a tendency eventuates in some instances. The commission salesman and the pieceworker, for example, may strive harder and achieve a higher living scale as a result.

(4) But probably the fourth possibility is the most valid, that of limiting the size of the family. As was stated previously, individuals are influenced by various environmental factors (including advertising) in the establishment of certain standards of living. They are able to achieve a higher scale per individual family member by the simple expedient of limiting the number of individuals making up the family group. Hence the average American influenced by advertising chooses to forgo the large family in order that he may acquire more or better worldly goods.

There is little doubt that advertising (either directly or indirectly) affects both standards and scales of living. Each of the aforementioned has some validity. The last—limiting the size of families—has probably the greatest significance.

8. Final Criticism.—Though all advertising cannot be condoned, certainly all cannot be condemned. Theoretically, at least, " . . . any occupation or undertaking is productive if it adds to the utility of consumable goods either by increasing the units of goods possessing want-satisfying qualities or by increasing the utility of individual units. . . . [By this standard of measurement, advertising] may at times be (1) destructive, (2) neither destructive nor productive, (3) less productive than some other combination or approach would provide, or (4) more productive than any other combination or approach. . . . "[1] The student will recognize the fact that some types of advertising will fall into one category whereas other types may fall into an entirely different classification. The use of advertising to disseminate information to the medical profession concerning the use of sulphanilamide in the successful treatment of streptococci infec-

---

simple and were easily satisfied as a result of working a few days out of each week. He solved the problem by picking out the prettiest girl in the factory, presenting her with a pair of silk stockings, and explaining that each worker would be given a similar gift if her attendance were regular. By offering portable phonographs and other luxuries, subsequently, he succeeded in raising their living standards to such an extent that steady work became essential to those wishing to maintain the standard thus established.

[1] C. H. Sandage, "Advertising—Theory and Practice," p. 19.

tions is of definite social advantage; the use of advertising in the sale of pornographic literature is socially disadvantageous.

When one invokes a strictly economic test—the effect of advertising upon prices—one must be equally eclectic. Increased sales brought about by the medium of advertising may raise or lower prices, depending upon the circumstances. The statement made by advertising men that advertising pays for itself through cost and price reductions is not completely tenable. The incidence of advertising costs depends upon the type of production operations obtaining in the industry, the distribution of increased volume among the several plants in the industry, and the extent of the monopolistic power built up and exerted by the advertisers.

It must always be borne in mind, however, that (if, indeed, we are to condone *any* sales effort in our economic system) advertising may aid in accomplishing a selling task at a lower cost than if personal sales effort were utilized exclusively. There are at least two ways in which this may be brought about by advertising. (1) By utilizing the device for economically seeking out prospective buyers or sellers. For example, retail advertising has as its major purpose the bringing of prospects to the market place so that the sales task may be completed by salespeople; a salesman selling some household device from door to door may advertise that he will be glad to demonstrate the device if interested persons will telephone or drop a card; a bibliophile in searching for a book long out of print may save much time, effort, and money by indicating his requirements in the columns of *Publishers' Weekly*. The end in each of these cases is the same—that of bringing buyers and sellers together. (2) By supplying information to, and reducing sales resistance of, prospective purchasers so that the costly time of the salesman may be saved. In other words, if the prospective buyer can be partly "sold" by means of advertising, the time taken by a salesman who calls subsequently will be materially reduced, thus cutting down the cost of selling. In the sale of consumers' goods to dealers, moreover, the latter is more apt to buy the well-advertised commodity if he knows that the consumer, in turn, will be amenable to suggestion and thus more easily sold.

There is little question as to the general effectiveness of advertising in the sale of individual commodities, although, as was suggested previously, results differ with circumstances. For some products (cancer "cures," for example), this sales-promotional device is in fact much too effective. For others (industrial items in time of depression), advertising is probably quite ineffective. That consumers read retail advertisements there is little doubt.[1] That they actually utilize the advertisements as a guide to their purchasing is equally certain.

It should be recalled finally that ours is a modified capitalistic economic system based upon private property rights and freedom of individual enterprise. This means that the system depends upon competition, and advertising is just one of the many methods used by sellers in their competitive struggle. Although there are admittedly certain devices in the competitive system that seem wasteful, the system taken as a whole is thought to be more economically effective than others. We must, in some instances, therefore, accept apparently undesirable phases of a superior system because they are part of that system.

Nor should advertising be totally condemned simply because it is being misused. The writers submit, however, that advertisers should lay more stress on objective performance and less on an appeal to the emotions, that the advertising fraternity should see fit to raise its standards of ethics and taste, and that certain types of advertising should be legally proscribed. But as long as competition is the core of our system, advertising

[1] Retail advertising is of particular interest to the consumer. In a study by Harold A. Fry ("A Study of Customer Opinion of the Advertising of Toledo Retail Merchants," University of the City of Toledo) it was found that the reading habits of the consumer were as follows:

Read retail newspaper advertisements	Percentage of men	Percentage of women
Daily	60.3	79.0
Thrice weekly	7.3	4.4
Twice weekly	5.9	2.2
Once weekly	11.8	4.9
Occasionally	4.4	1.7
Very seldom	4.4	1.7
When making specific purchases	4.4	4.4
Miscellaneous answers	1.5	1.7
Total	100.0	100.0

will be used by vendors to strengthen their own position in the market. Instead of condemning the device, then, we should be thinking in terms of raising advertising standards and where necessary circumscribing its use.

Questions

1. Compare in the current magazines the advertisements of different companies for a similar product such as toilet soap, face cream, or cigarettes. Are the claims essentially similar? What factual information is given? Could the product be recognized from the advertising if the name were deleted?

2. The cooperative creameries in Minnesota propose to advertise butter, securing their funds by a deduction from the cream checks of their farmer patrons. Would the farmers be wise to support or oppose this movement? How would such a program affect the consumer?

3. In what fields has advertising been relatively successful? Where unsuccessful? Give the reasons for your answer.

4. What relationship, if any, is there between advertising and the elasticity of demand for a commodity?

5. Is advertising ever directed to any other purpose than securing a monopoly?

6. Would an advertising-less society be to the advantage of the consumer? Discuss fully.

CHAPTER XII

STUDIES OF FAMILY EXPENDITURES

We are able to gain some information on the manner in which people spend their income from studies of family expenditures. There have been a great many of these studies made, both in this country and abroad. They can seldom be directly compared. They have been made in many different ways and include families living under quite different circumstances. Moreover, the families that have been included in the studies usually have been selected in a particular manner and for a particular purpose and may not be representative of the community as a whole. When the data of these studies are arranged in certain forms, however, there is a marked similarity among them. This similarity appears most strongly in the proportions of the income expended in the various lines of expenditure as the incomes become larger and the changes in the proportions of the income expended in the various lines of expenditures as the family changes in size. We may be quite sure of our conclusions in these respects since they appear in all the data despite their diverse characters.

1. Some Early Studies.—Some of the studies of family expenditures are quite old. Sir William Petty, for example, in 1672, used estimates of the purchases of the average workingman's family in judging the possibility of trade with Ireland. David Davies,[1] an English clergyman, in 1795 published data on the living of the families of 137 agricultural laborers from various sections of England, Wales, and Scotland. He endeavored to learn why two-fifths of his parishioners were receiving aid from the parish. Another early English study was published in 1797 by Sir Frederick Eden,[2] who was anxious to prove in the years of distress which attended the high price of corn that increases in the poor rate were not necessary. None of these early studies used statistical analysis or generalizations.

[1] David Davies, "The Case of Labourers in Husbandry," 1795.

[2] Sir Frederick Norton Eden, "The State of the Poor," London. 1797.

About 1850, extensive development of expenditure studies along two sharply different lines began. These were individual case studies of the Le Play type and statistical studies of selected groups of families. Frédéric Le Play[1] was a French mining engineer who spent his vacations living with some typical family in various parts of the world. These families were carefully selected after consultation with local clerical, educational, and other authorities. Le Play then lived some weeks or months with each of the families and in his monographs presents in minute detail the facts regarding the financial and domestic conditions both past and immediate of the particular family. The reports are so exhaustive and so remarkably well done that, even now, a person can get a vivid impression of the circumstances and manner of life of these individual families. The method has subsequently been followed by other investigators, and 75 studies of the Le Play type are known for France, 61 for the rest of Europe (mostly Belgium and Italy), 6 for Asia, 9 for Africa, and 3 for North America.[2] This method of careful observation of selected cases is valuable only when the cases are typical and the investigators are highly skilled. These conditions are rarely found, and more reliance is to be placed generally upon other methods.

The first use of what may be termed the *statistical method* in expenditure studies was made by Ernst Engel in 1857.[3] Engel was then head of the Statistical Bureau of Saxony. His contributions were in the classification of expenditures under systematic headings, arranging families by income levels, averaging the family totals for each item of expense at each income level, and getting expenses per capita for each heading and then translating these average figures into the form of percentages of total expenditures.

2. Studies in the United States.—There are more than 450 known studies of family expenditures in the United States. They have been made by many different investigators, for dissimilar groups, and under such a variety of methods that com-

[1] Frédéric Le Play, "Les Ouvriers européens," 1855–1879.

[2] See "Studies of Family Living in the United States and other Countries," *U.S. Dept. Agr. Misc. Pub.* 223.

[3] Ernst Engel, "Produktions und Konsumptionsverhältnisse des Königreichs Sachsen," 1857.

parisons among them are difficult. The most extensive studies have been made by the U.S. Bureau of Labor Statistics or by it in conjunction with other Federal agencies. There have been four investigations covering a large number of families in different states. The first was in 1889–1890 of 6,809 families connected with certain industries in which there was international competition. The second in 1901 included 25,440 families distributed in the various geographical divisions of the United States in relation to the industrial population. A third study made in 1918 included 12,096 white families located in 92 industrial centers. The last study, that of 1935–1936 including 53,000 families, is the most elaborate undertaken in this country. For this study, a preliminary short schedule was obtained from a random sample of about 336,000 families. A longer schedule covering information on expenditures and savings during the year, on ownership of important types of durable goods, and on other aspects of consumption was secured from a controlled sample of some 53,000 families, drawn largely from the random sample. Records were secured from urban groups in cities of various sizes and from village and farm groups in various types of farming areas. Seven occupational groups, 20 income classes, and 5 family types are also distinguished and records secured from each. Certain budget groups have been more elaborately examined for a smaller number of families. For example, special records of food consumption were secured from about 3,000 of the families to secure data on the nutritional adequacy of the diet. For these families, records were kept for one week at each season during the year. They were accompanied by records of the incidence of sickness of the members of the family in order to make possible an analysis of the relation of diet and health. This study provides more complete data on family expenditures in the United States than any heretofore available. The bureau has also made a number of smaller studies which involve only a particular locality or group of workers.

In addition to these studies of the bureau, there have been a great many studies made by other agencies. One of the most important of the studies made by these other agencies is the so-called Chapin Report on the Standard of Living in New York.[1]

[1] R. C. Chapin, "The Standard of Living among Workingmen's Families in New York City."

This report was published in 1909. The data were 400 family budgets obtained in 1907 and were excellently analyzed. The Chapin study has probably received as much attention as any budget study made since the time of Engel. Another important study is a national survey of the costs of living in the United States, which was made by the Great Britain Board of Trade[1] in 1909, covering 7,616 families in 29 cities and dealing principally with food and shelter. The same method of conducting surveys was used by them in surveys of living costs in Great Britain, Germany, France, and Belgium. This material makes possible some sort of international comparison.

3. Trends of Expenditures.—When the expenditures of families of essentially similar composition and location, but with different incomes, are examined, it will be found usually that the higher income families spend more on each of the expenditure groups than do those with the lower incomes. A typical example is given in Table 23 from the 1918–1919 study of the U.S. Bureau of Labor Statistics.

TABLE 23.—AVERAGE ACTUAL EXPENDITURES OF FAMILIES IN THE UNITED STATES WITH DIFFERENT INCOMES[1]

Income	Average yearly expenses per family						
	Food	Clothing	Rent	Fuel and light	Furniture and furnishings	Miscellaneous	Total
Under $900	$372	$112	$122	$57	$30	$150	$843
$900 and under $1,200	456	156	150	64	48	201	1,076
1,200 and under 1,500	516	206	180	73	62	262	1,301
1,500 and under 1,800	572	257	207	79	84	335	1,537
1,800 and under 2,100	627	307	232	87	97	404	1,756
2,100 and under 2,500	712	384	284	93	117	500	2,055
2,500 and over	860	503	260	102	133	608	2,467
All incomes	549	238	187	74	73	306	1,434

[1] Adapted from *U.S. Bur. Labor Statistics Bull.* 357, p. 5.

Some of these increases are more rapid than others with the result that, when families are arranged according to income level and the individual expenditure groups are expressed as percent-

[1] Great Britain Board of Trade, "Cost of Living in American Towns," summarized in *U.S. Bur. Labor Bull.* 93, March, 1911.

ages of either the total expenditure or the income, certain well-defined trends are disclosed. These are shown in Table 24 for families whose actual expenditures are given in the preceding table.

TABLE 24.—PERCENTAGE DISTRIBUTION OF EXPENDITURE AT DIFFERENT INCOME LEVELS BY FAMILIES IN THE UNITED STATES

Income	Food	Clothing	Rent	Fuel and light	Furniture and furnishings	Miscellaneous	Total
Under $900	44.1	13.2	14.5	6.8	3.6	17.8	100
$900 and under $1,200	42.4	14.5	13.9	6.0	4.4	18.7	100
1,200 and under 1,500	39.6	15.9	13.8	5.6	4.8	20.2	100
1,500 and under 1,800	37.2	16.7	13.5	5.2	5.5	21.8	100
1,800 and under 2,100	35.7	17.5	13.2	5.0	5.5	23.0	100
2,100 and under 2,500	34.6	18.7	12.1	4.5	5.7	24.3	100
2,500 and over	34.9	20.4	10.6	4.1	5.4	24.7	100
All incomes	38.2	16.6	13.0	5.2	5.1	21.3	100

Some studies express the expenditures as proportions of the total expenditure, others as proportions of the total income. There is little difference in the case of the lower incomes where the savings are small; but for the larger incomes quite a difference may arise, and a more accurate picture of the larger incomes is obtained by expressing the relations in terms of total income. The majority of the expenditure studies have reference to the smaller incomes. There are very few data on the expenditures of the large incomes.

The rates at which expenditures on a particular item or group change relative to changes in income are of importance. The relationship may be expressed by a coefficient and is termed the *elasticity of consumption.* The size of this coefficient may be taken generally as indicative of the relative urgency of consumption of the item or group. The higher the elasticity of consumption, the greater are the differences in expenditure on the item at different income levels. The greater the change in expenditure with changes in income, the less essential the particular item is to the family consumption. Conversely, the smaller the differential, and hence the more essential the item, the lower is the coefficient. Table 25 shows the coefficients derived for a number of studies.

Bowley and Allen[1] have suggested another method for this analysis. It consists of fitting a line by the method of least squares to dollar expenditures on the item and the total income. The resulting line $Y = a + bx$ gives the requisite data regarding

TABLE 25.—COEFFICIENTS OF ELASTICITY OF CONSUMPTION FOR SELECTED GROUPS IN EXPENDITURE STUDIES OF UNITED STATES CITY FAMILIES[1]

	0.24 and under	0.25–0.49	0.50–0.74	0.75–0.99	1.00–1.24	1.25–1.49	1.50–1.74	1.75–1.99	2.00 and over
Food	..	1	22	1					
Clothing	..	..	1	11	10	1	..	..	1
Housing	..	..	..	8	15	..	..	..	1
Fuel, light, and refrigeration	..	..	6	11	6	..	..	1	
Other household operation[2]	..	..	..	1	3	5			
Furnishings and equipment[3]	..	..	..	..	1	5	10	5	2
Automobile[4]	..	..	1	..	..	1	5	7	8
Medical care[4]	..	..	..	1	8	9	3	1	
Recreation[4]	....	..	..	2	11	8	1		

[1] These data have been calculated by the formula

$$\frac{\log C_1 - \log C_2}{\log I_1 - \log I_2}$$

where C_1 and C_2 are the expenditures in the extreme income classifications I_1 and I_2.

[2] Reported separately in nine studies; included in fuel, light, and refrigeration in other studies.

[3] Classification omitted in one study.

[4] Classification omitted in two studies.

the expenditure.[2] When a is positive, the commodity may be termed a *necessity;* when a is negative, a *luxury.* The percentage expenditure at any income level is readily computed, and the elasticity of consumption or income elasticity may be computed for any income level.[3]

[1] R. D. G. ALLEN and A. L. BOWLEY, "Family Expenditures, A Study of Its Variations."

[2] In this line, Y is the dollar expenditure on the item, b is the slope of the line or change in dollar expenditure for each dollar change in income, and x is the income in dollars.

[3] The percentage expenditure $p = (a/x) + b$.
The elasticity of consumption $\eta = bx/(a + bx)$.

An example of the results of this sort of analysis for a group of Chicago families included in the 1935–1936 Consumers' Purchases Survey is given in Table 26. Examining the *A* values, we find food and clothing indicated as the most urgent items for both groups of families. Transportation and clothing, however, have high relative urgency for the business group and are low for the wage earners, and the other items show differences in relative rank. The elasticities for most of the included groups run higher in the wage earner families than for the business group. The exceptions are housing and the fuel, light, and refrigeration groups.

TABLE 26.—SELECTED LINEAR REGRESSION CONSTANTS FOR EXPENDITURES BY INCOME FOR WAGE-EARNER AND SALARIED BUSINESS FAMILIES, CHICAGO, 1935–1936[1]

	Wage-earner families			Salaried business families		
	Intercept *A*	Slope *B*	Expenditure elasticity at the mean	Intercept *A*	Slope *B*	Expenditure elasticity at the mean
Food	$249	.201	0.636	$595	.067	0.347
Clothing	−27	.102	1.140	72	.073	0.827
Housing	207	.050	0.344	305	.073	0.532
Fuel, light and refrigeration	74	.018	0.350	65	.010	0.410
Transportation	−70	.112	1.402	93	.058	0.748
Recreation	−23	.038	1.386	50	.021	0.663
Education	−11	.013	1.624	−2	.010	1.048
Earnings	−337	.216	3.549	−1,155	.449	2.197

[1] Adapted from A. D. H. KAPLAN, "Expenditure Patterns of Urban Families," *J. Am. Statistical Assoc.*, vol. 33, p. 97, March, 1938.

4. Expenditures and Size of Family.—The division of expenditures among the budget items is also influenced by the size of the family. As the family becomes larger, physical necessities require larger expenditures for food and for clothing, with a consequent usually large reduction in the other items of expenditure. The general trends for these expenditures are shown in Table 27 by the budgets for normal families collected by the U.S. Bureau of Labor in its 1890 study.

Similar tendencies appear in data available from other countries. The adjustments which are forced to be made in the

TABLE 27.—PERCENTAGES OF INCOME SPENT FOR DIFFERENT BUDGET GROUPS BY FAMILIES OF DIFFERENT SIZES[1]

	Food	Clothing	Rent	Fuel	Lighting	All others
Husband and wife......	38.45	13.78	16.11	5.04	0.95	25.67
Husband, wife, and one child...............	38.96	14.88	14.92	5.03	0.90	25.31
Husband, wife, and two children.............	41.83	15.04	15.62	5.20	0.93	21.38
Husband, wife, and three children.......	41.91	15.97	15.02	4.93	0.88	21.29
Husband, wife, and four children............	43.70	16.72	13.89	4.78	0.86	20.05
Husband, wife, and five children.............	45.11	17.17	12.93	4.86	0.82	19.11

[1] "Eleventh Annual Report of the Commission of Labor," pp. 2008–2009, 1891.

budget because of the larger families are in the direction of lower scales. The data of the 1890 study are instructive in this respect.

TABLE 28.—AVERAGE ANNUAL EXPENDITURES FOR FAMILIES WITH $500 TO $600 INCOMES AND VARYING NUMBERS OF CHILDREN UNDER FIFTEEN, 1890[1]

Number of children in family	Expenditure for food per adult equivalent male	Expenditure for clothing			Average number of rooms per dwelling	Average expenditure for rent and operation	Average for miscellaneous
		Husband	Wife	Average per child			
None....	$98.37	$31.95	$30.17	......	4.74	$151.92	$68.92
One......	91.71	30.72	25.48	$14.16	5.03	146.10	71.12
Two.....	84.10	25.82	19.55	11.84	4.98	139.02	80.87
Three....	77.16	29.22	21.52	10.19	4.55	121.42	76.79
Four.....	73.37	27.08	18.68	10.95	4.55	120.23	67.21
Five.....	69.41	26.60	16.03	11.56	4.80	116.58	62.03

[1] H. KYRK, "Economic Problems of the Household," p. 361.

When the food cost per unit is compared with the number of units in the family, there is uniformly found a decided negative correlation. A similar situation exists with the clothing expenditure; while the total expenditure increases, the cost per unit decreases with an increase in the number of units in the family. The decline in the wife's clothing expenditure is especially marked. Expenditures for rent also decrease, as do those for sundries and miscellaneous.

The variations in composition of families have made comparisons among them difficult, and some investigators have devised scales for measuring the size of the family to facilitate comparison. Most of these scales relate to food and usually are based on the energy requirements of persons of different age and sex. Several important scales are shown in Table 29. The most famous of the general scales was that originated by Engel in 1882, in which the unit was named a *quet* in honor of Quételet. The Atwater and the Lusk scales have been widely used in analyzing family living data both in the United States and other countries. The Bureau of Home Economics has prepared several scales showing the quantities of each of several nutrients which may well appear in nutritionally adequate diets for individuals in different age, sex, and activity groups. The tendency seems to be toward a diversity of scales rather than the development of a single scale. An international standard of *family coefficients* was

TABLE 29.—SCALES FOR MEASURING SIZE OF FAMILY

Age	Engel's quet system (1883)	Energy requirements for food			Cost of food		Items other than food
		Atwater (1902)	Lusk (1918)	Bureau of Home Economics (1933)	Snydenstricker, and King (1916)	Stiebeling and Ward, liberal diet (1933)	Bowley housing (1912)
Under 1	100	30	50	40	28	47	
5 years	150	40	50	50	44	56	25
10 years	200	60	83	80	56	77	50
15 years	250	90	100	100	84	104	75
Moderately active adult man	350	100	100	100	100	100	100
Moderately active adult woman	300	80	83	83	86	85	100

developed at a conference in Rome in 1932 in order to facilitate international comparisons of dietary investigations. The conference was of the opinion, however, that no general scale could be formulated that would correspond exactly to the relative food consumption of family members in all countries and in all circumstances of life. It was hoped that although research workers would prefer to use other scales in making their particular dietary studies they would also calculate food intake per consumption unit in terms of the international scale. Much less work has been done and fewer scales developed for other lines of expenditure than for food.

5. Variations in Expenditures.—The data on trends of expenditures with differences in income and in size of family may create the impression that there is considerable similarity in the family consumption among each of the groups. There is, however, a large variation found among families both in the proportions allotted to the various budget classifications and in the consumption of particular items. Few studies have arranged their data to show these relationships, but some examples are given in Table 30.

6. Food Expenditure and Income.—Total expenditures on food customarily increase with higher incomes, but the proportion of the total expenditure taken by food is less on high than on low incomes. The relationship is among the more stable of the income-consumption relationships and the elasticity of consumption is found in many recent studies to be about 0.67. Low-income groups in the United States spend as much as 40 per cent of their total expenditures for food, an ordinary proportion for the middle-class group would be around 25 per cent, whereas in high-income groups the proportion falls as low as 15 per cent.[1] These changes, although of different magnitudes, are found generally throughout the world, and the proportion of the income spent on food furnishes a rough indication of the relative well-being of different groups.

A portion of the increase in food expenditure is due to the larger number of calories purchased on the higher income levels. Data are meager, but they indicate an elasticity of consumption

[1] Retail food sales were estimated at 21.4 per cent of total nonagricultural income in 1929. See "Monthly Indexes of Non-Agricultural and National Income," *U.S. Dept. Agr. AAA*, August, 1937.

TABLE 30.—COEFFICIENTS OF VARIATION FOR DIFFERENT GROUPS OF FAMILY EXPENDITURES

	Expenditure	Food	Housing	Household operation	Clothing	Recreation	Personal care	Medical care	Transportation
Families of husband and wife only, New York, 1934–1936[1]	......	20.7	21.2	29.9	47.4	48.0	26.9	48.0	79.5
Husband, wife, and two to four children, New York, 1934–1936[1]	......	7.6	21.0	27.7	79.0	28.2	30.8	39.7	44.0
Clerical, Washington, 1932–1933[1]	$1,700	21.7	35.8	41.8	36.0	56.3	46.3	87.5	64.0
Professional service, Washington, 1932–1933[1]	$3,200	30.3	33.4	47.8	43.0	48.5	45.4	91.1	74.8
Liverpool workers, 1929[2]	£132	....	30						
London School of Economics Budgets, 1932[2]	£436	25	39	....	35				

[1] FAITH M. WILLIAMS, "Variations in Family Expenditures," *J. Am. Statistical Assoc.*, vol. 32, pp. 44–45, March, 1937.
[2] R. D. G. ALLEN and A. L. BOWLEY, "Family Expenditure," p. 69.

of perhaps 0.20.[1] The greater portion of the increase in the cost of food is due to a greater variety and the inclusion of more expensive foods, in terms of calories, in the diet. The greatest increases in consumption are found in fruit, vegetables, dairy produce, meat, and eggs. The consumption of potatoes, bread, and sugar does not appear to differ greatly. These are changes that are desirable, since they improve the quality of the diet. That they are due very largely to exigencies of the comparative prices may be seen by examining the proportion of calories derived from different sources in the diets worked out by the Bureau of Home Economics as the best available at various costs.

Table 31.—Percentage of Calories from Various Sources in the Four Standard Diets

	Restricted diet for emergency use	Adequate diet at minimum cost	Adequate diet at moderate cost	Liberal diet
Bread, flour, cereals	43	35	24	15
Milk	12	18	19	19
Fruit, vegetables	14	15	18	18
Fats	17	17	18	18
Sugar	9	7	9	9
Lean meat, fish, eggs	5	8	12	21

The cost of food in terms of calories is hardly a proper measure of its relative value in the diet, since a food expensive from a

[1] The following figures are extracted from "Final Report of the Mixed Committee of the League of Nations," pp. 247, 253, Nutrition, 1937:

Sweden: Workers and lower officials, per consumption unit:
- Income under 700 Kr., 3,120 calories.
- Income over 145 Kr., 3,840 calories.

Germany: Workers, per consumption unit:
- Income under 800 Rm., 2,530 calories.
- Income over 1,500 Rm., 3,193 calories.

United Kingdom: All classes, per head:
- Income under 10 *S.*, 2,317 calories.
- Income over 45 S., 3,326 calories.

United States: Per nutrition unit:
- Weekly food expenditure, $1.33 to $1.99, 2,540 calories.
- Weekly food expenditure, $4.00 to $4.66, 4,130 calories.

calorie viewpoint may be inexpensive as a source of certain minerals or vitamins. The following table is included, however, to show the wide range in the cost of calories in the various types of food.

Low incomes and the resulting necessity of purchasing the so-called *energy foods*, which are low in calorie cost, rather than the *protective foods*, which are relatively high in calorie cost, lead to a progressive deterioration in the quality of the diet as the income declines, unless unusual skill is exercised in the selection of foods. The incidence of nutritional diseases increases, in consequence, in the lower income classes in the high-income countries such as the United States and is widespread in the poorer sections of the world.

TABLE 32.—COST OF 100 CALORIES IN VARIOUS TYPES OF FOOD[1]

Food	Switzerland 1936, centimes	Belgium 1932, francs	Italy 1933, centesimi	Denmark 1936, öre	United States 1937, cents
Flour (wheat)	1.04	....	4.67	...	0.22
Bread	.....	0.06	.....	2.8	0.71
Sugar	1.07	....	15.69	...	0.29
Lard	2.36	0.12	.....	2.1	0.34
Butter	6.12	0.24	15.00	3.0	0.94
Milk	4.37	0.28	15.86	4.4	1.77
Beef (veal)	25.00	0.77	34.59[2]	9.7	5.10[3]
Eggs	12.06	1.00	48.05	8.8	4.12
Potatoes	2.28	0.13	8.21	1.4	0.43

[1] Adapted from "Final Report of the Mixed Committee of the League of Nations," Nutrition, pp. 248–249.

[2] Forequarter.

[3] Sirloin.

The following data from a Bureau of Home Economics study of 897 dietaries of employed wage earners and low-salaried clerical workers give an indication of the extent and deterioration in the quality of the diet as income is lower in the United States. The *A* diet is one that meets the average minimum requirements with a wide margin of safety in all respects. A *B* diet is one that meets average minimum requirements in all respects with an uncertain margin of safety. A *C* diet is one that fails to meet minimum average requirements in one or more respects.

For the United Kingdom, Sir John Orr[1] estimates that the average diet of the 10 per cent of the population with the lowest incomes was inadequate for perfect health in all the constituents considered; that the diet of the next poorest 20 per cent was adequate only in total proteins and total fat; that the next 20 per cent had a diet adequate in energy values, protein, and fat, but below standard in minerals and vitamins; that the next 20 per cent was adequate in iron, phosphorus, and vitamins, but probably below standard in calcium; and that in the 10 per cent of the population with the highest incomes the standard requirements were exceeded in every case. In the countries with lower average incomes than those of the United States and Great Britain, the proportion of inadequate diets is, of course, much greater.

Table 33.—Quality of Diets at Different Levels of Food Expenditure in the United States[1]

Weekly food expenditure for food-cost unit	Number of records	Percentage of diets		
		A	*B*	*C*
$1.33 to 1.99	335	4	35	61
2.67 to 3.32	456	35	59	6
4.00 to 4.66	106	77	20	3

[1] Hazel Stiebeling, "Diets of Families of Employed Wage Earners and Low-Salaried Clerical Workers Living in Industrial Communities of the United States, 1934–1936," Bureau of Home Economics, February, 1937.

7. Clothing Expenditure and Income.—The expenditure on clothing is flexible and subject to considerable variation among families. The most usual proportion of the total expenditures, however, would be about 15 per cent. Most of the surveys of the lower income groups show elasticities of consumption slightly above 1, whereas the coefficients tend to be below 1 for the higher income groups. On the lower incomes, the husband's expenditure for clothing exceeds that of the wife, but the wife's expenditure rises more rapidly than that of the husband and on moderate incomes equals or exceeds the husband's expenditure. On the high-income levels, the wife's expenditure generally exceeds that of the husband. The daughter's expenditure on clothes usually exceeds that of the son at all ages and on all income

[1] Sir John Orr, "Food, Health and Income."

levels. The expenditures of grown sons equal or exceed those of the fathers, and the expenditures of grown daughters exceed those of the mothers, and the trends in both cases increase with income. The expenditures for the younger children are much less than for the adults and maintain a fairly constant relation to the expenditures on the fathers' clothing. The Bureau of Labor Statistics study of 1918–1919 gave the clothing expenditures in considerable detail, and the ratios in Table 34 have been computed from it.

TABLE 34.—RELATIVE CLOTHING EXPENDITURE FOR VARIOUS MEMBERS OF THE FAMILY[1]
(Husband's expenditures = 1.0)

	Income level					
	Under $900	$900 to $1,200	$1,200 to $1,500	$1,500 to $1,800	$1,800 to $2,100	$2,100 and over
Husband	1.0	1.0	1.0	1.0	1.0	1.0
Wife	0.8	0.8	0.9	0.9	0.9	0.9
Son, 15 and over	...	0.9	0.9	0.9	0.9	1.1
Daughter, 15 and over	...	1.0	1.1	1.1	1.1	1.3
Son, 12 and under 15	...	0.7	0.6	0.6	0.6	0.6
Daughter, 12 and under 15	...	0.7	0.6	0.6	0.6	0.7
Son, 8 and under 12	0.6	0.6	0.6	0.5	0.5	0.5
Daughter, 8 and under 12	0.6	0.6	0.6	0.5	0.5	0.5
Son, 4 and under 8	0.5	0.5	0.5	0.4	0.4	0.4
Daughter, 4 and under 8	0.5	0.5	0.5	0.4	0.4	0.4
Son, under 4	0.3	0.3	0.3	0.3	0.3	0.3
Daughter, under 4	0.4	0.4	0.3	0.3	0.3	0.3

[1] H. KYRK, "Economic Problems of the Household, p. 351.

An increase in income raises clothing expenditure by increasing the number purchased of articles already being bought and the price paid per article and in some cases leads to the purchase of entirely new articles hitherto lacking in the wardrobe. Indices, based on the important clothing items, are given in Table 35, showing the change in price and quantity of clothing for certain family members as the income increases. It appears that increases in quantity were greater than those occasioned by changes in price in the expansion of the clothing budget for all of the included groups.

TABLE 35.—INDICES OF PRICE AND QUANTITY OF CLOTHING FOR VARIOUS MEMBERS OF THE FAMILY[1]
(Expenditure on income level of $900 and under = 100)

	Husbands		Wives		Boys, fifteen and over		Girls, fifteen and over	
	Price	Quantity	Price	Quantity	Price	Quantity	Price	Quantity
Under $900....	100	100	100	100	100	100	100	100
$900 to $1,200	110	125	107	132	106	136	117	122
1,200 to 1,500	120	145	119	154	108	152	126	143
1,500 to 1,800	129	157	129	177	114	161	136	161
1,800 to 2,100	134	169	137	187	122	176	142	179
2,100 to 2,500	135	178	143	193	129	181	148	189
Over 2,500.....	137	173	137	190	136	188	161	214

[1] Based on the data in "Cost of Living in the United States," *Bur. Labor Statistics Bull.* 357. The indices are of the so-called Fisher *ideal* type.

Expressed in terms of dollars, the minimum level in clothing that provides suitable protection and decency in dress will require about $225 to $250 for the family. About $70 each is required for the adult members of the family, $40 for children from eight to twelve, and about $30 for a child up to four. If variety is added to these basic requirements, the cost will rise considerably. Where we reach a level that requires fabrics of good quality and of standard designs, the cost will have risen to (say) $700 to $900. This level is maintained by those with incomes of from $4,000 to $5,000. Here the man will require $175 or more, the woman $200 or more, and the children from $60 to $150, depending upon their ages. Clothing expenditures of those with very large incomes are too varied to permit generalization.

8. Housing and Income.—The cost of housing varies greatly among different sections of the country and economic groups. In 1930, the Bureau of the Census for the first time gathered data on rentals paid for all nonfarm houses. The median monthly rental for the United States was $27.15, or on an annual basis about $325. This would indicate that the median nonfarm family spent about 20 per cent of its income on housing.

Over half of the nonfarm population in the United States is housed in dwellings renting for less than $30 per month, or in owned homes valued at less than $5,000. Rentals and house values are distinctly lower in the South than in the North, and in smaller towns and cities than in the larger metropolitan areas. In only 12 states did the median monthly rental of rented urban homes exceed $30. In 3 states—New York, Michigan, and Illinois—it was more than $40. In 27 states, it was between $20 and $30, and in 9 Southern states it was below $20.

TABLE 36.—NONFARM HOMES IN THE UNITED STATES BY RENTAL GROUPS AND VALUE, 1930

Annual rental	Percentage of homes	Value of owned homes	Percentage of homes
Under $120	12.7	Under $1,000	7.6
$120 to $179	10.8	$1,000 to $1,499	5.4
180 to 239	10.5	1,500 to 1,999	5.1
240 to 359	20.6	2,000 to 2,999	11.1
360 to 599	25.8	3,000 to 4,999	22.3
600 to 899	12.2	5,000 to 7,499	21.9
900 to 1,199	2.8	7,500 to 9,999	9.4
1,200 to 1,799	2.8	10,000 to 14,999	8.6
1,800 and over	.8	15,000 and over	6.6
Median	$325.80	Median	$4,778

The Financial Survey of Urban Housing, conducted by the U.S. Bureau of Foreign and Domestic Commerce in cooperation with the Civil Works Administration in 1934, permits an examination of the relation of income to housing expenditure. This study was made almost in the depth of the depression and may be biased because of the inability of families to adjust their housing expenditures or because of the maintenance of these expenditures at a higher level under expectation of a subsequent change in income. The data from every one of the 51 cities included, however, indicate that the cost of housing absorbed a large portion of the income in the lower income groups and that this percentage falls rapidly as the family income increases to higher levels. In the group with family incomes below $500, the percentage allotted to rent was on the average as great as 40 or even 60 per cent, and owned homes were valued at five

TABLE 37.—VALUE OF OWNED HOMES AND RENTALS OF RENTED DWELLINGS BY INCOME GROUPS IN CITIES IN THE UNITED STATES, 1934

Income group	Owned homes				Rented dwellings			
	Ratio value of property to income	Value of houses per person	Value of house per room	Number of rooms per house	Ratio of rent to income	Annual rent per person	Annual rent per room	Number of rooms per dwelling
$1 to $249	15.3	$817	$542	5.2	96.3	$47	$41	3.9
250 to 499	7.9	848	548	5.5	48.0	51	44	4.0
500 to 749	5.2	891	576	5.6	34.9	57	50	4.2
750 to 999	3.7	897	626	5.6	27.3	67	54	4.5
1,000 to 1,499	3.1	964	659	5.9	23.4	78	60	4.6
1,500 to 1,999	2.3	1,069	684	5.9	20.0	97	70	4.8
2,000 to 2,999	2.1	1,302	823	6.3	17.9	118	81	5.2
3,000 to 4,499	1.9	1,667	951	6.9	15.3	148	94	5.6
4,500 to 7,499	1.7	2,222	1,175	7.7	12.3	190	112	6.2
7,500 to 8,000	1.2	3,659	1,619	8.6	8.5	267	134	6.2

or more times the annual income. In the range of family incomes above $5,000, the average reported rental expenditures were 10 to 15 per cent of the annual income, and house valuations were less than two times the annual income.

The cost of housing rises with the income both because the number of rooms per dwelling unit increases and because the rental or value per room increases. The nature of these changes is illustrated by the data in Table 37.

9. Further Classification of Expenditure Data.—Studies of family expenditures have thus far been content to analyze the data on the basis of the usual budget items. It is evident, however, that a recasting into other grouping and certain analyses of internal relationships might be fruitful. For example, if a single measure of the economic position of a family is to be available, the proportion of the income spent on food is perhaps the best indication. Similarly, the ratio of the woman's to the man's clothing expenditure may furnish an indication of social activities outside the home. Also, an analysis of the durable income-bearing objects held by the family would tell a great deal about the extent of the decline in real income in a depression, etc. An estimate for an analogous classification has been made by Lough and is shown in Table 38. The increasing importance of durable goods in the consumption of the higher

TABLE 38.—REPETITION OF PURCHASE AT CERTAIN INCOME LEVELS[1]

Type of purchase	Proportion of income		
	$1,500	$2,000	$2,500
Frequent	50.3	48.0	45.5
Less frequent	40.4	39.7	38.9
Infrequent	9.3	12.3	15.6
Total purchases	100.0	100.0	100.0

[1] W. H. LOUGH, "High Level Consumption," p. 192.

income groups is indicated, and since these purchases are made at infrequent intervals this consumption is likely to be of a highly variable character. Moreover, such a classification on the basis of time shows an increasing relative importance of the infrequent purchase elements in consumption.

Questions

1. How would you expect expenditures of a family having at present an income of $2,400 a year to compare with a similar family with an income of $2,400 in 1913?
2. Which budget groups show the greatest rise and fall?
3. What classifications of expenditures other than the usual budget classifications might be significant in showing the characteristics of family life?
4. In what lines of expenditure are differences in income most apparent?
5. How significant do you think that the computed elasticities of consumption would be as indicators of probable changes in demand following changes in income?
6. What relations, if any, would there be between the elasticity of consumption and elasticity of demand for a commodity?

CHAPTER XIII

VARIATIONS IN CONSUMPTION

The demands for particular products by consumers bear certain relations to one another. Certain groups of products may be said to have *competing demands; i.e.*, the consumption of one product means that some other products will not be consumed. Commodities that are substitutes for one another fall into this class, the most important example of commodities of this kind being food.[1] The national per capita consumption of food, when considered on a calorie, or thermodynamic, basis, remains quite constant. Calorie consumption, of course, varies with different nations and among classes within the nation. These differences are due to certain climatic differences and to differences in the character of the population. People living in cold climates, for example, require more calories than those living in warm climates. The nature of the occupations of people also affect their calorie consumption. Those doing vigorous outdoor work consume more calories than those engaged in sedentary occupations. Habits in housing and clothing, as well as waste in food preparation, will also affect consumption. People's size and their distribution among the various age groups will have some effect. These factors appear to be sufficient to explain international and sectional differences in calorie consumption. It was estimated before the World War, for example, that the daily per capita consumption of Italy was around 2,560 calories, the United Kingdom 2,860 calories, and the United States 3,650 calories.

Among the normally prosperous nations, such as the United States, the total consumption of foodstuffs measured in calories remains fairly constant, regardless of variations in the national income. Changes take place in the selection of foods that go to make up this calorie intake, however. In prosperous times,

[1] See A. E. Taylor, "Consumption, Merchandising, and Advertising of Foods," *Harvard Business Rev.*, April, 1924.

some of the undernourished may be brought up to normal, but for the majority there will be no increase in calorie consumption. The shift in such times is rather to more desirable foodstuffs. More meat is consumed, and less cereals and potatoes. Similarly, in less prosperous times, there is a change in kinds of foodstuffs composing the diet, but little change in its calorie volume. When times are hard in the North, the use of flour increases, and the consumption of meat declines. In the South, the use of corn increases, and that of wheat declines. There is everywhere a substitution of cheaper calories for higher priced ones.

This has an important bearing on the introduction of a new foodstuff into the diet or on the enlarged consumption of one already there, since it means that this foodstuff does not constitute a new addition to the diet but acts as a substitute for some food already there. Thus the addition of a new food means an approximately equal calorie-value reduction in the consumption of some other food or foods. Advertising of their product by a group of producers, which results in an increase in the consumption of that product, means necessarily a decrease in the consumption of something else.

The demand for certain products may be said to be *complementary; i.e.*, in some cases when one product is consumed a great deal more satisfaction can be obtained from it if another commodity is consumed with it, and a similar relationship exists with the other commodity. Bread and butter, a phonograph and its records, and a dress suit with the proper shirt and tie are all examples of this rule. A change in the demand for one is likely, because of this relationship, to be accompanied by a similar change in the demand for the other. The demand for other products may be said to be *individual; i.e.*, a demand for such goods has little relation to the consumption of other goods for the satisfaction derived from them.

Variations in consumption may be considered in four ways: (1) as among individuals or groups, (2) as among income classes, (3) as among periods of time, and (4) as among places. Each of these types of variation involves special economic problems; consequently each will be considered separately.

1. Variations in Consumption as among Individuals or Groups.

1. *Standards and Scales of Living.*—A comparison of the consumption of individuals reveals a striking similarity in the con-

sumption habits and goods of the individuals composing a particular social or industrial group. People of a particular class consume nearly the same sort of goods as their neighbors. Our clothing, food, and even the houses in which we live are much the same as those of our associates. This is particularly true of the parts of consumption that come under the observation of others. Among classes, however, the situation is quite different. The commodities that bank clerks as a class consume are in a large part similar and yet are quite different from those of garage mechanics. In the same manner, it is possible to distinguish characteristics of classes all the way through society. Broad comparisons may be made on the basis of these habits, and some important generalizations can be drawn from them.

As has been suggested in another connection, the actual commodities and services that a person or group consumes may be termed the *level of consumption* of the person or group. The level of consumption is to be contrasted with the *standard of living*. The standard of living is a desired manner of living and is not necessarily the level of consumption.[1] It is the level of consumption that people feel belongs to them and that appears to be reasonably within their efforts to attain. It is a psychic thing which may be or may not be realized. The level of consumption in contrast is the actual way of living. The standard of living is not the best imaginable way of living but is the way of living which people feel is incumbent upon them to realize, and without the attainment of which they will be oppressed by a feeling of dissatisfaction. The standard of living is largely a social product and, from the viewpoint of the individual, appears as something that is imposed upon him from outside.

There are, of course, important relationships between the standard of living and the level of consumption. If the level of consumption is below the standard of living, there is a feeling of privation and dissatisfaction; if above, a feeling of security and plenty. The whole problem of the restlessness of industrial groups is inseparably bound up with this relation between the standard of living and level of consumption. The standards of living of many of the very poor are pitiably low, as is evidenced by their contentment with their level of consumption. "If only the poor were discontented," say many social workers.

[1] See Hazel Kyrk, "A Theory of Consumption," pp. 174–176.

Over a period of time, there is a constant tendency for the standard of living and the level of consumption of a particular group to become adjusted. Thus if in a certain group the income decreases so that the level of consumption is considerably below the standard of living, those in the group are likely to marry later and have smaller families. Moreover, we are less likely to find the children remaining in the same group, with a result that subsequently, with relatively smaller numbers, the members of the group earn more than in the previous generation, with a consequent raising of the level of consumption. Increases in income are likely to result in higher levels of consumption and in higher standards of living as well. The effect of the increase in income depends in part upon the character of the individuals and in part upon the manner and suddenness of the increase. When the increase in the level of consumption results in higher standards of living, the increased level is likely to be maintained, but if the standards of living remain the same, the group is likely to expand in size in the next generation enough to lower the level of consumption to the old standard of living. Sudden and large increases of income are seldom of much fundamental benefit to the recipients. Much of the increase will probably be squandered in ways that yield little lasting satisfaction, and often in ways that are detrimental. If, on the contrary, the increase has been gradual, or, better yet, if it is unrecognized, coming in the form of a gradual decrease in prices, the larger income will probably be well used and result in a higher standard of living as well as a higher level of consumption.

Levels of consumption and standards of living are not fixed things. They change, however, only slowly in their main outlines. They rise, or include more commodities, somewhat more easily than they decline. To decrease one's level of consumption, at least those portions which are visible to others, is looked upon as a public confession of failure and a thing seriously to be avoided. In consequence, restrictions in consumption following a decrease in income frequently lead to the continuation of the consumption of articles visible to others even though these may not be essential and to the discarding of articles necessary for efficiency but that are not visible. Further evidence of the power of society over the consumption of the individual is found in the arrangement of the consumption of many persons. The things that society can see and approve are often stressed at the expense of the less visible items that go to maintain bodily health and vigor. The heavy expenditures of poor families for elaborate funerals at the expense of the proper nourishment of the family and the shopgirl's choice of silk stockings at the expense of warm undergarments are examples of this tendency.

The reason for the inclusion of the goods which we find in our present standards is an interesting speculation. Many are supposed to have been selected as the result of a trial-and-error discovery, made early by human beings. It is thought that these particular goods possessed survival value. Those who experimented with unfamiliar foods or other strange things often met with death, and the goods that met the test became incorporated in the standard. Primitive people are extremely conservative and cling with great tenacity to their habits. Survival value has ceased, however, to have much importance as a basis for inclusion of new things in our present standards. Life is now too complex to allow us to work things out in this manner.

Another great source of our standards is in the consuming of goods for their prestige value. There are some goods that are included as symbols of status and accomplishment and to meet the desire for distinction and recognition. Society has devised few ways of indicating economic power other than "conspicuous leisure and conspicuous consumption."[1] Goods utilized for this purpose are not included in consumption as opportunities, but as symbols of a class. The higher the economic class, the larger these items bulk. Only the few groups where other insignia of rank are available, such as the academic professions and the military, escape this sort of display. The lower ranks ape the higher, and the display in some of its forms reaches the very lowest ranks.

2. *Fashions.*—The phenomenon of the downward diffusion of fashions illustrates the power of this source. It is thus possible for a comparatively small group of acknowledged leaders with economic power and professional position to exercise a dominant influence over a considerable portion of the consumption of the great majority. Fashion as an influence on consumption will probably become more pronounced as society becomes more completely organized on a pecuniary basis, with economic position

[1] See T. Veblen, "Theory of The Leisure Class," Chaps. III and IV.

becoming more completely established as a factor distinguishing the classes, and will also become more pronounced as incomes, in general, grow. This element of our consumption may or may not be detrimental; it depends upon which class society sets out to follow and upon the inherent worth of the insignia of that class. Much is to be accomplished in awakening the rich to the responsibilities of their consumption, since in general the lower income classes tend to conform to modes established by the wealthy.

Fashions are semirecurring ways of doing things[1] and are to be distinguished from progress, which, involving change, does not recur. Fashions seem to start among those who, because of their wealth or talents, distinguish themselves from others. They are acts of differentiation, modes of setting oneself apart. The fashion then proceeds in a regular cycle.[2] Those who possess considerable incomes imitate the leaders. And the imitation proceeds successively down to the lower classes. When, however, the fashion is generally accepted, it sows the seeds of its own obscurity, for it now becomes necessary for the leaders to differentiate themselves again. Hence the paradox that the

[1] Professor Paul H. Nystrom, "Economics of Fashion," distinguishes style and fashion. Style is a mode or method of expression in some art—painting, writing, dressmaking, golf playing, what not. Fashion, on the other hand, is the prevailing style at any one moment of time. Thus the clothes of the nineties are of a certain *style*, but they are not in *fashion*. Fashion can be explained if one looks for the physical and psychological motives underlying the phenomenon. On the physical side, the seasons offer points at which changes actually are necessary. Hence, in clothing, instead of purchasing items identical in style, there is an opportunity to select something different. On the psychological side, there is a combination of factors that make for a desire for changes. Among these are the desire for display, the experiencing of fatigue or boredom, the desire for new sensations, a real desire for improvement. Add to these the fact that the wealthy both want and are able to rebel against convention and that the impecunious, curiously enough, have a fear of being unconventional, and you have the psychological basis of fashion.

[2] The fashion cycle can be measured objectively by means of fashion counts. When the data are plotted, the resulting figure is a graphic representation of the acceptance, rise, culmination, and decline of a style. Fashion cycles can be broken by catastrophe, war, or weather changes at the end of a season. However, fashions starting late in the summer and becoming quiescent by virtue of the season's end are likely to continue the following year. Moreover, the *use* and *purchase* cycles are not precisely contemporary; the former lagging behind the latter.

success of the fashion is to be judged by its subsequent popularity but that that very popularity leads to its own destruction. Fashion is accelerated by widely diffused income, by population mobility, and by agencies of mass impression. The fashion cycle is slowed down somewhat by the conservative group who cling to the old styles as long as possible and who change to the new in the most moderate manner possible rather than adopting the extreme of the style.

One of the most interesting problems in the whole fashion picture is that having to do with the origination, adaptation, and acceptance of styles. Styles, it must be recalled, are not plucked out of thin air. The more one studies the subject, the more convinced one becomes that "there is nothing new under the sun." Many styles are inspired by works of art (halo hats by old Italian paintings); others by current events (Chinese prints and hat styles by the prominence of Sino-Japanese activities); still others by related items (women's slacks by beach pajamas). Many other styles are merely reversions to the modes of earlier years (turtle-neck sweaters from the fashion current over two decades ago). Some, to be sure, are purely utilitarian adaptations (the capes designed for the purpose of preserving the "fluff" in the huge leg-of-mutton shirtwaist sleeves of yesteryear).

A *couturier* upon designing a garment of course may or may not achieve success since public acceptance determines the fashion. In other words, every style does not become a fashion. Just how much of the success of a fashion is due to the motif is imponderable. Certainly public interest in Sino-Japanese affairs makes acceptance of pseudo-Oriental styles more likely at least. If a style does become popular and is adaptable in other lines of merchandise, such will be the result. Witness the adaptation of the tricolor motif (inspired by the French Colonial Exposition) in practically all wearing apparel and accessory lines in the early 1930's.

With respect to the geographical origin of styles, there is much argument. According to some experts, Hollywood is now the style center; according to others, New York is predominant; and according to still others, Europe continues to "set the styles." The data in Table 39 are the result of a more or less successful attempt to find the answer. The items were so selected that the name of each was sufficient to suggest its exact nature. The

TABLE 39.—ORIGIN OF A SELECTED GROUP OF FASHION ITEMS, 1935

Item	Place and approximate time of origination	Comments
Men's:		
Midnight-blue tuxedo	England, middle 1920's	Received impetus about four years ago after acceptance by the then Prince of Wales; especially popular in Hollywood owing to photographic qualities
Mess jacket	British tropical provinces and Riviera, late 1920's	Worn for years by British army officers in tropics; popularity has not been lasting owing to too rapid acceptance and similarity to waiters' costume
Tyrolean hat	Austrian Tyrol adaptation, England; date not known	First introduced into England by English hunters returning from shooting season abroad
Deep-tone shirt	England, early 1930's	Inspired by popular shades in polo shirts; first introduced by custom shirtmakers; popular acceptance followed rapidly
Brown buck shoes	England during World War	Inspired by reversed-calf trench boot; acceptance rapid, adopted by English sportsmen. Success probably due to early adoption by the then Prince of Wales, subsequent adoption by America's most popular dancing cinema star, and their unusual practicability
Jockey shorts	French Riviera, late 1920's	Adaptation of a bathing trunk introduced originally on the Riviera
Women's:		
Sport-back suit	France, early 1930's	Adapted from men's sport suits, acceptance probably due to trend toward mannishness in women's out-of-door attire
Slacks	Deauville, early 1930's	An adaptation of the beach pajama introduced some years ago at Deauville, acceptance probably due to mannish trend, comfort, and greater out-of-door activity
Flat-heeled evening shoes	France, about 1933	Probably a manifestation of the sports influence; *Vogue*, Dec. 15, 1933, refers to them as the very latest in shoes
Halo hats	Paris, about 1934	Inspired by one of Mantegna's paintings, Renaissance Art Exhibit; gained almost immediate popularity in the United States
Tennis shorts	Deauville, late 1920's	When first introduced they were knee length; at first used only for beach wear, but by 1932 fashion periodicals began to suggest them for tennis use
Knee-length hose	Paris, about 1934	Reintroduced in Paris by Clarks Laboratories, offering to United States trade followed almost immediately

material was gathered from periodicals and from communications and interviews with various fashion commentators. The fact that the dates could be determined only approximately characterizes quite clearly the will-o'-the-wisp nature of the phenomenon.

One or two interpretive comments can be made regarding the material contained in the table. In the first place, it will be noted that in every instance the style originated or was first adapted in Europe; that men's styles are predominantly British in origin and women's are predominantly French. If we may accept this sample as adequate, the indications are that those who hold that most of our styles now originate at home are in error. In the second place, though many items *originate* in Europe *adaptation* takes place in the United States and the "end item" might be quite different from the original. Compare, for example, the original Tyrolean hat with the adaptation manufactured and sold by American firms.

The social and individual costs of fashions are high. In the case of durable goods, fashions may lead to the discarding of articles that are still suitable for use but are made obsolete by the change. If a coat, for example, is a serviceable one, it still continues to be useful regardless of the fashion change. To the extent that goods capable of rendering efficient service are cast aside because they are no longer fashionable, fashion is wasteful. The uncertainty as to changes in fashion and the unpredictableness of the particular style that is going to prove popular increase the risk and hence the cost of the merchant's business. The degree of risk depends to some extent on the stage of acceptance of a style, however. Thus, those selling a newly accepted item assume a greater burden of risk than those selling a well-established item.

The manufacturer also incurs risks because of style changes. The goods he produces may often prove unsalable. Also, more expense may be involved in the production of the goods because of the special methods required. For example, in the case of style shoes, the cutting must be done by hand, whereas the cutting for standard models can be done by machine. The discarding of goods before they have completed their usefulness means that a greater number of productive forces are necessary to produce them; hence means of production are drawn away from other uses where they might be employed to increase the quantity of goods to be consumed and in consequence the total product of society is lessened.

Producers endeavor to maintain as much control over fashions as possible, in order to lessen their risks and to manipulate the changes to their advantage. The production of styles in women's clothing has, for example, become highly commercialized. New designs are shown at the openings of the *couturiers* in February and August. If the design can be sold to a royal or titled person or a popular actress, the design may prove a success. Another means of attracting attention to the design is to exhibit the clothes on models or mannequins who appear at the races or on the boulevards of Paris. Cloak and suit makers, buyers for department stores, and representatives of American textile mills make a practice of attending functions at which the creations of the *couturier* are displayed.

Manufacturers of specialized raw materials are anxious to see styles demanding the use of their products and, in consequence, often carry on aggressive campaigns in favor of certain styles. For example, in 1919, a large shoe-button manufacturing concern conducted a campaign through unnamed advertising in trade journals purporting to be announcements that buttoned shoes were returning to vogue. At the same time, a campaign to maintain the style of high shoes for women was being carried on by a manufacturer of kid leather, which is the only kind of leather that can be used successfully in the tops of very high shoes. At the same time that this effort was being expended in high-shoe propaganda, another campaign was carried on by a number of companies favoring large numbers of colors in women's shoes. All the companies taking part in this campaign were engaged in the manufacture of colored leather. Besides these campaigns for special interests, the shoe trade and other trades have carried on campaigns in behalf of the whole industry in regard to certain styles or style policies.

The fashion cycle has an important effect upon merchandising in that a merchant must decide upon the particular phase of the cycle in which he is to operate and must adjust his sales appeals and policy accordingly. In the first portion of the cycle, goods are sold to the leaders or determiners of the fashion. Here the appeal must be to distinctiveness or differentiation from others. The second phase appears when those who closely follow the changes adopt the styles. Here the sales appeal is directed to emulation or to the up-to-dateness of the article. Finally comes the stage of general adoption, reached when the style becomes set and sales become large and fairly certain and can be made at lower prices. The appeals of this stage are generally those of economical emulation and are based on the idea that a person can now inexpensively follow the style leaders. The individual merchant must decide in which of these phases he is to operate, as his establishment must become associated in the mind of the public with one of these particular phases. Attempts to operate in more than one phase are rarely successful.

It is interesting to note that Americans are probably the most fashion-conscious of all peoples. This situation is not difficult to explain. (1) There is a greater diffusion of wealth here than elsewhere. That is to say, people can buy new things if they so desire. (2) Americans are, on the whole, more cognizant of what is going on about them. In other words, because of education, newspaper and periodical reading, travel, movies, etc., they know almost immediately about the new things offered. (3) Americans are freer from custom and tradition than most peoples. This means that desires are not checked by reactionary influences.

The American people are not quite so irrational in fashion matters as they once were, however. Practicability has become extremely important as a factor conditioning the success of a fashion. The reason for this, of course, lies in the modern trend toward freedom of movement and out-of-door activities for young and old. Thus, we would never expect a reversion to the hobble skirt in this day and age. Moreover, consumer-buyers are displaying a more rational attitude toward fashion in other ways. For example, the white vestee extremely popular in high- and medium-priced dresses some time ago proved unpopular in the very low-priced dresses because in the latter the vestee was machine-stitched and could not be removed for cleaning, which meant that the buyer of a $3.95 dress had to incur a cleaning cost of $1 every time the vestee became soiled. Again, fur coats in swagger lines received wide acceptance among those with higher incomes in the early 1930's but when executed in lower priced garments had to be toned down because the lower income classes demanded a coat that would not be conspicuously out of fashion within a relatively short time.

Thus, there is evidence leading to the conclusion that Americans are not victims of fashion to the extent that it is popularly supposed. Practicability—a rational factor—is making definite headway as an important determinant of style acceptance. This, indeed, is an encouraging sign.

2. Variations in Consumption as among Income Classes.—Though the subject of consumer expenditures is more properly discussed in another connection (Chap. XII), it seems advisable at this point to inquire into the effect of income on the consumption of certain types of items. Since the Federal government has allocated the WPA funds for investigatory work, much interesting information is at hand on this subject. One of their studies, "Consumer Use of Selected Goods and Services, by Income Classes,"[1] is particularly pertinent in this connection. The basic data were collected by means of a house-to-house property inventory of 64 cities and reveal many interesting facts.

There is little question of a very definite relationship between income and the consumption of particular items. For example, automobiles, though now a necessity for a large percentage of the nation, are not owned by 40 to 60 per cent of the reporting families. As might be expected, most of the families that have no automobile are of the low-income groups. More specifically, approximately three-fifths (or more) of the no-car families have incomes of less than $1,000. Since, in every city, even the lowest income class have many car-owning families, the influence of income on car ownership is more effectively revealed by the steady decrease, noticeable throughout the range of income classes from the lowest to the highest, in the percentages of families having no car.

The relation between income and the use of mechanical refrigerators is similarly manifest. This is revealed by the fact that despite the relatively low percentage of groups having incomes of $2,000 or more, two-fifths of the families reporting mechanical refrigerators in each city have incomes of not less

[1] The one from which the information in this section is drawn—*Market Res. Ser. No.* 5.12—covers Cleveland, Ohio; Decatur, Ill., Lincoln, Neb., Sioux Falls, S.D., Topeka, Kans., Wichita, Kans., Asheville, N.C., Greensboro, N.C., Hagerstown, Md., Wheeling, W.Va., Baton Rouge, La., Wichita Falls, Tex., Boise, Idaho; Butte, Mont., Phoenix, Ariz., Sacramento, Calif.

than $2,000. Moreover, the percentage of users in any one income class (below $5,000) tends to exceed the percentage of users in any lower group. Since, however, there is a relatively small number of families in the higher classes, the bulk of mechanical refrigerators is held by those with incomes between $1,000 and $3,000.

One would think offhand that everyone now has the benefit of modern bathing facilities. But such is not the fact. Though in some cities the percentage not having such facilities in their homes is only 4 per cent, in others it is much higher. Indeed, in Greensboro, N.C., according to the study, bathtub or shower installations are lacking for 43 per cent of all reporting families. The absence of installed bathing equipment is definitely associated with low incomes. Irrespective of race, most of the families reporting no installed equipment have incomes of less than $1,000. As a general rule, furthermore, the percentage of families without installed bathing facilities tends to diminish in each successive income group from the lowest to the highest. Conversely, there is a general tendency for each successive higher income class to have a greater proportion of families with two or more tubs.

Income has a direct bearing on the use of heating facilities also. This relationship is indicated by the fact that, in those cities where central heating plants are used to an appreciable extent, the percentage of families reporting the use of heating stoves tends to decrease in each successively higher income class. Moreover, from 60 to 80 per cent of all reporting families using stoves have incomes of less than $1,000. Conversely, there is a definite tendency for each successively higher income class to have more homes equipped with central plants than the group immediately below.

The income-and-consumption relationship obtrudes itself even at the level of the bare necessities. In the use of fuel for heating, the relatively few wood-burning families are those having less than $1,000 per annum. Oil is used in a larger percentage of families as incomes increase. In the matter of cooking fuel: in each city of the study, the proportion of people using gas for cooking in any income class below $3,000 tends to be larger in each higher income group. In those cities showing an appreciable use of electricity for cooking, a similar relationship is indicated.

Income, then, materially conditions the consumption of certain commodities. Wants arising out of fundamental requirements are satisfied in varying ways according to the amount of money available for expenditures. Moreover, there are many individuals whose wants are satisfied in a very inadequate manner at the present time. Some of this, no doubt, is due to depression conditions. Some, however, is probably due to the chronic economic ineffectiveness of the breadwinner of the family. In some instances, no doubt, consumption difficulties arise out of inefficiency in purchasing and through poor household management. That is to say, the family with small income chooses to maintain a motorcar (say) rather than to provide more effectively for their more fundamental requirements.

3. Variations in Consumption as among Periods of Time.—The consumption of a particular commodity over a period of time varies because of changes in the demand for the commodity or because of changes in its price. These causes are so closely connected in practice that it is nearly impossible to distinguish between them. The principal causes of changes in demand are (1) changes in the income of the people, (2) the growth of population and changes in its composition, and (3) changes in the habits of the people. The results of changes in the incomes of consumers have been outlined in Chap. III; the results of the growth of population and the changes in its composition are considered somewhat at length in Chap. XIX; some of the demand relations of commodities and results of their changes are taken up in the present chapter.

Changes in the prices of products, in the sense in which we are dealing with the problem here, to some extent at least arise from changes in production costs of a given quantity of product. When these costs are compared over a long period of time, many changes are found to have taken place. Inventions and improvements have reduced the cost of many commodities, formerly luxuries, until they are now necessaries. Two general classes of goods stand out, those which have historical decreasing costs of production and those which have historical increasing costs of production. These costs are not absolute but are relative to one another. There are very few commodities for which the absolute costs have risen. The general group that represents the commodities having historical increasing costs is agricultural products.

Manufactured products as a group represent historical decreasing costs. When an index of prices of agricultural products and an index of the prices of manufactured products are compared for any considerable period of time, the price of agricultural products is found to rise steadily, relative to manufactured products. This means, of course, that the costs of producing manufactured products have fallen much more rapidly than the costs of producing agricultural products.

General changes in the consumption of particular articles are evident wherever we have the data. Unfortunately, these data are somewhat meager, and all that can be done at present is to show the situation with regard to certain products. Within recognized data limitations, an attempt is made to show three sorts of regular changes: (1) long-time changes, called *trends*, (2) fluctuations above and below the long-time trend, called *cyclical fluctuations*, and (3) regular fluctuations within the period of a year, called *seasonal fluctuations*. Besides these regular changes, there are occasional irregular or sporadic changes.

In an economic society such as ours—a society based upon freedom of enterprise—tremendous changes occur over a period of time. Consumption habits change owing to the introduction of new commodities, to changes in the income of the members of society, and to altered conditions of life. Thus, automobiles, radios, rayon, and electrical refrigeration are the product of the present century, and their introduction has had a marked influence on consumption patterns. Moreover, these products have displaced other products (horse-drawn vehicles, phonographs, silk, and ice). Progress thus makes for dislocation of industry but is necessary if we are to accept improvement.

Table 40 gives indices of the value of product of certain industries for the years 1923–1929. Although this period is very short, the changes shown are quite striking. Thus, increases of at least 35 per cent have appeared in proprietary drugs, rayon, and mechanical refrigeration in a period in which population was increasing at a rate of only 1½ per cent per annum and general prices remained approximately the same.

For some of these products and for some others, additional data obtain. For example, the per capita consumption of silk in the United States increased almost 400 per cent during the quarter century 1900–1925. Within the last decade, however, artificial silk has gained tremendous headway until by 1935 the value of rayon manufactures was 35 per cent higher than the value of silk manufactures. Cigarette production has also shown a phenomenal advance, increasing some 150 per cent even in the past decade.

TABLE 40.—INDICES OF THE VALUE OF SELECTED ITEMS MANUFACTURED IN THE UNITED STATES, 1923–1929[1]
(Except for rayon and mechanical refrigeration, 1923 = 100)

Products	1923	1929
Book and job printing	100	134
Patent and proprietary medicine	100	135
Rayon	100[2]	137
Rubber tubes and tires	100	120
Mechanical refrigeration	100[2]	167
Cigars and cigarettes	100	130

[1] Adapted from data in "Statistical Abstract of the United States," Table 738, 1934.
[2] 1927 = 100.

Consumption patterns have altered greatly in other fields as well. For example, the ready-to-wear business, practically unknown 50 years ago, is now one of our foremost industries. Indeed, from 1914 to 1925 alone, per capita production of women's clothing (not including custom-made garments) increased one and one-half times.[1]

Similar changes have occurred in other phases of our economic activities. Thus, although the number of passenger automobiles (and taxis) registered in 1910 was only a little over 450,000, that figure had reached 26,500,000 a quarter of a century later. As further evidence of the dynamic nature of our society, the 1930 figure for passenger mileage of automobiles, hardly in existence at the turn of the century, was estimated to have reached the astonishing total of 332,000,000,000.[2] The increase in the use of radios is another twentieth-century phenomenon. One can hardly credit the changes that have occurred in this field. Here is an industry, practically nonexistent in 1920, which during the subsequent decade had placed enough sets in homes so that by 1932 over 16 million were in use. No wonder that the motion-

[1] Adapted from data in PAUL H. NYSTROM, *op. cit.*, p. 406.
[2] "Recent Social Trends in the United States," p. 178.

picture industry which was considered to be "depression-proof" in earlier years now finds itself in the trough of recession.

Accompanying the foregoing changes have appeared others equally important. Although there are few data showing the growth of newspaper and periodical consumption over an extended period, the few figures we have indicate important changes here also. For example, the circulation of newspapers in the United States increased 36 per cent from 1921 to 1931.[1] Periodicals—weeklies, class, general monthly, and women's—also showed changes. Indeed, in the four years 1927–1931 there was an 18 per cent increase in circulation of periodicals of this type.[2]

Changes have occurred even in living-accommodation requirements. "Changing manners of living in regard to such matters as permanency of tenure and size of home unit affect directly certain types of consumption. In 1920 only 2.1 per cent of the families in the Borough of Manhattan owned their homes (either free or encumbered) as against 30.7 per cent in New York State as a whole and 65.3 per cent in North Dakota; the Middle Atlantic states ranked lowest as a group with 37.2 per cent, while the West North Central group was highest with 56.4 per cent. Increased building costs, coupled with the desire to invest in other things than spare rooms and space within the home, have operated in the direction of smaller living units. Reviewing current trends in Denver, the University of Denver *Business Review* for January, 1931, said: 'The smaller number of children per family, lessened interest in the home as a social center, . . . the transfer of space-using kitchen and laundry activities to commercial enterprises, and the decreased portion of the family income available for home purchase and maintainance are typical changes which lead to the insistent demand for smaller and smaller living units.' Actual trends in new construction of different types and sizes of housing units in Denver are reflected by the percentages of dwellings of each type (in the summary from the same source as shown in the table on p. 220).

"The increases in small apartments and in small houses indicated here are particularly significant. New apartments built

[1] Adapted from figures presented by MALCOLM M. WILLEY and STUART A. RICE, "Communication Agencies and Social Life," p. 160.

[2] *Ibid.*, p. 166.

in New York City in 1913 averaged 4.19 rooms; this figure had declined to 3.63 in 1925 and 3.34 in 1928."[1]

Changes in consumption habits are not confined to durable consumption goods. Interestingly enough, actual trends can be

Types of housing units	Prior to 1901	1901–1915	1916–1925	1926–1930
One story, single houses	29.2	34.5	70.5	58.8
Two or more stories, single houses	24.9	20.9	4.1	4.0
Apartments:				
With no bedroom	2.1	4.7	6.1	9.8
With 1 bedroom	4.6	9.8	4.8	18.6
With 2 or more bedrooms	1.6	2.2	1.6	2.0
All others[1]	37.6	27.9	12.9	6.8

[1] Including terraces, double houses, 2-family houses (chiefly remodeled 1-family houses), shacks ("houses now valued at less than $200 by the Tax Assessor"), and rebuilt apartments (chiefly large single houses made over); data on the last three indicate the period of original construction, not time of remodeling or of depreciation to the shack classification.

discovered in eating habits. Table 41 indicates such changes. Thus, it can be seen that increases have occurred in the consumption of ice cream and sugar; decreases in that of pork, milk, beef, flour, and butter. Indeed, from the other sources one is able to conclude that the per capita consumption of meat has declined during the first 30 years of the present century. Part of this is due, it is thought, to a reduction in the need for a heavy diet resulting from increased use of the automobile, part to the use of small apartments in which meats are inconvenient to prepare, and part to installment selling and its rigid enforcement of economy in food purchase.[2] Whatever the causes, there is no gainsaying the partial replacement of meats by fruits, vegetables, and salads in the dietary program of consumers.

As was mentioned previously, the consumption of goods varies with the ebb and flow of business activity also. Though cyclical variations in consumption have not been studied very completely, we know that such variations are largely matters of changes of income. All articles are not, of course, similarly affected. Staple food products remain relatively constant, but clothing

[1] "Recent Social Trends in the United States," pp. 864–865.

[2] Ralph F. Breyer, "Commodity Marketing," p. 205.

and shoes fluctuate quite definitely. In general, as is indicated in Chap. IV, the volume of transitory goods acquired remains relatively constant in time of depression whereas the volume of durable consumption goods acquired declines drastically, although there are some exceptions. The sales of the latter

TABLE 41.—PER CAPITA CONSUMPTION OF CERTAIN FOODS IN THE UNITED STATES AT 5-YEAR INTERVALS

Year	Beef,[1] pounds	Pork,[1] pounds	Milk, and cream[1] in cities and villages, gallons	Flour,[2] barrels	Butter,[1] pounds	Ice cream,[1] gallons	Sugar,[1] pounds
1900	67.4	71.9	....	1.134[5]	19.9[5]	....	72.6
1905	71.4	70.6	....	1.131[6]	....	....	76.6
1910	70.6	62.4	....	1.073[7]	18.4	1.04	78.6
1915	57.4	67.3	....	1.071[8]	17.4[3]	2.08	79.7
1920	59.2	63.5	....	0.889[9]	14.8	2.46	99.6
1925	59.9	67.3	....	0.898	17.6	2.80	114.9[4]
1930	48.7	67.0	40.1	0.852	17.3	1.96	103.8
1935	52.9	48.5	37.0	0.775	17.1	1.56	101.3

[1] Estimates of the U.S. Department of Agriculture.
[2] Estimates of the Food Research Institute.
[3] Factory production only.
[4] For the crop year beginning July.
[5] For 1899.
[6] For 1904.
[7] For 1908.
[8] For 1914.
[9] For 1921.

type of products are, of course, only an imperfect index of their consumption. What actually happens, in some instances, is that old durable goods are utilized longer in time of depression. Utilization, therefore, might actually remain constant even with a drastic decline in sales volume.

The last type of consumption variation in point of time is that which appears more or less regularly within the year. Thus, the consumption of many articles varies seasonally and though retail sales are not always concomitant with consumption they indicate consumption fairly satisfactorily in some instances. For most retail products there is a marked seasonality in sales. Table 42 shows the seasonal variations in retail sales for a number of different types of stores.

TABLE 42.—SEASONAL VARIATIONS IN RETAIL SALES IN DIFFERENT TYPES OF STORES[1]

Kind of store	Jan.	Feb.	Mar.	Apr.	May	June	July	Aug.	Sept.	Oct.	Nov.	Dec.
Department...	87	77	100	104	103	100	75	78	91	112	113	160
Mail order....	99	91	115	100	87	84	74	77	97	128	126	122
Grocery chain	100	95	106	101	98	96	98	97	97	105	102	105
Five-and-ten cent........	72	75	95	95	96	92	92	96	94	108	94	122
Cigar chain...	88	86	96	96	101	96	99	97	99	107	100	135
Drug chain...	97	91	100	98	98	98	101	100	99	102	94	122
Shoe chain....	75	68	96	121	116	106	95	79	92	113	110	129
Music chain..	84	85	93	86	82	78	75	88	102	119	121	187
Candy chain..	84	85	96	102	97	92	98	101	100	103	95	147

[1] H. B. VANDERBLUE, "Problems in Business Economics," p. 65.

In most of these lines, there are pronounced seasonal movements. There are generally two periods of dullness in most

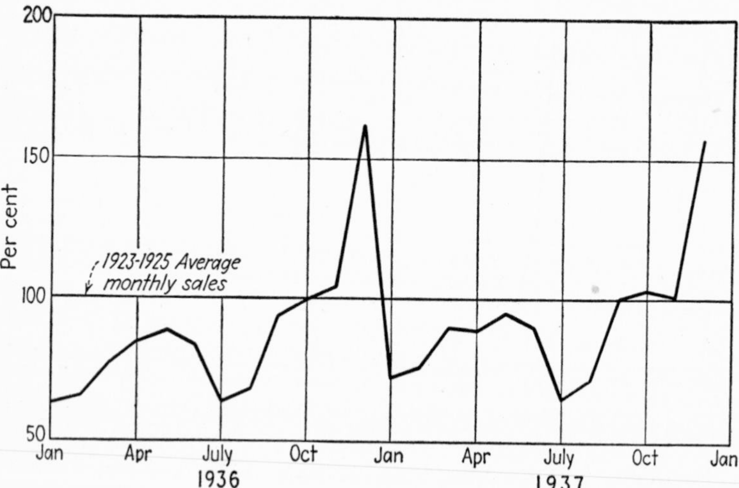

FIG. 6.—Seasonal variation in department store sales in the United States, 1936–1937.

lines, the first during January and February, and the second during July and August. There is usually a considerable volume during the spring months and an increase in volume during the fall, which reaches a peak in December. The winter dullness is most pronounced in the five-and-ten-cent and shoe stores. The midsummer inactivity affects the department stores, mail-order houses, and music stores particularly. The candy- and drugstores have considerable hot-weather business. Figure 6 shows the variations during 1936 and 1937 in the sales by department stores located in various portions of the United States. This graphic presentation of seasonality illustrates both the reasons for and the relative lack of success of department-store special events. The various lines making up the total sales have different seasonal variations as is shown in the accompanying figure of the sales of men's clothing and women's dresses in New England department stores.

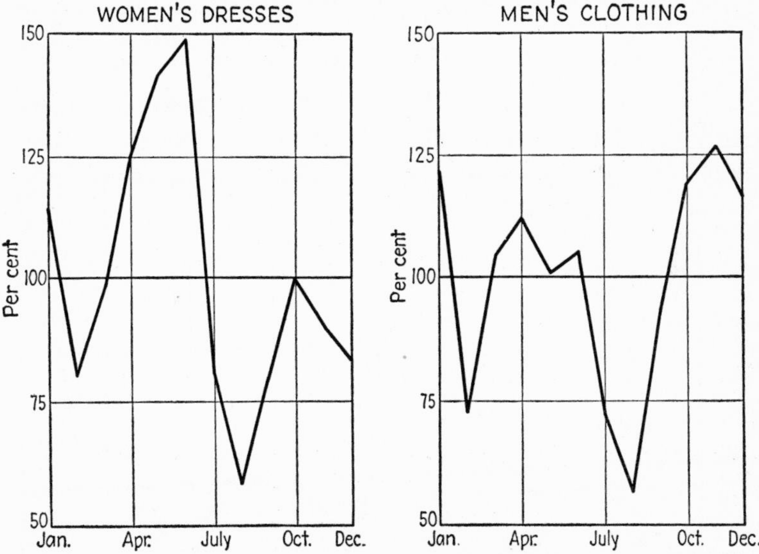

FIG. 7.—Seasonal variation in sales by New England department stores, 1926–1930.

Particular commodities, likewise, show distinct seasonal variations in consumption. The accompanying charts show some of the variations in the consumption of milk and cream in greater New York City. Milk and cream are particularly good examples, because a constant price is maintained throughout the year and variations in sales show true changes in demand. The graph for milk shows a peak of consumption in the warm months with consumption falling off on either side in the cooler months.

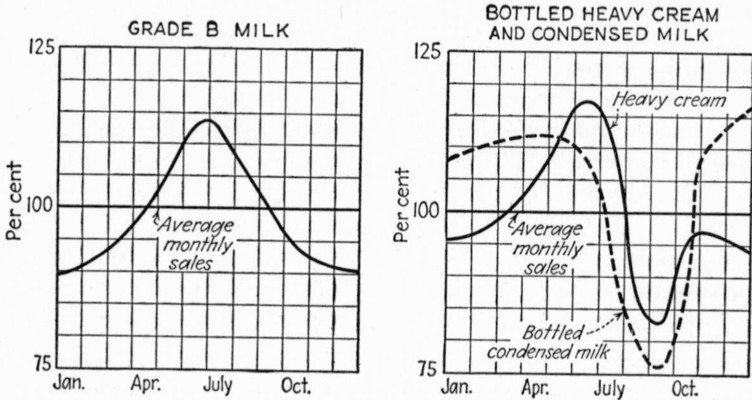

FIG. 8.—Seasonal variation in sales of dairy products in greater New York.

The heavy-cream curve shows a peak in May and June during the berry season, with a very great slump in August and September during the vacation period. Consumers of heavy cream are in a high enough income group customarily to take vacations. The condensed-milk-sales curve is explained by the variations in coffee drinking, bottled condensed milk being purchased by many New York consumers for use in their coffee instead of cream. Coffee drinking, of course, falls off materially during the warm weather.

4. Variations in Consumption as among Places.—Finally, the consumption of articles varies greatly as among places. A great many factors are responsible for these differences. Differences in nationality, income, price of products, climate, occupation, age, and composition of populations are all important. As was suggested previously, one of the most important conditioning factors is income, since, without it, goods may not be acquired even though they are desired.

There appear to be vast differences in income in different places. Thus, as can be seen in Table 43, income varies tremendously in various countries. These differences are explained to a large extent by differences in the extent and quality of natural resources. Some of them, too, are due to differences in technical skill among the workers of the several countries.

Variations in the degree to which capital equipment is used and the efficiency of the type of production organization under which industry works are also important. That the United States leads in most of these matters there is little doubt. That income is higher in the United States than in other countries is similarly manifest.

TABLE 43.—PER CAPITA INCOME ESTIMATES FOR VARIOUS COUNTRIES[1]

Country	Year	Per capita income, current dollars	Per capita income, 1913 dollars
United States	1928	749	541
United Kingdom	1928	411	293
Germany	1928	279	199
France	1928	192	188
Italy	1928	121	96
Russia	1929	107	62
Japan	1925	89	53

[1] SIMON KUZNETS, National Income, "Encyclopaedia of the Social Sciences," vol. 11, p. 206.

Income is not uniformly high in the United States, however. Nor are consumption patterns the same from region to region. Table 44 is proof of this contention. As can be seen, personal income in one section of the country (Middle Atlantic) is over three times as great as that in another (East South Central).

Tremendous differences in consumption patterns are also clearly indicated from the figures in Table 44. Some of these differences, without doubt, are due to factors other than income. For example, it is not reasonable to assume that people on the Pacific coast eat three times as much or as expensively as those located in the East South Central section of the country. Part of the difference in sales volume, without question, is due to the fact that the latter on the average produce much of their own food. Part of the differences in apparel sales can be similarly explained.

The same situation does not obtain in connection with furniture and automobiles, however. But even here the *use* of furniture and automobiles is not revealed by the sales figures. These data, at most, indicate the relative value of *new* merchandise acquired.

The figures in Table 45 are somewhat more revealing. These at least indicate *use* of certain items. Again there are striking variations among areas. On the Pacific coast, for example, per capita passenger-car registration is over three times as great as

TABLE 44.—INDICES OF PER CAPITA INCOME AND OF PER CAPITA SALES CLASSIFIED ACCORDING TO THE KIND OF STORE, FOR UNITED STATES REGIONAL DIVISIONS, 1929[1]
(East South Central figures = 100)

Region	Per capita personal income[2]	Total retail sales	Food including restaurant	Apparel	Furniture and household	Automotive
East South Central	100	100	100	100	100	100
South Atlantic	135	122	139	154	120	119
West South Central	138	139	139	131	130	170
West North Central	160	185	179	238	150	209
Mountain	193	192	208	177	170	233
East North Central	242	205	260	315	200	205
New England	261	210	295	331	210	186
Middle Atlantic	318	227	320	423	270	172
Pacific	290	249	302	331	250	296

[1] Adapted from "Recent Social Trends in the United States," p. 891 (except income data).
[2] Adapted from "America's Capacity to Consume," *op. cit.*, p. 173.

TABLE 45.—INDICES OF PER CAPITA PASSENGER-CAR REGISTRATIONS, 1934, SUBSCRIPTIONS TO TELEPHONE SERVICE, 1935, AND WIRED HOMES, 1930, FOR THE SEVERAL UNITED STATES REGIONAL DIVISIONS[1]
(East South Central figures = 100)

Region	Per capita passenger-car registrations 1934	Residence telephones 1935	Wired homes 1930
East South Central	100	100	100
South Atlantic	140	136	134
West South Central	161	147	125
West North Central	250	339	212
Mountain	219	208	207
East North Central	229	280	288
New England	195	322	328
Middle Atlantic	183	264	316
Pacific	329	356	368

[1] Adapted from "Consumer Market Data Handbook," pp. R22, R39, 1936.

in the East South Central section. Similar contrasts appear in respect to residence telephone subscriptions and wired homes. Differences between certain other sections are almost as striking.

Obviously, automobile registration indicates at least an *opportunity* to consume. Telephone-subscription and wired-home figures are similarly indicative. Wired homes is a particularly important index of consumption in that certain types of goods can be consumed only if the home is wired. To put it in a negative way, electrical appliances, most mechanical refrigeration, and modern radios cannot be consumed if electrification is absent.

Some of these differences are, again, due to differences in income; some, of course, to differences in environment. For example, in certain places automobiles are not so essential as in others. Also, telephones are probably much more of a necessity under certain circumstances than under others. Differences in the percentage of wired homes cannot be explained quite so easily by nonincome factors. In other words, most of the differences here are probably due to differences in income among the several regional divisions.

These differences among areas are to be found in other items also. For example, in January, 1932, according to an estimate, there were over 16 million radio sets in use in the United States. The distribution of these sets varied from rural to urban sections; from region to region. The largest proportion of families with radios appeared in the Middle Atlantic states; the smallest in the East South Central section. Differences were strikingly manifest among various states as well. For example, ownership in New Jersey was 63.3 per cent; in Mississippi, only 5.4 per cent. Highest percentage of ownership appeared in the Eastern, Northern, and Pacific states; lowest in the South.[1] Part of this variation is due, doubtless, to educational differences. Part, too, is due to differences in adequacy of power facilities in various sections of the country. Most of it, however, probably is due to differences in economic status.

Thus we see that variations in consumption occur from group to group, from time to time, and from place to place. Some of these differences are desirable; some of them definitely undesirable. For example, changes in consumption in point of time probably on the whole are advantageous. More and better goods presumably emerge from the dynamic economic process. On the other hand, the differences that are manifest as among income and geographical groups are very disturbing. It is

[1] "Recent Social Trends in the United States," p. 211.

particularly discouraging when one recalls the fact that there is some tendency for poverty to engender poverty.

Questions

1. Discuss the sources of prestige value in the consumption of goods in modern society.
2. Do you think that the prestige values of the future will be more or less rational? Give the reasons for your answer.
3. How does it happen that fashion is more important than ever before in the United States? Can its existence be justified socially? Explain.
4. Distinguish clearly scales and standards of living. What is meant by the American standard of living? What determines living standards? Scales?
5. There are striking variations in consumption as among places, times, and groups. What are the most important factors giving rise to these differences?

CHAPTER XIV

CONSUMERS' PURCHASING HABITS AND THE MARKETING SYSTEM

Marketing is the group of activities that are involved in the flow of goods and services from the point of production (in the narrow sense of the term) to the point of consumption. Marketing has to do with the creation of time, place, possession, and information utilities; *i.e.*, it actually produces want satisfactions since the mere creation of form utility does not complete the production cycle. The consumer should dispel the notion that the marketing system is a useless appendage to a very vital production system. There are many invaluable tasks that must be performed in order that goods and services be made available to consumers. Anything that affects the efficiency of the system is worthy of consumer attention. The marketing system has been the target of a great deal of adverse criticism by layman and economist alike. It is essential that the person interested in consumer problems should have a sound understanding of the organization and operation of the system. Without such a grounding, competent criticism is impossible.

The tasks performed by the marketing system are termed *marketing functions*. To these we shall turn our attention for a moment.

The functional approach to the subject of marketing is useful since not only is it a timesaver in that one no longer needs to study the marketing systems of scores of commodities in order to understand fundamentals, but it also gives one perspective in thinking about the subject since the basic functions must be undertaken by someone *regardless of the economic order under which the marketing system works*. There are, in other words, certain fundamental tasks that must be undertaken if goods and services are to be completely produced. These tasks are as follows:

I. Functions of Exchange.
   1. Buying:
      a. Determining the consumer requirements—amounts, styles, sizes, etc.
      b. Seeking out sources of supply.
      c. Assembling goods at the proper time and place.
   2. Selling:
      a. Seeking out buyers.
      b. Informing and persuading prospective buyers.
      c. Arranging prices and titles.
      d. Dividing, packing, and arranging delivery.

II. Facilitating Functions.
   1. Financing:
      a. Furnishing capital for purchasing merchandise.
      b. Arranging credit.
      c. Carrying accounts.
      d. Making collections.
   2. Standardization (the setting up of tests—size, quality, or what not—for the purpose of making grading possible).

III. Physical Functions.
   1. Grading (classifying goods according to accepted standards):
      a. Making possible sale by description and sample.
      b. Reducing storage and transportation costs by eliminating unsalable products.
   2. Transportation (the medium making specialization of area possible):
      a. International and interstate and intercity movements of goods.
      b. Intracity deliveries.
   3. Storage:
      a. Making possible supply of goods at the time and place required by the consumer.
      b. Improving or protecting quality of goods.
      c. Making possible the awaiting of more favorable demand conditions.

IV. The Universal Function.
   1. Risk-bearing—marketing institutions must bear the risks of:
      a. Price changes.
      b. Physical damage or deterioration.
      c. Changes in demand.
      d. Liability, etc.

From the preceding tabulation it can be seen readily that there are actual necessary services which must be performed by the marketing system in order that goods be made available for consumption. As to the question of who performs the various functions, no satisfactory generalization can be made. Presumably all marketing functionaries aid in some degree. Were it not so, competition would force them out of the system although it must be admitted that this elimination process might be quite slow. Channels of distribution are made up of various types of individuals and institutions, and the specific method of distribution of any one product depends upon relative costs and the relative effectiveness of the several alternative methods that are available.

It is often argued by the layman that costs of marketing are much higher than they should be because there are too many middlemen. Such a statement reveals a lack of understanding of the system. Though it may be true that there are too many middlemen in some instances, it might well be argued that there are too few in others. Many commodities could not be efficiently distributed by direct methods. Certainly no one would argue that the California grower of iceberg lettuce would be better off if he were to market his commodity directly to consumers located in New York City. Anyone taking such a position fails to recognize the tremendous economic gains to be derived from specialization of effort.

1. The Marketing Process.—The goods that the consumer purchases fall quite readily into three classes when considered on the basis of his buying habits. These are called *convenience* goods, *shopping* goods, and *specialty* goods. Convenience goods are those which the consumer purchases in the most convenient manner possible. They generally comprise things of low unit value, purchased at frequent intervals. Such things as bread and tooth paste fall into the convenience-goods class. Shopping goods include those things which the consumer desires to compare in price and quality in a number of establishments before purchasing. They are usually relatively expensive items purchased infrequently. Style goods, such as women's clothes and furniture, are examples of such goods. Specialty goods, finally, are those which are sufficiently different from other goods in the same class to possess reputation enough to cause the consumer to go to considerable inconvenience—usually to a particular firm—to purchase them. Automobiles, typewriters, and radios fall into this class. Hence, grocery stores are known as convenience institutions; department stores as shopping institutions; and radio shops as specialty institutions.

For the purposes of the student of consumption, little need be said about actual marketing technique. Suffice it is to say there are literally scores of different types of functionaries involved—brokers, jobbers, wholesalers, retailers, advertising agents, and what not; that some are *functional middlemen* (nontitle takers) and others merchants; that each specializes and presumably justifies his existence at any one time by producing his service in an efficient manner; that markets are of two general types—industrial and consumer.

Tables 46 and 47 give in condensed form the essential facts regarding marketing channels. Table 46 indicates that direct methods are utilized to an appreciable extent in the sale of some items (*e.g.*, industrial commodities) but that middlemen are

TABLE 46.—PERCENTAGE DISTRIBUTION OF SALES OF MANUFACTURING PLANTS IN THE UNITED STATES BY CHANNELS, 1929–1933[1]
(Based on selling value f.o.b. factory)

Channels	1933		1929	
	Amount, thousands	Percentage of total	Amount, thousands	Percentage of total
Total goods distributed by manufacturers	$28,088,000	100.0	$63,409,200	100.0
Sales to wholesalers	....	32.0	....	29.6
Sales to industrial users and large consumers	....	27.8	....	31.3
Sales to retailers and manufacturers' own retail branches	....	21.3	....	20.5
Sales to manufacturers' own wholesale branches	....	16.0	....	16.1
Sales to home consumers	....	2.9	....	2.5

[1] Adapted from census figures. T. N. BECKMAN and N. H. ENGLE, "Wholesaling," p. 112.

utilized for approximately 60 per cent of the total value of goods handled; that the wholesaler still has a definite place in the marketing picture. Indeed, it will be noted that wholesalers carried a greater proportion of total volume in 1933 than in 1929, which indicates that there are some conditions—*e.g.*, situations of depressed volume—in which the manufacturer cannot afford to utilize more direct methods but must employ agencies whose total volume is large enough to absorb the burden of overhead.

Table 47 shows the percentage of sales through various retail outlets. It is interesting to note in this connection that independent stores in general still do 73 per cent of the total retail business although the chains are continuing to make gains. As will be seen later (Table 53), the chains have made much greater inroads in some fields than in others. Incidentally mail-order houses, representing a more direct method of distribution, handle

TABLE 47.—PERCENTAGE DISTRIBUTION OF SALES IN DIFFERENT TYPES OF STORES, 1929, 1933, AND 1935[1]

Types	1935, total retail sales, in thousands, $33,161,276	1933, total retail sales, in thousands, $25,037,225	1929, total retail sales, in thousands, $49,114,654
Independents	73.1	71.3	77.5
Chains	22.8	25.4	20.0
Mail order	1.3	1.0	1.0
State liquor	0.5		
Direct selling	0.4	0.4	0.2
Leased departments	0.4	.....	0.3
Utility operated	0.4	0.3	0.3
Others	1.1	1.6	0.7
Total	100.0	100.0	100.0

[1] Census of business, 1935, "Retail Distribution," vol. I, p. 1-22.

a relatively small volume. Table 48 indicates the percentage of retail sales volume done by each of several types of commodity institutions. It is an interesting commentary on the modern way of life that in the United States in 1935, although the food-store volume was the largest, sales by automotive and motor-fuel outlets accounted for almost 20 per cent of the total retail sales volume.

One other phase of marketing that should be understood by the student of consumption economics is the nature of the market in the geographical sense. This requires a brief description of market areas. A trade or market area may be of any one of several types, depending upon the stage that a product has reached in the marketing process. A manufacturer's trade area, for example, is usually very extensive; it may be coterminous with the boundaries of the United States or even larger. A wholesale trade area, on the other hand, is generally less extensive, and a retail area is usually still narrower.

Retail market areas vary in size according to the economic importance of the trade centers that serve them, the number and types of highways tapping the area, the mobility of the residents, the wealth and the standard of living of the population, and the number, importance, and proximity of rival trade centers. The general trade area of a trade center is made up of the individual trade areas of the individual stores in that city. The sizes of these individual trade areas vary even as among

TABLE 48.—PERCENTAGE DISTRIBUTION OF RETAIL DOLLAR SALES VOLUME BY BUSINESS GROUPS, 1929–1935[1]

Business group	1935	1933	1929
Food stores	25.22	27.07	22.07
General merchandise	13.93	15.54	13.12
Automotive	13.89	11.53	15.94
Apparel	8.01	7.68	8.63
Eating and drinking	7.21	5.71	4.33
Filling station	5.93	6.12	3.64
Lumber, building, hardware	5.62	5.36	7.83
Furniture, household	3.89	3.83	5.61
Drug	3.72	4.26	3.44
General stores	3.35	4.38	5.23
Second hand	0.34	0.42	0.30
Others	8.89	8.10	9.86
Total	100.0	100.0	100.0

[1] Census of business, 1935, "Retail Distribution," vol. I, p. 1-08.

different stores handling the same types of merchandise, some (as a result of superior reputation or what not) enjoying a wide patronage and others having to be satisfied with a much more circumscribed clientele.

An individual market area is a link in a chain, the whole of which is a market in the price-making sense. Because of the influence of external demand-and-supply conditions, no one market area is a self-contained unit. A person living within the limits of a certain retail trade area does not necessarily make all his purchases within that area. If prices vary enough, he will shift his patronage from one place to another. Because of overlapping areas and the mobility of the average consumer, this usually is not difficult.[1] Nor is the market *center* self-contained from the point of view of supply. Prices charged the retailer by the wholesaler result from supply-and-demand conditions throughout a large area, perhaps the whole of the United States, the conditions in any one component trade area having in itself no great amount of influence upon the resulting price.

An individual market area, however, has a great deal of influence upon the *price policy* of the merchants located in the trade center. Commodities are produced in innumerable quality lines. Price lines which the merchants feel will be popular with their clientele may vary from town to town and even from store to store. The class of consumer—his income and way of living

[1] During the past fifteen or twenty years, "the average trade area for consumers outside the urban district has been increased from a radius of five or six miles to one of thirty to one hundred and fifty miles. This change is the result of a number of circumstances, all interrelated, no one of which can be considered without regard to the others. The causes of the widening of retail trade areas in a general way can be said to have two aspects, the technological and the psychological. Technological improvements have led to reduction of prices of many commodities and, at the same time, have been important factors in the trend toward increased incomes. A recent study shows an increase of 25 per cent in per capita real income in the United States from 1919 to 1929. The decrease in price of automobiles over a period of years may be cited as an example of reduced prices resulting from technological improvements. The psychological aspect is reflected in a higher standard, as distinguished from scale of living. This change is due in part at least to certain inherent traits in human nature and in part to a tremendous psychological effect of improved communication. The most important specific causes of widening retail trade areas, having in varying degrees technological and psychological implications, are as follows: (1) The increased number and improved quality of automobiles, making it possible for the consumer to travel thirty miles in the time that he formerly traveled five. (2) The increased number of improved highways, which reduces the irksomeness of long distance travel. (3) Increased motion picture attendance, increased number of radio receiving sets, and wide reading, all of which make for increased knowledge and stimulate interest in the newest types of merchandise. (4) The expansion of rural free delivery routes, which now makes it unnecessary for the rural dweller to go to the village for his mail. (5) The tendency of wide areas to become still wider, due to the fact that where trading is concentrated in larger centers rather than scattered among many it is economically practicable to establish chain stores and mail order branch retail concerns, which in turn draw more people from the smaller near-by towns to the larger, more distant towns." RALPH CASSADY, JR., and HARRY J. OSTLUND, "The Retail Distribution Structure of the Small City," pp. 21–22.

—in the trade area determines to a great extent the class of merchandise that will be offered for sale, since the merchant selects the merchandise he believes his customers will be able to buy. Thus, although the prices among several cities or towns may vary greatly, the quality of the merchandise handled, except for standard items, probably varies roughly in proportion. Since competition is far from perfect, however, some price differences exist not only among stores in different towns but among stores in the same community. Some stores, indeed, enjoy a quasi monopoly as regards location.

To summarize the discussion thus far, then, marketing is a very necessary part of the production system since the mere manufacture of goods does not make them available to those wishing to consume them. In the complete marketing process, there are certain essential tasks which must be performed. The performance of such functions is assumed by various functionaries —individuals or institutions—whose existence is justified by their ability to undertake efficiently certain portions of the marketing burden. The manufacturers choose their marketing channels on the basis of the relative effectiveness with which the job can be accomplished by various combinations of functionaries.

The consumer-buyer is part of the retail market area within which is a market center. To this center come goods from which the consumer makes choices. Owing to a combination of factors, retail prices among various areas are very similar, though the price lines that each group of merchants features may be quite different since they depend upon the incomes and desires of particular classes of individuals.

2. Increasing Marketing Costs.—From the evidence obtained currently, it would appear that marketing costs are increasing. Although the costs of marketing some commodities have perhaps declined during the past 20 years (*e.g.*, costs of staple groceries), many others have increased. In 1929, for every dollar spent in the manufacture of goods, some 85 cents was spent in the marketing process. In general, the marketing process probably takes a greater share of the consumer's dollar than heretofore. The reasons for such a situation are worthy of some attention.

Probably the most important cause underlying increased costs of marketing is that the techniques of production (again in the narrow sense of the term) have improved to such an extent that greater and greater quantities of goods have been produced. In other words, the manufacturing side of the system has, by means of an improved technological process, been enabled to increase production, and the resultant increased product has been turned over to the marketing system to sell. Though manufacturing is, in a manner of speaking, of a decreasing-cost nature, marketing is more a constant- or increasing-cost type. Marketing is largely without benefit of technological aids and, hence, must carry the burden by means of the increased use of labor. Evidence supporting this increased use of man power in marketing is found in Table 49. Though in 1870 only 10 per cent of those gainfully employed were employed in marketing, by 1930 this figure had increased to over 20 per cent. Between the same years, the percentage of those engaged in manufacturing had declined from 69 to 53 per cent.

Table 49.—Percentage of Those Gainfully Employed in Production, Marketing, and Professional Occupations, 1870–1930[1]

Year	Production	Marketing	Professional, clerical, and domestic
1870	69.0	9.9	21.1
1880	66.1	10.8	23.1
1890	62.7	14.6	22.7
1900	60.0	16.4	23.6
1910	63.5	16.4	20.1
1920	59.7	17.6	22.7
1930	52.8	20.4	26.8

[1] Adapted from census data. Paul D. Converse, "Elements of Marketing," rev. ed. p. 11.

The more goods there are to distribute, the greater the attempts to manipulate demand. The buying public is thus importuned on every hand, by newspapers, radio, magazine, and billboard, to buy more, better, or different goods. Every type of sales-promotional device imaginable has been utilized in an effort to sell more goods. At the same time, unfortunately, advertising effectiveness tends to be reduced owing to the offsetting effect of competitive campaigns and to consumer resistance which accompanies the attempt to load the consumer with more goods than he can conveniently purchase.

Another factor giving rise to increased marketing costs is the fact that goods are being carried greater distances now than heretofore. It is a well-known fact that transportation makes specialization of area possible and that specialization of area is a definite characteristic of our modern economy. Instead of a system giving rise to self-sufficient small areas, the law of comparative advantage makes for specialization and a subsequent exchange of goods. This condition gives rise to greater use of transportation facilities. Furthermore, many manufacturers are successful in differentiating their several brands of products with the result that such products are demanded by consumers regardless of their origin. Hence, while many New Englanders are purchasing shoes manufactured in the St. Louis area, the residents of the latter region may be buying shoes produced in New England. All of this gives rise to cross shipping; and, since transportation is a phase of marketing, the added cost is allocated to the marketing process.

Fashion has also had an important effect on marketing costs. In days gone by, it was possible for a retailer to purchase merchandise for 6 months ahead. This meant that it was necessary for salesmen to make (say) only two calls per year. It meant, furthermore, that shipments could be made at carload rates. Not only have rapid fashion changes caused an increase in costs of selling and transportation, but they also have made it necessary for retailers to adopt expensive stock-control systems and to assume the burden of costly markdowns on merchandise that suddenly loses popularity. The tendency of fashion changes is to give rise to higher marketing costs.

There is little doubt of the existence of intense competition in the marketing field. Competition, though tending to keep prices close to the cost level, tends also to give rise to certain items of additional cost. For example, many types of stores continually feel the necessity of obtaining increased sales volume. Such institutions are faced with the choice of cutting prices, increasing advertising, or improving service. Many retailers have felt that the last course is most effective for this purpose. As a result, departments and specialty stores, particularly, have vied with one another to prove the contention that the customer is always right. Free delivery (of any amount of goods to almost any point), children's playrooms, extended credits, and return of unsatisfactory merchandise are some of the items of service extended. Although these are costly, people have now become accustomed to them and consequently demand that they be continued.

One can get some notion as to the costliness of such services if he considers for the moment the cost elements entering into the return of "unsatisfactory" merchandise by a customer. One must recognize the fact that the time spent by the salesperson, though paid for, has proved completely ineffective; that the item has had to be delivered and picked up; that for sales purposes, while the item is out of the store, another has to be in stock; that the item may have become shopworn as a result of excessive handling. All this effort is completely wasted, and the cost of the waste effort is manifested in the expense percentages of individual merchandising institutions.

The competitive system also gives rise to another type of cost. There is, in many types of marketing institutions, an *optimum size.* That is to say, very small and very large concerns often have higher costs as a percentage of sales than concerns of so-called optimum size. In the retail field, particularly, are to be found thousands of high-cost enterprises most of which are of extremely small volume. Not only are these concerns inefficient in themselves, but also, because each takes a portion of the volume that would go to others, some of their more efficient competitors suffer as well.

There have been, of course, significant countertendencies at work to offset, at least partly, increasing marketing costs. Hence, " . . . chain stores have reduced the costs of retail and wholesale marketing in numerous lines; and some of the cooperative associations of farmers have succeeded in cutting marketing costs. Undoubtedly, the application of more scientific methods will result eventually in large economies in marketing."[1]

An increase in marketing costs in itself is not necessarily an indictment of the system in any case. It must be recalled that marketing is a part of production (in the broad sense of the term) and that, whereas manufacturers create form utilities, distributors create time, place, and possession utilities. It should be recalled further that, though manufacturers may call machinery into play when they decide to increase production,

[1] "Recent Economic Changes," p. 421.

distributors, in general, must resort to increased man power if the increased product is to be marketed. Now if, by forcing the marketing system to assume an increased burden, the manufacturers are able to cut down their cost by a greater amount, there is a net advantage to society.

Much the same reasoning may be utilized in pondering increased transportation costs among specialized areas. Although the result makes marketing more costly, the gain to manufacturing in many instances is more than enough to offset that increase.

In some instances, specialization of person likewise makes for increased marketing costs. The farmer who used to produce most of the goods he required (such goods being charged with no marketing costs whatsoever) now often specializes in one or, at most, a few commodities and purchases his other requirements through regular marketing channels. The commodities so purchased presumably are charged with various distribution costs including that arising out of transportation.

It is not enough to state, however, that an increase in marketing costs is justified by virtue of a resulting increase in the relative efficiency of the whole production system. There is still the question as to whether there are not points of actual inefficiency in our existing marketing process. In other words, admitting that recent increases in marketing costs may be justified, are there not possibilities of offsetting such tendencies through technical and other types of improvements? The several possibilities along these lines will be explored in subsequent sections of the present chapter.

3. Wholesale and Retail Costs.—Marketing costs are expressed as a percentage of sales. That is to say, if the expenses of doing business of a retailing concern are 20 per cent, this means that 20 cents out of every consumer's dollar spent in that establishment goes for costs of retailing the commodities handled by that institution, the balance going to cost of the goods sold and to profit, if any.

Tables 50, 51, and 52 show representative costs of various types of marketing institutions. From these it can be seen that frequently 50 per cent of the consumer's dollar goes to marketing. Table 50 gives figures for expenses in wholesale concerns; and Tables 51 and 52, for those in retail establishments. There are certain specific conclusions that may be drawn from these data.

(1) It will be noted that wholesale costs are lower than retail costs in the same line of business despite a lower base price for

TABLE 50.—TOTAL OPERATING EXPENSE AS A PERCENTAGE OF NET SALES FOR WHOLESALERS IN SELECTED TRADES, BY VOLUME OF BUSINESS, 1929[1]

Size of concerns, (net sales, thousands)	Type of business				
	Drug	Dry-goods	Groceries	Hardware	Paint and varnish
Total	13.3	10.3	9.8	18.5	21.8
Under 50	17.8	13.5	13.8	24.3	28.2
50 to 100	14.8	12.8	8.9	21.5	24.0
100 to 200	16.1	10.0	9.0	20.4	22.5
200 to 300	13.7	10.3	9.6	19.0	23.8
300 to 400	12.9	9.4	8.9	20.1	22.9
400 to 500	14.2	9.0	8.7	20.4	20.5
500 to 1,000	13.6	9.7	9.5	18.7	22.0
1,000 to 2,000	13.3	10.0	9.7	18.1	19.3
2,000 to 4,000	13.1	9.8	9.6	17.9	18.0
4,000 to 8,000	12.8	11.6	11.8	17.3	
8,000 to 15,000	13.4	12.1	14.8	16.7	
15,000 to 25,000	....	....	....	20.8	

[1] N. H. ENGLE, *Am. Econ. Rev.*, supplement, March, 1933, p. 101.

TABLE 51.—AVERAGE RETAIL EXPENSES OF SELECTED BUSINESSES, 1935[1]
(Expressed in percentage of sales)

Kind of store	Total reported expense, excluding allowance for service of proprietor	Total pay roll	Other expense
Jewelry	34.8	15.1	19.7
Furniture	31.9	14.7	17.2
Department	29.2	14.2	15.0
Women's specialty	28.8	13.0	15.8
Variety	26.6	11.7	14.9
Drug	23.7	11.6	12.1
Combination grocery	14.9	7.3	7.6

[1] Census of Business, 1935, "Retail Distribution," vol. I, p. 1-16.

the former. The main reasons for this condition are that wholesaling institutions ordinarily are able to do a larger volume of

TABLE 52.—Operating Expenses, Margins, and Net Profit of Department Stores by Annual Sales Volume, 1935[1]

Items	Less than $150,000	$150,000 to 300,000	300,000 to 500,000	500,000 to 750,000	750,000 to 1,000,000	1,000,000 to 2,000,000	2,000,000 to 4,000,000	4,000,000 to 10,000,000	10,000,000 to 20,000,000	Over 20,000,000
Gross margin.......	30.4	31.5	32.9	33.2	34.8	34.1	35.3	36.1	36.8	36.7
Total expense.......	31.4	32.3	33.0	33.7	34.1	34.5	35.5	36.8	36.3	36.0
Cost of goods.......	69.6	68.5	67.1	66.8	65.2	65.9	64.7	63.9	63.2	63.3
Net profit or loss....	*L*1.0	*L*0.8	*L*0.1	*L*0.5	0.7	*L*0.4	*L*0.2	*L*0.7	0.5	0.7

[1] CARL M. SCHMALZ, "Operating Results of Department and Specialty Stores in 1935," Harvard Business Research Bureau.

business per employee owing to larger orders, less personal service, etc.; that locations required by wholesale institutions are of the less expensive types; and that space can be more intensively utilized in the wholesale phase of marketing operations.

(2) The retail marketing of convenience items, particularly staple foodstuffs, is much less costly than the handling of shopping items, a condition that arises partly out of lower priced locations, partly out of a more effective use of space, and partly out of more intensive utilization of selling time.

(3) From the data in Tables 51 and 52, one may infer that operating costs vary with volume of sales. In some instances, indeed, there is a clear-cut indication of optimum size. Such a condition seems to obtain in grocery wholesaling, for example, at about a half-million-dollar volume. It seems to be equally true in the retail grocery field, as is indicated by the following sales and expense data adapted from the Harvard figures:

Sales of Volume	Expense, %
Under $30,000	19.9
$30,000 to $49,000	17.9
50,000 to 99,000	17.5
100,000 to 149,000	18.0
150,000 to 249,000	18.2

That it does not always work out in the same fashion can be seen from some of the other data. In department stores, for example, expense percentages seem to *increase* with volume.

This introduces a question of prime importance in this connection. Can operating expenses be accepted as an adequate index of merchandising efficiency? This question has been given little consideration by the economist but is, according to the view of the authors, of prime significance from the social standpoint. Let us assume a hypothetical example designed to compare the operating results of two imaginary establishments *X* and *Y*. The former, let us say, is the smaller store, the latter the larger. Under the assumed situation, *Y*'s expenses in terms of percentage of sales are higher than those of *X*. The assumed cost-of-goods-sold figure, however, is greater in the case of *X* than in that of *Y*. The results follow:

Store *X*		Store *Y*	
Sales	$100	Sales	$100
Cost of goods sold	73	Cost of goods sold	70
Gross margin	27	Gross margin	30
Expenses	28	Expenses	29
Net loss	1	Net profit	1

In this hypothetical case, store *X*, whose expenses percentage is definitely lower than that of *Y*, had a net loss of 1 per cent, whereas *Y* (despite greater expenses) earned a net profit of 1 per cent. This condition is obviously due to some sort of purchasing advantage that is enjoyed by store *Y*. Although the foregoing is only a hypothetical example, the actual figures given in Table 52 seem to bear out the theory admirably.

The specific reasons for a situation of this kind are worthy of some attention. In the first place, the larger store buys in larger quantities and hence earns greater discounts. This, in turn, is due in part to the use of group and central merchandising techniques and in part to effective aid given the manufacturer by the large retail distributor. In the second place, the buying talent is more efficient owing to the fact that larger stores are able to draw the best men and to practice specialization of effort. Indeed, many chain buying specialists become more expert in production techniques than the industrial manufacturers themselves.

The advantage accruing to larger establishments by virtue of this apparently anomalous cost situation is of social as well as individual significance. It would be advantageous to the consumer, in other words, if the savings coming about as a result of higher but more intelligent expenditures were shared with the consumer in the form of lower prices. Indeed, this condition frequently occurs. The possibility of this occurrence is easily appreciated when it is recalled once again that the consumer's dollar is divided into three parts going respectively to cost of goods, operating costs, and net profits. If, by spending a larger proportion of the consumer's dollar for operating expenses, the management is able to increase its volume and therefore buy more advantageously, an increase in net profits and a decrease in consumer's prices may occur coincidentally. It is, of course, possible that a shrewd buyer in a small establishment may be quite as efficient as his competitor in the larger, but such a situation is not typical. The latter with his triple advantage of an ability to find the best "buys," earn larger quantity discounts, and buy to price lines with less likelihood of markdowns is frequently able to offer the consumer better values despite higher operating expenses.

4. Integration in Marketing.—In an important sense, our marketing system is in a constant state of flux. Better methods, though perhaps slower in developing than technological changes in industry, are constantly appearing. Such changes usually take the form of new methods designed to carry the functional burden in a more efficient way. Often the resulting increase in efficiency is advantageous socially as well as individually, though this is not necessarily so. Indeed, at times the basic reason for "improved" methods is that of controlling the product all the way through the marketing process for the specific purpose of "price stabilization."

Though the wholesaler actually performs important marketing services,[1] the tendency in recent years has been toward integration. Hence, such integrated institutions as department stores, chain stores, and, in some localities, supermarkets, have become increasingly important in the distribution picture. Table 53 shows the importance of chain distribution in our marketing

[1] For example: bringing together products at convenient points so they can be supplied on short notice, offering credit, advising both manufacturer and retailer as to items most in demand, storing commodities not required at the moment, taking the selling burden from the shoulders of the manufacturer, etc.

TABLE 53.—RELATIVE DISTRIBUTION OF RETAIL SALES AMONG INDEPENDENTS, CHAINS, AND OTHER TYPES, 1929, 1935[1]

Types	Independent		Chain		Others	
	1935	1929	1935	1929	1935	1929
Hardware stores	95.4	....	4.3	....	0.3	
Jewelry stores	90.3	93.0	8.9	6.4	0.8	0.6
Furniture stores	86.0	83.9	13.5	14.2	0.5	1.9
Restaurants	84.0	86.1	14.5	13.6	1.5	0.3
Filling stations	77.8	66.0	21.5	33.8	0.7	0.2
Women's ready-to-wear	72.3	74.3	25.2	22.7	2.5	3.0
Drug stores (with fountain)	71.1	....	28.8	....	0.1	
Department stores	61.4	72.1	26.7	16.7	11.9	11.2
Cigar stores	61.1	73.5	35.8	25.1	3.1	1.4
Grocery and meats	60.5	67.6	39.1	32.2	0.4	0.2
Shoe stores	43.3	53.5	50.0	38.0	6.7	8.5
Variety stores	9.2	9.8	90.8	90.1	....	0.1
All stores	73.1	77.5	22.8	20.0	4.1	2.5

[1] Census of Business, 1935, "Retail Distribution," vol. I, p. 1-24.

system for the years 1929 and 1935. Thus, one is enabled to draw some inferences regarding chain growth in particular fields as well as to make comparisons with respect to the success of chain merchandising as among fields. As can be seen from the figures, though only about 23 per cent of the *total* retail business in 1935 was done by chain establishments, almost 91 per cent of the variety business was carried by chain enterprises. Groceries chains having only about 40 per cent of total grocery business in the United States in 1935 have managed to make much greater strides in certain localities than others. It is quite evident from the figures, moreover, that chain methods seem not to lend themselves to certain commodity fields at all.

Let us inquire somewhat specifically into the reasons for chain-store development. Probably the most important basic reasons for their success are: (1) a more efficient merchandising system, (2) lower buying prices due to volume, and (3) the success of the practice of shifting some of the marketing functions onto the shoulders of consumers.

Recent inquiries by the Federal Trade Commission have revealed that special discounts—trade, cash, advertising allowances, etc.—have frequently been made to chain organizations by manufacturers. These discounts have in many instances amounted to more than the decrease in marketing and manufacturing costs arising out of large-order business. Such discounts of course have been of definite advantage to chain establishments in the past but are now controlled by the operations of the Robinson-Patman Act, which circumscribes the buying and selling relationships of the retailers and manufacturers by making discriminatory discounts (those exceeding actual savings in marketing and manufacturing costs) unlawful.[1] Legitimate savings arising out of volume purchases may still be extended large buyers by the sellers, however.

As was previously stated, the chains have also been successful in their attempt to induce the consumer to assume certain of the marketing functions that had hitherto been carried by the retail establishment. Thus in many types of retail enterprises, service is conspicuous by its absence. Although the cost of carrying credit accounts and delivering merchandise has not been so great as is often assumed, still there have been actual savings to be derived which could be passed on to the consumer in the form of lower prices.

The most important advantage of chain operation, however, lies in its greater operating efficiency. One of the typical organization fundamentals in chain-store operation is the separation of planning and doing. That is to say, the central management specializes in the planning of all major activities, and the decentralized workers specialize in the execution of the plans. In chain operation, selection of personnel is given careful attention in order that plans can be efficiently carried through. The question of selection of location on a scientific basis is studied, since the attainment of an establishment of optimum size leads in many merchandising fields to a condition of lowest cost. Chain management, therefore, selects locations according to population concentration in order to ensure the attainment of an effective sales volume. The layout of chain

[1] The act, in brief, amends Sec. 2 of the Clayton Act and makes it more specific. Hence, under the new law (1) variations in prices to different buyers must bear a *determinable* relationship to variations in sellers' costs and (2) services extended various buyers must not be discriminatory but must be furnished all buyers on proportionally equal terms. In fine, the law proscribes price discrimination among various buyers of goods of like quantity and quality if the result is that of injuring a competitor.

units also has been scientifically studied in order to allow the handling of a large volume per sales person.

Although the grocery field cannot be considered as completely typical of all chain operation, it is illustrative of chain principles. In a study of grocery retailing made by Prof. Roland S. Vaile of the University of Minnesota, it was revealed that the difference in efficiency between the independent wholesaler and retailer setup and that of the chains as indicated by expense figures was very marked.[1] The main differences were in pay roll, in interest expense, and in trucking costs, although there were also minor differences in the items of taxes and supplies. By far the most important point of difference was in pay-roll expense. This can be explained in two ways: (1) by an actual difference in salaries and wages paid chain employees (made possible by the assumption on the part of chain employees that they receive a psychic income in the form of a chance for advancement); and (2) by a difference in terms of percentage of sales due to a greater sales volume per sales person. The latter is due in turn, for the most part, to better locations and more effective store layout. The difference in interest and taxes is probably due to a more effective stock policy based upon scientific selection of wanted items, and simplification of the stock structure. That is to say, chains have a policy of selecting only a limited number of brands on which to concentrate their sales effort, thus making possible carrying on operations with a relatively small stock. The effect of this policy, incidentally, is that of shifting part of the marketing burden to full-line independents.

Thus, chains direct their attention toward the control of distribution costs and, at the same time, toward the purchase of their merchandise requirements at the lowest possible cost. To the extent that they are successful in this two-point program, to that extent do they have an advantage in the market place.

How much of the increased efficiency arising out of chain operations is passed on to the consumer has not been clearly demonstrated. According to studies that have been made, there are important differences between chain and independent prices. Studies made by economists and by government agencies in various localities indicate differences of between 5 and 14 per cent in groceries and 9 and 11 per cent in drugs. Many of these

[1] "Grocery Retailing," p. 46.

studies, however, were based on a group of specific branded items common to the several stores under investigation, and one wonders whether the so-called *representative* items were actually representative. In the grocery field where privately branded and nonbranded items are not taken into account at all, one cannot but doubt the validity of the measuring device. Regardless of the limitations of the measuring techniques utilized in price studies, some difference between chain and independent prices undoubtedly exists, although the exact difference is imponderable. Indeed, a measurement of price differences existing at the moment is not of great social importance in any case, since the level of efficiency has already improved materially as a result of chain competition. In other words, one cannot measure the social effectiveness of chain operations by a mere measurement of price differentials at the present time, since chain competition undoubtedly has increased the level of efficiency in the industry as a whole and thus has had a depressing effect upon the level of prices of the independents. Though efficiency differentials are somewhat narrower than they once were, the beneficent effect of chain competition should not be underestimated.

The tremendous growth of chain stores has given rise to legislation designed to curb their activities. This activity has taken at least three forms: state tax laws, resale price maintenance laws, and antidiscrimination legislation. Where states have placed a discriminating tax burden upon chain operations, the main purpose is to reduce operating efficiency differentials between chain and independent establishments. Such legislation is, to say the least, reactionary and actually penalizes efficiency. It would be much better if, instead of lowering the level of efficiency of the low-cost institutions, someone would attempt to devise a method of raising the level of efficiency of the high-cost firms.

Legislation making legal the maintenance of resale prices by manufacturers is now in effect in over 43 of the 48 states. Although this subject is discussed in detail in another chapter (Chap. XV), it is important in this connection to understand that it makes impossible the sale of merchandise at prices lower than those named by the manufacturer, the effect being that of eliminating retail-price differentials between independents and chains. In other words, the efforts of the chains to pass efficiency savings on to the consumer are definitely circumscribed as a result of price-maintenance legislation.

The Robinson-Patman legislation is perhaps more justifiable economically. It is designed, ostensibly at least, to eliminate unfair buying advantages possessed by the chain institutions. Certainly one could not justify chain buying advantages arising out of the exertion of quasi-monopolistic power in demanding price concessions. Such advantages are unsound economically under a system depending upon competition to bring about economic efficiency. If, however, advantages accruing as a result of production savings are made unlawful, the result is that of "freezing" an existing situation, thus penalizing economic progress. The danger of such legislation lies in the possibility of the failure of its administrators (the Federal Trade Commission) completely to recognize efficiency savings. If such a situation eventuates, the level of efficiency will be forced downward and inefficiency will be perpetuated.

5. Critical Evaluation of the Marketing System.—The marketing system in the United States is a product of a competitive economic system. There are undoubtedly many phases of it that are economically ineffective. There is, in other words, opportunity for improvement in the economic efficiency of the existing system of market distribution.

Though marketing under a completely regimented society would have to bear the functional burden, there is little question but that such a system (everything else remaining equal) would result in reduced marketing costs. Consider, for a moment, the increase in technical efficiency that would arise if the consumer were instructed to appear at a certain specific time at a specified place to receive goods which had been selected for him by some governmental agency. Such a system would eliminate freedom of selection with its attendants, incompletely utilized store facilities and idle clerical time.

Aside from the fact that such a system would be unbearable and unacceptable to the population of a country whose institutions have been based upon a relative freedom of economic activity, a limitation appears that might well affect the apparent economic advantage suggested above. As has been suggested in another chapter, savings may accrue in a static situation that would be more than offset by an absence of improvements that ordinarily arise out of a dynamic situation. That is to say, a regimented society practically eliminates competition and, though competition is wasteful in some ways, there is no gainsaying the progress (measured in terms of improvements in techniques) that is made under it. The history of the automobile is suggestive in this connection. If Henry Ford had had a monopoly of car building, it is quite possible that we would still be riding around in Model T's. Competition has forced progress in the refrigeration field, in the railroad industry, and in many another. Monopoly seems to be reactionary, seems to make for complacency. Competition either of the intra- or interindustry type brings about improvement. Though its effects are not immediate, competition is a force the results of whose continual operations become manifest in time.

Existing methods of marketing are continually tending toward change. Integration offers many possibilities for improved economic efficiency. The department store is an integrated type of concern, combining wholesaling and retailing functions. The chain is another. The newly established supermarket, combining as it does all types of food marketing under one roof, holds many possibilities. The average expenses of such institutions are lower than those of small single-unit establishments. For example, the grocery departments of the larger supermarkets are able to do business, at present, at an expense rate of around 11 per cent in contrast to a rate of over 16 per cent for smaller service institutions. From a social viewpoint part of this advantage is more apparent than real for at times either (1) the grocery department is operated on a "loss leader" basis, the difference being made up in other departments, or (2) the supermarket owner who is also operator of the grocery department leases other departments at figures which allow him to charge himself only a small amount for rent. A substantial part of the cost differential, however, undoubtedly is real. In some sections of the country, the small independent cannot continue to exist in competition with this new type of retail concern. Thus, in time, better methods increase the efficiency of the whole system by forcing competitors to improve their techniques or to withdraw from the field.

But regulation is probably necessary also. Unfair marketing practices, such as false advertising, fraudulent failures, and commercial bribery, are socially costly since by such practices uneconomic units are perpetuated. The racket whose underlying philosophy is to create a hazard against which, for a fee, it "protects" the businessman is also exceedingly costly since the prices of commodities are affected by such activities.

Regulation has even been suggested to limit by license the number of retail outlets in each field. Retail failures in some lines run as high as 50 per cent the first year and are, to a great extent, due to incompetence.[1] That there is a tremendous amount of waste involved in failures there can be little question. Whether licensing prospective entrants on a basis of experience is advisable, however, is doubtful.

There is much room for research in the field of marketing. Further research effort along the lines of less costly methods of marketing should be undertaken. Though much has been done by government agencies such as the U.S. Bureau of Foreign and Domestic Commerce, most of this effort has been expended to aid individual business firms. Although such research activity is of undoubted value, a program of research undertaken from the social point of view would be much more worth while to the consumer. Many problems suggest themselves. There is, for example, room for further studies on simplification; shipping methods; and differences in cost accompanying variations in size of individual orders, in sales volume, and in types of institutions.

There are also some possibilities of controlling costs through consumer education. It is a well-known fact that certain types of retail institutions are going too far with their slogan, "The customer is always right." The volume of returned merchandise in some retail establishments, for example, amounts

[1] A study of grocery retailing in the Twin Cities (*Ibid.*, p. 42) showed the following with respect to the experience of new Minneapolis independent proprietors in that field:

Length of Grocery Experience	Percentage of Total Returns
None	51.69
Retail:	
Under 3 years	8.99
3 to 5 years	12.36
over 5 years	19.10
Wholesale	4.49
No answers	3.37

to 20 per cent of net sales. The consumer should be made to understand that a condition of this type can result only in increased costs of doing business and probably is reflected in higher retail prices. There is in addition evidence leading to the conclusion that small consumer purchases are very costly; that larger average orders can be handled at lower costs. Such information should also be made available to the consumer perhaps by joint effort on the part of the retail institutions. Consumer ignorance and thoughtlessness very probably lead to considerable marketing waste.

Questions

1. When will a saving in marketing costs be passed on to consumers in the form of lower prices and when retained by the organizations making the saving?
2. Are chain stores bad for a community? What criteria should be utilized in making a decision about this matter?
3. Are marketing costs higher now than (say) 50 years ago? If so, does the fault lie in marketing inefficiency? How far is the present trend toward an increased proportion of the gainfully employed in distribution likely to go?
4. Small retailers frequently remain in business for only a short time before failing. Does this increase the cost of goods to the consumer?

CHAPTER XV

RETAIL PRICES OF CONSUMERS' GOODS

Price in the competitive economy is the regulator of production and consumption. That is to say, the amount of any commodity offered by producers will, in the long run, be governed by prices and their relation to cost. Likewise, the amount of the commodity taken by consumers will be governed by the price of the commodity offered. Hence, price has the twofold purpose of determining the amount of goods that will come onto the market and the amount that will be drawn off.

Perhaps the most familiar price phenomenon, to students of economics, is that of the normal price analysis. Normal price, it will be recalled, is "the price that would prevail if only the more permanent forces affecting price-making were operative and if sufficient time were allowed to permit these forces to bring about a completely stable equilibrium of demand and supply."[1] It will be noted that the definition clearly states that normal price is that price that *would* prevail *if* completely stable equilibrium conditions obtained. Under such conditions, price would be identical with the cost of production of the marginal producer. Differentials naturally accrue to the more efficient enterprisers; losses to the submarginal concerns. The latter, of course, would be expected in time to disappear from the competitive picture although at any one moment of time there might be concerns operating at or below the margin.

The student of consumer problems is interested in *market* prices. Market price, unlike normal price, is an extremely realistic phenomenon. Though normal price is one that *would* result were demand-and-supply conditions allowed to work themselves out, market price is an actually existing price. Market price, in other words, is the price that actually exists in the market place at any one moment of time, the price at which a commodity actu-

[1] F. B. GARVER and A. H. HANSEN, "Principles of Economics," rev. ed., p. 97.

ally is sold. The analysis of market price takes into account only short-run factors, the actual supply-and-demand conditions obtaining at the moment. Cost of production, for example, is an unimportant factor in the market-price analysis, since, in the short run, immediate adjustments in long-run supply factors (shifting capital, etc.) cannot be made. Cost of production, therefore, for all practical purposes is of minor significance as a price factor in the short run. One has only to recall the many instances of producers or distributors selling their product for "whatever they can get" to grant the truth of this assertion. Picture, if you can, a vendor, attempting to convince a buyer that the latter should pay $1 for a certain commodity on the ground that that was its cost of production when because of a glut in the market a similar article could be purchased from other vendors for 50 cents. While one must insist that the cost of production is of relatively little aid in analyzing market prices, one must be equally insistent that it is one of the major determinants of normal price. Moreover, normal price is that price toward which the market price tends in the long run.

If a perfect market existed,[1] there would be only one market price at a given moment of time. If, in addition, all commodities were nondifferentiated (as wheat is), no element of monopoly would exist in market prices. Markets are not perfect, however; goods, in many instances, are differentiated. Hence, price differences exist many of which result from quasi-monopolistic conditions. Thus *X* product, though actually identical with *Z* product (except for the container, perhaps), is offered at a higher price than is *Z*; or retailer *A* is able to sell *Z* brand (say) for several cents more than his competitor since he enjoys the advantage of a superior location.

1. Producer, Wholesale and Retail Price Relationships.—Under competitive conditions, there seems to be a more or less definite relationship between producer and wholesale and retail price movements. Although there are exceptions, we usually expect that changes in producers' prices will lead wholesale price changes and wholesale will lead retail. The reason for this condition is

[1] Several individuals acting independently on both the selling and the buying sides, equal information to buyers and sellers alike, rational action on the part of all traders, and equal ability to trade at the most advantageous moment.

twofold. To begin with, fundamental changes in supply conditions take place not in the retailers' and wholesalers' but in the producers' markets. That is to say, changes in the supply of wool or wheat or tin take place in the raw-materials markets, and any change in price resulting from such shifts *first* takes place in these markets. The supply situation in the retail market, on the other hand (except in relatively rare cases of temporary isolation due to floods, say), is adjusted by the simple expedient of ordering additional quantities from suppliers. Hence price changes coming about as a result of changes in supply conditions usually take place in the producers' markets first, then filter through to the retailers' markets. In some instances, indeed, the retailer elects (or is forced) to absorb part or all of any such change. Consequently retail prices fluctuate less violently than do those of the producer and of the wholesaler.

Price changes taking place as a result of a change in demand conditions (except in cases where goods are physically or economically highly depreciable) usually occur first in the producers' markets, likewise. The change in demand, however, is felt first in the retail market. That is to say, an increase in consumer demand will be manifested in the form of a more active retail trade. As a consequence, the retailer increases the size of his orders. Suppliers thus keenly feel this concentration of buying orders and, in turn, place a larger volume of orders with the producers. The producers, therefore, are the ones who receive the full impact of the change in demand. Consequently, changes in prices coming about as a result of changes in demand take place first in the producers' markets, too, despite the fact that the actual change in demand was manifested first in the retail market.

Again, as in the supply-change situation, the retailers, upon receiving notice of producers' or distributors' price changes, may or may not pass on such changes to the consumer depending upon the circumstances. In the case of an increase, the retailer may find it *impossible* to pass the advance on. In the case of a price decline, on the other hand, he may find it unnecessary to share the saving.

2. Factors Affecting Retail Prices.—Though it is true in some instances that retail prices are set by the producer,[1] more often

[1] See discussion of resale-price maintenance later in this chapter.

prices in the retail markets are set by the retailer himself. In setting his prices, the retailer finds himself beset by many considerations. Usually the retailer sets a reservation price which he hopes will be effective in moving his stocks. Intelligent pricing transcends the use of a system of automatic markups. Though cost is taken into account, many other important elements are given consideration also. These factors are worthy of the attention of the student of consumption economics.

1. Merchandise cost (invoice cost of merchandise plus the average cost of doing business) may be used as a guide to pricing, as has been indicated. At most, however, merchandise cost can be used only as a guide. Some types of commodities never return a price that covers cost plus average expenses. Sugar is an example of such a commodity. Moreover, since expense percentages differ from store to store, the more efficient type of enterprise often will dictate prices. Indeed, some stores price merchandise at *less than invoice cost* for the purpose of advertising. The inefficient enterprise, hence, often finds it impossible to price merchandise on a cost-plus-expense basis. The cost factor, therefore, should not be given too much weight in an analysis of the factors entering into retail pricing.

2. Competition is a tremendously important factor in retail pricing, however. Particularly is this true in the retailing of so-called shopping merchandise. As we shall see later, although there may be price differentials in identical merchandise as among stores in the same market area, such differentials unless justified on some basis, such as superior location, store reputation, or additional service, cannot long exist. The tendency of competition is to force retail prices down to the cost level of the more efficient enterprisers. The more effective the competition, the less chance of making unusual gains.

3. The type and desirability of merchandise is also an important factor. For example, when a particular line of merchandise is extremely popular and when competitors have been somewhat slow in stocking such goods, a store may be able to earn a wider margin than would be possible otherwise. Conversely, if goods that promised to be popular have been purchased in large quantities and the expected popularity does not materialize, there is nothing to do but sell the goods at a lower than average

markup.[1] Merchandise subject to rapid fashion changes is usually priced at a point designed to take care of markdowns since a decline in popularity makes necessary a sharp revision in the prices of any such merchandise left in stock.

Incidentally, the amount that can be sold at a price has to be taken into account in retail pricing also. Thus, although a certain lot of 1,000 units of merchandise might be very desirable at a price of $1.00, 5,000 units would be a drug on the market unless offered for (say) 50 cent. Elasticity of demand, then, is a factor to be considered in retail pricing.

4. The type of merchandising establishment and its method of doing business are of no little importance in the setting of retail prices. As has been suggested, some types of retail concerns confine their efforts to the sale of high-quality fashion merchandise. Such establishments provide elaborate fixtures and furnish complete service. Their prices are often higher than average (for the same quality of merchandise) mainly because they enjoy a quasi-monopolistic advantage in the market. Others have very plain fixtures and furnish practically no service.[2] Such stores are geared to mass merchandising and, therefore, appeal on the basis of price. Their aim usually is to sell merchandise at less than market.

[1] Likewise, manufacturers make mistakes in prognosticating consumer wants from time to time. Merchandise so manufactured is sold at a price having no very great relationship to cost.

[2] Such a store is S. Klein's in New York City. In a recent year, this store sold 3,000,000 dresses, 1,500,000 coats, and 750,000 women's tailored suits for a total sales volume of $25,000,000. "All day long an army of women 100,000 strong, tramples through the barnlike hall of S. Klein. They come not for the decorations (the walls are adorned only with signs, the floors bare), not because of comfort (there is little ventilation, practically no private dressing rooms) nor on account of service (no sales people, no deliveries, no credit) but for one reason only: values. From the very first, S. Klein has had one big idea and one only: to sell clothes as cheaply, quickly and in as big volume as possible. With the fanaticism of a monomaniac he hewed to this line. 'Why don't you put chairs in the millinery department?' he was asked. Instantly came the reply: 'People come here to buy hats, not to sit down. This isn't a party.' . . . Klein estimates his cost of doing business as about 7 per cent of net sales. Therefore, he can make money with an average markup of only 10 per cent, as against markups of from 40 per cent to 75 per cent which the big stores uptown must—for a hundred reasons—put on their women's clothing." Adapted by Fred E. Clark from *Fortune*, July, 1932, for "Readings in Marking," rev. ed., pp. 349–354.

5. Quasi-monopolistic control of the market by the producer has now attained a high degree of importance as a factor in retail pricing. Even in the absence of price maintenance, highly regarded nationally advertised merchandise often is sold at a higher than market price (as compared with other merchandise generically the same). And now through "fair-trade" legislation the producer may legally set a price below which the retailer may not go.

6. Custom likewise has an important influence on the price of some products. Some merchandise, in other words, is sold at what is termed a *customary* price. Such items as gum, packaged candy, and periodicals fall into this category. The retailer has little control over the retail prices of such products regardless of the cost to him.

One may conclude that in most instances retail prices are set not according to formula but according to the position of the retailer in the market. Although the retailer may arbitrarily set his prices at any point he pleases (except for those articles whose retail prices are maintained by the producers), he may not do so with impunity. Competition, the desirability of and the elasticity of demand for the merchandise offered, as well as the reputation of the retail establishment, are all important price factors. The importance of each element depends upon the type of product and the market in which the retailer operates.

3. Price Lining.—The student of consumption economics should be cognizant of several other phases of the retail-price problem. One of these has to do with the lining of prices. The student is very apt to think that merchandise is first purchased and then priced. In shopping lines, often, just the opposite is true. The wise retail-store buyer recognizes that there are price grooves in which consumers prefer to purchase. For example: A study of price lines in a number of cities a few years ago revealed that most popular-priced comforters fell into the following price groups:[1]

Comforters	Most patronized price lines	Second most patronized price lines	Third most patronized price lines
Cotton filled, cotton covered.	$2.95 to $2.98	$1.98	$3.95 to $3.98
Wool filled, cotton covered...	$3.95 to $3.98	$4.95 to $5.00	$5.95

[1] Hugh B. Killough, "Economics of Marketing," p. 279.

The store buyer then goes to the market with the idea of buying merchandise to sell at a particular price. Manufacturers cognizant of this situation consequently often produce goods to sell in particular wholesale price lines. In the short run, in some lines price actually determines cost of product rather than the reverse. That is to say, the quality of the merchandise produced (and hence its cost) is determined by the price line in which the goods are to be placed.

Popular price lines are limited in number. Usually, the wise store buyer will concentrate his sales effort on a very few lines—five or six at the most. When such a rule is adhered to, the vendor and consumer may be both benefited since the latter is less apt to be confused by a large number of items possessing minute quality gradations and the former finds his selling costs reduced since he can do business with smaller stocks and need not spend so much time with each customer.

The consumer should compare merchandise *quality* between the price lines of each store as well as that of the lines offered by the several retail outlets. Goods that appear identical at first glance often reveal marked differences when examined carefully. Moreover, when price levels move upward, price lines often remain stable with the result that standards of merchandise quality suffer.[1]

4. Special-sales Prices.—Special sales, common in large retail institutions selling shopping merchandise, are those in which special inducements are offered the consumer in the form of lower than usual prices. According to Prof. Paul H. Nystrom ("Retail Store Operation," p. 199), 25 to 35 per cent of all furniture and home furnishings are sold at special sales as well as large proportions of radios, furs, and apparel. From the standpoint of the retail institution, the special sale is a way of securing greater sales volume. That the consumer has not complete faith in special-sales claims is suggested by the data in Table 54, which indicates customer reaction to statements appearing in special-sales advertising.

According to Professor Nystrom, " . . . it is very difficult to justify a special sales price on any rational ground. If it is a

[1] When absolute standards of quality exist—such as obtain in respect to butter—changes in the supply-and-demand relationship must reflect themselves in price fluctuations.

markdown from a higher price [he argues] it can be interpreted in either of two ways. It either indicates that the store has made an error which it desires to correct by repricing, or the store is trying to buy custom by offering a premium in reduced prices. If the store has made a mistake in its judgment of the value of the merchandise, then it may be necessary to try to find customers at lower price levels. A thing is worth what it will sell for and if it won't sell at the first price it isn't worth that price. To claim such a value is a misstatement.

TABLE 54.—EVALUATION OF NEWSPAPER ADVERTISING[1]
(Percentage of total)

Residential sections of those interviewed	Do you believe statements in special sale advertisement to be:				
	Dependable	Partly dependable	Not dependable	No answer	Total
Exclusive	34	56	8	2	100
Good	37	52	10	1	100
Fair	36	46	13	5	100
Poor	32	56	8	4	100
Total	36	51	10	3	100

[1] *Retail Ledger*, February, 1934, p. 20.

"A second reason for a marked-down price is to pay or bribe people to come to the store. You spend money in advertising in telling them to come . . . [in] . . . the hope that you may be able to sell them some goods on which you can recoup your advertising expense and, if possible, make a little money besides. If markdowns and comparative prices do not represent mistakes of judgment and are not intended to serve as gifts or bribes, then . . . what are they?"[1]

Professor Nystrom's view though acceptable in the main fails to emphasize certain aspects of the device that are of particular significance to the consumer. Some special sales, for example, are of the clearance type, special inducements being offered for the purpose of moving merchandise quickly. Purchases under such circumstances may be advantageous to both vendor

[1] P. H. NYSTROM, "Retail Store Operation," pp. 207–208.

and consumer. If a shopper is discriminating and does not mind purchasing merchandise which is not in complete favor with respect to style or for which there is not a full stock of colors and sizes from which to choose, he can make excellent "buys" at special sales since prices then are cut deeply in order to move goods immediately. Again an astute store buyer, working closely with a friendly source, will from time to time be able to arrange for the manufacture of certain commodities during a quiet season. Such merchandise can be offered at less than market because all costs need not be covered. This is beneficial to the manufacturer, since his loss is less than it would be if he failed to obtain this business. The store gains as well, since it utilizes its facilities more intensively. The lower-than-usual price obviously benefits the customer also.

Quiet buying seasons in the retail market also give rise to special sales at times. In the sale of furniture, some seasons of the year are not active buying seasons. In order to utilize the store's facilities at a time when they are incompletely utilized, special inducements are made. If the response is favorable, the tendency is to reduce retail costs as a percentage of sales. The result may be mutually beneficial to retail concern and consumer under these conditions, also.

It should be pointed out, however, that the consumer in order intelligently to take advantage of special offerings must select the store carefully and must also keep merchandise standards firmly in mind. The latter is tremendously important since the reason for a special price on an item might actually be the fact that the merchandise has proved unsatisfactory.

Little justification can be offered for special sales of the "bribe" variety. If the *regular* store customer fails to purchase specially priced merchandise during such a sale, however, he may indeed pay a penalty in the form of higher average prices throughout the year.

5. Resale-price Maintenance.—By resale-price maintenance is meant the setting of retail prices by the producer and his insistence that this price be maintained, even after the article has left his hands. That is to say, the producer is allowed to control the price of his product right through the channels of distribution. Under such a system, then, the retailer is obliged to sell the product at a price specified by the manufacturer.

Until 5 years ago, the maintenance of resale prices by means of a contract between manufacturer and distributor was definitely illegal. Vendors not only were legally proscribed from entering into contractual relations with buyers regarding the maintenance of resale prices but they were not even allowed, by implication, to solicit agreements from buyers to uphold retail prices. Any cooperative arrangement between producer and distributor designed for the purpose of informing a producer of instances of price cutting was declared illegal as well. The courts decided, furthermore, that all articles, regardless of patent or copyright privileges, had the same status with respect to resale-price control. Patent or copyright privileges, in other words, carried with them no special rights with respect to retail-price control. From this it can be seen readily that resale-price maintenance in interstate transactions, at least, had little legal support under previously existing conditions. Even in this earlier period, however, the courts held that a producer

1. Could announce his retail prices to the trade.
2. Could refuse to sell to those who did not adhere to the prices so announced.
3. Could even threaten to refuse to sell to price cutters.
4. Could inform himself of the existence of price cutting by means of the public prints.

Aside from this somewhat impracticable method of maintaining resale prices (that of refusing to sell), the vendor had several other more or less satisfactory methods that could be utilized in an attempt to maintain prices. He could, for example, reason with price cutters, explaining to them that price cutting would eventually have an adverse effect on the retail market since others would follow and margins would thus become narrower. He could, if it seemed advisable, use exclusive dealerships and assign to each dealer a definite territory, a sort of quasi monopoly in the sale of this particular item. The theory behind this was that the dealership would become so valuable that the dealer would take no chances on offending the vendor, lest he lose his valuable property. Finally, a producer-vendor could establish genuine agencies and, since an agent acts for his principal without transference of the title to goods, the original vendor could set and maintain any price that he chose.

For the most part, the methods that could be utilized in the maintenance of resale prices before the enactment of fair-trade laws were impracticable. Manufacturers and independent retailers, therefore, fought for legislation that would legalize an effective price-maintenance program. California was in the vanguard in enacting laws for this purpose; and, since the 1931 legislation (amended in 1933) in that state, 42 other states have followed the California lead.

The so-called *fair-trade laws* in the various states have more points of similarity than points of difference. Indeed, many states have copied the California act verbatim.[1] This act, in effect, legalizes contracts between vendors and vendees regarding the maintenance of prices set by the manufacturer of branded merchandise. Not only are parties to the contract held to its adherence, but all others who resell the manufacturer's product as well; which means, of course, that even though chain distributors refuse to enter into such contracts they must sell their product in accordance with the contracts signed by others in the trade.

The law specifies, however, that no *horizontal* agreements can be entered into. That is to say, distributors may not (according to the law) band together for the purpose of maintaining retail prices. Moreover, the law specifies certain exceptions even in the case of vertical contracts. Thus, goods, "may be resold without reference to such an agreement in the following cases:

1. In closing out the owner's stock for the purpose of discontinuing delivering any such commodity.
2. When the goods are damaged or deteriorated in quality and notice is given to the public thereof.
3. By any officer acting under the orders of any court."

In June, 1937, a Federal statute—the Miller-Tydings Law—came into existence making legal interstate price-maintenance agreements between states having fair-trade laws. This law supports the intrastate legislation and presumably makes valid (1) contracts between vendors and vendees located in different states and (2) the extension of control past state lines where

[1] Even to the extent of copying typographical errors, of which one section in its original form was mere gibberish.

contracts exist in any one state. Hence, the legal status of resale-price maintenance is now quite clear.

In evaluating resale-price maintenance from an economic standpoint, the various conflicting interests should be examined. On the one hand, the manufacturer of branded merchandise argues that price cutting is definitely harmful to him for at least two reasons: (1) His good will is utilized by the price cutter to the manufacturer's disadvantage. The price cutter, in other words (the producer argues), uses his product as a leader, often selling the item for less than invoice cost. The consumer, as a result, accepts the cut price as the standard, refuses to pay more. (2) Because of this condition, independent retailers attempting to sell the consumer merchandise at suggested price, find it so difficult that they either refuse to handle the manufacturer's product or exert strenuous selling effort in another direction.

The price cutter (the large merchandising institution), on the other hand, argues that his costs of doing business are less because of large volume and efficient management and he should be permitted to pass part of these "efficiency savings" on to the consumer. In any case, he argues, when he makes an outright purchase of goods he should be able to dispose of them at any price he pleases.

The independent retailer (and, obviously, the wholesaler, too) feels that the large-scale price-cutting institution is ruining his business since the price advertising of such concerns diverts customers from his own to the chain institution. The consumer, he contends, patronizes him only for stamps and magazines and for items forgotten on a shopping expedition. He insists that he is entitled to legal protection from his more efficient competitor. That effective resale-price maintenance *tends* to increase the independent sales of (say) nationally advertised drug items at the expense of the chain institutions there can be little doubt, although this tendency appears not to have manifested itself in the comparative independent and chain retail drugstore figures given in Table 55. It may of course be that chain-store growth has leveled off as a result of price-maintenance legislation. However, the chains may be achieving success in offsetting a decline in the sales of price-maintained items by an increase in sales of non-price-fixed merchandise.

Regardless of the effect of such legislation, one may challenge the soundness of a scheme whose purpose is that of subsidizing the less efficient distributive outlets at the expense of the more efficient.

TABLE 55.—PROPORTION OF CHAIN AND INDEPENDENT DRUG SALES IN CALIFORNIA, 1933 AND 1935[1]

Type of establishment	1933	1935
Independents	28.6	27.5
Chains	71.4	71.7
All others		0.8
Total	100.0	100.0

[1] Adapted from Census of Business data for 1933 and 1935.

The consumer's position is from our standpoint, however, the most important and should therefore be evaluated carefully. The intelligent consumer will recognize that less-than-cost selling is not clearly socially beneficial if only for the reason that specialists, some of whose positions in the field are economically justifiable, tend to be forced out of existence. Competent and conveniently located pharmacists and well-informed and helpful booksellers, perhaps, fall into this category.

Such protection, however, should not go too far. Though legislation designed for the purpose of enforcing fair competition may be justifiable, that having as its purpose the "freezing" of existing techniques is definitely undesirable. The independent should not be protected on the ground that he is being forced out of business by more efficient retail institutions, since such a course would tend to perpetuate inefficiency. He might be so protected, however, if the large-scale retailer is competing *unfairly* in the market. The drawing of customers by means of less-than-invoice-cost prices in order to sell them goods of a higher-than-average markup probably cannot be defended economically. The sale of goods at low average prices as a result of low distribution expense probably can. Such a conclusion would indicate that resale-price-maintenance legislation is not justified but that a prohibition of less-than-cost selling is.[1]

[1] Another type of legislation (known as the Unfair Practices Act in California) exists in many states also. This type has as one of its major purposes the prevention of sales below cost. Cost in the field of production is

What is the immediate effect of fair-trade legislation on the consumer-purchaser? Fortunately, from the standpoint of the consumer, "unidentified goods, approximately 50 per cent of the total retail business, are not legally subject to control under the acts. Producers' or owners' marks on many products are merely passive symbols of indentification and not active selling instruments. In many instances the producers' interest in his mark does not run beyond the initial purchaser. [Moreover] . . . Fair trade laws cannot effectively apply to perishables, style lines, finished goods affected by prices of raw materials, the second-hand market, and lines which bulk large in the consumer's budget and in which a small price rise will divert demand to another product."[1] In fact, the great majority of the contracts in existence are in the fields of drugs, cosmetics, books, and liquors.

Even when one confines one's analysis to an industry in which price maintenance is generally practiced, one should examine the situation from the point of view of several classes of consumer-buyers. From studies made by Prof. E. T. Grether,[2] the prices of drug items in cut-rate establishments from 1933 (before contracts were legalized) to 1934 (after such legalization) advanced over 30 per cent. Obviously, since different times are taken, extraneous influences—*e.g.*, a rising price level—might have had some influence on prices. Allowing an arbitrary

---

defined to include raw materials, labor, and overhead expenses; those in the field of distribution to include invoice cost of goods plus expenses of doing business. It has been the general practice in California when the Act has been applied, however, to use invoice or replacement cost of merchandise plus a somewhat arbitrary 6 per cent partly to cover distribution expenses. Exceptions to less-than-cost selling are made in the cases of "closing-out" and seasonal-goods sales, in the case of deteriorated merchandise, in the sale of merchandise by order of a court, and sales for the purpose of meeting competitors' prices in the same market area. This law has found its most active supporters in the retail grocery business but even here has met with only indifferent success owing to difficulties of policing and enforcing. Recently (in July, 1938) the California Supreme Court found the California Act constitutional.

[1] Summary of a *Printers' Ink* article, Feb. 7, 1938, E. T. Grether, "Why Most Retail Prices Will Escape Control under Fair Trade," in *J. Marketing*, p. 336, April, 1938.

[2] E. T. Grether, "Experience in California with Fair Trade Legislation Restricting Price Cutting," *Calif. Law Rev.*, September, 1936.

fifth of the total difference for the effect of such influences, however, the increase still is almost 25 per cent. Differences in certain classes of products were very much greater than average, others much less; Table 56 indicates the extent of some of these changes and reveals that the increase was less than 10 per cent in mineral oils, over 100 per cent in soaps.

TABLE 56.—COMPARISON OF ADVERTISED PRICES ON CERTAIN LINES OF DRUG PRODUCTS IN SAN FRANCISCO DURING THE PERIOD JAN. 1–JUNE 30, 1933, WITH 1934 CONTRACTUAL PRICES FOR IDENTICAL ITEMS[1]

Class of product	Number of products	Number of quotations	Percentage of average actual price to contractual prices	Percentage of increase, 1934 over 1933
Mineral oils	2	10	91.39	9.4
Antiseptics	9	58	84.34	17.3
Dentifrices	6	49	82.10	21.8
Cosmetics	25	100	72.81	37.3
Deodorants	6	33	70.37	42.1
Food tonics and digestive aids	2	4	69.62	43.6
Salts	1	26	52.34	91.1
Soaps	3	36	46.19	112.2

[1] Adapted from E. T. GRETHER, "Experience in California with Fair Trade Legislation Restricting Price Cutting," *Calif. Law Rev.*, September, 1936, p. 661.

In the same study, Prof. Grether discovered that there was little difference between the 1933 and 1934 *independent* store prices. Indeed, if anything, there was a slight decline in the price of the commodities making up the index between 1933 and 1934. Therefore, one is able to conclude tentatively, at least, that

1. Those consumers who typically purchase nationally advertised drug items from independent retailing establishments have not been adversely affected by fair-trade legislation.

2. Those who regularly purchase from cut-rate establishments must now pay almost a third more for nationally advertised proprietary items.

3. Those who have been buying substitute privately branded merchandise are probably not affected one way or another.[1]

[1] This conclusion is not completely tenable, however, for sellers of privately branded merchandise may have felt that, since the prices of nation-

As to the long-run effects of resale-price-maintenance legislation, no one can formulate them with any degree of assurance. To the degree that manufacturers can, by means of advertising, obtain consumer insistence for their brands, to that degree will they be successful. When this condition obtains, the contractual prices that are set are quasi monopolistic, not competitive. If the consumer insists on Bayer aspirin, he has no alternative but to pay 59 cents per 100. Legalized price maintenance indubitably fosters more effective brand monopolies. Socially, such a tendency is undesirable.

Now that price maintenance is legalized, the consumer should be doubly skeptical about vendors' claims of product superiority. As has been mentioned previously, privately branded merchandise in many instances is of equal quality with the nationally advertised product and is priced at a much lower figure. For example, a recent study of the drug field made by one of the authors reveals that, on the average, privately branded merchandise can be purchased for about one-half the price charged for nationally advertised merchandise. The greatly increased differential, incidentally, makes for greater chances of success for the sellers of substitute brands. It may indeed be that national advertisers will, in time, rue the day that they decided to maintain their prices at an excessively high level.

Large distributors have already begun to inform the consumer regarding equal-quality substitute products at materially lower prices. Sears, Roebuck in a recent catalogue, for example, suggests that the consumer "look for Sears own products marked X and save."[1] Macy's in New York, always militant opponents of resale-price maintenance, are doing somewhat the same thing. In a series of advertisements—national and local—Macy's have called the consumer's attention to the high price of nationally

ally advertised goods had been boosted, the price differential between these nationally advertised items and their own now were greater than necessary and thus may have increased them.

[1] The notice in the drug section of the catalogue continues, "Laws recently enacted in most states permitting the manufacturer of trade-marked articles to fix minimum selling prices in those states . . . have required us to raise the retail prices of those items to the prices set.

"If you are interested in buying quality merchandise at money-saving prices (and who isn't) . . . we suggest and recommend that you buy Sears own guaranteed products at prices not fixed under any State Laws, all marked branded merchandise and have suggested that he purchase Macy's private brand and save money.[1] Recently incidentally this store launched a campaign designed to break fixed retail book prices. Setting up a "book club," they offer consumer-buyers a 30 per cent discount in the form of a credit applying to the purchase of *any* book, based upon the purchase of every group of four club books. Needless to say, booksellers and publishers view this new move with alarm.

The large chains presumably have been directing the attention of the consumer to non-price-fixed merchandise also. As a result of such effort, a better informed body of consumers may be expected to develop. Presumably such consumers will, in time, realize that privately labeled merchandise can be purchased advantageously. If so, one cannot but conclude that brand monopolies will lose some of their power, with the result that contractual prices on nationally advertised merchandise will decline. Consumers may aid in hastening the day by setting up defenses against emotional appeals and by selecting their merchandise on a more rational basis.

6. Retail Market Prices.—For most commodities in a given market at a given time there is not a single retail market price, but a number of retail prices. Yet the differences among the prices charged for the same article by various shops are kept within fairly definite limits. In other words, although the retail prices at which articles are sold by different shops on the same day in the same locality are not identical in the majority

---

with this emblem X which stands for First Quality at a Saving. This sign in a Sears' catalog means

X The identifying mark on Sears own goods
X A quality product
X The way to greatest savings
X Unaffected by any price fixing laws."

[1] For example, in a Macy advertisement appearing in *Time* magazine, May 3, 1937, and headed, "The Consumer Will Now Decide," a detailed comparison is made between two brands of aspirin—a "well-known nationally advertised" brand and Macy's own. The consumer is informed that Macy's carries both; that each is manufactured in accordance with standards laid down by the U.S. Pharmacopoeia and are practically identical; but that the nationally advertised brand has been price-fixed by law and, hence, must be sold for not less than 59¢ while Macy's own is priced at 18¢ which includes a fair profit to Macy's and to the manufacturer.

of cases, they bear a close relationship to each other. That is to say, while there is no single retail market price for identical articles, there is what might be termed a retail *market price zone.*

At any one time in any retail market, there are two sets of opposing forces at work. One set of forces creates a tendency toward a uniformity of retail prices for identical merchandise; the other, much stronger, makes for a disparity in retail prices.[1]

The forces underlying the tendency toward a quasi uniformity of retail prices are worthy of consideration. The one-price policy of retailers, for example, has the effect of eliminating wide disparities. Seventy-five years ago, bargaining between vendor and the consumer-vendee was quite common. Hence, while retail prices may have been nominally uniform under such conditions, actual prices were likely to be poles apart. This absence of higgling, then, tends toward a uniform differential as among retail establishments. To put it in another way, where higgling exists there is a complete absence of retail-price uniformity.

Branding and advertising tend toward a uniform price situation (although there are some exceptions to the general rule), especially since price-maintenance legislation now allows contracts calling for minima below which no retailer can go. Even in the absence of such contracts, retail advertising keeps people informed with respect to prices. This also tends to iron out differentials.

Shopping habits of individuals are now more effective than ever in keeping price differentials among establishments down to a minimum. Automobiles and good roads now make it possible for the consumer to take advantage of lower price offerings at some distance. The retailers, consequently, must keep their prices in line, certain types maintaining comparison shopping bureaus for the purpose. Obviously, price lining makes for a tendency toward retail-price uniformity, since each similarly situated retailer uses the same factual basis upon which to set his prices.

The foregoing should not be construed as a contention that there is an absolute uniformity in prices as among establishments.

[1] M. P. McNair, C. I. Gragg, and Stanley F. Teele, "Problems in Retailing," pp. 137–140.

The consumer has only to look about him to see that retail prices in most lines are not identical. Its purpose is merely to explain why there is *any* degree of uniformity in the prices of various retail establishments.

Because of an infinite number of possible quality variants, price differences appear greater than they actually are. Silk stockings, for example, can be purchased for 49¢ or less or for $4.95 or even more. Unobservant buyers are apt to think in terms of prices only, assuming a uniformity of quality, when such an assumption is definitely untenable. This, of course, gives rise to statements made by consumers to the effect that though one store is charging $1 for a certain item they can get "identically" the same thing at a competitor institution for 49 cents. While this is true at times, often it is not.

As has been suggested, however, there are actual price differentials as among various institutions for the same items. As has been mentioned (Chap. XIV), the market for any type of commodity is made up of thousands of trading areas. Some cities have a score or more of miniature market areas. Conditions from area to area differ with respect to income of residents and their buying habits, the degree and type of competition, etc.; although the existence of interarea competition keeps prices from getting completely "out of line," differences can obtain because consumers find it inconvenient to go too far out of their way to make purchases. Thus grocers or druggists located conveniently to a certain residential district may price merchandise 10 or even 15 per cent higher than downtown shops.

Closely allied to the foregoing situation is the fact that when buying goods the consumer purchases not only the bare product, but with it a bundle of services. One of these services is the factor of convenience. Others such as credit, dependability, pleasant surroundings, carefully trained salespeople, telephone orders, free delivery, however, are equally important. Many people are quite willing to pay higher prices under these conditions, since they are in effect purchasing goods plus, to them, valuable service. Conversely, as has been suggested previously, many consumers demand commodities stripped of all service. Chain establishments often cater to the latter type of clientele. The fact that there are such differences makes for a lack of price uniformity.

Different retailers have varying policies regarding changing their prices to conform with wholesale movements. Hence, some absorb such price changes; others alter prices immediately upon receiving notice of a change by their suppliers; still others postpone action. Moreover, variations in the timing of special-sales events make for price differentials. Some retailers have monthly or semiannual events. Some, indeed, avoid special events entirely, taking markdowns as they are required. Millinery syndicates, for example, mark merchandise down daily As a result, at any one moment of time prices differ as among stores.

Uniform prices are nonexistent even for identical staple articles offered by stores in the same trading district. For example, a study of grocery prices in New York State reveals price differences of several types:[1] (1) those existing *between sales prices and regular prices* on identical items in the same store; (2) those occurring on the same day in *different stores;* and (3) those appearing on *different quantities* in the same store.

"To what extent individual buyers can profit by these differences in prices, depends upon the goods to be bought and the selling practices of the stores that can be patronized. With the various means of saving, however, most buyers have opportunities for taking advantage of some differences in prices on a large part of their groceries.

"Since grocery articles are relatively inexpensive, buyers cannot expect to save more than a few cents on each unit by taking advantage of differences in prices. These small price differences, however, are significant because the number of units bought at one time or over a period of time, as a month or a year, is usually large enough for the savings to make a sizable total. A difference of 10 to 15 per cent in the year's expenditures for groceries, through buying at the most advantageous prices, may result from the small savings on individual articles."

Considering the fact that there exist actual price differentials in identical items, the consumer, in order to obtain the best values, must perforce shop. This means that the astute consumer-buyer must investigate various retail sources in convenience goods, as well as shopping lines. An investigation into

[1] L. Doman, "A Study of Price Differences in Retail Grocery Stores in New York State," *Cornell Univ. Agr. Exp. Sta. Bull.* 665, p. 46.

comparative prices of grocery or drug items is perhaps just as desirable as one comparing prices and qualities of merchandise handled by department stores.

Moreover, in drug products particularly, substantial savings may be effected by purchasing privately branded merchandise in place of the nationally advertised brands. When comparing merchandise *values*, however, the consumer must consider not only prices charged but product quality offered and the service rendered by the seller. Each consumer must individually evaluate these several elements. Until this is done, intelligent utilization of comparative price data is impossible.

Questions

1. Are retail prices of identical articles the same in the same market area? If not, how can such differentials exist?
2. Name the one or two most important elements entering into the retail price of the following: high-fashion fur coats; Bayer aspirin; red roses in January; lettuce; bread; nonbranded men's shirts.
3. In your opinion, can legalized resale-price maintenance be justified?
4. How much would a fully informed consumer buying public do toward improving the quality of competition? What other factors are also of importance?

CHAPTER XVI

INVESTMENT AND INSURANCE

Each family or individual usually needs to set aside a portion of income to provide for exceptionally large necessary expenditures, often unforeseen, encountered during the prospective earning life, and for an income during nonearning periods such as those due to unemployment, disability, or old age. In addition, in some instances an endeavor will be made to provide an estate of some sort for the present dependents or prospective heirs. There should be a definite plan carefully worked out and adjusted to the particular conditions. The nature of the plan, the amount to be accumulated, and the rate of accumulation will, of course, vary with the individual circumstances, and few generalizations can be made. The problem for an individual, for example, will be quite different from that for a family.

1. General Considerations.—The consumer in saving is making an exchange of a portion of present purchasing power for a prospective future purchasing power. His first consideration naturally is that this purchasing power should be available to him at the time when he wishes to use it. This necessitates a form of saving that is safe, *i.e.*, that will return his principal to him, and likewise that is readily marketable so that he may secure a conversion into purchasing power at the desired time. A second consideration is that the exchange be made on as favorable terms as possible, *i.e.*, that the realized future purchasing power be as great as possible. This means that the saving should be in such form as promises to yield the largest return, both from the viewpoint of an increase in principal and of yield during the period of holding. The relative importance of these considerations varies with the purposes for which the saving takes place and the period of time under consideration.

A transfer of purchasing power over a considerable period of time must involve careful consideration of the device selected for this transfer. This is necessitated by the possibility of changes in the general level of prices. The transfers are of two general types. The first are those in which, in return for the present payment of dollars, promises of the return of specified sums in terms of dollars are secured. An ordinary bank deposit is of this type, likewise the contracts sold by insurance companies and government and corporation bonds and mortgages. The simple hoarding of cash is of a similar kind. The other type of transfer is the purchase of property or the rights to a share of the returns of income producers. Thus one might purchase a farm, or a house, or stocks of corporations. The significance of the distinction lies in the influence that the movements in the general price level exercise upon the prices of the two sorts of investments. The first, being promises to pay in dollars, remain unchanged or change little in price, and in consequence the owner loses in purchasing power in a price rise and gains in purchasing power when prices fall. Where property or the rights to the returns of income producers are held, however, both the returns and the values would be expected to rise with an increase in prices and to decline as prices fall, thus tending to maintain purchasing power.

If it were possible to foretell the movement of the general price level, the proper policy to be followed by the consumer would be clear. In periods of falling prices, the holdings would be promises to pay in terms of dollars, since these would increase his purchasing power with each decline in price. In periods of rising prices, property, which will increase in price, should be held so that purchasing power will be maintained or possibly increased. The magnitude of the changes occurring over a 10-year interval are shown in Table 57 for wholesale prices. In 81 out of the 129 years, prices were more than 25 per cent higher or lower 10 years later. Wholesale prices have been used in the absence of suitable cost of living indices, but the data are sufficient to show that the purchasing power of a contract which returned a saving in dollars would have changed materially throughout most of the period. The difficulty with the suggested policy lies in the virtual impossibility of forecasting the movements in the general price level. Even the best qualified technical experts have been wrong in the forecasts of price movements nearly as often as they have been right, and the ordinary man probably will find himself mistaken on a number of occasions. This suggests that the proper policy for an individual would be to have investments of both types so that a price movement either up or down would find him gaining in purchasing power on a portion of his holdings while losing on the other portion. The balance might be shifted as one thought one foresaw a general price movement in a particular direction.

Table 57.—Relative Level of Prices in the Tenth Year Following for Each Year from 1800 to 1926
(Given year = 100)

Price level 10 years later	Number of years	Relative purchasing power in later period
Under 65	9	Over 154
65 to 75	17	143
75 to 85	23	125
85 to 95	13	111
95 to 105	10	100
105 to 115	11	91
115 to 125	14	83
125 to 135	9	77
Over 135	23	Less than 75

2. The Accumulation of Reserves.—When funds are to be accumulated as reserves for special emergencies, such as sickness or misfortune, or for special expenditures such as a pleasure trip or the purchase of a car, or simply built into a sum sufficient for the purchase of some item in the investment program, one of the various savings institutions will ordinarily be utilized. The more important of these are the savings banks or savings departments of commercial banks, the postal savings system, credit unions, and savings and loan associations. Practically all these operate under supervision of various Federal and state authorities.

Two sorts of savings deposits in banks are possible, those in a savings bank and a savings account in a commercial bank. Savings banks are found in 18 states. They differ from ordinary banks in the special regulation of their investments. In New York, for example, the law prohibits savings banks from investing in stocks of any kind, in foreign securities of any nature, and in corporate securities other than steam railroad and public utility enterprises. The results of these restrictions have been to strengthen the banks and curtail losses from failures. Mutual or trustee savings banks are found mainly in New England and the Eastern states. The mutual or trustee savings bank does not possess any capital stock. The depositors are the mutual owners of the bank. All the earnings of the bank, less administrative expenses and apportionment to the guarantee fund or surplus, are divided among the depositors in the form of interest. The funds of the institution are derived solely from the deposits. The institution is managed by a body of nondepositing trustees. They usually hold office for life and are generally prominent businessmen who render this service as a public duty. There are about 560 of these institutions in the United States with total deposits of over 10 billion dollars. The stock savings banks are primarily a Middle West institution. They differ from mutual savings banks only in their ownership. The stock bank usually pays its depositors a stipulated rate of interest, and the profits, if any, accrue to the stockholders. The stockholders at times have a double liability for their stock; *i.e.*, they may be called upon to furnish an additional amount equal to their stockholdings in case the bank encounters difficulties.

Many commercial banks maintain separate savings departments. It is also evident that, in the 30 states that do not have savings banks, depositors are obliged to open an account in a commercial bank if they desire to keep their funds in a banking institution. The Federal Reserve Bank and the banking departments of the various states require a separate accounting of these deposits, and the reserve requirements and investments of this portion of the funds are regulated. The assets of the bank, however, are the common property of all depositors, whether in savings or in checking accounts, and, since savings banking is ordinarily less risky than commercial banking, there would be less risk with funds in a regular savings bank than with funds in the savings department of a commercial bank. The element of risk has been greatly reduced in those commercial banks in which deposits are insured with the Federal Deposit Insurance Corporation. This insures deposits up to a maximum of $5,000 in each account.

The Federal government now provides through the U.S. Post Office Department a savings institution operated by the United States government. Any person, ten years of age or over, may open a postal savings account at any post office authorized to accept deposits. A person not near such an authorized post office may open an account at any depository office by mail. The deposits are acknowledged by postal savings certificates of $1, $2, $5, $10, $20, $50, $100, and $500. These certificates are nontransferable and nonnegotiable. Interest is credited at the rate of 2 per cent annually. There is a maximum of $2,500 on the amount that any depositor may have to his credit, exclusive of accumulated interest. Withdrawal of all or any part of the deposits may be made by the depositor at any time from the post office where the deposits were made. Amounts less than $1 may be saved by the purchase of postal savings stamps at 10 cents each. Postal savings cards with 10 savings stamps affixed are accepted as a deposit of $1. The postal savings system has never occupied a large place in American finance. On Jan. 31, 1938, deposits totaled $1,272,000,000.

The United States government also offers through the post offices United States savings bonds which are a direct obligation of the Federal government. The maturity values of the bonds are $25, $50, $100, $500, and $1,000. The bonds are sold on a discount basis whereby the interest accumulates during the lifetime of the bond and the maturity value includes both principal and interest accumulated over a period of 10 years to maturity. The issue prices are $18.75, $37.50, $75, $375, and $750, which would yield an annual interest of about 2.9 per cent. These bonds are nontransferable. They may be redeemed at any time subsequent to 60 days after issue at stipulated prices rising according to the period for which the bond has been held. In event of redemption before maturity, the realized rate is less than 2.9 per cent. These bonds are an unusually attractive investment for those who desire a maximum of safety and convenience on their savings and who do not require any income return during the life of the bond. In January, 1938, there were about 1 billion dollars in bonds outstanding.

Another popular form of saving in the United States is provided by the purchase of shares in savings and loan associations. These associations are mutual organizations designed for long-term savings. Previous to 1933, these associations were chartered by the states, but legislation enacted in that year authorized the granting of Federal charters. Both Federal and state institutions are now found in the field. Investment is made through the purchase of shares, ordinarily with a par value of $100. The shares usually are bought by regular monthly payments at the rate of 50 cents per share. Dividends are paid proportionate to the amount paid in. Full payment for the shares usually requires about 12 years, when the dividends are around 6 per cent. Other methods of purchase less frequently used include irregular payments in amounts of $1 or more, prepayment of a considerable portion of the share, and purchase of fully paid shares through a single payment of the full stated value of the share. The funds of the associations are invested almost exclusively in first mortgages on owner-occupied small homes. In consequence, the associations are known in many sections of the country as building and loan associations. Associations meeting Federal specifications may secure insurance on accounts up to a maximum of $5,000 for each person in the association. There are said to be nearly 10,000,000 personal accounts in the associations in this country, and the total assets of the associations aggregate nearly $6,000,000,000.

The differential in interest (or dividends) between savings banks and building and loan associations often is an important consideration for the consumer. In some districts, for example, savings banks pay only 2 per cent while building and loan associations pay 4 per cent. There are at least two reasons for this: (1) Savings banks invest to a great extent in unusually safe securities, but building and loan associations invest largely in mortgages. Theoretically, at least, the former offer a greater safety factor. (2) Savings banks ordinarily offer a greater amount of service; *i.e.*, savings deposits may actually be withdrawn without notice (though legally the banks may require notice). Building and loan associations (perhaps owing to the nature of their investments) often cannot be so prompt in this respect. As has been mentioned in another connection (Chap. VIII) however, depositors (or shareholders) in each are insured by a Federal government corporation. Hence, each is considered quite safe.

3. Insurance.—Mankind is exposed to the possibility of many serious losses, such as those resulting from physical or mental disability or premature death. In the case of the individual, the exact time that such loss may occur is impossible to foretell. On the other hand, when a large group is considered, it becomes quite possible to foretell fairly accurately the happenings within the group. Thus the possible life span of a particular man thirty years of age is extremely uncertain; but, if 100,000 men at age thirty in sound health are taken, it is quite possible to determine from available statistical data with a very small degree of error the number who will die each year. Although premature death or disability itself cannot be allocated or dealt with by the individual, the financial consequences of such hazard can be distributed over a large group of individuals by a system of individual contributions, the total of which contributions, being scientifically calculated, is sufficient to reimburse the individual for the financial hazard to him or her. This is the so-called *spread of risk.*

The standard device used in this country for calculating the probability of death is the American Experience Table of Mortality. Starting with 100,000 persons at age ten, it gives the number of living and dying during each year. The table was compiled nearly 70 years ago and is very liberal in that fewer die than the table indicates. Since it errs on the conservative side, it has been retained as the basis of estimate. Large companies will seldom have an actual mortality experience as high as that indicated by the table. The following extract shows the data for the first 2 years and by 10-year periods:

TABLE 58.—AMERICAN EXPERIENCE TABLE OF MORTALITY

Age	Number living	Number dying	Expectation of life
10	100,000	749	48.72
11	99,251	746	48.08
20	92,637	723	42.20
30	85,441	720	35.33
40	78,106	765	28.18
50	69,804	962	20.91
60	57,917	1,546	14.10
70	38,569	2,391	8.48
80	14,474	2,091	4.39
90	847	395	1.42

Expectation of life means the number of years on the average those living at a particular age may be expected to continue to live. It is the sum of the additional years each person lives divided by the number of living at the age taken.

These data enable the insurance company to write a great variety of contracts. From the standpoint, of the individual, the insurance contract consists of an agreement with the company whereby the latter agrees to pay a designated party, the beneficiary, a stipulated sum upon the maturity of the contract, in return for which stipulated sum the insured contracts to pay certain sums, called *premiums*, at specified times.

To clarify a field in which there is so much haze, it might be well briefly to analyze the premium—the amount of money paid by the individual to the company for a certain amount of insurance protection, investment return, or both.

If an individual pays $10 yearly to a fire insurance company for $1,000 of fire protection, his yearly premium is $10, and the amount of protection he has for that property is $1,000. In the event of total loss, the man who pays the premium receives $1,000. If he sustains no loss, his $10 has been used to pay fire losses, to lay up reserves for future losses, and to pay expenses of operating the business of the company. This kind of insurance is *term* insurance in the field of fire insurance, since it provides protection for a definite time only. At the end of this time, the protection ceases, unless it is renewed for another period of time by the payment of an additional premium. The individual who thus has property protection against loss to him by fire insurance might also have a savings account at the bank. He might pay a fire insurance premium of $10 yearly and at the same time deposit $10 annually in a savings bank, which $10 deposit would thrive at compound interest. Or he might pay his fire insurance premium without having a savings account, and he might have a savings account without having fire protection. The two accounts might be absolutely separate, or they might be treated under one head.

In life insurance, we can divide the almost numberless contracts into three distinct groups.

1. *Term Insurance.*—This is sometimes called *death insurance.* The individual pays the company (say) $10 a year, in return for which the company agrees to pay the family of the individual or his estate $1,000 if he dies. During the year, the $10 premium, similar to the fire insurance premium, has been used up to pay

losses, death losses instead of fire losses as above, and operating expense.

There is a great variety of term contracts. The simplest, and supposedly the least expensive, is the *yearly renewal term,* renewable to a certain age, as fifty-five, sixty, or sixty-five. The premium for this contract steps up yearly. Then there is the 5- or 10-year *renewable and convertible* term. The premium for this contract steps up every 5 or 10 years and may sometimes be renewed to age sixty or sixty-five without evidence of insurability. The regular 1-2-3-5-10-20-year term, term to fifty, sixty, sixty-five, or seventy, are some of the many forms of term contracts. Almost without exception, any term contract may be converted to a higher premium contract without evidence of insurability and at either original age of issue or at attained age. It must be remembered that term contracts provide insurance for a stated period only, at the end of which period the policy expires and the obligation of the company is canceled. No portion of the premium is set aside in a savings or sinking fund; the premium paid represents the cost of protection.

2. *Retirement Annuity.*—This contract is an agreement between the purchaser and the company to the effect that, at a stipulated date in the future or before or after such date, the company will return to the purchaser a certain amount of cash or, in lieu of cash, a certain income for a stipulated number of years or for a lifetime. Some few companies offer no cash option but only the income option at maturity. The purchaser agrees to make certain deposits periodically with the company. The contract, if not carried to maturity by the purchaser, may be surrendered for its cash surrender value or for a reduced paid-up contract. In the event of death of the purchaser before voluntary maturity of the contract, the gross deposits plus dividends are usually returned to the heirs of the purchaser. It must be remembered that there is no protection or *term* element in this contract. Therefore, death cost is not taken into account. The contract may be bought by a single deposit and the return annuity may begin at once or may be deferred for a period of years, or it may be bought by a series of deposits and the return annuity may be deferred to some definite future time. For those who are unable to secure a contract that requires insurability or for those who do not need protection insurance, this is a splendid contract.

3. *Combination Contract.*—This contract combines classes 1 and 2. The number and varieties of such contracts are legion. We have here the elements of each of the other contracts combined in different forms and amounts.

The principal objections to term insurance are (1) increasing cost with advancing age, (2) arbitrary termination of the contract by the company at the end of the term period, (3) no sinking or investment fund created. These objections are all overcome by contracts in class 3.

The lowest level-premium contract in class 3 is the *ordinary life contract.* Technically, this is an endowment at age ninety-six. When we speak of *endowment,* we mean that the amount of the insurance is payable to the purchaser. In this case, therefore, $1,000 is payable to him at ninety-six. In this contract at age twenty-five we might have a gross premium of $20:

$10	$10
Term-insurance element	Savings element

If a mutual company, the company guarantees to keep this premium level or decrease it; it cannot terminate the contract prior to age ninety-six, and a sinking fund or cash value is being created, which is guaranteed to amount to $1,000 at age ninety-six. Should the purchaser prefer, he may purchase this type of contract over a definite period of years, 5, 10, 15, 20, or more, instead of over his lifetime. He would then have a 5-, 10-, 15-, or 20-payment life contract. On the other hand, he may wish to have the face of the contract, the $1,000 guaranteed to him, in 5, 10, 15, or 20 years or at age sixty. If so, he would buy a 5-, 10-, 15-, or 20-year endowment or an endowment at age sixty. It is all a question of how long he wishes to make the investment, or savings, line in the illustration.

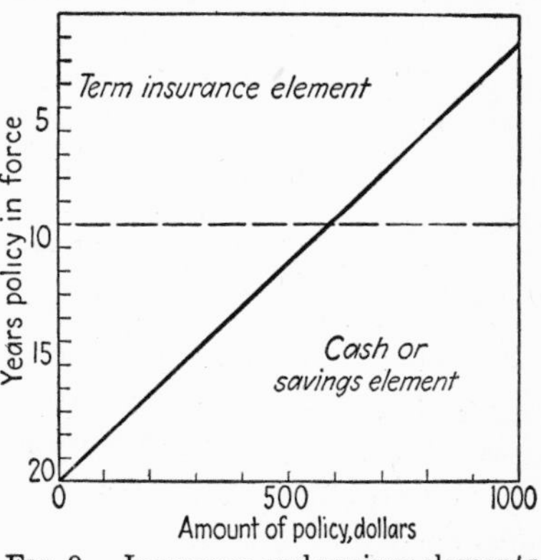

FIG. 9.—Insurance and savings elements in a 20-year endowment policy.

All the contracts in class 3 are, therefore, a combination of decreasing term and increasing sinking fund. In the illustration of a 20-year endowment with a yearly deposit of $48, the amount of term insurance varies from $1,000 the first year to $70 the nineteenth year, and the cash value varies from nothing the first year to $1,000 at the end of the twentieth year. In the event of death before the end of the twentieth year, the heirs of the purchaser receive $1,000. Suppose he died in the tenth year: We have now a cash value of $407 and individual term insurance in the amount of $593. The company returns the $407, the cash value or sinking fund, together with the $593 which is taken from the mortality fund. Thus there is at all times available $1,000 to be returned to the heirs if insured dies before the end of twentieth year, or $1,000 to himself if he survives to the end of the 20-year period.

The premium outlay for these contracts varies with the age of the person involved. The funds that are to be paid must be obtained from the group, and the probable period over which premiums can be collected or payments are to be made by the company are indicated by the mortality table. Thus for a group issued ordinary life insurance at age 30, the average expectation of life is 35.33 years, and this is the average number of years over which it may be expected that premiums will be collected. If the age of persons on whom the insurance were issued was 40, then the average number of years over which premiums would be paid would be 28.18 and the annual premiums would need to be enough higher so that the required sums could be accumulated in the shorter period. The premium for ordinary life insurance will thus rise with the age at which the policy is originally taken out. The contrary situation is true for an annuity. The expectation of life now indicates the average number of years over which the company will be forced to make payments. The older the annuitant, the larger the annuity the company can agree to pay in return for the deposit of a given sum, since the number of payments to be made is smaller.

Contracts differ in their manner of premium payment. Each may be purchased by the payment of a lump sum at the beginning or by periodical deposits such as annual, semiannual, quarterly, or monthly payments. Immediate annuities are always purchased by a lump-sum payment at the beginning of the contract. Many deferred annuities and much life and endowment insurance are also purchased by this single-deposit plan. However, the bulk of insurance in classes 1, 2, and 3 is bought on the installment plan.

Policies differ as to the number of persons that they insure. Insurance policies are commonly written on the life of a single individual, but occasionally *joint life policies* are written, which cover the lives of two or more persons and are payable upon the death of the first. Insurance also is written upon larger groups and is known as *group insurance.* Group policies differ from joint life policies in that they are not terminated by the death of one of the individuals. Employers often secure blanket insurance against the death of their employees, payable to the families of these employees on their death. Such policies are called *group insurance policies.* The cost of this type of insurance is borne either by the employer alone, by the employees alone, or by equal or unequal contributions by both employer and employee. They are not written on specific individuals but on all who are employed by this particular employer, and often only during their period of employment.

The great bulk of the insurance written in this country is written on the legal-reserve basis although there is some provided by fraternal or assessment associations. Roughly, insurance companies fall into two groups, known as *stock* and *mutual* companies. The volume of business done by mutual companies is in excess of that of the stock companies, although the latter exceed the mutual companies in number. Mutual companies are, as the title suggests, owned and controlled by the policyholders, whereas stock companies are, of course, owned and controlled by the stockholders. Policies vary according to the right they convey to share in the profits of the company. *Participating* policies provide for the return to the insured of a portion of his premium, known as a *dividend,* in the event that the earnings of the company justify such a dividend. The term *nonparticipating* policies simply means that the profits accruing are paid not to the policyholder but to the stockholder in the stock company.

The level-premium plan involves charging during the early years of the policy a net premium which is larger than is necessary to pay for the insurance in those years, with the result that a fund is accumulated to meet the costs of the insurance incurred in the later years. These overcharges are credited to the policy and constitute the reserve. The reserves are the source of the cash surrender values and loan values now a regular feature of practically all life policies, except term policies, written by legal-reserve companies and which become available to the insured usually after the third year of the life of the policy. An example is given in Table 59.

TABLE 59.—GUARANTEED VALUES OF AN ORDINARY $1,000 LIFE POLICY TAKEN OUT AT AGE TWENTY-FIVE

Years policy has been in force	Cash surrender value	Paid-up life insurance	Extended insurance	
			Years	Days
2	$12	$34	1	214
3	26	71	3	159
4	36	95	4	249
5	45	119	5	355
6	55	142	7	111
20	230	457	19	166

Three methods of payment of the surrender value are generally provided: cash settlement, paid-up insurance, and extended insurance. Under a cash settlement, no insurance remains in force. Under extended insurance, the policy remains in force for a limited period of time, and, under the paid-up insurance settlement, the face of the policy is reduced and the policy remains in force throughout the life of the insured. Under both of the latter settlements, the amount of the insurance is such as the cash surrender value will purchase as a single net premium. The loan values represent the amounts the company will loan on the security of the policy to the insured.

Insurance policies differ in their premium outlay depending upon the nature of the policy. Premiums vary with the age of the insured. The higher ages have greater risks of death than the lower ages, and, in consequence, for a given type of policy the premium rates increase with the age at which the insurance is taken out. The most inexpensive policy, from the standpoint of the annual outlay required, is the term policy; and the shorter the term, the lower the annual premium. Straight life will cost more than term insurance. Limited payment will necessitate a larger premium than straight life, because the period during which the fund to pay the insurance is accumulated is limited, rather than extending over the entire life. Premiums for endowment insurance will be much higher than those of the preceding types, since, in addition to the insurance provided, a fund equal to the face of the policy must be built up during the policy life to provide the endowment at the end of the period. Other types of policies will vary in cost depending upon their particular features. An example of the quoted rates is given in Table 60. These are to be taken only as indications, and some differences will be found among companies. Comparison among companies is usually made on the basis of net cost upon surrender, *i.e.*, on the basis of total premiums minus total dividends minus surrender value, and the company showing a low net cost is usually considered the better company, other things being equal. The purchaser of insurance should always keep in mind that he is buying a contract. Instead of buying by net cost upon surrender only, he might well examine the provisions

TABLE 60.—ANNUAL COST OF $1,000 OF INSURANCE

Type of insurace	Age when insured	
	25	45
5-year term	$9.68	$14.82
Ordinary life	20.14	37.09
20-payment life	30.07	45.69
20-year endowment	48.03	54.15

in the contract upon which such cost is based. There is not much difference between the best companies with regard to net cost, but there is a great difference between the best and the worst.

Two principal problems confront the purchaser of insurance, the choice of a type of policy and the choice of a company. The choice of the type of policy depends upon the individual situation, and few generalizations can be made. It usually is a question of the proportion to be directed toward insurance and toward accumulation. As is indicated in Table 61, the same expenditures may be divided between insurance coverage and accumulation in varying degrees. If the primary consideration is insurance, as is usually the case with younger family groups, some form of term contract should often be recommended to give the family as much protection as possible for the minimum premium outlay. As soon as the family can afford a reasonable amount of protection and in addition to such protection can also set aside a small investment fund, then the ordinary life contract is to be recommended. The choice of the best company requires analysis beyond the resources of the ordinary insurance purchaser.

TABLE 61.—AMOUNT PURCHASED WITH AN ANNUAL GROSS PREMIUM OF $300 IN A LARGE MUTUAL COMPANY AT AGE 25[1]

Type of policy	Premium per $1,000	Insurance	Cash surrender value			
			5 years	10 years	15 years	20 years
Ordinary life.......	$20.14	$14,895	681	1,474	2,389	3,434
20-payment life....	30.07	9,977	953	2,085	3,431	5,034
20-year endowment.	48.03	6,246	1,158	2,548	4,219	6,246

[1] The cost less dividends, based on past experience, would have been about two-thirds of these figures.

The purchaser may make his own investigation by consulting *Best Life Insurance Reports*, or some other good handbook, or may consult a reliable broker on the various points. The following are important considerations, and a good company should stand up well on all of them:[1]

1. Adequate size. The company should be large enough to obtain diversity of investment, a sound risk basis, and low cost. There are good small companies, but the preference of the non-expert must be for the larger organization.

2. The quality of assets. The investments should be well diversified. Liquidity is also important.

3. Reserve basis. The more conservative companies operate on the "full level premium American experience 3 per cent basis."

4. Surplus position (ratio of surplus to liabilities). Good companies fall between 5 and 10 per cent. Mutual companies operating on less than 5 per cent may be questioned, while

[1] This check list was devised by Prof. John C. Clendenin, University of California at Los Angeles.

those with over 10 per cent may be building surplus at the expense of policy dividends. Nonparticipating policies are of course strengthened by large and growing surpluses.

5. Net cost (total premiums minus total dividends minus surrender value). The company showing the lowest net cost over a period of (say) 20 years is usually considered the best, other things being equal.

6. Interest earnings. Average earnings are the important figure. Both high earnings and low earnings are indications of an undesirable situation.

7. Mortality. This is usually about 60 per cent of the American Experience Table of Mortality, a deviation of 5 per cent either way not being unusual.

8. Expenses. Comparisons may be found in "Unique Manual—Digest," or "Best Life Reports." The following comparisons may be used: total expense to total receipts, non-first-year expense to non-first-year income, or expense per $1,000 of insurance in force.

9. Types of business written. A company that writes excessive amounts of disability income insurance is not too desirable from the standpoint of safety. Retirement annuities, too, may be undesirable from a safety standpoint, since the span of life is definitely increasing. On the other hand, the company concentrating on life contracts (other things being equal) should become stronger with the passage of time. If the company has disability policies and retirement annuities, it should have a considerable volume of life contracts as an offset.

10. Management and reputation of the company. The quality of the management of the company may be gauged by the measurements suggested above, but its reputation for generosity and service is to be judged separately.

4. Investment.—The holding of funds, other than those in the immediate reserve, as a source of additional current income or for later use as, for example, a retirement fund, requires an investment policy. The "ideal investment" is one that has a high degree of safety of both principal and interest, yields a large return to the investor, and is readily marketable. It is impossible to secure all these qualities in their highest degree in a single investment. For example, the bonds of the United States government carry a high degree of safety of principal and interest, but a low yield; certain bonds of foreign governments promise high yields but carry little safety of principal and interest; real-estate mortgages may yield well but may not be readily marketable. The most important attribute of an investment from the standpoint of a beginner is safety. Safety is a relative term and should be thought of as such. Even the strongest guarantees of a return of principal and interest are subject to the risk of a change in purchasing power because of changes in the general price level. The importance of the latter factor makes a consideration of types of investments on the basis of whether they involve promises to pay in dollars or are claims to the income produced by properties a primary consideration.

The principal investments promising a definite return of principal in dollars and specified interest returns are annuities, bonds, accumulations in cash surrender values of life insurance, and savings in the types of organizations discussed in the section on the Accumulation of Reserves. For those who desire a dollar income for themselves for the low earning period of old age, the annuity contracts of insurance companies are entitled to first consideration. For those who are well along in years and have no posterity to consider, the annuity is a valuable means of securing them the largest possible certain dollar income for their entire life. The interest rate at which the insurance companies figure earnings is low, and, in consequence, for young people annuities do not yield more than could be earned by other investments. For older people, the rate becomes high, passing 8 per cent some time between ages fifty and sixty. The following table shows the average annuity returns for 15 American companies for males of different ages:

Table 62.—Average of the Returns Yielded by Annuities Taken at Various Ages in 15 American Companies[1]

Age	Per Cent Yielded by Annuity
Forty	5.83
Fifty	7.03
Sixty	9.21
Seventy	13.27
Eighty	19.35

[1] C. O. Hardy, "Risk and Risk Bearing," p. 278.

The bonds of the United States government are regarded as the safest available to the American investor. The savings bonds, previously discussed, are unusually well suited to the needs of the small investor. State and municipal bonds are less desirable ordinarily. There are likewise a large number of bonds of business corporations of a desirable type. Bonds are usually issued in denominations of $1,000, although there are a great many at $500, and some at $100. The latter are commonly designated as *baby bonds.* They do not differ materially from the $1,000 bonds since these are usually issued at the same time, with the same security, with identical maturities, interest, and other features. There is a difference in their marketability, however, the smaller bonds selling on the market at a slightly lower price and being purchasable only at a slightly higher price than the larger bonds.

Mortgages on both farm and city property may also often be advantageously used as investments. They have the advantage of calling for a definite amount to be paid both in interest and in principal. They have the disadvantage that the appraisal of the property securing them may be incorrectly made, that they usually can be sold at a forced sale only at a large discount, and that, in case of default of payments, foreclosure is costly and may result in a loss. They generally yield a higher return than bonds. Though mortgages are used extensively by insurance companies as an investment, this does not mean that they prove good investments for the small investor. The fact is that there are great differences between individual mortgages, hence they require too technical a knowledge of property values to be purchased without the advice of competent disinterested parties.

The advantages of the foregoing types of investments and deposits in the institutions for accumulation of reserves is that with the exercise of a moderate discretion the investor may be fairly certain to secure the return of his principal and a low but sure interest return. The danger of a price rise that would lessen the purchasing power of his savings is always present, and, although his first investments should be primarily of this type, after some accumulation he should consider purchases of income property or rights to the earnings of properties as a hedge against such a price rise. These latter purchases are of a much more hazardous character and require the exercise of a great deal of judgment. In case the income of the family is derived from the ownership of a business, then this type of hedge will be amply provided by the opportunities for reinvestment in the business. The more usual consideration will be the question of purchasing a home or buying stocks in some company.

Renting is usually less expensive than home ownership if full allowance is made for all costs. Home ownership, however, often provides a psychic return to the family in excess of that derived from renting. Home ownership is also entitled to consideration on the grounds of the probable appreciation in value of the property with a price rise. The purchase of a home requires such a large investment or commitment to make certain payments that utmost consideration must be given not only to the probable value of the property itself but also to the size of the total investment. The purchase price should not exceed two or at the most two and one-half times the annual income of the family; otherwise the burden of ownership will become excessive. The ordinary family will rarely make an investment of this size in any other way during its life. For this reason, the most careful consideration will need to be given to it.[1]

Informed observers are practically unanimous that stock speculation is an "unbeatable game." Probably not one out of a hundred who "play the market" are eventually successful. This does not mean, however, that a portion of the small investor's holdings may not be held properly in the form of shares in carefully selected corporations. These stocks should be purchased only after examination of the reports of some reliable, disinterested rating service such as Moody's Investment Service or Standard Statistics, should be securities listed on one of the larger stock exchanges, and should be purchased outright.[2]

[1] For an excellent discussion of the considerations to be taken into account when faced with the problem of whether to rent, buy, or build a home, see the article by Albert Mayer on this subject in Consumers' Union Reports, January, 1938, pp. 7–11. The same issue of the reports announces additional future articles on the community, on the site, orientation and plan of the house, on furnishability and style, on various types of materials, and on the maintenance of the home.

[2] DAVID F. JORDAN, "Managing Personal Finance," lists the following as 10 high-grade stocks: American Telephone and Telegraph, E. I. Du Pont, Eastman Kodak, General Electric, General Motors, International Harvester, Pacific Gas and Electric, Pennsylvania Railroad, Standard Oil of New Jersey, and Union Pacific Railroad.

The unit of trading for stocks on the New York Stock Exchange is 100 shares. Lots smaller than this are known as *odd lots* and comprise 30 to 40 per cent of all the trading. Certain traders on the exchange specialize in handling these odd lots and handle shares at a differential of from one-eighth to one-fourth of a point, depending upon the marketability of the stock, charging a higher price if buying and remitting a lower price if selling. The investor may thus purchase as little as a single share in the largest corporation.

The purchaser of stocks has secured some safeguards through the Security Exchange Act of 1934. This law provides that all important stock exchanges shall be registered with the SEC as national security exchanges. The registered exchanges become subject to Federal rules and regulations, and the individual securities listed on these exchanges likewise must be registered. The public must have made available to it accurate and complete current information with respect to those securities. Speculative manipulation of security prices is forbidden. These advances in the protection of the security purchaser have been highly desirable, but the individual should not rely upon the law to protect him; he must continue to exercise good judgment in his selection and be wary of fraud.

Questions

1. In view of the possibility of a rise in the general price level and the growing feeling of social responsibility for the aged, do you think that young people are justified in making any serious attempt at substantial saving?
2. What influence would changes in prices have upon the value of an annuity?
3. If a person should decide to cash in or surrender his insurance policy, what alternatives would be open to him?
4. What bearing do the earnings of a company have on the probable relationship of the price of its preferred and common stock?
5. If you should inherit $10,000, how would you invest it at the present time? Justify your answer.
6. At what period of the business cycle would you advise the purchase of stocks and at what period bonds?

CHAPTER XVII

THE PROBLEM OF PURCHASING CONSUMERS' GOODS

The division of the income among the budget groups and the decision as to the direction and kinds of expenditures do not complete the problem of the administration of that income. Commodity selection is essential to the complete consumption cycle since scales of living may be impaired by a dissipation of money income resulting from unintelligent consumer buying. In the case of purchases, the problems of where, when, how much, and what to buy become very important. There is, in addition, the question as to what method one should select in paying for the goods. All these are important consumer problems. Each becomes more complex as the variety of products increases and as conflicting claims continue to be made regarding commodities and the several channels of distribution.

There is no question that there is tremendous effort expended by business to persuade consumers to purchase higher quality merchandise than they require; to buy on the bases of fear, pride, and snobbery as substitutes for rational judgment; to utilize certain service features—*e.g.*, installment contracts—which, in many instances, are extravagant and wasteful. It is the opinion of the authors that the efficiency of consumer purchasing could be increased materially if a sort of skepticism could be created in the mind of each buyer. The consumer, in other words, should avoid the acceptance of vendor claims without careful investigation. An experimental attitude on the part of the buyer will lead toward a more careful selection of goods and services. Wherever possible, information derived from dispassionate investigation should be substituted for biased claims of producers.

1. The Amount of Purchasing by Women.—The problem of buying falls principally upon the housewife. In the majority of homes, fully two-thirds of the purchases made will be at her direction or with her advice. Articles entering directly into the consumption of other members of the family are often purchased by the housewife, for example, the shirts and ties of many a husband. We may gain some idea of her importance from the following table which shows the percentage of different articles purchased by various members of a group of New York families:[1]

2. The Problem of Where to Buy.—Identical goods are often sold at different prices in the stores of the same community. These differences are quite substantial in many instances. They are likely to be more pronounced in convenience than in shopping goods, and, in consequence, while the difference on a particular purchase may be small, the total saving, if all items were purchased at the lowest possible prices, would be quite significant. Table 64 gives figures for comparative prices between independent and chain drug and grocery stores.

[1] That the head of the family has a great deal of influence in most of the consumer purchasing, however, there is little doubt. The following excerpt from an advertisement designed for the purpose of selling advertising space in *Time* magazine, though humorous and somewhat biased, illustrates the importance of men's influence in purchasing: " . . . shrewd advertising men know that he who talks only to the woman is only half doing his selling job . . . let the men who read this ponder well whether Woman (the natural purchasing agent to be sure) really *determines* the purchase of 85% of everything which goes into the home . . .

"When the wife of a business man—*your* wife, for instance, wants an automatic refrigerator does she just trip out and pay $400 for the best looking one? Or do you first authorize the expenditure, and secondly, look into the mechanics and upkeep of the different makes yourself? . . .

"When a roof leak is discovered, does your wife call in a contractor, on her own and tell him to put on asbestos shingles? Very seldom, very seldom. Isn't she actually a passive buyer of oil burners or furnaces, of lumber, stone, copper, pipes, paints? When the furniture was purchased for the new house didn't you decide how much would be paid for it and have considerable to say in the selection of it?

"When the family wants a radio, do you or don't you do some short and long waving about it yourself? Do you have something to say about the car you drive or is it your wife and the bright-eyed children who decide the matter while you stand by and utter a check?

"Women may actually put the money on the counter, sign the check, or give the order for 85% or 99% of everything that goes into the home, but can there be a doubt that a great part of the time she is specifying this radio tube, that gasoline, that breakfast food, or this varnish, not only with the *approval* but at the direct *instigation* of her husband? After all, most women will honor their husband's wishes. Nor should it be forgotten (even at the risk of seeming brutal) that it is the man who pays, and paying, calls a considerable number of the tunes."

TABLE 63.—A COMPARISON OF THE PROPORTION OF THE PURCHASES OF CERTAIN ARTICLES MADE BY MEN AND WOMEN[1]

Class of article	Percentage by men all alone	Percentage by women all alone	Percentage by both	Percentage by neither
Men's clothing	65	11	23	1
Women's clothing	1	87	12	0
Druggist's articles	10	48	41	1
Kitchenware	2	89	8	1
Pets	19	5	15	61
Dry goods	0	96	4	0
Vehicles	23	1	15	61
House furnishings	4	48	46	2
Musical instruments	13	7	20	60
Raw and market foods	0	87	13	0
Package foods	3	79	14	4
Miscellaneous	6	22	68	4
Average	12.2	48.3	23.2	16.2

[1] H. C. HOLLINGWORTH, "Advertising and Selling," p. 296.

TABLE 64.—RELATIVE CHAIN AND INDEPENDENT SELLING PRICE AS REVEALED BY THE FEDERAL TRADE COMMISSION CHAIN-STORE INVESTIGATION[1]

City	Year	Selling prices	
		Independent	Chain
Part A: Grocery Study			
Washington	1929	106.42	100
Cincinnati	1929	108.84	100
Memphis	1930	108.28	100
Detroit	1931	110.47	100
Average	....	108.5	100
Part B: Drug Study			
Washington	1929	124.15	100
Cincinnati	1929	120.35	100
Memphis	1930	120.69	100
Detroit	1931	117.48	100
Average	....	120.67	100

[1] CHARLES F. PHILLIPS, "The Federal Trade Commission Chain Store Investigation: A Note," *J. Marketing*, January, 1938, p. 191.

At the time of the Federal Trade Commission study, independent prices exceeded those of chains by an average of 8½ per cent for groceries and about 20 per cent for drugs. This seems to check with most of the other studies that have been made to determine relative prices between independent and chain establishments.

Fair-trade legislation coming into existence since the inauguration of these studies has probably altered the situation considerably. Particularly is this true in the drug field. The grocery price differential, however, has probably changed very little. In a study of grocery items made at the University of Minnesota in 1933, it was concluded that "the prices charged in ownership chains are markedly lower, grade for grade, than the prices in other types of retail outlets. The average price of grade A products is 16 per cent lower in ownership chains than in all the stores combined. Ownership chain store prices of grade B and grade C goods are, respectively, 10 and 20 per cent lower than the corresponding prices in all stores. These lower prices are offset in part [however] by poorer quality. Ownership chain value, based on a combination of price and quality figures, is 14 per cent higher for grade A products and nearly 10 per cent higher for all grades combined than the corresponding values in all outlets. This greater value in relation to price [the survey found] is offset by the fact that ownership chain prices are for cash and carry service rather than for credit and delivery service, as is the case with most of the other outlets. This finding with respect to price harmonizes rather closely with the studies of prices of identical goods and strengthens the conclusion that consumers may save about 10 per cent on their staple grocery expenditures by patronizing the cash and carry ownership chain stores."[1]

Differences in prices between the types of stores are due largely, though not entirely, to differences in the services that are furnished with the goods. The thing that the consumer purchases in a retail store is not simply a package of raisins (say), but a package of raisins at a particular place and with certain services. The chain store, for example, is usually a cash-and-carry store. It has no credit expense, or loss from bad debts, or delivery

[1] Roland S. Vaile and Alice M. Child, "Grocery Qualities and Prices," pp. 13–14.

expense, and can, in consequence, afford to sell goods on a narrower margin to those who do not demand these services. An idea of the effect of these services can be gained from the differences in prices charged by grocers in New York City for seven standard fruits and vegetables. Unit stores furnishing credit and delivery services charged an average price of 27 cents for such products; the cash-and-delivery unit stores, 24.9 cents; and the cash-and-carry units, 23.3 cents.[1]

Department stores do not often push their grocery departments. Together with some of the other strictly convenience-goods departments, they are customarily operated at a loss as individual departments. Where they exist, they are maintained because they add completeness to the stock of the store, and a reputation for completeness is an important department-store asset; in this way, the grocery department contributes to the sales of other departments.

Among particular stores of the same class, price comparisons on the basis of single items may not be completely fair. A store sells a wide variety of articles and is likely to be higher on some and lower on others than its competitors. Thus one store may be low on staple groceries and high on canned goods, or low on fruit and vegetables and high on flour and sugar.

Consumers do not generally shop around for each of these classes of goods but choose a store for the general level of its prices, if even this enters into their calculations. In a total of 2,860 housewives included in the U.S. Department of Agriculture's study of consumers' preferences in the case of meat, 56.9 per cent stated that they never shopped among stores in purchasing meat, 31.2 per cent that they shopped among stores sometimes, and 11.9 per cent stated that they shopped among stores a great deal.[2] A study of about 3,100 Columbus housewives by the Ohio State University Bureau of Business Research showed comparative shopping in foods to be the greatest in the case of vegetables, next in meats, and least in the case of general groceries.[3]

[1] "Expense Factors in City Distribution of Perishables," *U.S. Dept. Agr. Bull.* 1411, p. 24.

[2] "Consumers' Habits and Preferences in the Purchase and Consumption of Meat," *U.S. Dept. Agr. Bull.* 1143, p. 32.

[3] "A Study of Housewives' Buying Habits," *Ohio State Univ. Studies*, vol. 2, No. 16, *Bur. Business Res. Monographs* No. 3.

The retailers of strictly shopping lines make greater efforts to keep their prices in line with those of competitors than do the retailers of convenience lines.[1] This is very important in shopping lines, since customers are passing constantly from store to store, and sales and reputation will be lost if prices get appreciably higher than in other stores. As has been indicated in another connection, department stores in large cities maintain an elaborate system of "shoppers" who visit the stores of competitors, comparing prices and qualities of goods with those of the home store. When prices are unreasonably low, considerable quantities of goods may be purchased from the competitors without his knowledge as to their final destination and transferred to the shoppers' store to be sold at prices to meet the competitor's. Shoppers also keep watch for new goods and rapidly moving lines.

The prices of specialty goods show a wide range for the different lines. Thus there will be a wide range in the prices of different radios and washing machines. Many of these will be selling at prices out of all proportion to their cost. Any particular make of specialty good, however, is likely to be sold at the same price in the stores selling it. This is because price frequently enters into the advertising, and also because of the close control over the distribution which is exercised by the manufacturer in the case of specialty goods through the exclusive agency or his own retail outlets.

The consumer will do well to look for differences in price, if not constantly, at least at regular intervals. He may be able to save a significant amount, in other words, by purchasing at

[1] Even here, however, there are many opportunities for consumer savings due to an absence of perfection of competition and to differences in the efficiency of retail institutions. There are, for example, differentials between mail-order retail-store, and catalogue prices. One of the largest firms in the mail-order field explains the reasons for this situation as follows:

"1. There is no waiting for business.

Only a third to a half of a retail salesperson's time is spent in serving customers. Mail orders are filled on a 'factory-production' basis.

"2. Actual time spent in filling an order is much less.

A mail-order clerk can fill orders in less time than it takes a salesperson to sell the same amount of merchandise over the counter. All the mail-order clerk has to do is to fill orders—the customer makes his selection before he mails the order.

"3. Many mail-order operations are carried on by machinery."

the proper place. In choosing outlets, each consumer must often decide in the light of his own circumstances whether a saving is worth the inconvenience of paying cash and forgoing services.

3. The Problem of When to Buy.—Another possibility of saving lies in purchasing articles at the proper time. The prices of many products vary during the year, and purchases of these products need to be considered carefully. Food is an important group in this class. Fresh fruits and vegetables, for example, are

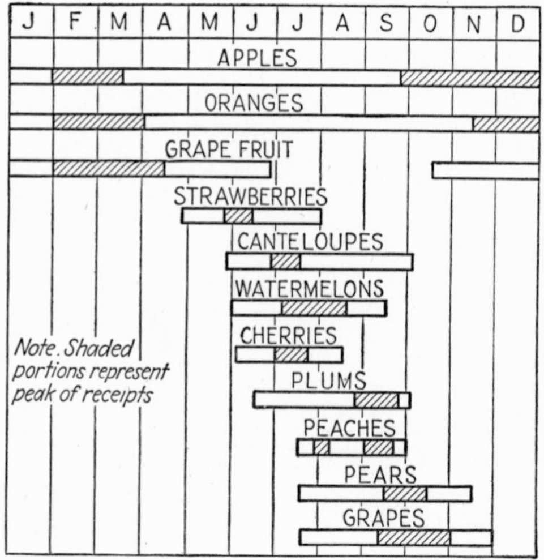

FIG. 10.—Period of carlot receipts of certain fruits in Minneapolis.

highly seasonal in nature, and there are limited periods in which each constitutes a proper purchase in the lower income groups. There is, likewise, a limited period in which they are sufficiently high in quality and low in price to be particularly suited for canning and preserving. These periods show some variation among years, but, in general, come at approximately the same time.

A valuable aid in proper seasonal purchasing may be obtained through the construction of a seasonal calendar which gives the time when foodstuffs are in season in the local market. Such a calendar would give a list of the products arranged in order, with the length of the season indicated and the period when it is at its height. Figure 10 will furnish an idea of the nature of such a chart of fruits. Articles that show considerable variation in price, but not principally seasonal, may be compared with competing products by calculating the ratio of the prices at which a dollar would purchase the same number of calories in each. These may quite profitably be calculated for the major food items. An illustration is given in Table 65.

TABLE 65.—RELATIVE PRICES OF MEATS AT WHICH EACH DOLLAR PURCHASES THE SAME CALORIES

Meat considered	Meat considered as a substitute Ratio which the price of the substitute must be to the price of the meat under consideration in order to purchase equal calories				
	Beef, flank	Beef, round	Ham, fresh	Pork, chops	Lamb, leg
Beef, flank	100	80	134	113	77
Beef, round	125	100	168	141	97
Ham, fresh	74	59	100	84	58
Pork, chops	88	70	118	100	68
Lamb, leg	128	103	172	146	100

When the price of the substitute meat is greater in proportion to the meat considered than the figures in the table, then the purchase of the substitute is undesirable, and when less it is desirable. Thus, if beef flank were 20 cents per pound and ham were 30 cents per pound, the price of ham would be 150 per cent of the price of beef flank and beef flank would furnish more calories per dollar of expenditure.

A somewhat similar situation occurs in the case of shopping goods. Style goods are often priced higher in the early part of the season than they are in the latter part of the season, and slow-moving lines are frequently sold below actual cost near the end of the season. Those who can afford to sacrifice priority of style can make important savings by purchasing at these later sales. Sales of particular lines of goods are conducted at regular seasons of the year by nearly all department stores, *e.g.*, sales of furniture, linens, and men's clothing. The times of these sales should be learned by the housewife and she should adjust her plans to provide for the year's requirements as far as possible at that time. Also, there are often sales in many specialty lines. The contract providing for an exclusive agency commonly permits a single sale, or possibly two during the year, below the manufacturer's established price. These occur often when a new model appears. Consumers who do not insist upon the "the latest" can effect definite savings at such times.

4. The Problems of How Much to Buy.—There is also the problem of the proper quantity to purchase. Many of the costs of retail services are related to the single sale and do not vary a great deal with the size of the sale. For example, the cost to the merchant of selling a peck of potatoes to one customer and that of selling a bushel to another are approximately the same. These differences are roughly adjusted by differences in the proportions of the prices of large and small quantities of the same articles. Thus a 100-pound sack of sugar will ordinarily be sold by a retailer at a price somewhat less than four times that of a 25-pound sack.

It would often be advantageous, in consequence, for the consumer to purchase in larger quantities than he customarily does. There are, however, a number of factors that must not be overlooked in reaching a decision as to whether to buy in the larger quantity. For example, one must consider the amount of discount to be gained from the larger purchase, the probable waste and deterioration that will arise from domestic storage, the care required to prevent spoilage, the storage facilities needed, the probable effect of the larger quantity on hand on the waste in cooking and at the table, and the investment involved in the purchase. Some goods, tinned foods, for example, often can be advantageously purchased for a year at a time when funds and storage facilities are available. It may be appropriate to purchase supplies of other things for shorter periods. Proper planning will enable quantity purchasing to save not only the household money but the time of the housewife as well.

There is some possibility of gaining the advantages of the lower prices on larger purchases through the combination of the purchases of a number of households. There are a number of cases of employees in particular plants making regular group purchases of special commodities, such as butter. These sometimes take the form of informal buying clubs, covering a wide range of purchase. However, such organizations depend for their success principally on the activity and vigor of their leaders, and except for short periods they are usually not successful.

5. The Problem of What to Buy.—The problem of what to buy is at once the most important and the most difficult of the several purchasing problems. It involves actual selection of merchandise from a wide variety of items which fall into innumerable price lines. The task of the consumer is that of matching offerings and requirements.

Not every buyer requires the highest quality merchandise. The consumer's job is to determine the quality required and then discover the item that promises to satisfy the requirements most exactly. This task is sometimes very difficult. For example, the several qualities of riding ease, smoothness, long life, economy, and beauty in automobiles are of varying importance to different individuals. Moreover, the several cars offered the consumer possess these qualities in varying degrees. A sound decision with respect to a combination of required qualities followed by a careful canvass of the field is essential to the successful culmination of the buying transaction. Many merchandise-selection problems are equally complex. Hence, guides to purchasing are of great importance.

Professor Jessie V. Coles of the University of Missouri has presented a number of guides to purchasing which, though possessing limitations, should be exceedingly helpful to the consumer-buyer.[1] An evaluation of these several guides follow:

1. *Price* though of some help to the consumer-buyer is not completely adequate as a guide. The reason for this is that the consumer market is so imperfect that the producer of overpriced merchandise often is not forced to revise the prices of his offerings. Indeed, quasi monopolies actually thrive on imaginary differences in quality and are nurtured by means of brand advertising. To be sure, the highest priced articles very often possess a high degree of quality, but the average consumer cannot afford a differential just for the purpose of quality insurance.

Available evidence, leading to conclusions regarding a close relationship between quality and price, are somewhat conflicting. For some products, one can assume such a relationship; for others, the correlation seems not to exist. For example, in their grocery study, Profs. Vaile and Child conclude that the differences in quality between the high and the lower grades of canned goods are almost exactly proportionate to the differ-

[1] Jessie V. Coles, "Standardization of Consumers' Goods."

ences in price. On the other hand, "Laboratory tests by the National Bureau of Standards of 111 pairs of silk hosiery showed that most of the hosiery selling for $1.00 was superior to stockings of the same weight selling for $1.65 and $1.85. . . . Manufacturers of dresses frequently use the same materials in goods selling at $6.75, $7.75, $8.75, $10.75 and $12.75. Some specialty shops buy dresses for $10.95 that are commonly retailed for $16.95 and put hand rolled hems in them and change an ornament or two and sell them for $29.50 and $39.50."[1] The correlation between quality and price has also been found to be low in boys' clothing, towels and sheeting, toilet goods, and razor blades.[2] And so it can be seen that price, though somewhat helpful in selecting certain types of products, is far from adequate, generally, as a buying guide.

2. *Inspection* is of some value in the selection of merchandise. It is definitely helpful in choosing books and in determining such qualities as the odor of perfume, the color of cloth, or the fit of garment. It is definitely limited, however, in that it fails to detect such things as an absence of fastness of color, the presence of weighting in silk, and inferior inner construction of furniture. There are the further limitations that the consumer has not the time to inspect all offerings and that some commodities cannot be inspected since they are put up in sealed containers. Inspection where practicable should be utilized in merchandise selection, however; and the better the training the buyer possesses, the more effective will be its results.

3. *Experience* is definitely helpful as a guide to purchasing and can be used to supplement inspection. The consumer-buyer should assume an unbiased experimental attitude in purchasing, recording results where necessary in order to derive the best results from purchasing experience. Though experience is an exceedingly valuable guide to purchasing, it also possesses certain limitations. For one thing, because of an absence of adequate time and energy, experience is often not broad enough. Moreover, the consumer, in many instances is unable properly to control conditions under which comparisons are made. That is to say, variations in the condition of use may affect the results

[1] NORRIS A. BRISCO and JOHN W. WINGATE, "Buying for Retail Stores," p. 145.

[2] *Ibid.*, p. 145.

one way or another. Furthermore, full advantage cannot always be taken of knowledge gained, because of an absence of product identification or because of quality changes which have been made in the goods that are offered.

4. *Testing* is closely allied to experimentation, and, although it is advantageous to large buyers, it is of limited practical value to consumer-buyers. Usually scientific testing requires time, technical knowledge, and equipment that consumers do not possess. Moreover, for some types of merchandise, samples are difficult if not impossible to obtain. Some advocates of testing seem to assume, for example, that obtaining a swatch from a $3.98 dress offers no problem! Testing as a guide to purchasing, then, leaves much to be desired.

5. *Trade-marks* as sources of buying information are inadequate in and of themselves but are of great value in facilitating the use of other buying guides, *i.e.*, inspection, experience, and advertising. They make possible not only the repurchase of satisfactory goods but also the avoidance of repetition in the purchase of unsatisfactory goods. The value of trade-marks for this purpose, however, depends upon uniformity of product quality which is not always existent. Moreover, lack of homogeneity (inherent in some kinds of products, *e.g.*, fruits and vegetables) might result from a change of source by the retailer or from a deliberate impairment of quality for the purpose of keeping prices uniform.

6. *Advertising* as it exists today is not in itself an adequate guide to purchasing. Noninformative advertising, indeed, is a misguiding and confusing influence. Much advertising is still of the noninformative type. An examination of 145 advertisements of textiles and clothing, for example, revealed that only 34 per cent were informative (regarding price, uses, specific facts on color, fibers, etc.) and that the remainder, 66 per cent, were noninformative (confining their statements to general claims of economy, smartness, newness, distinctiveness, etc.).[1] Advertising is, however, potentially of great value to the consumer-buyer. In fact, even as it exists today, advertising is useful in informing the consumer-buyer concerning the availability of goods, their prices, and their uses. And as a result of such information, other guides to selection (inspection, experience,

[1] Coles, *op. cit.*, p. 59.

etc.) are made more effective by indicating which goods should be examined.

7. *Labels* are often of greater aid to consumers than advertisements in that labels on certain types of commodities (owing to food and drug legislation) tend to be more accurate. Labels are not completely adequate, however. It must be recalled that, according to the old law, statements on foods need not be made unless there is a substitution in its ingredients or unless it contains narcotics; unless it is in packaged form, in which case the quantity of the contents must be stated and whatever statements are made must be truthful. The law regarding labels on drugs is somewhat more drastic.[1] Labels are often helpful as an aid to inspection in the case. Uses to which the goods may be put as well as directions for use are important to the consumer-buyer. Information as to the date of packing commodities subject to deterioration may be extremely important, and facts about the quantity held by a container and about the composition of the contents may be of great aid to intelligent commodity selection.

[1] The 1938 food and drug amendment, most provisions of which go into effect in June, 1939, has the following labeling provisions:

(*a*) For foods—

1. In foods for which no definition or standard of identity has been prescribed (and except for spices, coloring, or flavoring in which case they may be simply designated as such) ingredients must be named.
2. Except for butter, ice cream, and cheese, labels must declare artificial coloring, flavoring, or chemical preservatives.
3. Special dietary foods must have informative labeling as to vitamin, mineral, or other dietary properties.

(*b*) For drugs—

1. Labels of official drugs must reveal any differences in strength, purity, or quality from the official standards (U.S.P., N.F., or H.P.).
2. Labels of nonofficial drugs must list active ingredients.
3. Labels of drugs and devices must bear adequate directions for use as well as warnings against probable misuse.
4. Labels on drugs intended for use of man must bear warnings against habit formation if they contain any of a certain list of narcotic or hypnotic substances.
5. Labels on drugs subject to deterioration must have a printed warning to that effect.
6. Poisonous coal-tar hair dyes must bear warning labels (beginning 90 days after the passage of the new law of June, 1938).

8. *Guarantees* (specific or implied) may be of some value in selecting merchandise. Sometimes merchandise is guaranteed by the producer. Often, however, the dealer assumes this responsibility, the reputable dealer usually allowing the consumer the privilege of returning unsatisfactory goods. Though returning goods may be inconvenient and costly to the consumer, guarantees ensure the buyer against any substantial financial loss, a very important consideration in some instances. The purchaser, though, may have to pay a higher price for guaranteed merchandise. Whether it is worth while to do so depends upon the circumstances. Although there is certainly no evidence lending support to a contention that guaranteed merchandise is better than that which is not guaranteed, if other conditions remain approximately equal, it is probably better to purchase the former.

As can be seen from the foregoing analysis, the several buying guides that are available at present are not completely adequate although each can be used advantageously under certain circumstances. If utilized, however, it is necessary that the consumer use them intelligently. "Generally speaking, education of the household buyer which increases her information, intelligence and discrimination is an important method of increasing efficiency in buying. Teaching her how to know and use the available methods of choosing goods and how to identify and compare characteristics of particular goods, will aid the household buyer in meeting many of the practical difficulties of market selection."[1]

Much time and effort could be saved and more efficiency gained if standardization were more generally practiced in the production and sale of consumers' goods. For if standardization were in existence generally (assuming that consumers were properly educated with regard to the resulting grades), the buyer could effectively compare values and choose the items that would exactly satisfy his specific requirements.

6. Consumers' Information Services.—More and more specific information on purchasing is becoming available to consumers.[2]

[1] Coles, *op. cit.*, p. 29.

[2] In addition to that published by Consumers' Research and Consumers' Union (discussed in detail in the following paragraphs), valuable information on buying can be obtained from the following sources: Household Finance

Two very interesting agencies now exist having for their purpose the education and instruction of consumers in more effective purchasing. These are known as Consumers' Research, Inc., and Consumers' Union of the United States. Since they are essentially the same, they will be discussed as one.

The consumers' information services publish two types of information: (1) general consumer information on such subjects as the advisability of building a home and the pitfalls to be avoided if one does build; the maintenance and care of automobiles; (2) specific consumer information regarding various commodities. Each of the aforementioned agencies publishes a monthly bulletin containing information on automobiles, silk stockings, vacuum sweepers, safety-razor blades, cold remedies, fountain pens, etc. Each publishes periodically in addition a buyers' guide which summarizes in more usable form much of the information previously published.

In effect the consumers' information services tear the wrappers from the commodities and grade them, not according to the claims of their biased producers but according to the value of the product as revealed by tests. Ratings are based upon quality and price. Hence, products of good quality and low price would be recommended whereas those of low quality and low price or even good quality and high price may be rejected.

Each product tested by these agencies is eligible to any one of three ratings. Items are then classified as (1) those whose superior quality and low price earn them *best-buy* rating; (2) those whose values are neither high enough for *best-purchase* rating nor low enough to be condemned;[1] and (3) those which because of low quality or high price or both are considered unacceptable and hence are not recommended. With certain types of products (brake linings, say), very little explanatory

---

Corporation's series of booklets on "better buymanship"; National Better Business Bureau's series of pamphlets on various types of commodities (furs, jewelry, etc.); Consumers' Counsels' (AAA) "Consumers' Guide"; Home Economic Bureau's (U.S. Department of Agriculture) pamphlets on foods, diets, textiles, equipment, etc.; Consumers' Project's (U.S. Department of Labor) booklet on drugs, etc.

[1] Consumers' Union medium rating is somewhat different from that of Consumers' Research. The former designate the middle group as *also acceptable*.

information needs to accompany the ratings. With other types of commodities (*e.g.*, automobiles) lengthy explanations are required. The reason for this is quite clear. The former are rated on a very simple basis—length of life and price. The latter, however, must be rated, in addition, on the bases of riding comfort, ease of handling, gasoline mileage, general cost of upkeep, roominess, etc.

The careful consumer-buyer cannot afford to be without one of the two consumers' information services. Valuable advice is given with respect to home manufacture of certain types of commodities, the avoidance of the use of harmful products, the care of mechanical devices, a fuller utilization of motor lubricants. Best buys may be discovered in chain department stores, mail-order retail institutions, catalogue houses, or five-and-ten-cent stores. The market undoubtedly can be more effectively covered by these consumers' agencies than if each consumer were to undertake the task alone. As a matter of fact, the consumer can use the services to his advantage as a supplementary aid to his own inspection and testing activities. Through the work of Consumers' Research and Consumers' Union, the consumer-buyer has at his disposal, for a relatively small fee,[1] unbiased information concerning the things he buys. He has available, in other words, what might be termed a consumer's advocate.

The idea of furnishing the consumer with unbiased information concerning goods and services is not unique. For years the book review sections of the New York *Times* and the New York *Herald Tribune* (as well as others) have furnished expert quality information to buyers of books. In addition there are now in existence guides to current motion pictures which furnish summaries of plots and expressions of opinion regarding the quality of each production. The most recent suggestion along these lines would provide for an extension of consumers' information services into the field of investments.[2] The originator of the idea, Mr. Reis, was secretary-treasurer of Consumers' Research in 1932–1933 and was probably inspired by his experience in the field. His plan (which might well be termed *investors'*

[1] Each service is priced at $3 per year.

[2] Bernard Joseph Reis, "False Security—The Betrayal of the American Investor."

research) " . . . is to form a national organization with dues assessed to individual security holders according to their holdings. A paid staff of lawyers, accountants, and financial experts would analyze and evaluate new issues as applications were made to the S.E.C. for listings. Investors' Research would not only issue confidential bulletins to members but they would attend stockholders' and bondholders' meetings, play watch-dog on corporate activities, maintain . . . legislative lobbies to protect investors' interests. . . . "[1]

There are, of course, certain technical limitations to the type of consumers' information services outlined above. In the first place, the testing of certain types of products, particularly durable consumption goods, is extremely expensive. Considering the fact that neither of these agencies has a subscription list exceeding 75,000 (at the very most), one can readily see that adequate testing of certain types of products is impossible. Though it is true that these agencies have certain nonprofit research facilities at their disposal, some of the ratings actually are based upon opinions of users of the products reported on. These opinions may or may not be sound. In the second place, many of the products rated have many important qualities, not just one. In such cases, the consumer must take care that he understands the basis of the rating since what seemed an undesirable feature to one individual might be of no consequence to another. This does not vitiate the system, however, since a careful study of the bases of each rating actually can be made by the consumer. Finally, qualities and prices change from time to time, each change having the effect of vitiating previous ratings. Hence the consumer should utilize the existing agencies as guides only, not as final arbiters of product choices.

These agencies while imperfect are of invaluable aid to the consumer, however. They are particularly necessary in our present society since standardization is generally nonexistent and since, despite legislative devices, adulteration, misbranding, and false advertising actually are practiced from time to time.

If the consumers'-research type of activity were carried out to its ultimate conclusion, it would result in a more perfect market since the improvement would come in the ordinarily inadequately informed buying side of the market. Although there would be a

[1] *Time*, May 10, 1937.

conflict at first between advertisers' claims and information supplied by the consumers' agencies, in time, if the consumers' information services were a generally accepted device, untruthful advertising would cease to exist. Producers would have to turn to informative advertising, and those producing poor products would perforce improve the quality of their products, place them in lower price brackets, or be forced out of business.

7. Installment Buying.—Installment buying is based upon a form of credit that is paid off or liquidated by installment payments; *i.e.*, the payments are made piecemeal or in successive fractions under a plan agreed upon at the time the marketing transaction is initiated. Although this type of credit is based upon trust and confidence in the debtor's ability and willingness to pay, the object sold is very often utilized as a part of the security.

The use of installment financing in the sale of consumers' goods is not a new phenomenon. As early as 1750, for example, Chambers's "Encyclopaedia" was sold on this basis. Singer Sewing Machine Company has been doing a profitable installment business since 1850. There are many other similar cases. But the impetus to installment was received in the early 1920's. In other words, although the device itself is not new, installment-sales volume increased tremendously following the war. By 1929 installment-sales volume was over 12 per cent of total retail sales,[1] or between 6 and 7 billions of dollars.[2]

[1] In some industries, the percentage of installment sales to total sales is very high; in others, negligible. The U.S. Department of Commerce, several years ago, estimated the percentage of business (in terms of units) on an installment basis in certain products as follows:

	Per Cent
Stoves and ranges	73
Furniture	58
Musical instruments	55
Electrical applicances	49
Radios	29
Jewelry	17
Furs	11

[2] Some of the more important reasons for the increase in installment business following the World War were as follows:

1. Excess plant capacity following the war and postwar boom made necessary experimentation with various sales stimuli.

2. Increase in real wages from 1921 to 1925 made this stimulus effective

It is generally agreed that products which lend themselves to installment selling most satisfactorily, from an individual vendor's point of view, should possess:

1. Durability, since the product acts as security for the loan.

2. Relatively high and slowly declining resale value, in case of repossession.

3. Moderate degree of standardization, since resale depends upon a fairly wide market.

4. Fairly high initial cost, since the buyer, otherwise, usually finds little need for long-term credit.

Much can be said for and against installment selling. In its support, one must insist that in some instances installment credit merely replaces another type of consumer credit. That is to say, open book credit is replaced by the sounder, more formal, installment credit. Moreover, installment credit encourages saving in kind. For the purchase of ephemeral commodities, it substitutes, in part, the purchase of durable commodities. Without it, many individuals would dissipate their incomes on transitory goods. Again, it makes possible the purchase of better quality products since the purchaser is not limited in the amount to be spent, to the sum actually in his possession. Furthermore, it probably has made possible decreased costs in certain commodities since increased production often follows introduction of long-term credit terms.[1] And, finally, the argument is advanced by some that scales of living are raised through installment credit since an individual strives harder (and thus becomes more productive) when goaded on by the necessity of meeting the installments on his various purchases. The last two points are subject to some debate.

There are, however, several important indictments of installment selling. The first is that in installment selling many racketeering practices obtain. In New York State, for example,

---

since consumers were optimistic, hence, amenable.

3. Falling off in automobile sales about 1923 caused finance companies to seek new products to finance.

4. Interindustry competition (*e.g.*, automobiles vs. furniture) forced those industries not selling on time into the installment field.

5. Business-seeking methods of reducing sales resistance in order to make advertising more effective promoted installment buying.

[1] This may have affected other industries adversely, however. For example, home building may be affected by increased automobile sales.

by means of wage assignments, an installment creditor on default of contract may demand of a present or subsequent employer the entire wage due a debtor until the account is liquidated.[1] This, one must insist, leads to great hardship in many families. Repossession fees also lead to harmful results. In some contracts, if the commodity is repossessed the debtor must pay an exorbitant fee in order to regain the possession of the commodity.[2] Moreover, exorbitant interest and service-charge rates are demanded by many small local companies. Though one cannot indict the whole system on account of a minority of shady dealers, consumers should be warned of such dealings in order that they be enabled to protect themselves.

A second indictment of installment selling rests on the fact that by means of the device the consumer can be more easily influenced in the purchase of commodities since he no longer possesses the defense of not having enough money. That sales resistance is reduced when the insufficient-funds defense is removed there can be no doubt.[3] One must be equally insistent, however, that it is difficult, if not impossible, to protect the consumer against his own poor judgment even though high-pressure sales methods were proscribed.

[1] ROLF NUGENT and LEON HENDERSON "Installment Selling and the Consumer," *Ann. Am. Acad. Political Social Sci.*, May, 1934, p. 95, state that in New York City, eight representative employers reported that 1,900 powers of attorney to collect wages were received in 1931 against their 105,000 employees. Practically all these demands for wages were by installment merchants; six jewelry and clothing merchants accounted for more than half of them. A street railway company employing 17,000 men reported that an average of 3,400 notices of assignment a year were received against its employees between 1921 and 1932. Armour and Company reported that among its 5,380 plant employees, most of whom are Negro laborers, the number of notices of assignments from 1921 to 1932 was approximately one-half of the number of employees.

[2] NUGENT and HENDERSON, *op. cit.*, p. 97, report a case involving repossession of a car on which the last payment of $15 was due and for whose repossession a charge of $35 was demanded.

[3] Again quoting Nugent and Henderson, *ibid.*, p. 96, "A colored boy came into the Louisville Legal Aid Society for help because an installment company had attached the pay upon which his family's food depended. He was wearing a frightful purple checked suit, and we asked him how much he paid for it. 'Three dollars,' was his reply. Obviously this was the weekly payment, not the price · · · [The fact is] he had promised to pay $3 a week for thirteen weeks."

The third argument against installment selling is that the cost of financing is too high. As can be seen from the figures in Table 66, the interest and service-charge rates are, under certain conditions, very high. Though rates are unreasonably high in some instances, very often apparently excessive rates are not *unreasonably* high but are due to the necessity of meeting certain costs. These include:

1. Interest on borrowed funds.
2. Credit-investigation expense.
3. Expense of collecting on small notes.
4. Costs arising out of difficulties of repossession.
5. Losses on bad debts (ranging in a recent year from less than 1 per cent in the case of automobiles to over 7 per cent in clothing).

TABLE 66.—RANGES OF ANNUAL INSTALLMENT CHARGE RATES FOR VARIOUS TYPES OF ENTERPRISES[1]

Agency	Article financed	Range of annual rate of charge, per cent
A large automobile finance company....	Automobiles	14 to 38
A large Eastern public-utility company..	Electrical appliances	13 to 23
A large general finance corporation......	Electrical refrigerators	14 to 30
A well-known mail-order house.........	Miscellaneous merchandise	13 to 66

[1] Adapted by ROLF NUGENT and LEON HENDERSON in "Installment Selling and the Consumer," *Ann. Am. Acad. Political Social Sci.*, May, 1934, from LEWIS A. FROMAN, "The Cost of Installment Buying," *Harvard Business Rev.*, January, 1933.

In general (and within limits) the rate paid by consumers is higher when (1) the balance due is small and (2) the time over which payments are made is short. The reason for this situation is simply that basic accounting and investigation functions must be borne even if the balance were but $1 and the time over which the payments to be made were but 1 week. The principle of increased rates accompanying small unpaid balances and short-contract periods is illustrated by the figures in Table 67. There are, then, certain conditions under which the consumer should avoid the use of installment credit. Cash payment should be made under such circumstances.

One must conclude then that while installment credit is advantageous to the consumer in that it allows him to purchase better-quality merchandise, forces him to save in kind, and makes possible more intelligent budgeting, it has certain undesirable features as well. Since racketeering practices exist in the field, the consumer should approach the problem of purchasing goods "on time" with caution. Moreover, installment charge rates under certain circumstances are more than many consumers can afford to pay. Probably the average consumer cannot

TABLE 67.—RATES CHARGED BY ONE OF THE LARGEST AND MOST REPRESENTATIVE AUTOMOBILE FINANCE COMPANIES[1]

Unpaid balance	Company charge	Monthly payments	12-month rate, per cent	Rates on less than 12-month contracts, per cent			
				10 months	8 months	6 months	4 months
$205	$18	$19	17	19	20	26	38
$475	$39	$44	16	16	17	18	20
$1,975	$142	$179	14	14	14	15	15

[1] Adapted from LEWIS A. FROMAN, "The Cost of Installment Buying," *Harvard Business Rev.*, January, 1933, p. 230.

afford to buy low-priced merchandise on the installment plan since the rate for such service at times amounts to over 50 per cent per annum.

In any case, the consumer should know what rate he is paying for the credit service he is purchasing. This is important individually and socially. Without such information, in other words, the consumer cannot intelligently compare values among institutions, brands, or makes and cannot even intelligently decide whether to wait and pay cash or commit himself to a series of installment payments. Price competition thus becomes quite ineffective since those firms charging high rates are not forced to reduce them.

Consumers should be informed, not only of the true rate of charge for installment service, but also the comparable charges of competing companies. "Until all consumer credit agencies adopt a common method of stating the rate of charge, the intelligent consumer who wishes to shop around for the best terms will have to resort to mathematics. . . . whether the commodity sold is money or mattress, the consumer is entitled to know the actual true rate he must pay for credit."[1]

Household Finance Company, author of the foregoing statement, has prepared a pamphlet on credit costs for the consumer, a major portion of which is composed of a table of true interest rates corresponding to cost ratios and the number of installments. From this table, one discovers that "for example, on a $100 loan, to be repaid in ten equal monthly installments with a deduction of 6% discount and 2% investigation fee, the true interest rate is not 6% or 8% but, as the pamphlet shows, 1.55% per month or (even without compounding) 18.6% per year."[2]

One further phase of installment credit should be considered by the student of consumption economics. This concerns the effect of installment buying on cyclical business movements. One might think offhand that, since installment buying permits the purchase of merchandise by consumers who are not in possession of enough money to make an outright purchase, it would aid in cushioning the shock of depression conditions. This, however, is not true.

In general, installment buying probably has the effect of making for instability rather than for more stable conditions. The reason for this is quite clear. In good times, consumers have jobs and are optimistic about the future. Hence, they are willing to commit themselves to a series of monthly payments out of income. The result is that business becomes even more active momentarily (especially in durable-goods lines). To put it a little differently, boom conditions are intensified as a result of increased sales arising out of the optimistic attitude of buyers.

But when business activity slows up and optimism turns to pessimism (partly as a result of reduced wages and layoffs), consumers are unwilling to commit themselves to a series of future payments. Hence sales fall off and (particularly)

[1] Mimeographed letter from Household Finance Company, 919 North Michigan Ave., Chicago, accompanying their pamphlet "How to Figure True Interest Rates on Loans and Installment Purchases."

[2] Household Finance Company, "How to Figure True Interest Rates on Loans and Installment Purchases."

durable-consumption-goods industries are hit very hard. Industries of this type expand rapidly in boom periods and thus receive a greater impact from cyclical downswings.

"Consumers credit is not a device which enables consumers indefinitely to buy more than they could buy for cash. During the period while credit is in the process of expansion, consumers can buy more than they could for cash. But when credit is no longer expanding, even though it remains unimpaired, they can not buy any more than they could if they could pay cash and did not have to use their cash to pay for things bought weeks before. When consumer credit begins to contract and as long as it is in the process of contraction, consumers cannot buy as much as they could if they had no debts to pay and could use their incomes in making cash purchases. This expansion and contraction of consumer credit makes for economic instability."[1]

8. Buying Superstitions.—Many commodities—particularly food products—exist in a variety of qualities, and it is difficult to determine the proper quality of the particular article suitable for the individual family, even after the general purchase has been decided upon. The solution of this problem, as has been indicated, lies in the proper education of the consumer and in the working out and enforcement of proper standards by which the consumer may judge the true worth of the products that he buys.

At present, curious buying superstitions exist among consumers in different places. In connection with food, for example, there are a great many. In New York, consumers have paid higher prices for white eggs than for brown, whereas the reverse is true in Boston. Chemically, there is no significant difference between the two kinds of eggs. White bread is less nutritious than whole-wheat bread; yet there is a feeling that white bread is superior to whole-wheat bread. Rye bread indeed is considered even less respectable than whole-wheat. We find that the North demands yellow cornmeal, and the South desires white. Apples are customarily bought because they are red; some of the other varieties are equally good and much less expensive. The South wants yellow onions, but the North will take red ones too.

[1] Thomas Nixon Carver, "Consumer Credit and Economic Instability," unpublished at this writing, May, 1938.

Certain cuts of meat are thought to be much better than others. The cheaper cuts, however, generally yield much more in calories per dollar than the higher-priced cuts. As a matter of fact, many consumers are unable to judge the grades of meats they are purchasing and, in consequence, often receive poorer grades than those for which they paid. "The policy of lowering the grades of meats sold at a time of rising wholesale market and of restoring the former grades on a declining wholesale market, thereby furnishing meats to customers at prices more nearly uniform than would be possible if the same grade were maintained constantly, is followed by many dealers and is regarded with approval by persons of high business standards in the trade. The shifting of grades is somewhat easier to those dealers who usually carry more than one grade. Carrying more than one grade also enables an unscrupulous dealer to sell meat of a lower grade to a customer who is unskilled in judging, at the same price as meat of a higher grade to a discriminating customer."[1]

Similar conditions prevail in other lines of expenditure. The sale of rayon, for example, was much retarded during the early years of its introduction because it was labeled *artificial silk* and consumers attached an idea of inferiority to it. Consumers can, in consequence, secure relative bargains, if they properly understand the qualities of goods, by purchasing commodities that sell comparatively low in price because of these superstitions and avoiding those made comparatively high in price by these superstitions.

Prejudices, also, exist with respect to certain types of retail outlets. Some individuals penalize themselves by being susceptible to anti-chain-store propaganda. Others would not think of buying through the mail-order house. Still others feel it beneath their dignity to trade in basement establishments. Obviously, such prejudices are harmful to the consumer. The only way he can be assured of obtaining the best values is to keep well informed regarding offerings and to be willing to give his patronage to the institution offering the most for his money. A priori notions regarding certain types of institutions tend to narrow the field of selection. Such a tendency is inconsistent with consumer-buying efficiency.

[1] "Retail Marketing of Meat," *U.S. Dept. Agr. Bull.* 1317, p. 31.

Questions

1. Show that there are economic as well as technical factors involved in the proper designation of grades.

2. Would it be advantageous from the standpoint of the consumer to have a governmentally operated consumers' research organization?

3. Is the consumer's purchasing task more or less difficult than that of the industrial purchasing agent? Give reasons for your answer.

4. What are the most important elements making for efficiency in "buymanship"?

5. Considering both favorable and unfavorable aspects of installment selling, what should the policy of an enlightened commonwealth be in regard to it?

CHAPTER XVIII

CONSUMERS' COOPERATION

The consumers' cooperation movement, as conceived by its more enthusiastic supporters, embraces an entire economic and political philosophy. They see in it a means of reorganizing our economic structure and of eradicating many of the evils which are by-products of the capitalistic order. Chief among these would be the elimination of the profit motive as a stimulus to production and its accompanying evil, the desire to misbrand and adulterate goods. There also would be an elimination of high-pressure advertising and sales effort, which they argue would reduce marketing costs considerably. Many of the "unearned increments," then, would be the common property of society and would indirectly add to the incomes of all members of society. As a consequence, there would be a reduction in the disparity of real incomes.

Thus, rabid cooperators . . . "argue that if every ultimate consumer bought everything he used at a retail cooperative and received the accrued surplus back at the year's end in the form of rebates, there would obviously be no profit left in the retail trade. Manufacturers selling to the cooperative wholesales would, however, still be making a profit. But the wholesales could put an end to this by building their own factories. The end result would be that people would merely produce and perform services and receive produce and services in exchange. Capitalism would thus be subtly transformed into 'production for use,' a sort of glorified barter with money functioning solely as a medium of exchange."[1] As to the possibilities of such a program, the student should reserve judgment until he has well in mind not only the principles of consumers' cooperation but a conception of the extent of the movement in various parts of the world.

1. The Nature of Cooperation.—Not all forms of joint effort are of consumers' cooperative type. There are, chiefly in agriculture,

[1] "Consumer Cooperatives," *Fortune*, March, 1937, p. 144.

a great many cooperative endeavors carried on by producers. These usually take the form of marketing organizations or processing plants to which producers bring their products and where such products are handled and sold by paid workers. Contrasted to this type of endeavor there are the so-called *cooperative workshops* which are actually owned and managed by the workers of such establishments. Nor are these the only types of cooperative activities in existence. The Report of the Inquiry on Cooperative Enterprise in Europe 1937 (page 6), reveals that cooperative enterprise in Europe takes the following diverse forms:

1. Farmers' purchasing societies (for the purpose of supplying farmers' requirements of machinery, fuel, fertilizer, etc.).
2. Farmers' marketing societies (for the purpose of marketing farmers' products in an efficient and orderly fashion).
3. General-purpose farm societies (designed to receive and process commodities, sell such goods, and handle farm supplies and consumers' goods).
4. Workers' productive societies (groups of workmen owning and operating the enterprises in which they are employed).
5. Consumers' distributive societies (for the purpose of marketing consumers' goods).
6. Housing societies (whose purpose is to build and finance homes, often with aid of the government).
7. Utilities' cooperatives (for the purpose of building and operating telephone and power lines as well as that of buying or generating power to be sold to members).
8. Special service societies [for the purpose of supplying (say) burial and medical service for members].
9. Credit and banking societies (for the purpose of accepting and investing savings of members as well as that of borrowing money—sometimes from the government—to lend to members).
10. Insurance societies (for the purpose of writing life, accident, health, fire, livestock, and property-damage insurance for members on a mutual basis).

As can be seen, some of these cooperative organizations are primarily for the purpose of carrying on productive enterprises, while some are primarily for consumption purposes. There seem to be fundamental differences and conflict between consumers' cooperation and the other types of cooperative movements. Consumers' cooperation is essentially a social movement; it embraces all society. The aim of consumers' cooperation is to supply goods to its members at the most reasonable prices possible, to *save* the consumer money. The price relationship that is sought is essentially the relationship between the prices of the various commodities which the economist would speak of as a normal price relationship. Producers' cooperation and cooperative workshops, on the other hand, would seem to be essentially capitalistic movements. The cooperators form a group with an individual interest opposed to that of the other groups in society. The interest of the group is that of obtaining a high price for its particular product relative to the prices of others products. That is to say, the main purpose of the producers' cooperative is to *make* money. The essential conflict between these forms of cooperations is not so readily apparent when they are small relative to other forms of social direction but would of necessity appear if they increased materially in their importance.

2. Principles of Consumers' Cooperation.—It is generally acknowledged that the cooperative movement as we know it today was inaugurated in 1844 by 28 flannel weavers, in Rochdale, England. Each contributed £1 toward the capital of the organization, and with this small sum a cooperative store was established. Ten years later, its membership had expanded to nearly 1,000, and its yearly business amounted to considerably over £20,000. Consumers' societies vary in their organization but little from country to country, and whenever the movement has been successful, the principles evolved by the original Rochdale pioneers have been followed.

These principles, according to Dr. Warbasse,[1] one of the stanchest supporters of the consumers' cooperative movement, *evolved* from the school of experience and were not preconceived notions thought up on the spur of the moment. The contribution of the pioneers was that of selecting discriminatingly successful methods utilized by various cooperative societies and bringing them together in the form of a sound working plan. These principles are as follows:

[1] JAMES PETER WARBASSE, "Basic Principles of Cooperation," *Ann. Am. Acad. Political Social Sci.*, May, 1937, pp. 7–16.

1. *One Member, One Vote.*—Each member is entitled to one vote regardless of the number of shares held. No proxies are allowed, which means that consumers' cooperation is founded on genuinely democratic principles. There are, of course, inequities arising out of the *one-vote principle,* since it allows no additional voice to those who contribute (*a*) more funds, (*b*) more patronage, or (*c*) more time and thought to the organization. Consumers' cooperation is a movement designed for the benefit of all, however, and the one-vote principle is fundamental.

2. *Limited Returns on Capital.*—This provision has its purpose, that of limiting the rate of interest to the wages of capital. That is to say, the amount of interest paid should be only enough to draw capital into the enterprises. There should, in other words, be no element of profit in the return to capital. Speculation is thus eliminated and with it the type of individual who seeks to gain speculative profits from a successful enterprise. This too is a democratic principle.

3. *Sound Goods of Full Weight Sold on Cash Basis.*—Though Dr. Warbasse does not specifically mention "sound goods of full weight" in his list of principles in the article previously cited, it is usually considered the *sine qua non* of consumers' cooperation.[1] Buying and selling for cash was laid down as a principle on the grounds that efficient merchandising demands adequate amounts of working capital and that if working capital is dissipated business cannot continue. Furthermore, it is argued that credit

[1] One writer (J. B. Mathews, "The Cooperatives—An Experiment," *Atlantic Monthly,* December, 1936,) devotes a great deal of space to a criticism of the quality of cooperative products and analyzes, among other things, the advertising claims of such British Cooperative Society products as health salt, sulphur tablets, yeast tablets, typewriter ribbons, and razor blades. He finds that representations made by the society are, to say the least, exaggerated and that the quality of some of the products is definitely inferior. One conclusion derived from the study (p. 710) is that " . . . *most* of the European cooperatives' medicinal products would have difficulty with the Federal Trade Commission or the Food and Drug Administration in the United States. The British Cooperative Pile Ointment . . . carries the following plainly untruthful claim: 'If used as directed on the tube this Pile Ointment will not only be found effective in curing Piles, but also in preventing the conditions conducive to their return.' Such a claim has been illegal under the federal Food and Drugs act and in most of the states of the United States for thirty years."

business is inequitable since those who are granted credit are carried by those who pay cash. And finally one of the original purposes of consumer cooperation was that of freeing people from debt. Why should the institution that is attempting a reform encourage a violation of one of its tenets? There are, of course, several exceptions to the general rule. The main one arises out of the sale of large items. In the purchase of houses, for example, the consumer is extended credit, often, however, through a credit union set up for the purpose.

4. *Distributive Savings Allocated for Definite Purposes.*—In general the price policy of the consumer cooperative is that of selling at the market.[1] From the gross margin (the difference between cost of goods and selling price) are subtracted operating expenses, an amount (usually 2½ per cent) set aside for cooperative education, and a sum earmarked for reserve purposes. The resulting balance, if any, reverts to members on a basis of patronage; *e.g.*, a person making purchases amounting to 1 per cent of sales of the cooperative would be entitled to 1 per cent of the balance available for dividends. Hence those members responsible for the sales volume are given dividends in proportion to their patronage. Incidentally, patronage dividends amounting to more than $125,000,000 were returned to British members in 1936.

5. *Unlimited Membership.*—Democracy is again promoted by an adherence to this principle. The one exception is that of keeping out those who might harm the society, *e.g.*, those who wish to use the society for purposes of individual advantage.

Three other operating practices have now earned a place on the list:

6. *Neutrality.*—Because proponents of trade unionism, of socialism, of some religious sect might destroy consumer cooperation by creating a schism in the ranks of the society, the neutrality

[1] Obviously, there are certain conditions that make it impossible or inadvisable to charge market prices for goods sold by cooperatives. Indeed, at times, one is hard put to determine what the market price of a certain commodity actually is. Moreover, in such cases where the consumers' cooperative is attempting to break a monopolistic situation (such as those which obtained in Sweden for lamp bulbs, galoshes, and margarine) the invoking of the market-price rule would be ridiculous. In general, however, there is adherence to the rule if only to obviate a hostile attitude on the part of competitors and to induce nonmember customers to become members.

principle has assumed a great deal of importance. Consumers' cooperation, it should be recalled, is a united effort on the part of consumers for the purpose of raising the scale of living. It is not designed to further the ends of any one faction.

7. *Education.*—Since successful cooperation depends upon a clear understanding of the subject, all substantial societies put aside 2½ per cent of the surplus for this purpose. Educational activities take the form of lectures, pamphleteering, etc. And, since training is necessary for good management and training for profit business has been found to be inadequate for a successful execution of cooperative enterprise, courses for executives and employees are often offered also.

8. *Expansion and Union.*—"When a group of people have learned how to supply themselves with one commodity, it would seem natural that they use the same methods and experience to supply other needs."[1] Moreover, a union of societies is rapidly becoming an international principle in order that societies requiring it can be given aid and in order that competitive overlapping can be minimized.

As can be seen from the foregoing, the essential cooperative principles are democratic control, limited interest on capital, and saving returns in proportion to patronage. Unlimited membership, cash transactions, neutrality, etc., after years of cooperative experience have proved themselves, however, and as a result have been accepted as sound policies of consumers' cooperation.

Consumers' cooperation then differs greatly from ordinary profit enterprise. Consumers' cooperation is founded upon democratic principles. This is manifest in the membership policy, in the voting arrangements, and in the returns to participants. All are welcome to align themselves with the movement, each is given an equal voice, and everyone is granted an equal opportunity to earn participation dividends.

Private enterprise, on the other hand, is set up not for the benefit of the participants (customers) but for the stockholders. Indeed, in many instances, private concerns are organized for the benefit of only a small group of stockholders. An attempt is made to maximize returns through monopolistic practices so that the beneficiaries may receive greater dividends. Control is

[1] WARBASSE, *op. cit.*, p. 13.

exercised for the benefit of a minority group. Thus in private enterprise there is a fundamental conflict between patrons and enterprisers that does not exist in consumers' cooperation.[1]

3. Extent of Consumers' Cooperation.—Total world cooperative membership is difficult to estimate. Reports of the International Cooperative Alliance indicate, however, that there is a total membership of something in excess of 90 million. Consumers' cooperatives probably have a membership of some 40 million persons in over 30 countries. Consumers' cooperatives, says the Alliance, do an annual world business amounting to well over 30 billion dollars. This, of course, includes the transactions of cooperative banks and credit societies as well as those of the cooperative housing associations and of other cooperative enterprises outside of the field of consumers' goods retailing.

TABLE 68.—EXTENT OF CONSUMERS' COOPERATIVE ENTERPRISES IN SELECTED COUNTRIES, 1934–1935[1]

Country	Population total	Membership consumers' cooperative societies[2]	Production of consumers' enterprises	Retail trade of consumers' societies	Estimated percentage of total national retail trade
Denmark	3,705,559	354,000	11,205,135	63,400,500	
Finland	3,762,026	517,763	13,631,538	73,076,586	25–30
France	41,228,000	2,540,290	3,183,378	233,544,330	
Great Britain (including Ireland)	46,082,000	7,483,976	354,442,375	1,080,545,492	12.0
Norway	2,817,124	138,557	4,477,200	31,906,200	
Sweden	6,211,566	568,161	26,337,265	103,716,950	10.0
Switzerland	4,066,400	402,535	21,408,462	94,299,933	10–12.0

[1] "Report of the Inquiry on Cooperative Enterprise in Europe," 1937, p. 7.

[2] Although there is some duplication of membership, these figures in general may be taken as representing numbers of families.

[1] There might be some conflict between member-patrons and managers, however. For example, the typical consumers' cooperative enterprise is in competition with private enterprise. If the manager of the former is able to increase the business of the consumers' organization by selling goods of questionable quality because patrons (as a result of consumer ignorance) demand them, he may be granted higher managerial compensation. Indeed, since the consumers' cooperative enterprise is faced with such aggressive competition, it probably has to offer goods actively in demand (whether of highest quality or not) or be faced with a situation of excessive distribution costs resulting from small volume.

In many of the countries of Europe consumers' cooperation has attained a tremendous strength. In such countries as England, France, Sweden, Finland, and Denmark, for example, consumers' cooperative societies are now among the largest distributors of the necessities of life, particularly foodstuffs. The figures given in Tables 68 and 69 indicate the extent of consumers' cooperation in various countries.

TABLE 69.—MEMBERSHIP IN, AND PROPORTION OF RETAIL TRADE HANDLED BY, CONSUMERS' COOPERATIVES, 1933[1]

Country	Membership, percentage of population	Retail trade through cooperative channels, per cent
Soviet Union	44.06	66
Great Britain	15.97	12 to 15
Finland	13.52	25 to 30
Switzerland	10.29	12 to 15
Denmark	9.27	17 to 20
Sweden	8.90	10
Hungary	8.08	
Czechoslovakia	5.82	7
Belgium	5.75	5
Austria	5.12	
Germany	5.12	3.3
Norway	4.60	
United States	0.56	

[1] *U.S. Monthly Labor Rev.*, January, 1936, p. 102.

As can be seen, consumers' cooperation in Europe has made tremendous headway. It has been able to make greater headway in some lines than in others, however. In England, for example, the proportion of total grocery sales passing through cooperatives is much greater than that of any other single item. As can be seen in Table 70, dairy products, textiles, clothing, footwear, and coal also have made impressive showings. It is interesting to note, however, that the percentage of total trade enjoyed by cooperatives is much less than the percentage of population trading with cooperatives. This is due in part to the fact that many families do not trade exclusively with the cooperatives but trade where they can buy most advantageously and in part to the fact that cooperative custom is largely of the lower income class and, hence, its purchases are on the average smaller.

Consumers' cooperative activity in transatlantic countries is of course not confined to retail trade. "The first expansion beyond retailing [in England] was taken in 1864, twenty years after the Rochdale weavers opened their pioneering store. In that year a group of retail societies in Lancashire and Yorkshire joined together to establish their own wholesaling agency, which, after many early vicissitudes, is now firmly established as the Cooperative Wholesale Society. The C.W.S., as it is known

TABLE 70.—RETAIL SALES OF DIFFERENT TYPES OF COMMODITIES THROUGH COOPERATIVES IN GREAT BRITAIN, 1935[1]

Department	Sales	Percentage of total	Percentage of nation's trade
Groceries	£127,200,000	57.7	22.5
Meat	18,800,000	8.5	7.9
Dairy products	17,000,000	7.7	13.2
Fruit, fish, etc	3,600,000	1.6	1.1
Drapery goods	17,500,000	8.0	9.4 (drapery goods and clothing)
Clothing	6,000,000	2.7	
Footwear	5,700,000	2.6	9.1
Furniture	7,200,000	3.3	5.0
Coal	10,000,000	4.5	14.0
Drugs	1,300,000	0.6	6.2
Unclassified	6,100,000	2.8	
Total	220,400,000	100.0	10.7

[1] GEORGE DARLING, "Consumers' Cooperation in Great Britain," *Ann. Am. Acad. Political Social Sci.*, May, 1937, p. 156.

throughout Great Britain, originally confined its business to wholesale merchanting. As the movement grew in size and expanded its commercial activities, the C.W.S. was compelled to extend into other fields. It is now charged with the task of undertaking every kind of business involved in bringing salable articles to the retail store, and in creating finished goods from raw materials. It undertakes the merchanting, manufacturing, importation, and transport of goods; it undertakes banking, insurance, and the investment of cooperative funds; it is responsible for designing and building cooperative shops, factories, and warehouses; it owns farms and estates; it publishes books and periodicals; it conducts all kinds of consumer services—the pasteurization of milk, the administration of health insurance, provision of dental and optical treatment, and so on. On a smaller scale, the Scottish Cooperative Wholesale Society undertakes similar services for the retail societies in Scotland. . . .

. . . "The Cooperative Wholesale Society and the Scottish Cooperative Wholesale Society jointly own and control two other federal societies: the English and Scottish Joint C.W.S. which conducts the movement's trade in tea, coffee, cocoa and chocolate, and owns tea plantations in India and Ceylon. . . . . . . C.W.S. has 174 factories in different parts of England and Wales in which nearly every kind of domestic article is made, from aluminum ware to woolen cloth, from bacon to tobacco. It has warehouses and sales depots in most of the main urban centers. It employs nearly 60,000 workers. The Scottish C.W.S. has 56 factories with an aggregate output valued annually at over £6,000,000 and employs 13,000 workers. The total annual sales of the wholesale societies amount to £130,000,000."[1] This certainly is an impressive record for consumers' cooperative development. Much of the same type of economic activity is being carried on by consumers' cooperatives in the continental countries.

4. Consumers' Cooperation in the United States.—Consumers' cooperation in the United States has made relatively little headway. While the percentage increase in sales volume during the depression has been striking, the dollar volume in 1936 reached only the relatively insignificant figure of $500,000,000 or only about 1½ per cent of total retail sales. Furthermore, the business of the large farm purchasing cooperatives in the Dakotas, Wisconsin, Minnesota, Michigan, Kansas, Missouri, Indiana, Illinois, Ohio, Pennsylvania, and New York, is largely in oil and gas (for use, in part, in trucks and tractors), and in stock feed, fertilizer, seed, etc., which are likewise production goods. Probably three-quarters of the half-billion dollars of sales were made by farm purchasing associations. Most of the money spent in cooperatives, then, was spent in the interests of production for profit. "Consistent with the American character, consumer cooperation turns out to be, not a way of life, but a way of running the purchasing department of a business concern."[2]

[1] George Darling, "Consumers' Cooperation in Great Britain," *Ann. Am. Acad. Political Social Sci.*, May, 1937, pp. 161–162.

[2] "Consumer Cooperatives," *Fortune*, March, 1937, p. 144.

The use of the consumers' organization for the purchase of production goods seems to be completely out of line with the aims of consumers' organization. Dr. Warbasse contends, however, that there is no fundamental difference between this use of the consumers' cooperative organization and that to which it is ordinarily put. "The workingman patronizing his cooperative store, buying food and clothing [he argues], is supposed to be the real cooperative consumer. But as a matter of fact he is [in a sense] in profit business, just like the farmer. Instead of having commodities to sell, he has labor power to sell. And he wants to sell it at a profit. To increase the selling price he has his trade union, the same as the farmer has his marketing association. But neither of these solves their problem. They both have their cooperative consumers' organizations. The workingman uses his to reduce the cost of the things he employs to produce the labor which he sells. Through his cooperative he gets the food to make his muscles go, the same as the farmer gets his gasoline to make his tractor go. The workingman puts clothing on his machine and houses it for its protection. He keeps down the cost of all this by the cooperative consumers' method and the more he succeeds in keeping down these costs the bigger is his profit when he sells his labor."[1]

However, there seems to be no gainsaying the fact that consumers' cooperation in its pure form has enjoyed relatively little success in the United States. There seems to be a combination of reasons for this lack of development. In view of the fact that consumers' cooperation offers many possible advantages to society,[2] one should find it profitable to inquire into the possible reasons for its retarded growth in America. This is particularly pertinent in view of the contrasting phenomenal success experienced by consumers' cooperation in European countries.

It should be continuously borne in mind that in many European countries consumers' cooperation is a way of life. Owing to an absence of economic frontiers there is no alternative but economically to utilize existing resources. Consumers' cooperation

[1] WARBASSE, *op. cit.*, p. 15.

[2] For example, reduction of prices through cooperative competition, improvement in merchandising efficiency, improvement in family economy (by discouraging overspending and encouraging cash buying and the maintenance of family budgets), improvement of quality of products, and the development of members' knowledge of economics and business.

is aimed at reducing production and distribution costs in order to raise the level of life. In most European countries, homogeneity of population is the rule, so that consumers' cooperation not only is indicated but is practicable since the people are willing and able to work in a cooperative fashion. In the United States, on the other hand, the people are a heterogeneous lot. They differ not only as to race and religion but as to the geographical and climatic conditions under which they live. Hence, they are not nearly so cooperative-minded as their transatlantic cousins. Moreover, average earnings are higher in the United States, so that Americans do not feel so great a pressure on their pocketbooks for the basic necessities as do their European contemporaries.

As a corollary, in dynamic America—a country of tremendous natural resources—one has (or feels that one has) a good chance for individual economic improvement and can thus direct one's energies toward the earning of a higher income, rather than toward the conservation of a small income through more effective expenditures. The average American, in ordinary times, probably has little patience with an organization whose end is that of saving pennies.

There is in the United States, also, a more efficient system of retail distribution. "Consumer cooperation came into existence in Europe chiefly to protect homogeneous stable groups of workers of small income from an antiquated, inefficient system of retail distribution, which was free from Government regulation as to prices charged or character of goods sold and was supported by the doctrine of 'Caveat Emptor.'"[1] This means that there is not the same opportunity for gains arising out of consumers' cooperation in the United States as there is in countries where inefficiency prevails. Chain stores have developed with an increase in population mobility and are more firmly entrenched in the United States than ever before.

Consumers' cooperation in some countries acts as a "yardstick" by which the efficiency of distribution can be measured. Consumers' cooperatives, in such countries, assume a social responsibility regarding restrictive activities of private firms. In the United States, on the other hand, we have antitrust laws designed to restrain monopolistic control of business and enforce

[1] "Report of the Inquiry on Cooperative Enterprise in Europe," p. 110.

competition.[1] Food and drug laws, inspection and health laws, public utility regulations, etc., also have been provided in the United States. These, though somewhat imperfect, protect the consumer in some measure, at least. Furthermore, we are continually and optimistically looking to *improved* consumer-protective legislation. The people of the United States, in other words, have been looking to government for protection, rather than to cooperative effort.

One other reason for the lack of success of consumers' cooperation in the United States is that the movement has failed to draw and retain outstanding managerial talent. Probably one of the reasons is that American private business offers such tremendous premiums for good management. Prices of executive talent are so much greater in private business than in consumers' cooperation that outstanding executive brains are drawn to capitalistic enterprise. This makes for a condition that might be termed *a survival of the unfit* in cooperative enterprise. This weakness might be overcome in time if the importance of the psychic income arising out of cooperative endeavor can be instilled in the minds of young and talented leaders.

Consumers' cooperation has never been able to gain a firm foothold in the United States and, hence, has not had the advantage of a large and efficient wholesale business behind it. Full gains cannot be realized without such an organization. Cooperative enterprise has been given little encouragement by private business; in fact, private firms have actually made it difficult for cooperatives. The absence of a wholesale organization, inci-

[1] One of the important factors of consumers' cooperative development in Sweden, for example, is their success in curbing monopolies. Since the government is not concerned with the problem, the consumers' cooperatives are the only agencies giving fight to the trusts. Their efforts have been successful as regards the margarine, flour, galoshes, and electric-lamp-bulb monopolies. In each case, monopolistic prices were broken by the establishment of cooperative factories. According to Marquis Childs in his "Sweden—the Middle Way," the situation with respect to lamp bulbs was as follows: The industry was long controlled by an international trust. While the Luma (cooperative) plant was in the course of construction, the price of bulbs dropped from 37 to 27 cents. The Luma price was set at 22 cents which allowed a comfortable margin on which to work. So remarkable was Luma's success that when English cooperatives began *discussing* the possibility of a similar venture, the price of light bulbs in England promptly dropped 10 cents.

dentally, makes for a vicious circle in that without it top efficiency is impossible; hence, savings are insufficient to induce patronage. Moreover, without a large volume of business (resulting from such patronage) a wholesale organization cannot be maintained.

5. Critical Evaluation of Consumers' Cooperation.—Consumers' cooperation is to be contrasted in its aims and methods with socialism. Socialism, in general, is a political movement. It aims to overthrow the present order and to substitute for it another in which the main means of production are publicly owned and directed by government officials. There would be a centralization of authority and control from above. Many socialists advocate that the change be made quickly and at once. Consumers' cooperation, on the contrary, is essentially a democratic economic movement. It seeks to direct society not by means of political vote, but by the economic interests of the consumer. The control is decentralized, resting in the consumers themselves and passing upward. It hopes to achieve its end not at once or violently, but by a gradual expansion through the various fields that are devoted to ordinary profit-making business.

As to the relative efficiency of consumers' cooperation and private business, few conclusive statements can be made. There is some indication, however, that the well-managed cooperative enjoying active consumer support has some advantages with respect to operating costs in actual practice. For example: (1) Salaries and wages might be lower as a per cent of sales owing to donated time, high sales per sales clerk (owing to short business hours), and bulk sales of fast-moving items. (2) Rents might be lower, owing to the fact that best locations need not be utilized since members might be induced to go a considerable distance to trade in their own establishment. (3) Advertising might be a less costly item owing to the fact that less costly forms of publicity (such as lectures and pamphlets) may be utilized; that, in any case, volunteers often carry on some of these activities; and that cooperative effort in part is parasitic in that private manufacturers create a demand for a certain type of product (corn flakes, say) and cooperatives supply the demand so created. (4) Capital costs are often low owing to the fact that those who furnish it do so on a much less rational basis than those furnishing capital for private enterprise. (5) Credit losses are much less than those of many private concerns since credit service is not ordinarily extended. Other service costs are also reduced since patrons are often willing to carry some of the marketing burdens themselves.

Obviously, many of these so-called advantages would disappear in a society dominated by a cooperative system. Even granting the aforementioned advantages, however, the lot of consumers' cooperation is far from happy in the United States. Many cooperatives have been unsuccessful and have failed; some have been sold out to private persons, or have had to be reorganized. The main causes of lack of success seem to have been:

1. Poor or dishonest management (including bad bookkeeping, lack of proper audits, etc.).
2. Inadequate capital.
3. Credit extension.
4. Attempts at underselling private traders.
5. Declaring dividends too soon.
6. Lack of patronage or support of members.

These causes resolve themselves into (1) poor management, (2) a lack of adherence to fundamental cooperative principles, and (3) an absence of cooperative spirit within the membership.

As to the prospects of consumers' cooperation, it must be admitted that the movement contains many elements of strength although its expansion is likely to continue to be more rapid in Europe than in the United States. It is quite probable, moreover, that it will become relatively a much more important form of economic activity than at present. There are, however, certain inherent weaknesses in consumers' cooperation that will prevent it from entirely dominating the economic system. Cooperatives now customarily accept the market level of prices and price their goods accordingly, remitting to their members savings in the form of dividends. If consumers' cooperation were the exclusive system, then these prices would not exist, and there would be the difficult problem of determining the proper amount and type of goods to produce and the prices of such goods. Moreover, the cooperative is usually a follower rather than a leader in the development of new desires, and as long as there were no legal prohibition we would expect to find always a more or less wide group of businessmen developing new things.

The consumers' cooperative also faces problems in its relations to its employees. As long as there are more or less definite wage rates established in the competitive market and the cooperative consumes principally things that are not produced by its members, the problem is not serious; but if the cooperative absorbs the market and its goods are made principally by its own members for sale to it alone, these problems become vital. There will, in other words, be constantly a demand for better pay and working conditions advanced by the employees as a claim against the general profits of the organization. This has actually occurred with some of the larger cooperatives. This is, indeed, a clear conflict of interest and one that would necessarily arise if the movement were to take the place of the existing system. It is the opinion of the authors that while consumers' cooperation admittedly has a broad field, this field is not without limits and that the consumers' cooperative movement cannot be expected to expand sufficiently to dominate the economic order completely.

Questions

1. Distinguish specifically the consumers' cooperative organization and the corporation.
2. What are the three most important reasons for the success of consumers' cooperation in Europe and its absence of success in the United States?
3. Are there any *real* economic advantages resulting from consumers' cooperation? Must one have a specific country in mind in order to answer the question intelligently?
4. How do you account for the comparative success of cooperative oil associations and the failure of cooperative retail stores?

CHAPTER XIX

THE POPULATION PROBLEM AND THE CONSUMER

The relation of the number of people to the product of society is an important problem. It is, in many aspects, largely a consumption problem, since the population that a given area supports depends in a large measure upon the consumption habits of the people. Among plants and animals, the numbers are determined principally by the needs of subsistence. There is a strong tendency for a rapid increase in numbers until the population becomes so large that nature thins out the young before they reach maturity and the population becomes stationary. With mankind, these forces are complicated by considerations of the future that lead many to restrain their impulses and by influences that society throws about the individual. These act sometimes to increase and sometimes to decrease the growth of population.[1]

1. Factors of the Problem.—The population problem, at least among civilized people, is a dynamic one. The number of people is increasing, the product of society is increasing, and the consumption of the people is changing. There are, in consequence, three important aspects of the problem: (1) the rate of increase of the people, (2) the rate of increase of production, and (3) the changes in the consumption of the people. These are mutually dependent factors, a change in one necessarily affecting the others. Thus, in a settled community, an increase in the number of the people at a more rapid rate than the rate of increase of production can be accomplished only with a downward revision of the level of consumption of the people. Similarly, an increase in the level of consumption means that the rate of increase of the people will necessarily become relatively slower than the rate of increase of production. A uniform level of consumption means that the rate of increase of production is just equaling the rate of increase of the people.

[1] See A. Marshall, "Principles of Economics," 8th ed., p. 173.

These situations may be temporarily obscured by the accumulation or depletion of wealth produced but unconsumed by the people. This, however, will be temporary, and in the long run the relations that we have indicated will hold true.

2. The Growth of Population.—Three principal features characterize the growth of population in the United States: (1) The decline in the rate of growth in the total population. The decennial rate of increase has fallen since about 1860, and the annual increase in numbers has fallen steadily and rapidly since 1923. (2) Our increasing urbanization. In 1910, one-fourth of the total population was in 39 counties comprising 23,243 square miles, whereas in 1930 one-fourth of the population was in 27 counties covering only 14,431 square miles. (3) The marked differential between the rate of growth of the various social and economic classes. Lorimer and Osborn report that there is hardly a single urban group in which the majority of the young people enjoy the advantages of a high-school education and in which many continue their education through college that is now replacing itself from one generation to another.[1]

The probable population of the United States at certain dates in the future has been estimated by several investigators. The estimates of Reed and Pearl based on extrapolation of an S-shaped growth curve to the past population indicate a maximum population of around 200 million about the year 2000. Estimates by Dublin, Whelpton, and Thompson based on estimated birth rates, death rates, and immigration place the peaks earlier and the maximum lower, ranging from 148 million in 1970 to 190 million in 1980.[2] Industries, such as agriculture, which depend to a great extent upon population, for an increasing demand will face increasingly difficult problems of adjustment. In most lines, however, readjustment will not be difficult once business is convinced that population growth will slacken and is able to make estimates accordingly, since the changes will be gradual. Somewhat more important in its effect on demand is likely to be the changing age composition of the population. The proportion of young people in a stationary or declining population is much

[1] F. Lorimer and F. Osborn, "Dynamics of Population," p. 199.

[2] See O. E. Baker and T. B. Manney, "Population Trends and the National Welfare," U.S. Department of Agriculture, Bureau of Agricultural Economics.

less than in a growing population. Estimates of the age composition at different periods are shown in Table 71.

TABLE 71.—ESTIMATED PROPORTION OF POPULATION IN VARIOUS AGE GROUPS[1]

Ages	1880	1930	1980
Under 5	13.8	9.3	6.4
5 to 19	34.3	29.5	20.3
20 to 44	35.9	38.3	35.4
45 to 64	12.6	17.5	25.8
Over 65	3.4	5.4	12.1

[1] W. S. THOMPSON and P. K. WHELPTON, "Population Trends in the United States," p. 415.

Such changes must necessarily alter demand for things like educational facilities, recreation, and clothing. They will undoubtedly lead to increased pressure for public responsibility for the aged and to agitation for larger families.

We are becoming increasingly an urban people. It is estimated that fully one-half of the people in this country now live within an hour's automobile journey of a city of 100,000 or more.[1] Three-quarters of the national increase in population between 1920 and 1930 took place within the orbits of these large cities. The census classification of localities as urban and rural with all places having a population of 2,500 and over classified as urban is becoming increasingly less significant. Nevertheless, in 1900 the census reported 60 per cent of the people as living in rural areas and but 44 per cent in 1930. Much of this change was accomplished by migration from the country to the city in search of larger opportunities. The depression years following 1930 saw a reversal of these trends, but there is reason to suppose they will again become operative as times improve.

The increase in population does not come equally from all classes of society. A great difference exists among the birth rates of the various social and economic classes. The higher birth rates are to some extent offset by higher death rates, but not sufficiently to overcome the difference in birth rate. It is a well-recognized phenomenon that, as we descend the social

[1] "Recent Social Trends in the United States," Chap. 9, "The Rise of Metropolitan Communities," p. 493.

and economic scale, both the birth rate and the mortality rate increase. An example of family size is given in Table 72.

TABLE 72.—SIZE OF FAMILY BY OCCUPATIONAL GROUPS, 1930 CENSUS[1]

Occupation	Size of Family
Professions	3.01
Clerical	3.04
Proprietary	3.25
Skilled workers	3.51
Semiskilled workers	3.47
Unskilled	3.91
Farm owners	4.48
Farm renters	4.32

[1] "Recent Social Trends in the United States," vol. I, pp. 685–686.

The differential rate of growth among classes raises the important problem of whether the general inborn qualities of the people are decreasing. Certain groups in the upper and middle classes are not maintaining themselves, and the great increase is coming from the lower social and economic groups.

"The only groups in the United States which are at present reproducing at rates far above actual replacement needs are located in certain rural areas, and predominantly in communities that are at the lowest economic levels and most remote from those educational and cultural influences which are held typical of social progress in this country. And within the towns and cities, the lower occupational groups, especially those in marginal economic circumstances, and dependent groups, characterized by low ratings as regards cultural-intellectual development, are commonly found to have birth rates somewhat above replacement needs and far above the birth rates characteristic of neighboring groups with superior advantages."[1]

On the assumption that there is a considerable correlation between the possession of a low income and "poor" qualities and a high income and "good" qualities and that these qualities are hereditary, then the general quality of the population must be lowered progressively.[2] Certain things must not, however,

[1] LORIMER and OSBORN, *op. cit.*, p. 199.

[2] LORIMER and OSBORN, *op. cit.*, p. 175: "There are marked differences between occupational groups in their cultural-intellectual development as measured by intelligence tests. A great number of studies have been made on this subject, and with few exceptions the results obtained are extraordinarily consistent. The studies often show a difference of twenty or

be overlooked in reaching a conclusion on these points. The first is that the test of economic position may not be an entirely valid one. It is within the power of each society to reward liberally those members whom it judges to contribute most to that society. It is possible that the system of rewards in our present organization does not sufficiently repay those making the most lasting contributions to our civilization.[1] In the second place, these differences are undoubtedly due in a large measure to environmental and educational advantages. Though the precise part played by environment and heredity is incapable of differentiation, the environmental factor is undoubtedly large. The effects of these environments are inherited in a large measure, similar to the inheritance of hereditary characteristics.[2] Moreover, they are cumulative in their effects. If the environment of this generation can be improved, then the individuals are better than they would have been had they lived in a poorer environment. They, in turn, will be able to provide their children with a superior environment, and these, in turn, their children, etc. We may conclude, therefore, that, even though the innate quality of the people may have declined slightly, and this is indeed open to serious question, this decline has certainly been much more than offset through improved environment. We also find a clear tendency for the rate of increase of a class to decrease as its material well-being increases. If the rate of decrease itself

---

twenty-five points in average intelligence quotient between the uppermost and lowest of five main occupational groups. Classification by income, or by other indices of social status, usually yields somewhat similar results.

"There is much overlapping of individual abilities among all social classes. Nevertheless, the relatively high frequency of persons of unusual ability in the upper social groups and the relatively high proportion of mental defectives or persons with very inferior intellectual development in the lowest social groups is one of the striking results indicated in the survey."

[1] A. Marshall, "Principles of Economics," 8th ed., p. 598: "Many business men, whose inventions have in the long run been of almost priceless value to the world, have earned even less by their discoveries than Milton by his 'Paradise Lost' or Millet by his 'Angelus'; and while many men have amassed great wealth by good fortune, rather than by exceptional ability in the performance of public services of high importance, it is probable that those business men who have pioneered new paths have often conferred on society benefits out of all proportion to their own gains, even though they have died millionaires."

[2] See A. C. Pigou, "Economics of Welfare," 1st ed., pp. 98–101.

decreases as material well-being increases, then, as society increases its per capita income, its distribution remaining the same, the relative increase of numbers coming from the lower income groups would decrease. We may also definitely conclude that any less unequal distribution of income because of a relative increase in the income of the lower income groups must lower the proportion of the population coming from the lower income groups.

3. The Rate of Increase in Production.—The principal difficulty that arises in the case of production as population becomes larger is the general tendency toward diminishing returns. The broadest statement of this tendency is the so-called *classical law of diminishing returns; viz.*, that an increase in the capital and labor applied to land causes, *in general*, a less than proportionate increase in the amount of produce raised, unless it happens to coincide with an improvement in the arts in agriculture.[1] The reasons for this general tendency are that, as more products are obtained from the land cultivated already, the increased production can be obtained only at a greater cost of labor and capital per unit of product and that the cultivation of new land necessitates the utilization of poorer land. If it were not for improvements, then, we would find shortly that an increase of population could be obtained only at the expense of a lower level of consumption.

There are a number of factors that tend to offset this tendency toward a diminishing return. The development of productive technique and the discovery of new natural resources are important ones. They have been principally responsible for our great increase in productiveness during the past century and a half. It is a problem of how long this march of progress can continue. No one can predict. There are, however, two good reasons for supposing that it cannot continue indefinitely. The inventions and discoveries that have been effective in increasing production are those that make available new natural resources hitherto unused or that provide a better utilization of those already in use. Thus, the steam engine substituted the energy in coal for the muscular energy of man and horse, and the hydroelectric turbine more effectively utilized the energy in the streams and rivers than the old waterwheel. If there is a definite

[1] Marshall, *op. cit.*, pp. 407–409.

quantity of those resources, the discovery and utilization of each lessens the probability of future discoveries. Furthermore, improvements become increasingly difficult as the machine in use becomes more effective. It is much easier, for example, to raise the efficiency of utilization of coal from 5 to 15 per cent than to raise it from 15 to 25 per cent, each an addition of 10. This indicates increasing difficulties of expansion along these lines.

Another factor that lessens the sharpness of the action of diminishing returns is the advantage that a large population gains from large-scale production and specialization.[1] These advantages are quite considerable and have offset the action of diminishing returns for a considerable time in many places. They operate most markedly, however, in the early stages of a community's development and gradually lose their force as population becomes more dense. Although they offset, in part, the action of diminishing returns, they cannot be expected to do so completely.

Total production may be increased also by a growth in the amount of capital. If the rate of increase in capital is greater than the rate of increase in population, then each laborer will have more capital to work with than formerly and the per capita product will be increased. There has been a growing accumulation of capital in the world during the past century and a half, and this is a factor we may expect to become increasingly important, since incomes appear to be rising and greater portions of large incomes are likely to be saved than of small incomes.

There is, in addition, the possibility of increased efficiency in our utilization of human resources. A large portion of our increase in production was due to the greater trustworthiness of modern workmen as compared with old. Moreover, any population contains a large number who contribute little to the productiveness of society. A reduction of this proportion would add to the per capita production. Similarly, there are indications of untold resources in the way of human energy in the great spurt of production following the introduction of piece rates in many industrial establishments and in the impetus to production that seems to have followed the World War. Methods

[1] Henry George and Simon Patten have argued that this might completely overcome the tendency to a diminishing return. See HENRY GEORGE, "Progress and Poverty," Book II, Chap. IV.

that sustain the interest and enthusiasm of the workers would do much to increase production.

In the United States, we find, as yet, no clear evidence of the action of the general tendency toward diminishing returns. The rate of increase in our production has been greater than the rate of increase in our population, and we have had, in consequence, a continual rise in the level of consumption. Data on the rate of increase of our total production are not very satisfactory, but indices, prepared by several separate investigators, show nearly identical rates of increase over a considerable period of years.[1] Burns concludes, " . . . if there has been any decline in the rate of growth in the total physical production of this country, its extent has probably been slight, and it is even mildly probable that the rate of growth may have been increasing somewhat."[2] The principal increases in production have come from mining and from manufacture. Agriculture has about maintained pace with population growth, manufacturing has increased about twice as rapidly, and mining about three times as fast.

4. Changes in Consuming Habit.—Over broad sections of the world, certainly in considerable areas of Europe and the United States, food is no longer the principal factor limiting population. In Africa and Asia, food continues to hold the dominant role, and the great mass of the people is close to a bare subsistence level. The almost universally declining birth rates in the Western countries are ample evidence that new economic and psychological forces are at work. The emphasis of discussions on population has as a result been shifted from a consideration of factors limiting or determining the maximum population to a consideration of the optimum population.

There is no agreement as to what constitutes an optimum population. It depends upon the objectives of the group. For example, is the optimum for the individual or for the state? The state is a collection of individuals, but not only of present individuals but future individuals as well. What is best for those today may not be best for the long-run interests of the

[1] The Day-Persons index shows an average annual growth of 3.7 per cent during 1870–1930 and the Warren Pearson index a rate of 3.8 per cent.

[2] Arthur Burns, "Production Trends in the United States since 1870," p. 279.

state itself. Is the state to be a self-contained economic entity or to function in a world of free trade? If war is imminent, then a large population with consequent supply of available troops may be desired, even at the expense of a low level of consumption and poor quality of population. For an isolated country, where the danger of war is less, the ideal would seem to be a population of such size that with some chosen division of the day between work and leisure available production resources would be worked at the point of maximum sustained per capita output.

Levels of consumption are frequently compared on the basis of their cost or on the quantity of goods included in them.[1] A high level in these terms means one that has a high cost or includes a large quantity of goods, and a low level, one that has a low cost or includes small quantities of goods. These concepts are useful when we are dealing with economic welfare, since we usually may associate a high level of consumption with large per capita welfare and a low level of consumption with low per capita welfare. They do not, however, constitute the best levels of consumption when considered from the standpoint of the material progress of the nation. From the standpoint of material progress, that standard is most effective which produces the largest surplus, not total surplus, but surplus relative to the amount consumed. Thus, a high level of consumption that produced a given surplus would be less efficient than a low level of consumption that produced a smaller surplus if the production relative to the consumption on the lower level were larger. This, of course, omits any consideration of well-being, but in the absence of evidence to the contrary we must assume that a relatively high well-being accompanies relatively large material possessions.

The nation whose production exceeds its consumption progresses in an economic sense, whereas that whose consumption exceeds its production declines. This surplus will be greatest in any given nation with a given population when all consume so that the ratio of their production to their consumption is greatest. Production must be taken in the broadest sense. Many do not produce directly but act as the advisers or inspirers

[1] See T. N. Carver, "Principles of Political Economy," Chaps. XXXIX and XLII.

of others and in this way increase total production. Such people must be judged productive even though it may be difficult to isolate precisely their specific contribution. Similarly, we must judge a person by his entire life, rather than by a single period of it. The consumption of a child and of those who are receiving specialized training usually exceed their production but may be more than justified by the subsequent large surplus that they produce. Moreover, we must, for this purpose, adopt a material and ethical view of production and deem as production only those things which directly or indirectly result in material production.[1] Thus, the services of the educator or physician might be deemed productive since they enable others to increase the material product of society, but the activities of the robber or the purveyor of "fake" medicine could not be judged so.

Much of the validity of this test of an efficient standard rests upon the assumption that these accumulated surpluses of capital will increase subsequent production. It is a general principle of economics that a relative increase of any one factor of production reacts to the benefit of all the other factors and increases their productivity.[2] This will lead directly to a rising level of consumption. Because of the increase in capital, each laborer is now able to produce more in the community than he would have been able to produce if the quantity of capital had been smaller. This means that it is now possible to satisfy wants that were formerly relatively unimportant since they added little to men's ability to produce. But now, both because the productive cost of supplying these wants has decreased and because the greater productivity of laborers made possible by capital accumulations has made each increase of production, owing to the inclusion of a previously excluded good, larger than it

[1] Development of the opposite viewpoint may be found in H. J. DAVENPORT, "Economics of Enterprise," Chap. IX.

[2] See PIGOU, *op. cit.*, 1st ed., Part V, Chap. III.

P. H. DOUGLAS, "Theory of Wages," p. 487, says, "During the period from 1890 to 1922, an increase of one per cent in the quantity of labor in manufacturing in the United States, with the quantity of capital constant, would normally lead to an increase of three-fourths of one per cent in physical product. During this same period, an increase of one per cent in the quantity of capital in manufacturing, with labor constant, would normally lead to an increase of one-quarter of one per cent in physical product."

was before, there will be a constantly rising level of consumption necessary in the fulfillment of an efficient level of consumption.

There is a constant battle waged among classes, nations, and races on the basis of their levels of consumption. Those on low levels appear to multiply faster and crowd out those on the higher levels by literally eating them out of house and home. In one portion of Texas, for example, the whites were crowded out by the lower level blacks, and subsequently the Negroes by the still lower level Mexican peons. The real competing power of a level of consumption, however, depends not on whether it is high, but on whether it is more efficient. If people are proportionately more efficient in their production than they are in the amount of their consumption, then they can hold their own against the lower level group indefinitely. It is not the low level of consumption that is invariably successful, but the efficient level, which may be either high or low. As population increases, unless it coincides with a change in the arts or with a great accumulation of capital, there will be a diminishing productivity per capita. If this decrease of productivity is proportional on all levels of consumption, then the competing power of those who show the greatest excess of production over consumption relative to their consumption will be increased regardless of the actual level of consumption. The final test of the competing power of a level of consumption lies neither in the absolute level of the consumption nor in the present excess of production over the present level of consumption, but in the excess of production relative to consumption, and that group must win whose proportion is the greatest.

Countries peopled by races with high levels of consumption sometimes raise barriers against the competition of those with lower but more efficient levels of consumption. The latter with their more efficient living would shortly be able to buy out the farms and industries of the original inhabitants. Thus, we have immigration restrictions in this country and the actual exclusion of certain peoples. The problem is not, however, entirely solved by this exclusion but is transferred to another field. Competition between nations proceeds in the markets of the world and is just as real and bitter as competition between individuals; it proceeds more slowly but just as surely. The nation with the more efficient consumption must eventually drive the less efficient from the markets of the world. Wars and invasion may result when the pressure becomes great enough. Superior natural resources will give a particular people an advantage for a time, but some of these resources must finally be exhausted and with the exhaustion comes the severe handicap of a more costly level of consumption. There is, however, considerable point in excluding those with effective competing levels from entry into a particular country. If the population is kept small relative to the natural resources and capital of a country, then the per capita production will be high, and a high level of consumption may still remain an efficient one. It may be more efficient than that of the worker in the other country solely because the natural resources and capital that country provides is relatively small. Thus, we prohibit the immigration of the Chinese to this country as their low level of consumption is relatively very efficient when they are able to work with the large amount of capital and natural resources that we have relative to China. As long, however, as the Chinese working in his own country must compete with the American laborer working here, his production, because of the scarcity of natural resources and capital, will be so low that his level of consumption will not be so efficient as that of the American laborer, and we need have no fear of his competition.

In considering the consumption of a people in relation to their production, it is necessary to recognize two portions, that which is essential in maintaining their health and efficiency and that which is not. We may designate the first as the *level of life*. An increase in the level of life implies an increase in self-respect and energy, a more careful judgment in expenditure, and an avoidance of goods and activities that are unwholesome. We may designate the second as the *level of comfort*.[1] It includes those things which, while they add much to the enjoyment of life, do not add to, or may even detract from, our productive powers. A rise in either the level of life or the level of comfort will increase the product of the workers, but at different times and in a different manner. An increase in the level of life will increase the productivity of the workers, in consequence, their wages, and the total product of society. The laborers themselves and others of society gain. An increase in the level of comfort,

[1] See MARSHALL, *op. cit.*, 8th ed., pp. 689–690.

on the other hand, will raise the earnings of the laborers only through its effect upon their numbers. This cannot come immediately but must come through the smaller size of the subsequent generation. This will increase the product per laborer and his wage; but the decrease in numbers will more than offset the increased productivity, the total product of society will be smaller, and other classes will lose. Thus a rising level of consumption may or may not increase the total product of society and may or may not benefit other groups. Moreover, it does not necessarily follow that, because a population is small, it will have an efficient level of consumption, but simply that the level of consumption may be higher than if the population is large. When the level of consumption is close to the level of life, it is efficient, and, as the level becomes increasingly a comfort level, it becomes more inefficient the higher the level.

Questions

1. What is meant by the statement "The population is growing older"? Does such a tendency have a bearing on the rate of population growth? What other factors enter into the tendency toward population stability?
2. What industries are likely to feel the decline in the rate of population growth the earliest? Which may be affected ultimately?
3. Certain types of businesses and industries bear a close relationship to the population in a community; others show little association. Give examples of the two types.
4. What notable differences occur as to age distribution among the urban and rural-farm population? What are some of the educational implications in this connection?
5. Does the American laboring man have any concern with the level of consumption of the laboring class in other countries?
6. If a mechanical cotton picker should lessen materially the demand for the hand labor of the Negro in the South, how would the North be affected?

CHAPTER XX

THE CONSUMER AND NATIONAL POLICY

The government occupies an increasing prominence in economic life and in consequence exerts an influence on the consumption of the people. It provides the means of furnishing certain services which private business would find it unprofitable to supply or which for other reasons it has been judged undesirable to leave in the hands of the businessman. The system of taxation may serve as a vehicle for the transfer of income from the rich to the poor and may modify the relative prices of various goods. In addition, government provides the rules of conduct governing business transactions and maintains conditions determining the nature of the economic order. There is a distinct tendency for the services that the modern state provides its citizens to increase in number and quality. Public expenditures have been increasing for more than one hundred years. Many services previously poorly supplied now take large sums. Expenditures for education, police protection, sanitation, and public lighting have only recently come to demand large amounts.

1. Government Expenditures and Revenues.—Total governmental expenditures in the United States now amount to nearly $125 per capita. The largest spending agency is the Federal government, and this is a development of recent years. Formerly Federal expenditures were about one-third of the total, whereas now they are close to one-half. A good share of this change probably is temporary and due to the depression. Data for several years are given in Table 73. Compared with the national income, taxes have been about one-fifth of the total. This proportion of course varies with the amount of the national income as well as the size of the tax burden, and the high proportion of the 1930's is due in large measure to the decline of the national income in that period. Estimates are shown in Table 74.

The sources of revenue of the various governmental units differ greatly. The Federal government relies principally upon the income tax, and this is supplemented by customs and excise taxes. The local governmental units rely almost exclusively on the general property tax. The states depend upon property, motor vehicle, income, business, and license taxes largely. Up to 1933, the principal expenditures of the Federal government

TABLE 73.—GROSS GOVERNMENTAL EXPENDITURES IN THE UNITED STATES PER CAPITA[1]

Year	Total	Federal	State	Local
1923	88.94	34.83	11.14	42.97
1928	105.20	33.12	15.24	56.84
1933	105.88	41.85	17.02	47.00
1934	122.38	56.92	16.84	48.62

[1] National Industrial Conference Board, "Cost of Government in the United States 1933–1935," p. 7.

were payment for past wars and preparation for future wars, and for state and local governments the principal expenditures were for education and highways, with lesser amounts for protection to persons and property and social relief. Beginning in the 1930's, there was a great growth in expenditures for relief,

TABLE 74.—TAXES AND THE NATIONAL INCOME[1]

Year	Percentages that taxes are of national income			
	Total	Federal	State	Local
1903	6.7	2.5	0.8	3.4
1913	6.4	1.9	0.9	3.6
1923	11.1	4.6	1.4	5.0
1933	16.7	4.0	3.4	9.4

[1] National Industrial Conference Board, "Cost of Government in the United States, 1925–1926," p. 77; "Cost of Government in the United States, 1933–1935," p. 30.

especially by the Federal government. The funds for much of this expenditure were secured by borrowings.

The government necessarily modifies consumption through its system of taxation. This may be because the tax falls unequally upon the different members of the community and lowers some incomes more than others or because the relative prices of things are changed. It is, in consequence, pertinent to examine the circumstances under which these taxes may modify consumption and discover which modifications are desirable and which undesirable.

The taxes levied by the government may take different proportions of income from different people. Property is classified for purposes of taxation, and it is common for certain classes to be taxed at a higher rate than others. Even with a general tax, certain property may escape assessment and taxation. Thus it is argued that the general property tax bears most heavily on the farmer. Outside of the rural districts, the great mass of personal property consists of intangibles which as a rule escape taxation almost entirely. In the rural districts, on the other hand, the great mass of personal property consists of visible objects which cannot escape assessment. Another difference arises in the exemption of certain property from the tax. The income tax is not imposed on very small incomes, nor the inheritance tax on very small estates. In most jurisdictions, a small amount of personal property is exempted from the personal property tax. Taxes may also be progressive; *i.e.*, the rate may increase as the base on which the tax is imposed increases in amount. Our income tax is an example. As the amount of income grows larger, the rate of taxation increases. Most commodity taxes are regressive; *i.e.*, they bear more heavily on small than on large incomes, since the proportion of large incomes that is spent is smaller than that of small incomes.

The argument for progression in taxation rests upon the idea that justice in taxation means an equal sacrifice by all members of the community. This would require a larger proportion of the income of the rich to be absorbed by taxes than of the incomes of the poor, since an equal percentage deduction from the income of the poor and the rich means a greater sacrifice to the poor. The difficulty lies in the fact that we cannot set the precise rate of decrease in the significance of income.[1] In the United States, progression has been applied to both income and inheritance taxes.

The effect of taxation does not necessarily remain on those who originally pay the tax. They may be able to include the

[1] Irving Fisher has outlined a method for attempting this in his article, "A Statistical Method for Measuring Marginal Utility and Testing the Justice of a Progressive Income Tax" in "Economic Essays Contributed in Honor of John Bates Clark."

tax in the price charged for goods or buy some of the materials or services used in production at a lower price. If this can be done, then the tax is said to be *shifted*, and the settlement of the burden on the ultimate taxpayer is called the *incidence* of the tax. The tax may be shifted forward or backward, or only partly shifted. A payer of a tax will endeavor to shift that tax to others wherever possible. This can be done only when the supply of the commodity is changed. Thus a tax placed on the production of an article can be shifted to consumers in the form of a higher price (1) when it leads to a withdrawal of capital and labor from that field with a consequent reduction in the quantity of the good produced and (2) when producers reduce their output and sell a smaller quantity at a higher price. The former process is the more usual, and the producers may finally be able to shift the entire tax to the consumers. The original incidence of the tax may be felt by the producers for a considerable period of time, because they are not able to withdraw their capital from the business quickly. All capital, however, wears out in the long run; and, when the wearing-out process has begun to reduce the amount of capital, the shifting of the tax will begin. The reduction in supply necessary to raise the consumer's price by the amount of the tax will be small when the demand is inelastic and large when the demand is elastic. In consequence, the tax is likely to be shifted more quickly and more completely when the demand is inelastic.

There are a number of taxes in this country on particular consumable commodities. For example, we have taxes on beverages, tobacco products, automobiles, etc. Generally speaking, mass goods are more convenient and economical objects of taxation from an administrative standpoint than goods purchased in small quantities. Experience shows that a large number of taxes of small amount are relatively far more costly and inconvenient to collect than a few taxes of large amount. Mass goods are purchased largely by the poorer classes, and in consequence these taxes, when they are on necessities, are likely to take a much larger proportion of the income of the poor, and are very undesirable. An increasing number of these levies have recently appeared in the form of state sales taxes. Such taxes, though they are regressive in nature, are productive, inexpensive to administer, and certain; and their regressiveness is offset in the main by progressive features in the remainder of the tax system of which they form a part. Import duties form another sort of commodity tax; their effect has been discussed elsewhere.[1]

Taxes that cannot be shifted are those on objects the supply of which will not be decreased because of the tax. Thus taxes on the additions to the value of people's property that are not foreseen by them and are not due in any degree to efforts made by them or to capital "invested" by them cannot be shifted. Certain people have argued, in consequence, that the principal source of revenue should be taxes on the so-called *unearned increment* of land values, since these would fall on the unexpected portions of the owners' incomes and, properly placed, would not change the uses of land or the quantities of goods produced.

Taxes on income approach the character of this group of taxes and are particularly desirable forms of taxation from the standpoint of consumers in general. The supply of services will not be diminished unless the taxes are very high, and if the rates are low enough there will not be serious attempts at evasion. Another tax which, in general, affects consumers only indirectly is the inheritance tax. The only objection to such a tax lies in its possible effect upon savings. These effects are probably small, however, and heavy death dues can probably be levied on large estates without causing any considerable check to savings.

Judging from this analysis, we may reach the following conclusions with respect to the principal taxes levied in the United States. The personal income taxes and inheritance taxes are not shifted. This is true also of that part of the general property tax representing the levy against the unimproved value of land. The sales taxes, such as those on gasoline, tobacco, and liquors, are ultimately almost entirely shifted to the consumers. At the outset they fall on the producers, but subsequently are shifted, except for a slight burden on the producers and the owners of land producing these products. The burden of the general property tax in so far as it applies to man-made capital, the corporate income tax levied by the United States government, and the business income and license taxes of the cities and states is divided. An estimate has been made by the Twentieth Century Fund of the burden of taxes on specified

[1] See p. 79.

income and occupational groups, and some of these estimates are given in Table 75.

TABLE 75.—TOTAL TAX BURDEN, FEDERAL, STATE AND LOCAL AS A PERCENTAGE OF POTENTIAL INCOME FOR NEW YORK STATE[1]

Occupation	Income	Percentage of total income
Farmer	$500	12.0
Farmer	1,000	10.5
Farmer	2,000	9.7
Wage earners	1,000	15.4
Wage earners	2,000	14.2
Salaried workers	5,000	18.8
Salaried workers	20,000	30.6
Merchant	5,000	23.9
Corporation officials	100,000	44.0
Corporation officials	1,000,000	83.6

[1] Twentieth Century Fund, "Studies in Current Tax Problems," p. 32. The lowest proportion of the five estimates made on various bases has been recorded in the table.

The conclusions of the study are as follows:

"It seems safe to conclude that the tax system as a whole is regressive for those income groups not subject to income and death taxes. The regressive elements appear to be more numerous and more important than the progressive elements at the lower end of the income scales. It seems safe to conclude, further, that the tax system is progressive for the income groups subject to income and death taxes, for these taxes dominate all others for the higher groups. It seems safe to conclude, likewise, that no one escapes making a substantial contribution to our tax revenues, however well concealed his share in the burden may be. There are enough shiftable taxes on a wide enough variety of bases to insure this effect. It seems probable that the tax burdens of the higher income groups exceed half their income, unless they are evading taxes illegally. The burden will hardly reach this proportion, however, for incomes that do not exceed $1,000,000."[1]

2. State Action and Private Business.—There is a great difference of opinion as to how far the state should enter into economic life. The further state action is carried, naturally,

[1] Twentieth Century Fund, "Studies in Current Tax Problems," pp. 41–42.

the greater the influence on consumption. No one argues that the state should do nothing at all. Certainly it must provide the rules and their enforcement for the operation of business. Likewise certain activities, such as operation of the postal system, fire protection, and education, are generally agreed on as proper state activities. But whether the state should operate utilities, engage in housing activities, direct investment, and enter other businesses are debated questions. Under private business, only those goods and services are produced for which consumers are willing and able to pay a price sufficient at least in the long run to cover the costs of their production. Moreover, these goods go only to those able and willing to pay the going price. Certain services, however, it is believed should be available to all regardless of ability to pay, and certain activities are thought essential to society even though they do not cover their production costs in the market sense. The issue arises as to the circumstances under which the state can better utilize resources than they would be utilized under private enterprise.

If private enterprise is engaged in activities that are detrimental to the public interest, state action is clearly needed and no question is involved of superior competence on the part of the state officials. Many such circumstances are found in the modern economy. This is the case with monopoly where the action of the producers in restricting production is contrary to public interest. The state has a clear case for intervention to force a larger production at a lower price by such methods as may be most expedient. This may be by some form of control, by dissolution, or by direct state operation. The growing monopoly problem in modern society makes it imperative that adequate methods of control be provided. It is clear that these methods are yet to be devised.

We have already indicated that with respect to time the viewpoint of the state and the individual differ. The future is tied to the present for the individual by the length of his life and by his consideration for his own posterity, and even when these ties are strongest they seldom extend beyond the next generation. The state, however, is concerned with its future citizens as well as its present ones. Technically this means that the interest rate for the state will differ from that of the market and, properly, will be lower. There will thus be a tendency for the more rapid utilization of natural resources through private operation than may be felt to be justified by the state and various efforts for conservation will thus be undertaken by the state. Certainly the self-interest of one generation must be prevented from squandering resources that will be essential for the following ones. The same considerations apply to investments for future returns; the lower rate of interest properly applicable to state enterprises permits investments in forest projects, flood control, etc., that would not earn the going market rate of private industry.

Another difference between state and private investment arises with respect to the investment in human resources, which differs from ordinary investment in that the returns from that investment accrue to others than the investor. Thus, unless undertaken by the state, investment in the rearing and training of laborers will be made because of family affection or by the individual himself. The state, however, has an interest in a strong well-educated body of citizens and, in consequence, is led to investments in education, recreation, health, sanitation, etc., which no individual could afford to make for others. The advisability of such investment may be extended even to such things as housing and supplementing nutrition in the lower income groups.

It sometimes happens under the economic system that the full costs or damage of a person's action are not assessed against him, nor, conversely, does he always secure a full reward for or the benefit of his action. Thus without legal coercion the industrialist may not find it profitable to surround his workmen with adequate safeguards. Likewise, as Marshall pointed out, " . . . the struggle for survival tends to make those methods of organization prevail, which are best fitted to *thrive* in their environment; but not necessarily those best fitted to *benefit* their environment, unless it happens that they are duely rewarded for all the benefits which they confer, whether direct or indirect. And in fact this is not so."[1] An example might be found in some forms of cooperative associations.

The interests of the state again become prominent when we consider the maldistribution of incomes. Investment of resources in support of the lower strata will in many cases more than repay in terms of increased total productivity the amounts expended.

[1] A. Marshall, "Principles of Economics," 8th ed., pp. 596–597.

Certainly expenditures on proper nutrition for mothers and children will avert subsequent illness and loss of working time and improve the quality of the population, not to mention the individual benefits of such a program. Better housing may produce more alert and resourceful workers and lessen the cost of crime prevention. As was previously pointed out, however, a nice judgment is involved as to how much can be taken from the higher income group without leading to a decrease in the total national income.

In so far as the ends sought by private business are not contrary to the interests of the state, the case for interference must rest upon the assumption that the state can in some ways carry out these operations more effectively than private individuals under the stimulus of a desire for personal income. This assumption is certainly a doubtful one. There is little reason to suppose that the state can assemble better administrators than private business. Likewise, state officials are subject to pressures of interests and uninstructed public opinion, which makes action difficult. Moreover, there remains the attitude of the people toward government action. As long as the state and its activity are looked upon as the legitimate prey for all sorts of unscrupulous dealing, state operation must be ineffective as compared with private business.

3. Governmental Responsibility for Purchasing Power.—Some sort of failure in the purchasing power of consumers or its allocation among groups has been considered by a number of students as a major cause of our recurring stoppages in the economic system. In line with these views, it is urged that governmental action toward increasing purchasing power or redistributing it is essential to a smooth working of the system. Certainly purchasing power has occupied an important position in recent administrative attempts to cope with the depression.[1] In popular discussions, purchasing power usually means money, but for our purposes it will be necessary to keep money distinct from real purchasing power as we have formerly defined it in terms of goods and services.

[1] A stated purpose of the AAA was "to relieve the existing national emergency by increasing agricultural purchasing power" and of the NIRA, "to increase the consumption of industrial and agricultural products by increasing purchasing power."

If there is an increase in the money incomes of the people with no corresponding increase in the quantity of goods, then the result must be a rise in prices with total purchasing power remaining unchanged. If the increase in money incomes is unequally distributed or falls into the hands of a selected few, then, when prices rise, these may gain in purchasing power, and those whose money incomes remain unchanged or rise less rapidly than the increase in prices lose in purchasing power. Total purchasing power in such a case remains unchanged. There is simply a reallocation of the purchasing power in the community. It is perfectly natural for any group to feel that not only they but the whole community would be benefited by their larger expenditure, and, in consequence, an increase in purchasing power is argued as a reason for such things as the Townsend plan or a soldiers' bonus.

New money will evidently dissipate itself in a price rise and purchasing power remain unchanged unless it in some way stimulates production. It is, however, possible that the rise in prices or the anticipation of that rise may stimulate production, and, in consequence, real income or purchasing power may increase. This is evidently the theory under which the government has operated in its "pump-priming" activities. The authorities may be able to determine where new money injected into the system is to be spent first, usually through their credit operations, but there is no subsequent control of how the money is used by the successive recipients. A great deal thus depends upon the psychology and anticipations of the businessman, as well as other more fundamental elements that may be present in the particular period. There is therefore no assurance that such procedures will be successful.

One of the causes often cited as making it necessary for the government to pump money into the economic system is technological progress. Technological progress results in an increase in the volume of consumers' goods. If the total quantity of money remains unchanged, we would expect a fall in prices to follow the increase in production. It is now argued that this fall in prices makes it impossible to sell goods at a profit and forces curtailment of output, discharge of workers, and a resulting depression. But in so far as these increases are due to technological improvements, costs will have been lowered.

The fall in prices is then necessary to pass the benefits of these technological improvements on to consumers and to increase their purchasing power, and because of the decline in costs there is not necessarily a loss to the producer. There is no reason for gradual technological progress to result in a business depression.

It is also said that the use which the consumer makes of the money in his hands is an important factor in business fluctuations and that much depends upon what is spent and what is saved. Money that is used for the purchase of consumers' goods is presumed to occupy a strategic position, and it is supposed that by the process of saving we somehow lose purchasing power in the community. This notion probably arises because as individuals we tend to contrast what we spend and what we save. But, in general, when we save money it is usually invested, if not by ourselves, then by the bank or other agency through which we save. When invested, money pays for the production of factories, machines, or whatever a borrowing businessman uses funds for. New capital equipment requires labor and raw materials in its production, and these funds saved are simply transferred to others to be spent in different ways. The saved funds are spent as surely as expenditures made by consumers on shoes or flour. The difference lies in the direction of expenditure. Saving does not necessarily add to unemployment or to a decrease in purchasing power.

It is, however, to be pointed out that saving and investment in new capital equipment do not necessarily occur simultaneously, and idle reserves may be built up in banks or cash hoarded. During a depression when the spirit of enterprise is low, it is quite probable that savings tend to produce deflation and to prolong the slump. During such a period, savings exceed new investment because they are used to liquidate bank credit or are hoarded as cash or idle bank deposits. The money spent in the consumers' goods markets declines, and there is no corresponding increase in the capital goods market. But this is quite a different thing from saying that saving in itself was responsible for the original development of the depression.[1] The

[1] G. Haberler, "Prosperity and Depression," 1937, p. 116, "There is no evidence that an absorption of savings occurs during the boom or before the crisis; on the contrary, there invariably exists a brisk demand for

government may, of course, step in to spend the amounts that other people are failing to spend, but unless it takes over all of industry it has to rely largely upon creating conditions that make it profitable for businessmen to spend, and here such intangibles as expectations and confidence become important.

A further refinement of the theory that the division of money receipts between consumer expenditure and saving is responsible for depressions places the difficulty not at the time when savings increase but later. The savings which are made in the present find outlet in investment with no reduction in total money to take consumers' goods off the market. But as these investments become productive capital equipment later, the volume of consumers' goods is increased and there is now an excess of goods to be sold unless prices of consumers' goods fall. It is at this time, then, that difficulties are supposed to develop. The increased volume of saving, however, would result in a decline in the interest rate and a lowering of the cost of goods involving much capital. There would thus be no reason for the subsequent fall in prices to produce losses. The fall in prices is in fact necessary to pass some of the gains on to the consumers and to slow up the production of these goods. Whether investment has stopped at the proper point in a particular industry will depend upon the foresight of the entrepreneurs in calculating the results following their investment. It is thus not the fact of saving but errors in investment that produce undesirable results. As long as the changes are gradual, there are no necessary ill effects. Any large change or dislocation of processes in the economic system of course produces its repercussions. A sudden great burst of saving would result in strains; but this is not necessary with any gradual growth or change.

There is finally a group who hold that somehow in the economic process purchasing power is lost and does not reappear in the market for consumers' goods. In the United States, this idea is associated principally with Foster and Catchings.[1] They would

---

new capital, signalized by high interest rates. There is an excess of investment over saving and not the contrary. The situation changes, of course, completely after the turning point, when the depression has set in. Then there is an excess of savings over investment."

[1] Also with P. W. Martin of the International Labour Office in Switzerland and Major Douglas of England of social credit fame.

argue that industry fails to disburse to wage earners and investors an amount of money equal to the final sales price of its product. This is said to be because a portion of the profits is retained in the business and used to expand productive capacity, rather than being paid out as dividends. In addition the wage earners and investors do not pay out all they receive on consumers' goods but also save part of their income. Most of these savings likewise go into the production of capital equipment. Thus it is argued that some money is used *twice* for production before it is used for consumption, because of the savings by business enterprises and by consumers. The supply of goods thus outruns the money purchasing power of consumers, to the extent that it is used more frequently for production than for consumption. There is alleged in consequence an accumulation of stocks, a collapse of prices, and a depression, during which consumers use up these accumulated stocks at prices below their production costs.

There would be a considerable element of truth to this proposition if all business were one gigantic corporation making a single product, the manufacture of which required a definite period after the public had invested in the enterprise before the results could appear. Actually many processes and products are involved, and the adjustment is gradual and can be made without difficulty by shifts in relative prices provided that savings are not greatly different from formerly. In addition, there are many other factors that are sufficient in themselves to produce business fluctuations, and it is a mistake to attribute them entirely to a single cause such as this.

The majority of competent investigators would appear to hold that there is no necessity for the government to expand money purchasing power in order to maintain a smooth-working economic system. Technological progress, the act of saving by consumers, changes in the rate of saving—none of these necessarily results in money incomes inadequate to clear the market of goods without entrepreneurial losses. There is likewise no failure of the system itself to put into the hands of buyers sufficient money purchasing power for the goods produced by the economic system. The business cycle appears to arise principally from other causes, and the developments with respect to consumer purchasing power appear to be accompanying results. But in view of the time required for the development of productive capital equipment, the institutions between the consumer saving and final investment, and the fixity of certain rates or prices in the system, there are times when increased consumer spending might act to maintain production. There are then, at times, periods when additional money purchasing power may sustain or lead to an increase in production, but these increases of purchasing power are in the form of stimulants designed largely to produce psychological results and there is no necessity for sustained doses.

4. Provision for Higher and More Stable Income.—Our previous analysis has shown that there is no general deficiency of purchasing developed by the operation of the economic system necessitating a constant replenishment by the government. This is not to say, however, that there are no possible advantages of an increase in the purchasing power of the low-income groups at the expense of the more well to do from a purely ethical viewpoint and possibly in certain circumstances from a productive viewpoint as well. It has been noted elsewhere that consumption has an important bearing upon the quality of the people and that investment in human resources, not now made under the existing economic system, might yield larger returns than similar investments in capital equipment. It would appear to be a clear duty of government to maintain as high a level of consumption for the lower groups of the population as is possible without serious curtailment to the total volume of production.

One of the most usual proposals is to establish a minimum wage and maximum hours of work, at a level sufficient to provide some desired total income. The new Federal wages and hours law is set up along these lines. The wage-hour program aims at a national standard of a minimum wage of 40 cents an hour and a maximum work week of 40 hours, to be gradually attained in industry in 7 years. It approaches these goals gradually and permits considerable flexibility. The universal "floor" for wages, without provisions for sectional or other differentials, was set at 25 cents per hour for all affected industries operating in interstate commerce as soon as the act becomes effective. The standard is raised to 30 cents the second year. Similarly, the maximum work week is established at 44 hours the first year, 42 the second year, and 40 hours thereafter. Minimum-wage legislation has had considerable success in improving the position of the lower paid workers in a number of instances. There are, however, limitations to the extent to which it will be successful. The rate of wages of course may be set at any level, but employers may hire any number they wish at that rate. The total income of the laboring class depends upon both the rate of wages and the volume of employment, and the long-run elasticity of demand for labor appears to be quite high.[1] Unless judiciously applied, a law simply imposing higher wage rates is likely to lower rather than raise the money income of the laboring class. Higher wages lead to higher costs, and these higher costs lead to higher prices with curtailed output or to losses and shutdowns. They also result in increased advantages of mechanization and laborsaving devices. The higher prices lower the purchasing power of the other groups. There are exceptions, of course. Where labor is exploited, higher wages may be secured by squeezing profits out of entrepreneurs. These areas of profit are, however, in all probability relatively small. Where the entrepreneurs are inefficient or the industry overexpanded, needed adjustments are hastened, although these will be accompanied by temporarily increased unemployment. If the minimum is sufficiently high to affect more than a small portion of the laboring group, it must lead to increased unemployment. The problem of what to do with these unemployed will then still remain to be faced. Indeed, the situation may become worse, instead of better.

There is a growing feeling that government is responsible for providing work for those employables for whom the economic system fails to find a place and that this is especially the case during a depression. Federal responsibility for the financing of relief was first recognized in 1933, when the Federal Emergency Relief Administration was organized in May to administer relief on a nation-wide scale. During the first two years, direct Federal cash relief for the needy was provided with no distinction between employable and unemployable. Beginning in 1935, a division of responsibility was decided upon, and the Federal government assumed the provision of work relief for the employables and the

[1] Paul Douglas by statistical analysis arrives at a figure of between −3.0 and −4.0, ("Theory of Wages," p. 501), while A. C. Pigou through deductive reasoning estimates that it is "probably not less than −3.0" ("Theory of Unemployment," p. 97).

states and municipalities were left with the direct relief for the unemployables. The former, which has since been administrated by the WPA, has made a very creditable showing despite the magnitude and difficulty of its task.

There has been a divided opinion as to how relief for employable persons should be provided. One group would favor direct relief because it is cheaper than job relief. Those who favor the job-relief scheme maintain that dependence on direct relief over a period of time is injurious to the morale and skill of the workman and that the maintenance of his skill and self-respect is quite as important as mere physical sustenance. The numbers employed in the Works Program reached a peak of 3,836,000 in February, 1936, had fallen to 1,956,000 in October, 1937, but was 3,185,000 in December, 1938. From the beginning in August, 1935, to 1938, it has involved a grand total of 8½ billion dollars. About three-quarters of this expenditure has gone for construction work and the rest for less tangible things such as education, art, and research.

The provision of income for old age until recently has been the responsibility of the individual, but with the enactment of the Social Security Act in 1935 a vehicle for accumulation by the worker and his employer was established. The Federal old-age benefits established by the act provide monthly old-age retirement benefits, beginning at age sixty-five, for workers who have the following qualifications: total wages of at least $2,000 from what might roughly be termed industrial and commercial employment in at least five different calender years after 1936 and before the worker is sixty-five years old. The amount of benefit will vary for each individual depending upon his total wage. A person who has worked 10 years at $1,000 a year would receive $20.82 per month. The maximum monthly payment that anyone can receive is $85 and the minimum $10. If an individual dies before attaining the age of sixty-five, his estate is to be paid an amount equal to 3½ per cent of the total wages determined by the board to have been paid him for employment after Dec. 31, 1936.

To provide the reserves for these payments, a tax is levied on the wages received by the employee, which is deducted from his pay check and remitted to the government; and also a tax is levied on the total wage bill of the employer and is paid by the employer. These taxes begin at 1 per cent for the first year of the act and gradually increase to a maximum of 3 per cent for the year 1949 and following. Some interest attaches to the incidence of these taxes. The tax on the employee's wage is clearly paid by himself, but the incidence of the pay-roll tax on the employer is not so clear. It seems probable that in the long run it will be shifted to the laborers. If this is the case, it amounts to forced savings on the part of the individual. It has the advantage of forcing the laborer to provide for old age out of his own earnings. As yet the act leaves a considerable group unprovided for, but subsequent additions to the act may be expected, extending its area of application.

A beginning has also been made toward the development of unemployment compensation in this country. Unemployment-compensation benefits are not provided directly by the Social Security Act, but by programs of unemployment compensation adopted within the separate states and stimulated by provisions of the act. The act levies a Federal tax on the pay rolls of employers of eight or more employees within each of 20 weeks of any year. The same groups are included as with the old-age benefits; the tax was set at 1 per cent of the 1936 wages, 2 per cent of the 1937 wages, and 3 per cent of the 1938 wages, and for the following years. Each employer may credit against this tax, up to 90 per cent thereof, his contributions to a state unemployment-compensation fund established in accordance with a state unemployment-compensation law that has been approved by the Social Security Board. The Federal tax unassigned to particular states under this system goes into the general treasury for general purposes of the Federal government.

The effect of the law is that a state which passes an unemployment-compensation law is able to withdraw nine-tenths of this pay-roll tax for its own unemployed, by collecting it as contributions under its own law, rather than letting the Federal government collect it as a tax. The Federal government has granted the states funds to pay proper administrative expenses. These provisions have led to nearly universal enactment of compensation laws by the states. The benefits for total unemployment have customarily been about 50 per cent of the wages with a maximum of $15 a week, although there are many variations. The most common measure of benefit weeks to duration of previous employment is that they shall not exceed 1 week of benefits to 4 weeks of employment within the previous 104 weeks. The payments begin after a waiting period of various lengths, usually of 3 or 4 weeks.

These provisions for the greater security of income in the way of unemployment-compensation and old-age benefits are to be highly commended as desirable forward steps. Much of the actual benefit will depend upon efficient and honest administration, which will require time for development. The provisions of the wages and hour legislation also have merit, but as has been pointed out might be disadvantageous both to workers and to consumers if rates are set too high. The provisions for relief are necessarily temporary and to be replaced by other measures if a more permanent group of unemployed develop.

5. International Trade Relations.—One very important aspect of national policy directly influencing the consumer is the decision of the state with respect to whether the national policy will be in the direction of self-sufficiency or whether trade is to be sought with other nations. We have already indicated in Chap. VI that market exclusion is detrimental to the consumer.

When viewed from a social standpoint (taking into account all countries and assuming no barriers already in existence), restrictive barriers are completely untenable. The advantage to be derived from free trade arises from specialization and subsequent exchange. Underlying this advantage is the principle of comparative advantage. Comparative advantage, in its essentials, means that an advantage will follow specialization of effort and subsequent exchange—each country specializing in the thing or things it can produce most effectively even though one country may not be superior in any one thing. In other words " . . . the United States will import her total supply of fine-grade woolens in spite of the fact that American workmen can produce more yards of woolen cloth a day than British workmen can. On the other hand, although Great Britain will produce a part of her wheat supply, she will import most of it, since, except for the land most favorable to wheat production, her labor can be employed more profitably elsewhere. In the case of the coarser cottons the United States will import a considerable amount in spite of the fact that she has a natural advantage over Great Britain. A part of her domestic market will be supplied by her own labor—that part which can be produced under sufficiently favorable conditions to pay the wages which can be earned elsewhere."[1] Each, in other words, produces the things in which it has a comparative advantage. By so doing (and subsequently exchanging), the national product of each country is larger.

Protectionism has always flourished in certain areas, partly because of a misunderstanding of the incidence of the device. Part, of course, is a result of a particular purpose. Since the World War the situation has become worse than ever. Now, instead of instituting barriers for the purpose of nurturing home industries which promise to be economically self-supporting later on, much of the barrier building is for other reasons. For one thing, the totalitarian countries aim to be self-sufficient at any cost. Much of this is due to the aim of avoiding a repetition of World War conditions in which some countries suffered greatly because of an absolute lack of essential commodities. For another, the establishment of exchange controls (a type of trade restrictive device) has been found to be "necessary" because of market disruptions due, in turn, to shifts resulting from the war.

Many restrictions, of course, are retaliatory or protective. Some barriers have been aimed at countries which had constructed barriers against products sold by the first country; some have been thought to be necessary in order properly to allocate existing amounts of foreign exchange in such a way as to bring in the more "essential" commodities. Whatever the causes in the several individual instances leading toward the adoption of nationalistic policies, the world finds its economic intercourse obstructed by all manner of devices. As a result " . . . the price of wheat in France [for example] is three times the price in England. Butter costs over three times as much in Switzerland as New Zealand butter brings in the London market. The price of sugar is almost five times as high in Germany as in the world market."[2] A similar situation obtains in regard to many products in many countries.[3] This condition is clearly detrimental to consumer interests.

[1] Garver and Hansen, *op. cit.*, pp. 638–639.

[2] League of Nations, "World Economic Survey, 1934–1935," p. 81.

[3] According to *Index*, February, 1935: 36 countries at that time had exchange controls, 28 had import licensing systems, 28 had import quotas, and 17 possessed import monopolies on particular products.

The existing barriers include not only high tariffs but also, more recently, extensive use of such devices as quotas, import licenses, exchange controls, clearing and compensation arrangements, and many kinds of preferential agreements. They have been in a large measure responsible for the great decline in the volume of international commerce. They have caused surpluses to be built up in many countries; created shortages of essential products in others; and been instrumental in disorganizing prices and employment.

It is for this reason that the United States has been attempting to lead the world to a saner policy with regard to international trade. The device used is the so-called *reciprocal agreement program.* "Congress, after extensive consideration and debates, authorized the President to negotiate trade agreements designed to expand foreign markets for American products and, in return for concessions received, to proclaim modifications of our own duties in the course of a specified procedure, within carefully restricted limits and according to adequately defined standards that fully safeguard the interests of domestic producers in the home market."[1]

By the end of 1938, nineteen of these agreements had been completed.[2] Regarding these agreements, Secretary Hull says: "Important as are the immediate benefits of the trade agreements program in rebuilding, on a mutually advantageous basis, our foreign trade and the foreign trade of other countries, that program has another and even greater significance. We embarked upon it at a time when the world was caught in the toils of the most destructive economic war ever known in history. The disastrous consequences of this warfare were apparent not only in the field of economic activity, but also in the domain of social stability within countries and in the sphere of peaceful relations among nations. By pursuing our trade policy with

[1] Statement of Assistant Secretary of State, Francis B. Sayre, before the Committee on Ways and Means of the House of Representatives in the Course of Hearings on House Joint Resolution No. 96, commencing January 21, 1937, p. 5.

[2] These 19 countries included: United Kingdom, Canada, Netherlands, France, Cuba, Brazil, Belgium, Sweden, Colombia, Czeckoslovakia, Switzerland, Finland, Guatemala, San Salvador, Honduras, Ecuador, Costa Rica, Haiti, and Nicaragua. Agreements were pending with Venezuela and Turkey.

vigor and conviction, we are contributing our fair share of leadership in a movement which may have a decisive influence upon the whole future course of civilization—a movement away from the gathering fury of international strife and toward general appeasement which is indispensable to the well-being and progress of all nations. Other countries are increasingly adopting policies similar to ours and directed to the same ends, and are making earnest efforts toward evolving plans of appropriate action.

"Economic warfare is a basic aspect of international strife in general. It generates enmity and ill-will. It creates the vicious circle of retaliation and counterretaliation. It causes economic distress within nations, which, in turn, frequently leads to profound social unrest. Faced with a dismal economic future, nations can all too easily be misled into attempting to secure by force of arms that which, under stable world conditions and an intelligent organization of international relations, they would be able to obtain much more fully and satisfactorily through the constructive process of peaceful trade."[1]

The trade-agreement policy of the Federal government is clearly in the interest of the consumer in the United States and is entitled, for this reason, as well as others, to his full support.

6. Sumptuary Legislation.—Regulation of consumption by means of legal enactments has met with little success, and in modern times there are few attempts at such direct regulation. Such legal enactments, or sumptuary laws, have generally been directed along two lines, the maintenance of class status by prohibiting the use of certain articles by others than those of a particular class and the prevention of the introduction of new sorts of consumption. For example, in the later Middle Ages, knights were permitted to wear gold, but esquires only silver; the former damask, and the latter satin or taffeta.[2] The Scottish parliament in 1477 legislated that no merchant or his wife should wear clothes of silk or costly scarlet gowns. Laborers and husbandmen and their wives were limited to garments of cloth of their own make or of a value not in excess of elevenpence per clue.[3] During the nineteenth century, Japan tried similar

[1] CORDELL HULL, "Trade, Prosperity and Peace," Department of State release 64, pp. 5–6.

[2] WILHELM ROSCHER, "Political Economy," Book IV, Chap. II, Sec. 234, Note 3.

[3] C. ROGERS, "Social Life in Scotland," vol. I, p. 83.

sumptuary legislation and found it impossible of operation. Efforts were made in the sixteenth century to prevent the introduction of brandy, in the seventeenth, of tobacco, and in the eighteenth, of coffee. Governments shortly discovered the fruitlessness of their efforts toward such prohibitions. For example, a Turkish law of 1610 provided that all smokers should have their pipes broken against their noses. A Russian law of 1634 prohibited smoking under penalty of death. Similarly the use of coffee was prohibited in Turkey in 1633 under pain of death. As late as 1780, there was a Hanoverian prohibition of coffee trades in the rural districts.[1]

In the United States, such regulations have been restricted to the prohibition of only a few things generally acknowledged harmful. Thus we have laws limiting the use of narcotics to medicinal purposes. The prohibition laws with regard to liquor were widely violated and were later repealed.

Questions

1. Has the government any policy with respect to consumption? Is it politically possible for it to have any?
2. It is proposed to limit the working week to 30 hours. What influence, if any, would this have on consumption? Might your answer be different if the measure were considered as temporary rather than permanent?
3. Suppose the costs of shipping wheat to Europe were considerably lowered by the development of the Great Lakes Waterway. Who would derive the benefits?
4. A contemplated law in a Western state would pay all over fifty years of age $30 each Thursday. What economic results would follow?
5. Are the principles that underlie proper governmental expenditure different from those for an individual business organization?
6. If it is necessary to raise new governmental revenue, what forms of taxation do you think will be most probable? Most advantageous?

[1] Roscher, *op. cit.*, Book IV, Chap. II, Sec. 235, Note 1.

CHAPTER XXI

CRITIQUE OF CONSUMPTION

It is evident from the foregoing discussion that the level of consumption in no part of the world is sufficiently high so that concern with respect to it may be disregarded. Even in as rich a country as the United States there are large groups with levels that are depressingly low. The studies of family expenditures disclose vast potential demands for goods. At each successive income level, families are found to spend more for food, clothing, and shelter as well as the comforts and conveniences of life. These people would consume goods far in excess of our present productive capacities if given the opportunity. The power of the individual to consume is determined pretty largely by his personal money income. For society as a whole, however, it depends upon the volume of production. A fundamental proposition which we must keep before us at all times is that our volume of consumption is limited by our volume of production. At present this production, unfortunately, is not sufficiently large in any country of the world to provide the inhabitants with a very adequate level of consumption even though income were equally distributed. The solution to the consumption problem even in a country such as the United States is not to be found in a redistribution of the income from current production or in a sharing of wealth but lies much deeper in the necessity for a larger total volume of production. This cannot be too strongly emphasized.

Unfortunately for the consumer, many of the current tendencies are unfavorable for an expansion in the total volume of production. In the democratic countries, numerous politicians have misled the public with extravagant statements designed to convince people that a leveling down of the incomes of the well to do would materially improve the lot of the poor or that a free pension to the aged would increase the volume of available goods. In the dictator countries, vast quantities of labor and materials are used for unproductive purposes such as public displays and armaments with a progressive pressure upon the levels of consumption of the people. In the world as a whole, there has been not only an insane striving for national self-sufficiency but also the raising of embargoes and tariffs with a consequent loss of the advantages of specialization and exchange. Until these tendencies are overcome and there is realization that as a group we must work longer and harder, the broad upward thrust to our productive powers through improving knowledge and technique promises to be largely dissipated without material improvement in levels of consumption.

Even within the limits of the present volume of production, it is evident that consumption is not carried on in the best possible manner. Much of it is foolish and wasteful, and some of it is actually harmful and degrading. Perfection is not to be expected, but great improvements can be made and these are well worth striving for. Some of the errors in consumption are due to the nature of the economic order in which the consumer finds himself, some are due to imitation of the consumption of others without proper allowance for the differences in the circumstances under which consumption takes place, and others are due simply to a lack of knowledge on the part of consumers and to a lack of pride in efficient consumption.

The greatest handicap that the present economic order places upon consumers is that it brings into conflict the interests of producers and consumers. Producers voluntarily modify their conduct to the consumers' advantage only when such modification furthers their private ends. If it were not for the necessity of future sales, in most cases the selling of goods would proceed on an absolutely unscrupulous basis. The consumer would be cheated or sold shoddy goods whenever possible. Even the necessity of future sales does not completely protect him. He suffers a disadvantage because in many cases he does not know what he needs and, in consequence, is susceptible to suggestion by advertising and salesmanship and also because, even though he may know what he needs, he is unable in a great many cases to tell whether the thing he is purchasing will perform in the manner he expects, or is led to expect, at the time of purchase. As long as the consumer is unable to judge the performance of commodities before their purchase, he will be sold commodities unsuited to his needs and of lower qualities than he believes himself to be buying.

One of the most elementary rights to which the consumer is entitled is to know the truth about the goods that he buys. In our existing society the consumer is given relatively little opportunity to obtain such information. One remedy for this situation lies in increased standardization of commodities and of commodity performance. These standards must be worked out from the viewpoint of the consumer and must mean definite things regarding the services of the commodity for him. The problem is tremendously complex and difficult. Some progress is being made at present, but it is not sufficiently rapid. There is need for a large foundation or government department with ample funds for research and with fearless direction. The enmity of powerful producers must inevitably be incurred. The savings that a regime of complete standardization would effect are great. There would be a saving in the better ordering of consumption on the part of the individual consumers. There would also be a great saving in the effort expended upon advertising and selling. An advertiser would have greater difficulty in picking out some point irrelevant to the performance of his product and in building a sales appeal upon it. Moreover, competition would proceed more nearly upon the merits and price of the article than it does at present. Those producers delivering the greatest quality of product at the lowest cost would gain distinct advantages, at the expense of those producers who are efficient advertisers and sellers rather than producers. All this should result in some reduction in the price of products to consumers.

Another fundamental right of the consumer should be the right to purchase goods from the cheapest possible source. The extent of monopoly elements in the economic system has been fully recognized only recently. The growth of monopolies and the necessity for their successful control have become a major problem, and in the minds of many their control is essential for the preservation of the present order. It is certain that from the viewpoint of the consumer there can be little justification for market exclusion. Frequently technical conditions are such that, because of decreasing cost, size produces a monopoly. Such monopolies are desirable and are to be encouraged as a means of increasing the volume of production. A means must be found to prevent the resulting savings in cost from being retained solely by the producer and to force the sharing of this excess with consumers in the form of lower prices. Satisfactory means for monopoly control are not in existence, now, and the direction that these controls will take is not clear. The growth of monopolies, however, demands that adequate controls be found. Yet it is not to be thought that all these controls need be of a negative character. Under proper guidance, the monopoly may have considerable possibilities for social betterment through discriminative action among groups of consumers.

The order places special handicaps upon particular groups of consumers by limiting their money income. This is not in itself a general consumption problem but rather a problem in welfare economics. Whether these persons are to be provided with larger incomes is a matter of political and ethical expediency. Total income, as has been emphasized, is not sufficient to raise the income of everyone to even a moderate level without seriously endangering the total volume of production. Increased production rather than redistribution of income is the solution to the consumption problem of the masses. This means that the problem is much broader than consumption economics and involves such things as the means of lessening industrial fluctuations, provisions for increasing the health and education of children, rehabilitation of the industrially unfit, and provision for aid in old age and sickness. We do, however, possess sufficient income in our present stage of progress to warrant minimum levels in several lines below which the state has an obligation to see that no one falls. One of these is nutrition, especially that of children, We have ample production of food and ample total income to provide all with a minimum diet adequate to maintain health and strength. Some other countries are not so fortunate. To a more limited degree, this is also true of housing and medical care and health service.

The consumer himself is responsible for some of the errors in consumption. Some errors for which consumers are responsible arise from our imitation of the consumption of others. Fashions are the most striking example. Rapid changes in fashion are costly from the standpoint of both the manufacture and the distribution of products. They are costly to consumers in that they lead to the discarding of a great many goods before these goods have furnished all the services they might provide were it not for the change in fashion. These goods, moreover, derive their values in a particular manner: they are chiefly valuable because everyone cannot have them and, when everyone does, they cease to be valuable for this very reason. Some progress may be made in this respect if the rich and powerful can be shown their social responsibility in consumption and can be led to promote the consumption of articles that, in themselves, possess intrinsic values rather than solely prestige values. Unfortunately, there is no very great probability that this can be accomplished. The greatest hope lies in educating the lower strata to see the senselessness of the consumption of many of the goods consumed for their prestige value, and in putting emphasis upon the desirability of individuality in consumption rather than of being simply members of the herd.

Consumption is also inefficient simply because of a lack of intelligent attention to the problem by consumers themselves. There is great need for the development of a pride in efficient consumption. The businessman takes a distinct pride in the conduct of his business, the sportsman in the excellence of his performance, and, in a similar manner, there is need of a pride in the efficiency of consumption. Before such a pride can be developed, objective tests of what constitutes effective consumption will need to be developed. These tests are largely technical matters. They will need to be worked out by our various research agencies. Our colleges of home economics are making notable progress in this respect but are so limited in funds and personnel that sufficient progress cannot be made without national assistance. The increasing emphasis upon the problem in our schools and colleges is a step in the right direction. Each student should receive specific instruction upon the problem of personal finance, tests by which the consumer may judge the quality of goods, the advantages of standardization, etc.

The opportunities for wasteful expenditure increase rapidly as the income rises above the minimum of subsistence level. Our increasing power over productive resources and our rising level of income are complicating rather than simplifying the problem of efficient consumption. We must look forward to a loss of much of this gain in productive efficiency through poorly ordered consumption unless consumers, in general, can be educated to better modes of consumption and stimulated to a pride in efficient consumption.

Any extension of the economic activities of the state or an increase in the amount of central planning necessitates increased attention to the problem of consumption. Whatever else may be the faults of the present economic system, it does have the merit of providing a rapid registration of changes in the demand by those who possess the means of purchase. Goods cannot long be produced that consumers do not wish to buy. The rewards for anticipation of shifts in wants or new desires are so immediate and swift that great energy goes into their study. The substitution of collective for individual decision imposes upon those who mold that collective decision grave responsibilities for offering consumers a proper range of choice. A program of uniformity of consumption for all individuals can hardly be supported in view of the recognized differences among these individuals. Certain fluidity over time is required, and proper or best consumption is a changing thing. More knowledge than we now possess is essential before state guidance of any considerable magnitude is feasible.

Questions

1. In what ways would the intrusion of the state into business involve problems of consumption?

2. One writer has argued that profits are no longer a desirable form of motivation for our economic order since they are now largely derived from monopolistic positions resulting in curtailed production and from superior advertising, rather than from cheaper production of better quality goods. Would you agree?

3. How would you suggest developing in the community a pride in good consumption?

4. What faults or errors in consumption are the result of the inherent characteristics of the consumer himself, and what are to be laid to the economic order? Which bulk larger? Which are subject to remedial action?

INDEX